Where to Go

The regional chapters of this guide are ordered east to west, following the route of a traveller entering Somerset, passing through Devon and finishing up in Cornwall.

The first chapter, **Somerset, Bristol and Bath** begins with tours of two great cities, which together provide the perfect urban gateway to the rural pleasures beyond. They offer neatly contrasting attractions: Bristol buzzes with bars, hip new restaurants and the revitalization of its industrial heritage, while Bath promotes the studied appreciation of the old, welcoming thousands daily to admire its carefully preserved Roman and Georgian architecture. The nearby cathedral city of Wells is the perfect miniature base for gentle walks in the Mendips and tours of the local limestone landscape's great rain-cut wonders: Cheddar Gorge and the Wookey Hole Caves. The country gets wilder and more intense as you head west through the boggy Somerset Levels and its great mystical capital of Glastonbury into the poet-inspiring Quantocks and on to rugged Exmoor and its wonderful wooded coast.

Above: Roman baths, Bath, Somerset

Below: Clear sea off Tresco, Isles of Scilly

The **Devon** chapter also begins in urban fashion at Exeter, home to one of the region's most remarkable cathedrals with its impossibly intricate fan vaulting, before heading off along the south coast, passing through the big hitters of the 'English Riviera' and on to some of the region's most beautiful resorts – including swanky Dartmouth and Salcombe – before ending up amid the cheery modern bustle of Plymouth and its wealth of maritime history. Inland is perhaps the Southwest's most celebrated natural wonder, Dartmoor. The timeless rolling expanses of England's wildest wilderness invite extensive exploration on foot or horseback, and by bicycle or kayak.

Cornwall kicks off at Bodmin Moor, the county's miniature version of Dartmoor, which comes with its own collection of myths, legends and tors. Cornwall's south coast is dotted with villages – some of them, including Looe, Polperro and Fowey, among the most inviting in the Southwest – and also provides access to two of the nation's great horticultural wonders: the great domed rainforests of the Eden Project and Mevagissey's Lost Gardens of Heligan. The north coast is an angrier, less forgiving environment with its high wave-battered cliffs supporting brooding lonely castles, such as Tintagel, the supposed birthplace of King Arthur. But it also boasts some of the region's top-rated attractions, from the gourmet fish restaurants of Padstow to the art galleries of St Ives. At the end of the peninsula, Penzance, Britain's most westerly town, makes a good base for exploring the romantic offshore castle of St Michael's Mount, as well as Land's End, the nation's furthermost extremity, and the Isles of Scilly, the pretty stretch of islands 28 miles (45 km) from the mainland whose balmy(ish) climate has made them a popular beach-holiday destination.

01 INTRODUCING CORNWALL, DEVON & SOMERSET

Top: St Michael's Mount at sunrise

Above: Bowerman's Nose rock stack, Dartmoor

Like England but less so, the Southwest has long revelled in its otherness. It is the West *Country*, the nation within a nation, the supreme host welcoming visitors with an easy charm, but always staying slightly removed from the party; 'with' England, but not 'of' it, as Churchill once said of Britain's relationship with continental Europe. For tourists it presents two contrasting personalities, being both the country's most convivial holiday destination – all those resorts and holiday cottages and fish restaurants – and its most mysterious, rebellious region.

In the Southwest, myths and legends seem almost to seep from the ground. This is a land of swirling mists and lonely moors, its history filled with tales of legendary kings, smugglers holed up in secret caves and rebel leaders alighting on rocky shores ready to march on London. But it's also a place of cream teas and surfing, of sunning yourself on sandy beaches and bracing coastal walks, of gentle literary tours and bobbing boat trips, of cycling along narrow country lanes, chiff-chuffing steam train rides and fish suppers on the harbourside. It's a pirate in a kiss-me-quick hat. It's King Arthur eating a scone. It's a rebel leader with a plastic bucket and spade. Above all, it's a profoundly beautiful place with an endlessly varied landscape that warrants thorough exploration, from the gentle rolling hills of Somerset through the tor-studded moorland of Devon to the craggy headlands and cliff-top castles of Cornwall.

As you head west and the peninsula tapers down towards the looming Atlantic, so the influence of the sea becomes ever greater. Much of the north coast is wave-battered and wild, the great ocean rollers providing the country's best surfing conditions, which are harnessed to their most popular effect at Newquay, while the

Above: Minack Theatre, near Porthcurno, Cornwall

Opposite: Cornish coastline, near Padstow

south is calmer, more sheltered and lined with deep water estuaries, picturesque fishing villages and large sprawling resorts.

The weather in these parts can often be filled with mean intent, throwing thick obscuring blankets of fog across the moors and hurling waves with ferocious abandon against the rocky shore. But it has its kinder side too – all that coastal battering has left behind a collection of lovely serene beaches at places like Salcombe, Falmouth and Fowey. And when the sun shines and the mist and clouds depart, revealing the landscape in all its verdant, patchwork, craggy, sandy glory, there are few places more idyllic in the whole country.

While the Southwest is perhaps best known for its natural and rural wonders – its proud, embattled cliffs, its noble sweeps of sand, its forbidding moorland expanses dotted with thatched cottages – it has plenty of urban treasures too: the honey-coloured architectural primness of Bath, the buzz and bluster of Bristol, the art galleries of St Ives and the fancy fish restaurants of Padstow among them.

The Southwest is also where the nation's most determined eccentrics come to indulge their quirkiest passions, where wonderful follies and grandly odd projects are given life, where people create giant tropical greenhouses in abandoned quarries (the Eden Project), cut theatres into coastal cliffs (Minack Theatre) and build entire homes simply to showcase their collections of seaside knick-knacks (A La Ronde).

The Southwest is many things. It's a haven of regional gastronomy, a surfing mecca, a holiday-home paradise and a renowned artistic retreat. It's a place of tiny tasteful towns and giant rural sweeps, of modern cities and traditional fishing villages, a land defined by the sea, that boasts one of the country's most celebrated interiors. But most of all, it's a great place for an adventure. So do yourself a favour, hop in your car or climb aboard the Great Western Railway, and go and find yourself one.

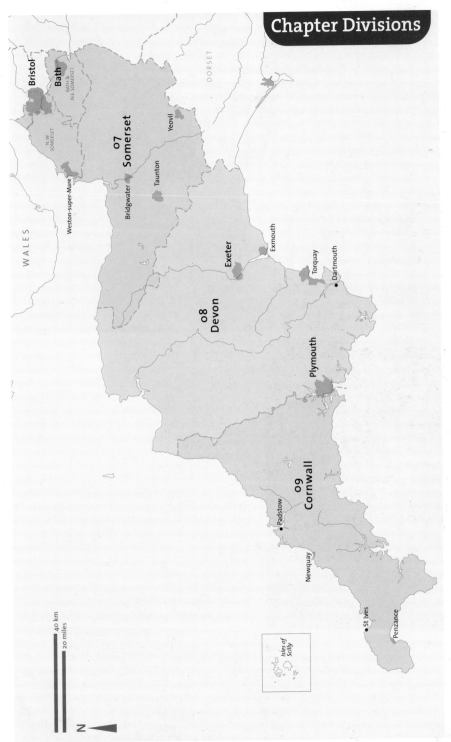

WALES

Bristol

Bath

BATH &
N.E SOMERSET

N.W
SOMERSET

Weston-super-Mare

Yeovil

07
Somerset

Bridgwater

Taunton

DORSET

Exmouth

Exeter

Torquay

Dartmouth

08
Devon

Plymouth

09
Cornwall

Padstow

Newquay

St Ives

Penzance

Isles of
Scilly

40 km

20 miles

N

Urban Treasures

In the great rush to hit the beaches or start tramping over moorland, the Southwest's cities and towns are too often overlooked.

- **Bath Abbey Church Yard.** The perfect sampler of Bath's charms – the Roman Baths, the medieval cathedral and the Georgian Pump Room, all within a few square metres, p.84
- **Exeter Cathedral.** In a region not exactly short of glorious medieval architecture, the virtuoso fan vaulting of St Peter's soars above the competition, p.118
- **The National Maritime Museum, Falmouth.** The country's premiere collection of small boats provides a fascinating overview of Cornwall's long and distinguished seafaring history, p.194
- **Plymouth's Barbican.** Amid all the modern, faceless post-war architecture, the Barbican is Plymouth's salty heart, a narrow, cobbled jumble of Tudor and Jacobean buildings from where, in 1620, the Plymouth Pilgrims set out for the New World, p.142

Top: Bath Pump Room and Bath Abbey

Above: Gothic vaulted ceiling, Exeter Cathedral

Opposite: SS Great Britain, Bristol; Tate Gallery St Ives, Cornwall

- **SS Great Britain.** Once the biggest ship in the world and a towering icon of the industrial age, the Brunel-designed SS *Great Britain* can be seen in all its metallic majesty in dry dock next to Bristol's Floating Harbour, p.74
- **Tate Gallery St Ives.** A treat for lovers of art and architecture, the great spaceship-like gallery examines the work and influence of the St Ives school and hosts regularly changing displays of 20th-century art, p.207

Moors and Gardens

The Southwest is famed for both its three great wildernesses and its carefully cultivated gardens where nature has been tamed, tended, tweaked and teased into position for your viewing pleasure.

Below, clockwise from top: The Cheesewring, Bodmin Moor; Burrator Reservoir, Dartmoor; Bluebells on Dartmoor at sunset

• **Bodmin Moor.** Go searching for the 'beast' and the myriad of other mystical creatures said to inhabit the Southwest's smallest stretch of wilderness, p.171

• **Dartmoor.** A great swathe of primeval countryside, dotted with prehistoric ruins, medieval villages and gnarly, fantastically-

shaped granite tors bathed in mysterious swirling mists – it's a walking, cycling and horse-riding paradise, p.148

- **The Eden Project.** The Southwest's very own rainforest, housed in a series of enormous greenhouses, is the region's most popular attraction. A veritable tropical jungle wonderland, p.180

- **Exmoor.** One of Britain's very first national parks and still one of the best. Exmoor provides a softer, gentler, more agricultural alternative to Bodmin and Dartmoor, with a network of well-worn routes taking you past the verdant fields, dry-stone walls, wooded combes and tinkling streams on the lookout for the abundant wildlife, p.111

From top: Tulips at the Eden Project, St Austell, Cornwall; Heather on Exmoor; The Lost Gardens of Heligan, near Mevagissey, Cornwall

- **The Lost Gardens of Heligan.** The exotic blooms, kitchen gardens and glasshouses of a 19th-century country estate restored to all their rampant glory, following five decades in the wilderness, p.181

- **Tresco Abbey Gardens.** A luxuriant subtropical garden in a 10th-century Benedictine abbey thriving amid the clement climate of the Isles of Scilly, p.215

Trips, Tours and Treks

The Southwest is primarily an outdoor destination, somewhere to get out in the sunshine and do something (although be sure to bring your raincoat, just in case) – take a trip, go for a ride or learn a new sport.

Top: Surfer, Newquay

Above: Dartmoor pony, Dartmoor

- **Go bird-watching on Lundy Island.** The southern and western cliffs of this narrow island, little changed since medieval times, are home to a huge wealth of wildlife – shags, kittiwakes, shearwaters and, of course, puffins – while offshore, seals and basking sharks patrol the waters, p.159
- **Go horse-riding on Dartmoor.** With the hard work done for you, you can concentrate on enjoying the views of England's largest remaining wilderness, p.148
- **Learn to surf at Newquay.** Or, if you fancy testing your board skills away from thousands of prying eyes, at the quieter surfing mecca of Croyde, pp.188-190
- **Sunbathe on Blackpool Sands.** The region's wonderful array of beaches is the main reason why the M5 is boot to bumper every summer bank holiday. Head away from the main resorts and enjoy the pristine sands at this quiet, unspoilt, empty stretch of coast, p.137
- **Take a combined river trip, steam-train ride and sightseeing bus tour.** The boat trip takes you from Totnes along the tree-

lined banks of the River Dart, the steam train jogs between Kingswear and Paignton, while the bus takes you back to Totnes, p.134

• **Walk (part of) the Southwest Coastal Path.** The country's longest footpath stretches for more than 600 miles (966 km) around the perimeter of the entire peninsula, taking you through a seemingly infinite variety of coastal landscapes, p.112

Top: Steam train, Totnes, Devon

Above: Blackpool Sands, Devon

Right: Cliffs at Bolberry Down on the Southwest Coastal Path

Itinerary 1: Two Weeks' Highlights

Day 1: Start big with a visit to **Bristol**, the region's largest and most vibrant town. Tour the sites by day – particularly the cathedral, Clifton and the SS *Great Britain* – and then at night hit the restaurants and bars.

Day 2: Make the short journey down to **Bath**. Spend as much time touring its glorious honey-coloured architecture and museums as your legs can take – be sure not to miss the Roman Baths, the Pump Room and the Royal Crescent.

Day 3: Head west to Bath's diminutive sibling, **Wells**, for a quick whiz round its famed cathedral and then head out to explore the natural wonders at the **Wookey Hole Caves** and **Cheddar Gorge**.

Day 4: Go wildlife-spotting in among the boggy wilds of the **Levels**, one of the country's most important wetlands, followed by a bit of new-age spotting at the area's capital, **Glastonbury**. Be sure to take in the views from atop the Tor.

Day 5: Take a drive along the A39 to **Lynmouth**, and then head out for a walk along the glorious wooded coast of **Exmoor**.

Day 6: Get back to city ways with a trip to **Exeter**. Visit the cathedral, tour the underground passages and hang out at the pubs and restaurants on the quayside.

Day 7: Take a steam-train ride and ferry to **Dartmouth** and then an idyllic boat trip up the River Dart to **Totnes**.

Day 8: Go for a drive, a walk or possibly even a horse ride into the depths of **Dartmoor**. **Hay Tor** is fairly easy to reach and offers great views all around.

Day 9: Spend the day lounging on the beaches or, if you've got the energy, exploring the wooded estuary around **Salcombe**.

Day 10: Enter another world entirely within the tropically heated biomes of the **Eden Project**.

Day 11: Tick off the region's third and final wilderness, **Bodmin Moor**, with a quick tour of its various famed sites including former smuggler's hide-out, The Jamaica Inn, and Dozmary Pool where King Arthur supposedly received the magical sword, Excalibur.

Day 12: Tame the Atlantic breakers with some board-riding at the country's premier surfing destination, **Newquay** (or, if you prefer, just hang out at the town's myriad bars).

Day 13: Have a quiet, reflective day of art appreciation at **St Ives'** various galleries, including the Tate St Ives and the Barbara Hepworth Museum and Sculpture Garden.

Day 14: Finish with the only fitting finale, a visit to **Land's End**, the official westerly conclusion to Britain. From here it's nothing but sea until you reach America.

Top: Bristol Cathedral

Above: Front entrance to Wells Cathedral

Below: Land's End, Cornwall

Opposite, top: St. Michael's Tower on Glastonbury Tor

Opposite, bottom: Hay Tor, Dartmoor

Above: Porlock Weir, Somerset

Below: Dramatic Dartmoor, as featured in Conan Doyle's The Hound of the Baskervilles

Itinerary 2: Joining the Literary Dots

The Southwest has been providing inspiration to the country's leading literary lights for centuries. Spend a week touring the locations that gave birth to the masterpieces.

Day 1: Start in **Bath** with a tour of the various sites associated with **Jane Austen** during her five-year stay in the city, including the Pump Room and grand Georgian terraces. The Jane Austen Centre organizes themed walks.

Day 2: Follow in the footsteps of **Coleridge** and **Wordsworth** with a wander in the **Quantocks** and visit Coleridge's former home at **Nether Stowey**. Spend a (hopefully uninterrupted) evening in **Porlock** following a trip aboard the West Somerset Steam Railway.

Day 3: Take a 'Lorna Doone Country Walk' through **Exmoor** in the footsteps of **R.D. Blackmore**'s famous heroine. Maps are available from all the local tourist offices.

Day 4: Explore the **North Devon Coast**, so beloved of **Charles Kingsley** and described in loving detail in *Westward Ho!* (although avoid the village of the same name), set in the reign of Elizabeth I.

Day 5: Hop aboard the 'Tarka Line' at **Barnstaple** for an idyllic train ride to **Exeter** through the countryside of **Henry Williamson**'s *Tarka the Otter*.

Day 6: Head southwest into the wilds of **Dartmoor**, to Foxtor Mire, the real-life inspiration for the deadly 'great Grimpen mire' featured in **Sir Arthur Conan Doyle**'s *The Hound of the Baskervilles*.

Day 7: Make your way down the peninsula's south coast to **Fowey** and the **Daphne Du Maurier** Visitor Centre. The author lived nearby and set many of her novels, including *Rebecca* and *Jamaica Inn*, in the region.

CONTENTS

Reference

History

O2

Ice, Stone and Iron

As rich as the Southwest's seafaring heritage is, there is little doubt that the first people to arrive here did so on foot, possibly as early as 50,000 years ago, in the sub zero midst of the last Ice Age when Britain and continental Europe were connected by a land bridge. They were hunter-gatherers who no doubt came in pursuit of the giant herds of mammoth and rhinoceros that then roamed the landscape and formed a major part of the Neolithic diet. Although these chilly nomads created no permanent settlements, there is plenty of evidence, in the form of flints, arrowheads and animal bones, to suggest that they used to shelter from the bitter cold in the region's caves. Indeed the oldest human bone (or possibly Neanderthal, the scientific jury is still out) yet found in Britain was discovered in **Kent Cavern**, near Torquay in the 1920s, while the oldest complete human skeleton – a mere whippersnapper at just 9,000 years old – was unearthed in one of **Cheddar Gorge**'s numerous caverns (*see* p.100). The large gap between these two dates reveals not a lack of human habitation in the intervening period, but rather an absence of evidence for it, which is why any description of prehistoric life and culture must necessarily be based largely on educated guesswork.

The end of the last Ice Age in around 8,000 BC, and the disappearance of the ice sheets blanketing the country, cut off the early Britons' continental escape route, but also greatly improved the living conditions of those left behind. Now no longer condemned to trudge behind the great woolly herds, the hunters became settlers, building small villages and farming the open grassland of the newly revealed moors, where they planted crops and raised livestock. These communities grew rapidly in sophistication and by the second millennium BC had established trading links with the continent, exporting some of the region's various metal deposits – notably the tin and copper that would make many a fortune in the millennia to come – in return for jewellery, weapons and other goods. Tellingly, the ancient Greek name for the British Isles was Cassiterides, the 'Islands of Tin', recognising the importance of the metal that would come to dominate the social and political life of the Southwest in the Middle Ages.

These Neolithic pioneers also developed a system of belief and built places of worship, erecting stones in various symbolic arrangements including circles, dolmens and quoits (which look a bit like giant stone tables), the most famous of which is Stonehenge, which lies just east of this region on Salisbury Plain. Exactly what these stones were used for remains a mystery. It is clear that some were laid out in reference to (and imitation of) celestial bodies in the night sky, while others may have been tombs, meeting places or sacrificial sites. No one really knows.

Their preservation – the moors of the Southwest have some of Europe's finest extant prehistoric landscapes – is due in part to a minor climatic catastrophe that took place around 1000 BC when temperatures once again briefly plummeted, covering the moorland in impenetrable ice and forcing the settlers to leave their monuments behind and head to the milder climes of the coast.

This icy intermission coincided with the arrival of the next wave of immigrants from the continent, the **Celts**. The diffuse, disparate Celtic culture had its origins in the central Europe of the early Iron Age. Waves of migration took the Celts right across the continent in the first millennium BC, from Ireland all the way to Turkey, establishing them as western and central Europe's dominant culture.

The Celts' sophisticated use of iron for making tools and weapons gave them a significant advantage over their territorial rivals, allowing them to sweep through Britain into the Southwest where they took over the land, establishing villages and farms, which were often protected by hill-top forts. By the first century AD, Celtic tribes were spread throughout the Southwest, even in some of the most inhospitable places, such as the wetlands of the **Levels** where they erected their settlements on land islands, relying on the surrounding bogs and marshes for defence. Here they developed a complex hierarchical society led by druids, who controlled the sacrifices and feasts of their polytheistic religion, and warriors who utilized their people's mastery of metal-working to adorn themselves with intricately crafted torcs and brooches and carried elaborately decorated shields and weapons, indicative of their high status.

Although they shared a common culture, each Celtic tribe was a separate entity with its own chief. There was no Celtic Empire under a single command. Rather the individual tribes constantly jockeyed for position, occasionally engaging in short-lived wars over territory. It was probably this lack of unity and inter-tribal organization that doomed the Celts to defeat when the ultra-regimented Romans arrived in the first century AD.

A Far Corner of Empire

The **Romans'** first foray into Britain was not a great success, whatever Julius Caesar may have said at the time. Far from coming, seeing and conquering, the Romans won some quick battles, replaced one Celtic chieftain with another more friendly towards Rome, and then went away again, leaving the Celts to get on with it. The Britons wouldn't get off nearly so lightly next time. When around a century later the bumbling, stuttering Claudius came to the Imperial throne, needing a military triumph to shore up his position, Britain, by then at the very edge of the Empire, was the obvious target for an attack.

In AD 43 around 20,000 Roman troops, under the command of future emperor, Vespasian, landed on Britain's southeast coast on a mission of conquest. The Romans defeated the Celtic tribes wherever they met opposition, although, in contravention of their warlike reputation, they were just as happy to do a deal as to fight. Unlike the Anglo Saxons who came after them, the Romans had no desire to force the native population from their homes and take over their land. They just wanted the natives to acknowledge Rome as their master, and if that could be achieved voluntarily, all the better.

Using this pragmatic strategy, the Romans persuaded the Dumnonii tribe who then occupied much of Devon and Cornwall to join the Imperial fold. They named the region **Dumnonia** in the Celts' honour, established a fortified garrison town at Exeter (known as Isca Dumnoniorum) to watch over things and then largely left the Celts to their own devices. The Romans were much more excited about exploiting the natural hot springs at **Bath**, building a complex of bathhouses that are today the region's prime remains from the period (*see* p.85). Indeed it seems the Romans found little in the Southwest to warrant further expansion. West of Exeter almost no evidence of Roman occupation has been discovered.

Over the next few centuries Celtic and Roman culture would grow increasingly intertwined in Britain. Following a period of resistance, and a fair few revolts, the Celts gradually came round to the ideal of Imperial living and the benefits it offered, including protection against foreign invasions and increased trading possibilities. Around the Imperial cities, many Celts were intrigued by the Romans' elegant, urban way of life, even going so far as to ape the manner and customs of their overlords, learning Latin (all the better to do business), wearing togas, bathing and living in Roman-style villas adorned with frescoes and mosaics. This happy hybrid culture would come to a jolting end, however, in 410 AD when Rome, under sustained assault from Germanic tribes, withdrew its legions and support from the province. Denied their Roman protectors, who had guaranteed their safety for more than three centuries, the Celts became easy targets for the various itinerant tribes then marauding the continent on the hunt for new land, including the Picts, the Jutes, the Fresians and, of course, the Angles and the Saxons.

It's All Gone Dark

The next period of invasion and settlement was significantly more brutal than that which had taken place under the Romans. The **Angles** and the **Saxons** were not sharers. They wanted the land, not control of the people, who were either killed or forced from their homes. With the Romans having taken their scholars back to Rome, little written evidence of these '**Dark Ages**' survives. However it does seem clear that from the fifth century onwards, waves of invaders arrived in the country, driving the Celts westward into Wales and the Southwest, which over the next few centuries became the principal strongholds of the old Celtic culture.

This was supposedly the period in which the great Celt, **King Arthur**, led the Romano-British resistance against the Anglo-Saxons, holding back the tide of invasion in the Southwest with a series of spectacular victories. While there is some (very limited) evidence for the existence of an important Celtic leader at this time, and there is no doubt that the tribes of the Southwest held out much longer than contemporaries in the rest of the country, most of the Arthurian tales were created at least 600 years after the event.

Almost as soon as they established themselves as the new dominant powers, the Anglo-Saxons came under attack from the next set of continentals to turn their acquisitive gaze towards England, the **Vikings**. The modus operandi of these Scandinavian adventurers was not conquest but pillage, stealing treasure from coastal towns, looting their way through the countryside and demanding tribute.

The Viking raids forced the Anglo-Saxons to improve their military organization and to expand their armies, which indirectly ended up being bad news for the Celts. In the early ninth century, resistance in the Southwest was finally broken by the newly enhanced Wessex armies of **King Egbert** who rampaged through the peninsula. By 927 AD the Anglo-Saxon and Celtic kingdoms had been brought together to form a single unified state, England. This was not just a political union, but a religious one too, combining the Celtic Catholicism of the west (born during the days of the Roman Empire and bolstered by subsequent visits from Irish missionaries) with the continental Catholicism of the Anglo-Saxons which took hold following the sixth-century mission of St Augustine.

Tin Men

The Anglo-Saxons had spent nigh on half a millennium bringing England under their control, but were to rule the kingdom for little more than a century. A single day's fighting at Hastings was all it took for the nascent English nation to be effectively absorbed into the Norman Empire of **William the Conqueror**. Any tentative moves towards Southwestern independence were quickly snuffed out following William's capture of Essex in 1068.

Under the **Normans** the Southwest enjoyed a building boom unprecedented in its history, as the country's new rulers sought to shore up their position with a network of castles at strategically important locations, including **Exeter**, **Totnes** and **Okehampton**, around which new towns began to grow up. Trade with continental Europe also increased dramatically in this period on the back of the burgeoning clothing industry, leading to an expansion of the region's ports. **Bristol** would lead the way, soon becoming England's second city after London.

This growing wealth would lead inevitably to increased displays of wealth, as towns and cities used their bulging coffers to erect great stone cathedrals – such as those at **Wells** and Exeter – to replace the simpler wooden Anglo-Saxon structures.

While farming and cloth manufacturing were central to the economy of Devon, Cornwall's fortunes became increasingly dependent on the mining industry. The county's great lodes of tin and copper, which had been extracted on a small scale since prehistoric times, were now mined with greater intensity and in much higher volume, both to supply the nation's coinage and to be sold abroad. Soon Cornwall was Europe's principal tin supplier. The mining towns grew wealthy and self-important on the back of this trade. The so-called stannary (tin making) towns of **Helston**, **Lostwithiel**, **Truro** and **Liskeard** in Cornwall, and **Ashburton** and **Tavistock** in Devon, were given special authority by the crown to run their region's affairs.

Industry also expanded along the Southwest's coastline, as improved marine technology allowed more effective exploitation of the bountiful surrounding seas. The coast became home to a thriving band of fishing villages, several of which, including **Beer**, **Brixham** and **Polperro**, still make their livelihoods in largely the same way today and retain their medieval layouts. Coastal activity was further bolstered by the introduction of customs duties in 1272, which created a new, albeit illicit, trade almost overnight – smuggling. The labyrinthine caves riddling the cliffs of Cornwall and Devon soon became the hide-outs for an army of smugglers.

The mounting wealth of the region received royal recognition in 1337 when **Edward III**, looking for a way of providing his son, the Black Prince, with a form of income, established the Duchy of Cornwall. Its benefits proved so great that all subsequent heirs to the throne have also become Dukes of Cornwall.

Rebels and Revolts

Cornwall had never been a willing or eager member of England, but the success and prosperity of the early Middle Ages had kept any revolutionary leanings in check. The mood changed, however, in the late 15th century at the beginning of the Tudor era, as the state became more powerful, more centralized and started extending its influence ever further into the lives of ordinary subjects. A rise in taxation, levied by **Henry VII** to pay for his war against Scotland, prompted 15,000 Cornishmen to walk on London to protest to the king, lead by Michael Joseph (also known as **An Goff**, 'The Smith', who is today one of the leading heroes of the Celtic Nationalist movement). Henry responded by sending his army to brutally crush the protestors. This created great resentment in the West Country and the perfect conditions for a rebel leader to rally the populace. That leader came in the unlikely form of **Perkin Warbeck**, who landed at Land's End three months later claiming to be Richard, Duke of York, one of the 'princes in the tower' who most people believed to have been killed by Richard III. He was nothing of the sort, but the Flemish fantasist somehow managed to get the people, by now seething with resentment, flocking to his cause, particularly when he promised to abolish the new taxes.

Warbeck had himself crowned King of England on **Bodmin Moor** and, supported by a impromptu army of some 6,000 Cornishmen, began marching towards London. But his ersatz reign soon came to an ignominious end. Despite successfully taking Exeter, Warbeck's would-be regal demeanour faded when he learnt that the real king's troops were advancing to meet him. He panicked, deserted his own army and was captured a few weeks later, whereupon he was taken to the Tower of London and executed.

More West Country revolts were to follow in the wake of the Reformation and the religious revolution that swept the country in the mid 16th century, which saw monasteries and abbeys dissolved across the region, including at **Glastonbury**, **Bath** and **Buckfast**. The Act of Uniformity of 1549, which insisted that the eucharist be conducted in English rather than the traditional Latin and that churches read from the new Book of Common Prayer, found particular resistance in Cornwall where many did not speak English as their native tongue. However, the resulting Prayer Book Rebellion fared no better than its predecessors with the rebels defeated in **Clyst St Mary** just outside Exeter.

Round the World

As the Middle Ages gave way to the **early modern period**, and England's maritime prowess grew, so the ports of the Southwest became ever more important. Having spent much of its history warding off unwelcome visitors from beyond, the region was now keen to do a little expansion of its own. Some of the very earliest attempts to connect the old world with the new were launched from the Southwest, beginning with **John Cabot**'s pioneering journey from Plymouth to mainland North America in 1497. **Plymouth**, along with the region's other major ports, also began to take increased responsibility for the nation's defence, a development that was given official recognition in 1509 with the formation of the Royal Navy by **Henry VIII**, one of the most antagonistic of all monarchs in a very antagonistic era. **Elizabeth I** expanded the navy further, which she saw as her most useful weapon for curbing the growing power of Spain, Europe's other great maritime power, and of cashing in on the trading links being established across the Atlantic.

However, for Elizabeth, it wasn't enough simply to forge new trading links or plundering opportunities in the Americas, those of Spain also had to be diminished. To this end she sanctioned a policy of official piracy, encouraging her greatest sailors to indulge in the euphemistic practice of 'private enterprise' – in other words looting Spanish ships, themselves filled with treasure looted from the indigenous populations of South and Central America. Many of these 'great' sailors were from the Southwest, by now firmly established as the nation's leading maritime region, including **Sir Richard Grenville** from Cornwall, **Sir Walter Raleigh** from Devon, **Sir John Hawkins** from Plymouth and, perhaps the greatest of them all, **Sir Francis Drake**, who in 1577 became the first Englishman to circumnavigate the globe.

Elizabeth's decision to increase the country's naval power proved its worth in 1588 when Drake and Hawkins engaged the fearsome Spanish Armada of King Philip II in battle off the Southwest coast, routing them at the Battle of Gravelines. However, for all their derring-do, these men also had their less savoury sides. They helped to establish the slave trade, which helped fund the growth of the region's most prominent ports, notably Plymouth and Bristol. Indeed in the 18th century Bristol would enjoy unparalleled success on the back of the trade in human beings, acting as the main nexus between the source, Africa, and the principal markets in America and the Caribbean (the so-called 'Triangle Trade').

As time passed the Southwest evolved into one of the main departure points for those looking to colonize the New World, beginning famously in 1620 when a group of puritans set sail from Plymouth aboard the **Mayflower** hoping to make new, austere, god-fearing lives for themselves in North America. They named their new settlement New Plymouth. Subsequent voyages followed their lead with the result that the eastern seaboard of the US is now dotted with doppelgängers of Southwestern towns including Portland, Portsmouth and Dartmouth.

In the 18th century Plymouth would play host to another world-changing departure when **Captain James Cook** set out from here for the South Pacific, in the process becoming the first European to lay eyes on Australia and New Zealand.

Brother versus Brother, Customs Officer versus Smuggler, Owner versus Worker

The Southwest saw its fair share of battles during the **Civil War**, albeit none on the scale of Naseby or Marston Moor. The region was largely, if not universally, on the Royalist side. Support was certainly considered strong enough have the royal mint moved to **Truro** in 1642–3. The Royalists got much the better of the early fighting, winning at Braddock Down, Stratton, Lansdown and Lostwithiel. However, as in the rest of the country, the story from 1644 onwards was largely one of reverse after reverse. The surrender at Tresillian, near Truro in 1646, marked the end of Royalist resistance in the region.

Rebellion flared up again briefly towards end of the 17th century with many in the Southwest supporting the Protestant Duke of Monmouth's attempt to seize the crown from the Catholic **James II**. The revolt ended in brutal fashion at Sedgemoor, the last major battle fought on English soil, and the subsequent trials, known as the 'Bloody Assizes', saw hundreds of rebels executed and many more imprisoned.

The decades of calm that followed the Glorious Revolution saw commerce continue to increase. The Southwest expanded its trading network, opening up new markets across the Atlantic. Bristol became its leading slaving port, Plymouth the country's main naval base, while Falmouth was established as the principal port for trade with the burgeoning British Empire.

Rising imports necessarily meant rising customs duty imposed by a state eager to capitalize on the region's success, which inevitably prompted a corresponding increase in smuggling. By now Cornwall's network of cliff caves were a veritable smuggling empire. Many in the region regarded smugglers as the successors to the rebels of yore, .standing up against official oppression. Their activities were broadly supported by the local population, and some smugglers even became local celebrities, seen in almost Robin Hood-like terms, stealing from the rich government in order to provide the locals with cheap goods, which in the early 18th century included an exotic new drink rapidly growing in popularity – tea.

Progress was also being made inland. Here the region's tin and copper mines, a source of prosperity since early Middle Ages, now benefited from a series of technological advances. First, the introduction of gunpowder in the late 17th century allowed miners to blast recalcitrant lodes of tin and copper to the surface. However, it was the increased mechanization offered by the Industrial Revolution that really sent the industry into overdrive. Powerful steam-driven beam engines allowed miners to dig deeper and work quicker than ever before. Many of the revolution's pioneers were local men, including Dartmouth's **Thomas Newcomen**, who invented an 'atmospheric' steam engine for pumping water out of pits, **Richard Trevithick**, who built the world's first working steam locomotive railway, and **Humphry Davy**, the inventor of the eponymous lamp which allowed miners to work safely in mines where methane gas was present (although his invention initially led to a rise in accidents, as miners were encouraged to work in mines previously deemed unsafe).

The expansion of mining did not benefit everyone to the same degree. Indeed the contrast in fortunes between the mine-owners, who were soon making obscene profits, and the miners charged with the difficult and dangerous job of extracting the metals, neatly demonstrated the huge social divisions being created by industrialization, not just in the Southwest but across the country.

The miners endured brutally hard conditions, working deep underground for between eight and twelve hours a day, in temperatures often exceeding 30°C, in an environment where roof collapse and gas explosions were regular occurrences. And their reward? A basic subsistence wage of a few shillings a week. To make ends meet, miners' wives and children were also often employed in the industry doing some of the more fiddly, cleaning and sorting jobs. Home life was equally squalid, with alcohol providing the only respite from the crushing barbarism of their lives. Pubs were always guaranteed to do good business in a mining town. The combination of extremely dangerous, unhealthy working practices and a self-destructive lifestyle meant that few miners made it into their forties.

Into this savage environment stepped **John Wesley**, the founder of Methodism who preached throughout the Southwest during the mid 18th century. His message of piety, self-reliance and, above all, temperance, seemed unlikely to win over the hard-drinking miners, but his idea of self-sacrifice in this life in return for heavenly reward in the next struck a chord with the downtrodden workers. A century later the majority of people in Cornwall were Methodists.

The 18th century also saw great urban expansion in the Southwest particularly in Bristol where the ugly profits of slave-trading were laundered into beautiful squares and houses for the city's plump, wealthy merchants, and at Bath where the rediscovery of the Roman Baths and a growing fashion for 'taking the waters' saw new streets laid out on extravagant lines as architects – notably John Wood and son – got to work fashioning elegant terraces and squares for the upper classes.

The Rise of Tourism

The early- to mid-19th century would prove the region's industrial zenith. By the 1830s Cornwall alone had more than 200 mines employing in excess of 30,000 people. In the decades that followed, the West Country would become a sort of giant workshop for one of the greatest figures of the industrial age, **Isambard Kingdom Brunel**, many of whose projects – including the railway between London and Bristol, the Royal Albert Bridge over the Tamar between Devon and Cornwall and the transatlantic passenger steamers, the *Great Western* and SS *Great Britain* – connected the Southwest with the wider world as never before.

Brunel's railways brought new visitors to the region, helping to expand a recent industry, tourism. The region's tourism began in a small, upper-class fashion during the

Napoleonic Wars when members of aristocratic society, denied access to their usual foreign holiday resorts, adopted many towns in the Southwest, including Torquay, Exmouth, Sidmouth and Lynton, as domestic replacements. The expansion of the train network from the 1840s onwards opened up the rest of peninsula, which until then had been little visited owing to the poor quality of roads. Soon the middle classes had joined the aristocratic vanguard, and by the late 19th century the Southwest was enjoying a tourism boom which saw many formerly down-at-heel fishing towns transformed into seaside resorts. In places like **Torquay** and **Dawlish**, seafronts once lined with modest cottages now boasted grand stuccoed hotels, boarding houses and piers. The Victorians became fixated with the idea of the health-giving benefits of a seaside holiday, and the range of ailments that could supposedly be cured by a spot of saltwater bathing and a few lungfuls of bracing sea air. As rail travel became ever more widely available, so the working classes also joined in the fun, although they tended to regard their holidays less as health cures as breaks from the monotony of their industrialized existences, giving them the chance to spend a few days cutting loose in pubs, music halls and amusement arcades before returning to the daily grind.

The region's economic and industrial peak would, perhaps inevitably, be followed by a long and deep decline. The bottom fell out of the metal mining industry abruptly in the mid 19th century when cheaper sources of copper and tin were discovered abroad, leading to the closure of many mines and the departure of many former miners to America and Australia. Today, there are no mines left. However, as one industry was dying, so another came to life, following the discovery of kaolin, or china clay, near **St Austell**, which was soon being exploited for use in the ceramics and paper-making industries. Today it is the only major manufacturing industry still operating in the region. However, this success aside, it was clear that, as 19th century gave way to 20th, the industrial rot had set in. Those tourists, originally a welcome source of a little additional money, were going to become an increasingly important (if not vital) part of the region's economy.

Making the Modern Southwest

Tourists weren't the only ones to discover the charms of the Southwest. In the late 19th and early 20th centuries, the picturesque vistas of the north Cornwall coast began attracting artists who founded influential communities, first at **Newlyn** and later at **St Ives**. The region also provided literary inspiration to a host of 20th-century writers including **D.H. Lawrence**, **Daphne du Maurier**, **Agatha Christie** and **Sir Arthur Conan Doyle**. Some even played a part in encouraging tourism. **John Betjeman**, the poet laureate, wrote guidebooks to Cornwall and Devon in the 1930s in an attempt to bring visitors to the county (he lived to regret it – when the hordes arrived he felt that they rather spoilt the place).

As with the rest of the country, the **First World War** marked a turning point in the fortunes of the Southwest, removing a large proportion of the male workforce. Fortunately the region suffered no direct damage. However, the same couldn't be said for the **Second World War** when many cities were heavily bombed, including Exeter and Plymouth, neither of which were rebuilt with any great care or aesthetic regard in the decades that followed. Post-war, as the British Empire was being wound up, so the region's ports, which had once played a prominent role in supplying the colonies, began to fall on hard times.

Since the 1950s people have been looking for tourism to fill the void left by the decline of trade and industry, not always successfully. Hand in hand with this has come a growing sense of environmental concern, the first significant signs of which saw **Dartmoor** and **Exmoor** designated as national parks in the 1950s.

The closure of many of the region's local branch lines following the Beeching Report of the early 1960s had perhaps less impact on tourism than might have been expected, largely because it took place at the same time as a large road building scheme. The M5, linking Birmingham with the Southwest, was opened in 1963 and extended over the next decade and a half until it reached Exeter, while the region's other major roads, particularly the A38 'holiday route' to Bodmin and the A30 to Land's End, were also improved. Despite all the road building, congestion has become a severe and growing problem here, particularly in the summer months, with supply never quite able to match demand.

Though fishing continues as a viable industry in many places, it's an industry facing problems, not least the decline of fish stocks and consequent imposition of strict quotas by the European Union, which has seen significant numbers of fishermen go out of business. Many farms have fared little better, and for both industries, tourism is often seen as a way of providing a new or secondary income.

Over the past few decades the Southwest has become a popular choice for second-home buyers, which has kept the estate agency industry buoyant, but has also priced many local people out of the housing market. And holiday homes that are left empty for several months of the year damage the local economy.

But tourism has also had its success stories, notably the wealth of top-class hotels and fish restaurants that have opened in the past decade (as exemplified by Rick Stein's seafood empire in Padstow), and the Eden Project, the giant artificial rainforest created just after the millennium which is now the region's most popular tourist attraction. But it's not been enough to plug the fiscal gaps. Indeed, Cornwall's economy reached such a low ebb that in 1999 it was declared one of the European Union's poorest economic areas, and was awarded more than £350 million worth of aid over the next half decade.

The trouble is, the people here know from bitter experience that, no matter how many hotels, restaurants and attractions you open, an economy based on tourism is only ever a single health-scare away from disaster. In 2001 a devastating outbreak of foot-and-mouth disease essentially shut the entire countryside down to tourism for months, closing moors, footpaths, cycleways, bridleways and beaches and sending many small holiday businesses to the wall. Thankfully, things have recovered in the years since, but the region remains ever wary.

Today, this proud region is searching for a new history – the one founded on trade and industry is over, the new one based on tourism and the service sector is not quite fit for purpose. There's a feeling that something big needs to step into the breech for the region to return to prosperity. The trouble is, no one is quite sure what that might be, yet.

Topics

03

Cultural Identity

The closer to the Atlantic you get, the stronger the Southwest's sense of cultural identity becomes. Cornwall has the clearest and most pronounced view of its own uniqueness, born of its strong Celtic roots. In the Dark Ages this was one of the principal enclaves for Romano Britons holding out against Anglo-Saxon incursions, and, despite grudgingly becoming part of England in the 10th century, it managed to maintain its own language and a largely separate culture throughout the Middle Ages and into the early modern period. Today, however, it could be argued that much of what made the county culturally distinct has faded away. The Cornish language died out in the 18th century, specific local crafts have been replaced by ubiquitous trades, the mighty tin-making industry – for centuries the basis of local political power – has crumbled, while the population, once made up almost entirely of people born in the county (a situation maintained for centuries by the region's notoriously poor roads) is now a mixture of locals and migrants from other parts of the country and beyond.

And yet, despite (or perhaps because of) this gradual watering down of the traditional Cornish way of life, recent years have seen a pronounced surge in regional identity, with many people proclaiming a new sense of pride in their Celtic roots. The striking St Piran's flags – a white cross on a black background – flies from homes across the region. Attempts are being made to revive the long dormant Cornish tongue, albeit on nowhere near the scale that has taken place in Wales. The Celtic nationalist party, Mebyon Kernow (literally 'sons of Cornwall'), which campaigns for greater Cornish autonomy, attracts widespread support in the county, and there are a good number of people here calling for the county to have its own regional assembly along the lines of those operating in Britain's other Celtic heartlands of Scotland and Wales. Some even argue for total independence.

The sense of regional identity is less clear cut elsewhere in the region. There are no pressure groups campaigning for Devonian or Somersetonian independence. But then, these counties never had their own languages and were opened up to the wider world much earlier than their more westerly neighbour, and are more clearly and more obviously English. Still, you'll find plenty of people here who are very proud of their heritage and highly vocal about their regional attachments. This often takes the form of a general Southwestern affiliation or a pronounced civic pride – identifying themselves closely with local towns and cities, such as Bath, Bristol or Exeter, rather than the county as a whole.

Ask anyone outside the Southwest to characterize the culture here and you'll no doubt hear the usual clichés about cider-drinking, surfing and combine-harvester riding. But there is no one Southwest identity, rather a myriad different ways of life: rural, urban, traditional, modern, that change and evolve with the passing decades, and together make up an endlessly fascinating whole.

The Economy

Fishing, shipbuilding, trade (of various dubious sorts including, for more than a hundred years, slavery), smuggling and mining have all played their part in creating the economy of the Southwest. But today, from Bath to Land's End, one industry towers above them all – tourism. Out of every five pounds spent here, one goes on some kind of tourist service. In many places tourism has supplanted the long-established industries (the last mine closed in the 1990s), and in those places where traditional trades continue, on the farms and in the fishing villages, tourism often provides a vital form of additional revenue. This is no doubt set to increase in the future unless farming and fishing can arrest their current decline.

Manufacturing hasn't been wiped from the landscape entirely. The extraction of kaolin, or china clay, for use in pottery and paper-making is still a going concern in Cornwall. Both Plymouth and Appledore maintain shipbuilding industries. And Bristol still has relatively healthy finance, technology and aeronautics sectors, which is just as well as the city has never been able to draw the paying punters in anything like the numbers of its more preened and pampered neighbour, Bath. Elsewhere, however, the demise of industry has often been replaced by a big gaping void. Cornwall endured such a pronounced decline in the 1980s and 1990s that the European Union was prompted to pour hundreds of millions of pounds of aid into the economy. The effect, however, has arguably been limited. Per capita earnings here are still on average 10% lower than they are for the country as a whole.

This is of particular concern because, not only is the Southwest a pretty sparsely populated place (out of Britain's 60-million-odd citizens, around 3 million, or just over a twentieth, are resident in these three counties, most of them in Devon), but those that do live here are not really of an age to kickstart the economy. The Southwest's population is old and getting older. There are more senior citizens here than anywhere else in Britain, with over a third of all residents aged fifty or over. It's a situation that is likely to get worse. The lack of opportunities for young people forces many to move out of the region, most heading to London and the Southeast. At the same time, the Southwest is fast gaining itself a reputation as England's retirement home. So it's a double whammy. Not only are the locals getting older as the younger generation seeks its fortunes elsewhere, but new arrivals are often at the end of their working life. This situation helps to make the Southwest a calm and placid place, but not a very economically vibrant one.

And just to throw another problem into the mix, many of the region's more desirable villages are now suffering from second home syndrome: wealthy professionals from other parts of the country buy up holiday cottages, which are then left vacant for many months of the year, damaging the local economy.

Of course, it's not all doom and gloom. Tourism has brought wealth to the region and provided work for many people. There's just a feeling that, on its own, it doesn't provide quite enough opportunities to stop the region's youth from seeking their fortunes elsewhere.

Art

These days art is one of the West Country's biggest draws, with thousands coming each year to visit the galleries of **Newlyn** and **St Ives** on the North Cornwall coast, which in the late 19th and early 20th centuries were home to thriving and highly influential artists' communities. The first painters arrived in Newlyn in the early 1880s attracted by the inspiring coastal landscapes, simple rural life and clean pure light. Trained in the Impressionist schools of France, the artists saw in Cornwall something reminiscent of the coastal villages of Brittany, or at least felt able to project the vision taught to them in Brittany on to the Cornish coast. However, it was the arrival on the scene of the Irish painter, **Stanhope Forbes**, that really set in motion the creation of a specific 'Newlyn School'. His paintings captured the rural customs and hardy lifestyles of the locals, particularly the fishermen, with whom he became increasingly fascinated. These sometimes rather sentimental portrayals of fishing life gained great favour, following exhibitions at the Royal Academy in London, and other artists soon followed in his wake, including **Norman Garstin**, who seemed to specialize in portraits of bedraggled people walking in the rain, most famously in *The Rain it Raineth Everyday*, and **Henry Scott Tuke**, whose almost obsessive outdoor studies of young nude males have seen him dubbed as a pioneer of gay culture and homoerotic art. Incidentally, most of the subjects in his portraits are not locals but models brought in from London. Cornish fishermen were having no truck with that sort of thing.

Above all, what these artists shared in common was a desire to move painting out of the studio (and indeed out of the city) into the open air, *en plein air* as the French put it, to paint people going about their everyday lives in pure, natural light. The Newlyn scene continued into the 20th century when a second wave of artists arrived in town, including Forbes' wife, Elizabeth, but its reputation was soon superseded by that of St Ives, just down the road, the new cool kid on the artistic block.

Artists and craftsmen had been settling and painting in St Ives for decades, but it was the establishment of a studio by the potters **Bernard Leach** and **Shoji Hamada** in the 1920s that brought the wider world's attention to the work going on here. The St Ives Pottery was almost singlehandedly responsible for the creation of Britain's studio pottery movement of the next few decades, a movement characterized by the creation of simple, plain pottery in a small studio, with all the processes controlled by a single potter. Leach's philosophy – largely derived from the mingei folk movement of Japan where he had spent much time studying – was that pots should be first and foremost utilitarian objects, not pieces of art, and that function must always dictate form.

The St Ives fine art scene began in the late 1920s with **Ben Nicholson**'s discovery and promotion of a local retired fisherman and amateur artist, **Alfred Wallis**, who had taken up painting just a few years earlier after the death of his wife ('for company'). Wallis' naive depictions of local fishing life, often painted on pieces of driftwood or bits of cardboard packaging, attracted a great deal of appreciation from artists both in St Ives and in London, although unfortunately not with the wider art-buying public. Despite Nicholson's earnest championing, Wallis was never able to make a steady living out of his art and died in penury in 1942.

His mentor fared considerably better. Nicholson became the figurehead of the **St Ives School**, which, though similarly inspired by the rugged, natural beauty of the area as its Newlyn predecessor, leaned more towards a non-figurative, semi-abstract approach to art, as highlighted by Nicholson's own work and that of his second wife, the sculptor, **Barbara Hepworth**, who was profoundly inspired by the contours of the Cornish landscape.

The couple split in the 1950s, with Nicholson moving to Switzerland, while Hepworth continued to live and work in St Ives, overseeing the rise of a new group of artists in the 1950s and 60s – including people such as **Peter Lanyon, Bryan Wynter, John Wells, Roger Hilton** and **Terry Frost** – and watching the movement undergo a split between those who still wanted to take a semi-realistic approach to their paintings and those, of whom Hepworth was one, who favoured abstraction (and who would form their own splinter group, the Penwith Society). Hepworth kept busy until her death in a fire in 1975. Her house and garden are today a museum dedicated to her work and influence (*see* p.208). In 1993 the importance of St Ives' artistic legacy was given further acknowledgement with the opening of the **Tate St Ives**, an outpost of the great London gallery dedicated to British art (*see* p.207).

Newlyn also boasts its own grand collection, the **Newlyn Art Gallery** (*see* p.204) , one of the finest for contemporary art outside of London. Other notable galleries in the Southwest include: the **Bristol City Museum and Art Gallery** (*see* p.70), which contains works by both Nicholson and Hepworth, a gallery of Pre-Raphaelite paintings and a whole gallery devoted to works by the Bristol School, a group of Romantic artists who practised in the city in the early 19th century; Bath's **Victoria Art Gallery** (*see* p.88), whose collection features works by some of the numerous caricaturists who came to the city in the 18th and early 19th centuries to capture and satirize society life, including John Nixon and James Gillray; and the **Plymouth Museum & Art Gallery** (*see* p.144), which has a wall dedicated to the city's most famous artistic resident and chronicler of pub life, **Beryl Cook** (*see* p.145), plus a gallery devoted to works by artists of 'St Ives and the Southwest'.

Bristol's streets and houses also provide an al fresco gallery for the protest graffiti and whimsical stencilling of local anonymous self-styled 'guerrilla artist', **Banksy**. If they haven't been painted over yet, works to look out for include a stencil of Charon, the ferryman for the dead, on the side of town's club boat Thekla, and the *Love triangle*, which shows a naked fleeing man hanging from a window at which his mistress and her husband stand (painted appropriately enough on the wall of sexual health clinic).

Literature

Many of the greats of English literature either have come from the Southwest or have used it as inspiration for their works. These have included:

Jane Austen (1775–1817). The foremost satirizer of Georgian social manners lived in Bath for around five years at the turn of the 19th century and set two of her novels here, *Northanger Abbey* and *Persuasion* (*see* p.87).

John Betjeman (1906–84). The poet laureate was born and laid to rest in the Cornish village of Trebetherick. All his life he maintained a great fondness for the West Country, producing numerous poems on the region and in the 1930s writing guidebooks, known as the 'Shell Guides', on Cornwall and Devon, aimed at motoring tourists.

R.D. Blackmore (1825–1900). Blackmore's most famous work, *Lorna Doone*, is set on Exmoor at the time of the Monmouth Rebellion (*see* p.111).

Agatha Christie (1890–1976). The world's bestselling crime writer was born in Torquay and spent her entire life in the region, from 1938 onwards residing at the Greenway Estate on the River Dart where she wrote many of her best-known works (*see* p.132).

Samuel Taylor Coleridge (1772–1834). The poet was born in Ottery St Mary, and wrote many of his best works, including *The Rime of the Ancient Mariner* and *Kubla Khan* whilst living in Nether Stowey, drawing inspiration from his nocturnal roamings in the Quantocks and on Exmoor in the company of his close friend, William Wordsworth (*see* p.105).

Daniel Defoe (1660–1731). Defoe reputedly met Alexander Selkirk, the real-life castaway who inspired his novel *Robinsoe Crusoe*, at the Llandoger Trow pub in Bristol (*see* p.71).

Sir Arthur Conan Doyle (1859–1930). The Scottish creator of Sherlock Holmes worked as a doctor in Plymouth and Portsmouth before becoming a writer. He was inspired to write one of his most famous Holmes' stories, *The Hound of the Baskervilles*, following a trip to Dartmoor (*see* p.154).

Charles Kingsley (1819–1875). The author of *The Water Babies* and *Westward Ho!*, and cheerleader-in-chief for the North Devon landscape, was born in the village of Holne on Dartmoor, and later moved to Clovelly (*see* p.165).

D.H. Lawrence (1885–1930). Lawrence lived in Zennor during the early years of World War I where he completed one of his best-known titles, *Women in Love*.

Daphne du Maurier (1907–1989). Though born in London, du Maurier spent most of her life in Cornwall and set her three most famous novels there, *Jamaica Inn*, *Frenchman's Creek* and *Rebecca*.

Henry Williamson (1895–1977). Williamson's best-loved novel, *Tarka the Otter*, which follows the adventures of the eponymous aquatic mammal, was set in and around the rivers of North Devon. Today you can follow the Tarka Trail along the banks of the rivers Taw and Torridge (*see* p.163).

William Wordsworth (1770–1850). Wordsworth lived at Alfoxton House in the Quantocks in Somerset for a year in 1797–8 where, in conjunction with his great friend and fellow poet, Samuel Taylor Coleridge, he produced the *Lyrical Ballads*, often described as the 'manifesto for Romanticism'.

Food and Drink

This is where the Southwest really comes into its own. Here they take food, particularly the sourcing of good ingredients, very seriously, which is probably why the region supports more organic farmers than anywhere else in the country. But then, with more than 600 miles of coastline, much of it teeming with fish, the people have long appreciated the benefits of a larder stocked with fresh produce. Together, the seas and fertile farmland inspire the region's restaurants to produce some of the finest cooking Britain can offer, based both on traditional, local recipes – often fiercely preserved and protected – and adventurous takes on more exotic cuisines. That's not to say that the Southwest's dining scene is one unmitigated joy. Its big resorts can offer the same low-end fast food found anywhere else. But you are perhaps more likely to find stylish, innovative eateries in places you wouldn't normally expect them, such as in small fishing villages and rural hamlets. Generally, the Southwest's culinary landscape – in contravention of the economic problems besetting many of the region's other industries – has expanded and improved dramatically over the past couple of decades, fuelled in part by the correspondingly rapid growth in tourism to the region.

Specialities: Food

Unsurprisingly, given the region's lengthy coastline, and the fact that few places are further than 30 miles from the sea, **fish and seafood** dominate the menus of the Southwest. There's both a great abundance (despite the relative decline of the fishing industry in recent decades, it's still a thriving business in many ports, ensuring a constant supply of the freshest ingredients) and a wonderful variety, from chip-shop classics, such as cod and halibut, to gourmet favourites like monkfish, sea bream, John Dory, oysters, tiger prawns, lemon sole and lobster. More than 40 local species are caught and cooked commercially. You'll find fish offered in the fanciest forms possible – such as 'marinated salmon with passion fruit, lime and coriander' at Rick Stein's celebrated Seafood

Restaurant in Padstow – and the simplest, as exemplified by the battered fish and chips and crab sandwiches offered in the region's pubs.

Lamb, reared on the region's rich grasslands, is the Southwest's meat of choice. Game, such as grouse hunted on Exmoor and Dartmoor, also has a sizable market, as does locally reared venison. The region's organic, handmade **sausages** are some of best around.

If you asked people to name a dish that summed up the Southwest, most would probably opt for the **Cornish pasty**. These days it's a near-ubiquitous fast food sold in outlets across the country, and not generally seen as particularly sophisticated fare. But just as a burger from McDonald's bears little relation to something organic, grass-fed and home-made, so the cellophane-wrapped gristly parcels sold at the nation's train stations are not good representatives of this fine baking tradition. For the best pasties, you need to head to a local bakery where you'll be sold delightful, tightly-filled envelopes of flaky pastry, carefully crimped around the edges (so as to form a sort of pastry 'handle' by which to hold it) and filled with the classic ingredients of steak, onions, potato and sometimes swede (known locally as yellow turnip) in a moist gravy. Avoid anything prepackaged in plastic or microwaveable. These days there are several other fillings available; some acceptable (pork and apple, lamb and mint), some not (chicken balti).

The food was invented in mining communities as a sort of ready-meal to be eaten underground on the job, and was originally supposed to be an all-in-one main course and dessert, with a savoury filling at one end and a sweet at the other, separated by a pastry wall. The pastry case not only made it easy to eat, so the workers didn't have to carry cutlery, but the thick crimped seam stopped them from contaminating the meat – the seam was usually thrown away uneaten.

The Cornish are justly proud of their pasties, and not a little grateful – these days it's a £150-million-plus industry, which probably goes some way to explaining why the Cornish Pasty Association are currently lobbying the EU to have the dish awarded geographical protection, like champagne or Parma ham, so that only pastry parcels created in the county can legally call themselves 'Cornish'.

Other savoury specialities of the region, albeit much less commonly encountered, include **cobbler**, a heavy hearty meat dish from Devon, a bit like a casserole topped with a thick scone, and the surreal-looking **star gazey pie**, a fish pie made using seven different species with the heads and tails left sticking out of the pastry (for ease of identification, apparently, *see* p.210 for more).

The West Country is also well known as the originator of the **cream tea**, although whether it was developed first in Cornwall or in Devon is still hotly debated. It's a simple offering, consisting of a selection of light, fluffy scones, thick locally produced jam (typically strawberry), clotted cream and a pot of good well-brewed tea, but done well it is a meal to rival any other. Unfortunately, it is done fairly badly fairly often, particularly at on-site cafés at tourist attractions. Head to the local village teashop to experience a real West Country cream tea.

Less well-known delicacies include **saffron cake**, a currant loaf coloured yellow, and lightly flavoured, with a little saffron, **Cornish heavy cake** – a stodgy fruity concoction – and various types of fudge.

Moving on to the cheese course, the region's many dairy farms produce a great variety of produce, from the nation's favourite, **Cheddar**, as served up in ploughman's lunches across the country – at its best in its tangy, sharp mature state – to the mild creamy **Cornish yarg** which comes wrapped in a mouldy (though edible) rind of nettles.

Specialities: Drink

The one drink everyone associates with the West Country is, of course, **cider**. The region is the world's major producer of the drink (at least the alcoholic version), which enjoys a centuries-old tradition. Once upon a time this was truly a cottage industry. Every farm would put aside a little land for the purpose of growing apples, and a little time each year for creating their own potent brew. Small producers do still exist, many turning out scrumpy, cider's cloudier, more tannic, more lethal sibling. Do take care if ordering a pint as it's often a good deal stronger than cider (sometimes more than 8 percent by volume) which can quickly take a toll on even the hardiest of constitutions. Most of the cider sold, however, is mass produced, a good deal of it by the Gaymers plant in Somerset – Europe's largest – which is responsible for some of the country's best-known brands including Blackthorn and Olde English (*see* p.109).

Though perhaps not as closely identified with the region, **real ale** has a popular presence in the pubs of the Southwest, a good deal of it made by a growing band of mini-breweries, turning out a raft of evocatively named tipples, such as Doom Bar (from Sharp's Brewery in Rock, Cornwall), Spingo (from the Blue Anchor Inn in Helston) and Betty Stogs, Cornish Knocker and Ginger Tosser (from Truro's Skinners Brewery).

Wine is not something the British traditionally do well, or rather don't really have the climate for. But the Southwest's relatively balmy summers give it a slight advantage over the rest of the country. These days some decent vintages are being produced, particularly at Devon's Sharpham Vineyard, which can offer reds, whites and, to finish, some very fine cheeses from its on-site dairy.

The strongest regional drinks of all, however, are the various brands of gin turned out by the Plymouth Gin Distillery, which has been serving up its beverages since the late 18th century. You can tour the plant to see how it's done (and get a few free samples, *see* p.142).

Geography
and Wildlife

04

Geography

A thin tapering peninsula jutting out from the mainland of England, the Southwest's defining feature, from both a geographical and a visitor's point of view, is its coastline which stretches for more than 600 miles, encompassing everything from high, wave-battered cliffs to soft sandy beaches and grass-covered dunes. The region is underpinned by a variety of different rocks. To the west, in Cornwall and Devon, these are mainly hard, igneous rocks, such as granite, which give the moors their distinct tor-studded appearance. These represent the oldest sections of the landscape, the results of rumbling volcanic activity around 300 million years ago which created the bulging, undulating intrusions that have only slowly, reluctantly been eroded into today's familiar hill-scattered landscape. To the east are softer sedimentary rock, such as sandstone, limestone, clay and chalk, all of which were laid down during later geological periods, and which give the countryside above them a gentler, more rolling aspect.

Industry, particularly tin and copper mining, once the dominating feature of the interior landscape, has faded into the background in recent decades, with much of the former infrastructure now either abandoned and being slowly reclaimed by nature or turned into wildlife reserves and tourist attractions – most notably in the form of the Eden Project in a former St Austell china-clay pit.

In the rural heartland, particularly on the lonely moors, the land can feel feral and untamed, although this is something of a bucolic illusion. Little of the land here is truly wild. Most has endured some reshaping by humans. Agriculture began here in prehistoric times, soon after the end of the last Ice Age, and over the millennia the needs of farming and industry have seen the region's once-thick woodland cleared for timber and fuel and to provide land for grazing, the grasslands divided up by hedgerows and dry-stone walls into a merry patchwork of fields, seams of metal pulled out of the earth and entire hillsides obliterated to provide stone for housing, harbours and roads.

Despite the influence of humankind, pockets of wild flora and fauna can still be found, albeit not in the abundance and diversity of times past. Modern, intensive farming methods have seriously degraded many environments. But human influence hasn't been entirely hostile. Recent decades have seen the local population waking up to the wonders on its doorstop – and the dangers facing them – leading to the creation of the protected areas and national parks that are now the region's main havens for wildlife.

Flora

The Southwest may receive no more sunshine than the rest of the country, but its Gulf Stream-aided climate nurtures a singular profusion of plants. Much of the flora is here as a direct result of – or has at the very least been obliged to adapt to – human activity. The farmlands of Devon and Cornwall in particular are crisscrossed by a network of ancient hedgerows, some dating back to before the Norman invasion, made of sturdy native shrubs such as hazel, hawthorn and elder, which provide habitats for an abundance of birds and insects. Though a good deal of the region's woodland and forest has been cleared to service the needs of housing and industry, patches remain on Dartmoor, Exmoor and Bodmin Moor, including some areas of Atlantic (or upland) oakwood. These were managed areas of trees carefully coppiced for charcoal and tanbark (to produce tannin for processing leather) between 1600 and 1800. In more recent times many of these areas have been replaced with plantations of fast-growing conifers and other commercial woods, or have been taken over by invasive shrubs such as rhododendrons. Those few surviving patches hold a great biodiversity, their thick canopies filled with birdlife and providing cover for a mulchy mass of ferns, fungi, mosses, liverworts and lichens. There's a particularly good example on Dartmoor, where the 777-acre Yarner Wood, growing around the site of a former copper mine, offers a dense selection of native trees. Among others, these include pine, oak, holly, ash, beech and larch.

Each area boasts its own particular tapestry of colours as flowering plants come into bloom. The flower-filled meadows of North Devon (known here as culm grassland) are awash with purples (foxgloves, devil's bit scabious, meadow thistle), pinks (campion), whites (cow parsley), blues (common speedwell) and oranges (hawkweed). The moors sprout great blankets of yellow (gorse) and purple (heather), while in summer coastal areas provide harbour to delicate, cowering clusters of bright mauve sea lavender, yellow kidney vetch, purple marsh orchids and pink wild thyme. Look out in particular, both on the coast and in local menus, for samphire, which has yellow flowers and spicy, aromatic leaves.

The nurturing effects of the Gulf Stream have perhaps been put to their best use in the Southwest's various gardens, many of which boast bright, subtropical blooms that seem almost out of place under England's grey, cloud-covered skies. Good examples include Trebah (see p.196), Heligan (see p.181) and Tresco Abbey Gardens on the Isles of Scilly (see p.215).

Fauna

Land

It has to be said, things aren't quite so exciting these days as they were a few millennia ago when bears, wolves and boars roamed the post-glacial landscape. Today the top predators are foxes – in increasing numbers since the introduction of the hunting ban in 2005 – badgers, who live in setts in the region's woodland, and otters, which hunt in, and live alongside, several of the region's rivers, including the De Lank and the Camel in Cornwall, and the Taw and Torridge in Devon. Their shy nature and largely aquatic lifestyle, however, means they're unlikely to be spotted without a good deal of patience and dedication. Also inhabiting the riverbanks are equally elusive communities of stoats and water voles. Still you've got a better chance of seeing all of these than you have of the native red squirrel which has been largely eradicated – both here and in the rest of the country – following the introduction of the larger, more aggressive grey squirrel from North America in the 19th century.

Moving down the food chain, the Southwest provides a generous, grassy home to hordes of hares and rabbits, as well as a couple of wild equine species, including the shaggy Dartmoor pony and its near neighbour, the Exmoor pony. Exmoor is also home to one of country's largest populations of red deer.

Close to the ground, keep an eye out for some of the region's various slippery residents, including slow worms, grass snakes and adders (the only poisonous snake in the UK) which inhabit areas of open grassland, and can occasionally be spotted sunning themselves on rocks, but will probably slither off into the undergrowth if approached.

Air

From the dragonflies and butterflies of the riverbanks, to the bats of the woodland and the nesting birds of coastal cliffs, your best chance of spotting wildlife in the Southwest is to look upwards. The region's meadows, hedgerows, riverbanks and reed beds are home to healthy populations of dragonflies and butterflies. Those you are most likely to see include the tortoiseshell, the clouded yellow, the red admiral and the painted lady. Those you are unlikely to catch a glimpse of include the Large Blue which has recently been introduced, in limited numbers, since being declared extinct in the 1970s. Hedgerows also provide nest sites for various native birds including the song thrush, blackbirds and bullfinches.

At the shore, much of the coastline is under the protection of the National Trust. Here the cliff-top grassland is home to nightingales (listen out for their distinctive whistley songs), while the cliff ledges host nesting colonies of guillemots – there's a particularly large population near Brixham – and razorbills, found in their greatest numbers in West Cornwall. The cliff ledges also provide roosts and nesting sites for the peregrine falcon, the nation's fastest bird of prey. Other seabirds common to the area include fulmars, kittiwakes, gannets and cormorants, as well as herring gulls, those ubiquitous seaside chip scavengers. The region's islands provide perhaps the best environments for marine bird spotting, particularly the Isles of Scilly and Lundy Island, both of which are home to colonies of puffins.

The greatest concentrations of wildfowl are found in the estuaries of Devon and Cornwall. Numerous wading species can be spotted at the refuge at Dawlish Warren, at the mouth of the Exe Estuary, including curlew, redshank, godwits, dunlin, oystercatchers and avocet, as well as wildfowl such as brent geese, shelduck and grebes (see p.126).

Moving inland, birds of prey patrol the skies above areas of open farmland and countryside. Although large species, such as eagles, are long since extinct in these parts, you can still see kestrels, often spotted hovering dead still above their quarry, as well as sparrowhawks, hobbies, goshawks, and honey buzzards (who despite their name actually eat insects, typically wasps and hornets). Woodland areas often harbour barn owls and tawny owls, although as they are nocturnal, you're more likely to hear their plaintive hoots than see them in action. More commonly spotted are the various species of bird living alongside the region's fast-flowing rivers – in particular the Taw and the Torridge in Devon. These include the likes of kingfishers, herons, dippers and sand martins.

Perhaps the winged creature you're most likely to spot isn't a bird at all, but a bat. The nation has 17 species, several of which live in the Southwest, including horseshoe bats,

National Parks

The Southwest has two national parks and nine Areas of Outstanding Natural Beauty (www.aonb.org.uk), which along with a network of private refuges and stretches of National-Trust-owned coastline, represent your best opportunities for watching the diverse range of wildlife in the region:

Blackdown Hills AONB, St Ivel House, Hemyock, Cullompton, DEVON; t (01823) 680681; linda.bennett@devon.gov.uk.

Cornwall AONB (including Land's End and the Lizard Peninsula)Fal Building, Treyew Road, Truro, Cornwall;t (01872) 323998; pwalton@cornwall.gov.uk.

Dartmoor, High Moorland Visitor Centre, Tavistock Road, Princetown, Yelverton, Devon; t (01822) 890414; www.dartmoor-npa.gov.uk.

East Devon AONB (encompassing the coastal landscape from Lyme Regis to Exmouth, the 'Jurassic Coast'), East Devon Business Centre, Heathpark Way, Honiton, Devon; t (01404) 46663; cwoodruff@eastdevon.gov.uk

Exmoor, Dulverton National Park Cetre 7–9 Fore Street, Dulverton, West Somerset; t (01398) 323841; www.exmoor-nationalpark.gov.uk.

Isles of Scilly AONB, Old Wesleyan Chapel, Garrison Lane, St Mary's, Isles of Scilly; t (01720) 424355; tkirk@scilly.gov.uk.

Mendip Hills AONB, Charterhouse Centre, Near Blagdon, Bristol, Avon; t (01761) 463357; sjackson@somerset.gov.uk.

North Devon AONB (encompassing the coast from Coombe Martin to the Cornish border), Bideford Station, East the Water, Bideford, Devon, t (01237) 423655; linda.blanchard@devon.gov.uk

Quantock Hills AONB, Fyne Court, Broomfield, Bridgwater, Somerset; t (01823) 451884; quantockhills@somerset.gov.uk.

South Devon AONB (encompassing the coast from Torbay to Devon), South Devon AONB Unit, Follaton House, Plymouth Road, Totnes; t (01803) 861384; robin.toogood@southdevonaonb. org.uk.

Tamar Valley AONB, Cotehele Quay, St Dominick, Saltash, Cornwall; t (01579) 351681; info@tamarvalley.org.uk

brown long-eared bats, common pipistrelles and noctule bats. They're best spotted near areas of woodland, or old farm buildings, come twilight as they emerge from their roosts for an evening's hunting. If near a body of water, keep an eye out too for Daubenton's bat, the 'water bat', which skims the surface looking for insects.

Sea

To have a chance of seeing the Southwest's largest creatures, you'll need to get in a boat. Colonies of grey seals inhabit many offshore islands, including Mousehole Rock and the Isles of Scilly, where you'll find them in their greatest numbers. A trip through local waters may also give you the chance of seeing them in the water, bobbing their heads above the surface to watch you pass. Groups of dolphins and porpoises can also be encountered in the English Channel, although numbers have greatly decreased over the past century owing to overfishing – this has not only depleted the stocks on which the animals feed, but has also caused innumerable deaths through dolphins inadvertently getting tangled up in fishing nets. It's too early to tell yet whether the EU's ban on drift nets (the 'walls of death') has allowed the populations to recover.

Moving down the likelihood-of-spotting scale, whales, including minke, humpback and even killer whales, are sometimes spotted in the waters around the Isles of Scilly, as are migrating leatherback turtles on their vast journeys across the oceans back to their breeding grounds in the tropics. One species whose numbers actually seem to be increasing – and which you have a reasonable chance of spotting during the summer months – are basking sharks, the world's second largest fish, who visit the area in summer to feed on vast swarms of seasonal plankton. Though measuring up to 40ft long, the sharks are completely harmless to humans (though deadly to plankton).

Planning
Your Trip

05

When to Go

Climate

As every tourist brochure to the region will constantly remind you, the Southwest enjoys Britain's most clement climate. This is chiefly because it receives the earliest and clearest benefit from the warm air and water pushed over the Atlantic by the Gulf Stream. And it's a good job that it does. Britain's latitude is officially Arctic, and without the kindness of the currents the climate here would be closer to Russia's than the Med's. The hottest months are July and August, which also correspond to the school holidays making them also the most congested times of year. However, even in summer you shouldn't expect uninterrupted sunshine, as this is also the wettest region in Britain (something the tourist brochures aren't quite so keen to advertise). There is no single wet season; downpours can occur at any time, so it's best to always be prepared. Such blazing sun as the region does get allows it to enjoy the country's highest sea temperatures, although you might be hard pressed to tell as you stand shivering in the shallows.

Spring and autumn will generally be cooler (and wetter), but you'll have much less company during your travels, making them perhaps the best time to visit. Winters can be cold and brutal, but beautiful, particularly after a big snowfall, although this will limit your movements rather.

Festivals

March

5 March, St Piran's Day, Cornwall. Each Cornish 'National' Day seems to be celebrated with more intensity and greater fervour than the last. Observance only began in the late 19th century and continued in a largely low-key form until the 1950s. Since then it has gradually become a truly county-wide affair with most towns and villages now joining in the festivities and iconic white and black flags fluttering from every available vantage point.

Mid March, Bath Literature Festival. Nine days of talks, reading and events. See p.91

May

1 May, May Day, Padstow. Padstow is the setting for the region's most famous May Day celebrations when one of the town's local men is given the dubious honour of donning a strange black, white and red costume to become the Obby Oss ('Hobby Horse'), the centrepiece of the town's centuries-old fertility rite. See p.185.

First Week, Flora Day, Helston. Elaborately costumed couples twirl through the streets performing the Furry Dance (or Floral Dance) to celebrate the coming of Spring. See also p.200.

First Week, World Pilot Gig Championships, Isles of Scilly. These popular rowing boat races featuring teams from across the Southwest have been held for more than a quarter of a century (www.worldgigs.co.uk).

Early–Mid May, Daphne Du Maurier Festival, Fowey. A week of events loosely themed around the local author – comedy, readings, exhibitions, dance performances etc (www.dumaurierfestival.co.uk).

Mid May, Bath International Music Festival, Bath. Over two weeks of concerts at venues across the city. See p.91

Late May–early June, Bath Fringe Festival. Though much less well known, Bath's fringe festival is the country's biggest after Edinburgh. Expect lots of comedy, theatre, dance and street performance (www.bath-fringe.co.uk).

June

Late June, Glastonbury Festival of Performing Arts. Although these days it competes with dozens of similar contenders, 'Glasto' is still the summer season's biggest and most prestigious event, attracting top names from the world of music. The announcement of each year's line-up is usually met with great fanfare by the press. It's not cheap – expect to pay £185 for a ticket – and bad weather and plentiful mud seem almost guaranteed, but that doesn't stop more than 120,000 people turning up to party over the long weekend in front of more than 80 stages playing host to in excess of 700 acts.

Midsummer, Golowan Festival, Penzance. Nine-day celebration of Cornish Culture centred around midsummer ('Golowan' in Cornish) with concerts, parades, an 'obby oss' procession and fireworks (www.golowan.org).

July

Second Week, Way With Words, Dartington. Prestigious literary festival amid the splendid surrounds of Dartington Hall. *See* p.135

Early–mid July, Eden Sessions, The Eden Project. In summer a large, curvy and appropriately biome-like stage is set up in front of the real things for a series of big name concerts by the likes of Oasis, Kasabian, Goldfrapp etc (*www.edenproject.com/sessions*).

Mid July, Exeter Arts Festival. More than 40 events, including comedy, dance, contemporary and classical music, theatre and special children's events over two July weeks (*www.exeter.gov.uk/festival*).

August

Early August, Relentless Boardmasters, Newquay. A celebration of everything Newquay-ish, this five-day event features concerts, bmx-ing, skateboarding, bikini competitions and, of course, surfing (*www.relentlessboardmasters. com*).

Early August, Sidmouth Folk Week, Sidmouth. Concerts, cream teas and crab sandwiches. All very gentle (*www.sidmouthfolk week.co.uk*).

Early August, British Fireworks Championship, Plymouth. The Hoe is the best vantage point for Plymouth's annual celebration of colourful explosions. Six teams compete over two nights to be declared Britain's Firework Champions (*www.britishfireworks.co.uk*).

Mid-August, Falmouth Week Regatta, Falmouth. Seven days of races in Falmouth Bay for all types of boats – multi-hulls, yachts, dragon boats etc. (*www.falmouthweek.co.uk*). August also sees regattas taking place at Paignton (*www.paigntonregatta.org.uk*), Fowey (*www.foweyroyalregatta.co.uk*), *see* p.178, and Dartmouth (*www.dartmouthregatta.co.uk*).

November

5 November: Bonfire Night – Ottery St Mary. Bonfire celebrations take place throughout the region, the most famous of which are held in Ottery St Mary where blazing tar barrels are carried through the streets to a gigantic bonfire topped with a flaming effigy of Guy Fawkes.

December

23 December: Tom Bawcock's Eve – Mousehole. Locals celebrate their continued survival against the elements with servings of star-gazey pie. *See* p.210

Tourist Information

Britain's main tourist information service, **Visit Britain** (1 Regent Street, London, t 0870 242 9988, *www.visitbritain.co.uk*) is a good source of national information while **Visit Southwest** (*www.visitsouthwest.co.uk*) can provide more region-specific knowledge. Both can give good up-to-date information on places to visit, events, where to stay and eat and local transport. The London office sells maps, guides and entertainment tickets and also operates an accommodation-booking service (also available online). Dartmoor (*see* p.149) and Exmoor (*see* p.113) National Parks offices can give specific advice on walking in the parks.

Disabled Travellers

Travellers with disabilities are generally well catered for in the Southwest, but difficulties do still arise because of the age of the region's infrastructure, including hotels, attractions and transport. For help and advice, contact **RADAR**, a mine of information. It publishes an annual guide, *Holidays in Britain & Ireland – A guide for Disabled People*, with advice on transport and accommodation. Much of the information is also available online. As a rule, they advise using newer, purpose-built hotels that have had to comply with modern building regulations regarding accessibility, which often means staying in blandly reliable chains like Travelodge, Travel Inn, Ibis or Holiday Inn.

The Tourist Board's official accommodation guide also provides a list of places to stay geared towards disabled people.

Trains and planes are supposed to provide practical help for wheelchair users or anyone who needs help getting on and off. Phone the airline or train-operating company in advance to find out exactly what help you can get, and book it.

The **National Trust** publishes an annual booklet, *Information for Visitors with Disabilities*, with details of accessibility, which can be downloaded from their website, **t** (01793) 817634, *www.nationaltrust.org.uk*. **English Heritage** produces a similar *Access Guide*, **t** 0870 333 1181, *www.english-heritage.org.uk* again available online, as does the **Dartmoor National Parks Association**: *Easy Going Dartmoor*, **t** (01626) 832093, *www.dartmoor-npa.gov.uk*.

Organizations for Disabled Travellers

RADAR (Royal Association for Disability and Rehabilitation) 12 City Forum, 250 City Road, London, **t** (020) 7250 3222, *www.radar.org.uk*.

Holiday Care Service 2nd Floor, Imperial Buildings, Victoria Road, Horley, Surrey RH6 9HW, **t** 0845 124 9971, *www.holidaycare.org.uk*. Provides information for disabled travellers about a whole range of holiday matters – transport, accommodation, attractions etc – around the UK.

Good Access Guide 38 Alexandra Road, Lowestoft, Suffolk NR32 1PJ, **t** (01502) 566005, *www.goodaccessguide.co.uk*. Information on leisure, lifestyle and holidays in the UK.

Getting There

By Air

Although increasingly frowned upon in these more environmentally-conscious times, flying into the Southwest has never been easier with the region served by a surprisingly large network of small domestic airports. If coming from abroad, you'll probably have to connect via one of the main international airports outside the region. Prices vary hugely depending on the time of year and how far in advance you book, from as little as £30 for a Ryanair flight from Stansted to Newquay, or £39 from Manchester to Plymouth with Air Southwest.

Airports

The biggest regional airport is Bristol which welcomes flights from all over the continent and further afield. Others, such as Land's End Airport, serve only domestic routes.

Bristol International Airport, BRS, **t** 0871 334 4344, *www.bristolairport.co.uk*.

Exeter International Airport, EXT, **t** 0871 282 0990, *www.exeter-airport.co.uk*.

Land's End Airport, LEQ, Kelynack, St Just, Penzance, **t** (01736) 788771, *www.landsendairport.co.uk*.

Newquay Cornwall Airport, NQY, St Mawgan, **t** (01637) 860600 *www.newquaycornwall airport.com*).

Plymouth City Airport, PLH, Crownhill, **t** (01752) 204090, *www.plymouthairport.com*.

St Mary's Airport, ISC, Isles of Scilly, **t** (0172) 042 2677, *www.scilly.gov.uk*.

Airlines Serving the Southwest

Note that telephone numbers beginning with 090 can cost in excess of £1 a minute. Book via the website instead, which will in any case usually get you the best deals.

Air Southwest, t 0870 241 8202, *www.airsouthwest.com*. Operates services to Bristol, Plymouth and Newquay from Cork, Dublin, London City, London Gatwick, Leeds, Manchester and Newcastle.

Bmibaby, t 0905 828 2828, *www.bmibaby.com* Operates services to Newquay from East Midlands and Manchester.

Easyjet, t 0905 821 0905, *www.easyjet.com*. Operates flights to Bristol from Inverness, Glasgow, Edinburgh, Belfast, Newcastle and over two dozen European cities, including Paris, Amsterdam, Berlin, Madrid, Rome and Prague.

Flybe, t 0871 700 2000, *www.flybe.com*. Operates flights to Exeter from Belfast, Dublin, Glasgow, Edinburgh, Aberdeen, Newcastle, Leeds, Manchester, Norwich and over a dozen European airports, including Málaga, Amsterdam, Paris and Nice.

Rynair, t 0871 246 0000, *www.ryanair.com*. Operates flights to Newquay from London Stansted.

By Train

Like the weather, England's rail network is often regarded as one of those unfortunate national idiosyncrasies that must be tolerated as part of the price of living here, with similarly troublesome characteristics, being unpredictable, highly changeable and often obliging you to alter your entire day's plans at very short notice. In fact, outside of the peak hours and major climatic disasters (such as a bit of snow), the country's trains are generally pretty reliable and offer a fairly comfortable way of getting from A to B. The Southwest enjoys good rail links with the rest of the country. Paddington is the main London station for westerly services.

Rail Companies

National Rail Enquiries, t 08457 48 49 50, *www.nationalrail.co.uk.* This should be your first port of call, listing the timetables, fares and contact details for all the various companies serving the region.

Cross Country Trains,t 0870 010 0084, *www.crosscountrytrains.co.uk.* Links many of major Southwest towns – including Penzance, Truro, Bodmin, Plymouth, Totnes, Torquay, Exeter, Taunton and Bristol – with the Midlands, Manchester, Northeast England and Scotland.

First Great Western, t 0845 700 0125, *www.firstgreatwestern.co.uk.* Links many of the major Southwest towns – including Penzance, Truro, Plymouth, Exeter, Taunton, Bath and Bristol – with London Paddington. It also operates various branch lines throughout the region.

Southwest Trains, t 0845 600 0650, *www.southwesttrains.co.uk.* Links several Southwest towns – including Exeter, Taunton, Bridgwater, Bristol and Bath with London (Waterloo).

Rail Tickets and Passes

The most expensive option is to pay the walk-up fare on the day of your journey. The further in advance you book, the cheaper things will be. Under-fives travel free, while those aged 6–15 pay half price. There is also a range of budget passes available to help you cut costs further, which entitle the holder (or holders) to up to a third off the standard fare for a period of up to a year. These can be bought from most rail stations or purchased online at *www.railcard.co.uk.*

Family Railcard: £26, a third off the adult fare and 60 per cent off the children's fares for up to four adults and four children.

Senior Railcard: £26, a third of the standard fare for anyone over 60.

Young Person's Railcard: £26, a third off the standard fare for anyone between the ages of 16 and 25.

Disabled Person's Railcard: £18, a third off the standard fare for anyone registered disabled.

International visitors can buy BritRail passes, which entitle them to a variety of discounts on the network, but have to be purchased prior to entering the country from the website (*www.britrail.com/uk*) or a travel agency.

By Coach

If you want to cut the cost of your journey and don't mind taking a little longer to reach your destination, coach travel is probably the way to go. The country's main long-distance coach carrier is **National Express** (**t** 0845 600 7245, *www.nationalexpress.com*), which operates services from all over Britain to the Southwest. The main London terminus is Victoria, from where coaches leave for Bath (from £5 one-way), Bristol (from £5 one-way), Exeter (from £5 one-way), Torquay (from £7 one-way), Plymouth (from £8 one-way), Truro (from £10 one-way) and Penzance (from £12 one-way). The earlier you book, the cheaper your fare will be.

A range of passes and discounts is also available, including half-price fares for over-60s, Family Coachcards (£16, two children travel free if accompanied by two full-fare paying adults) and 16 to 26 Coachcards (£10, giving young adults one third of all fares).

By Car

The most popular choice. More holiday-makers arrive in the Southwest in their cars than via any other form of transport, which can cause a fair few problems. Don't expect to arrive anywhere anytime soon if setting out on a sunny Bank Holiday weekend when the roads into the region will be bumper to bumper all the way down. The major arteries into the Southwest are:

M4 – linking London with Bristol and the M5.

M5 – Linking the Midlands with Bristol, Bridgwater, Taunton and Exeter.

A30 – Starts in London and heads straight through the region, passing Exeter, Okehampton, Bodmin and Penzance before finally winding up at Land's End.

Getting Around

By Air

Considering the expense and the brevity of the journeys – you'll no sooner be up than down again – air travel is an option only for the very rich or the very impatient. The exceptions are, perhaps, the offshore islands, as you can catch a small plane, operated by Skybus, to the Scilly Isles from various regional airports at a cost only slightly exceeding that of the ferry (*see* p.215). More expensive helicopter flights are also available, both to the Scilly Isles (*see* p.215) and to Lundy Island (contact the Lundy Shore Office, The Quay, Bideford, Devon, t 01271 863636, *info@lundyisland.co.uk*).

By Train

Trains are not only a fast and efficient means of hopping between the region's towns, but are also one of the most pleasant – not to mention eco-friendly – ways of exploring the countryside and coast, chugging along a network of lazy, meandering branch lines. Particularly scenic routes include the Severn Beach railway (*see* p.78), the Tarka Line between Barnstaple and Exeter (*see* p.162) and Plymouth to Liskeard. Check out *www.carfreedaysout.com* for details of further idyllic journeys in the region.

For some serious rail exploration, you might want to invest in a 'Freedom of the Southwest Rail Rover' pass, which entitles you to three days' worth of unlimited travel on the network for £70 (£35 child), although you'll have do a lot of travelling to make it worthwhile. It's available from CrossCountry Trains, First Great Western and Southwest trains (*see* p.47).

Trips down memory lane back to the golden age of railways are provided by the region's various steam railways, which include the Avon Valley Railway (*see* p.78), the Paignton and Dartmouth Steam Railway (*see* p.134), the South Devon Railway (*see* p.136) and the Bodmin and Wenford Railway (*see* p.170).

By Bus

If you're keen to explore the backwaters of the Southwest at a snail's pace, you will enjoy riding the buses. It can be a soporific experience, in the course of which you may forget where you're trying to go. Single-decker, double-decker and mini-buses are operated by a number of different companies, with services often infrequent outside towns. However, the buses also penetrate places not reached by the railway or anybody without a car. In the National Parks, walkers are actively encouraged to dump their cars and use the buses.

National Express (t 0845 600 7245, *www.nationalexpress.com*) links the region's major towns and cities, including Bristol, Bath, Exeter, Newquay, Plymouth, St Ives and Penzance. For more localized bussing, you'll need to switch to local bus companies. **First Group** (*www.firstgroup.com*) is the Southwest's dominant provider offering services in all three

counties via its subsidiaries, **First Devon and Cornwall** (t 0845 600 1420) and **First Bristol, Bath and the West** (t 0845 602 0156). Details of routes and fares are available on the main website.

By Car

Motoring is really the best way of getting to know the countryside, although not for visiting towns and cities. Hellish ring roads, awkward one-way systems, expensive car parks, scarce street parking and financially crippling fines for illegal parking are enough to put you off taking your car into town centres and persuade you to use Park and Ride services, such as the one operating in Bath, which enables you to park cheaply out of the city and catch a shuttle bus into the centre.

If you are travelling from any of the main English-speaking countries you will not need an international licence to drive in the UK, provided you can cope with manual-drive (stick-shift) cars, and working the gears with your left hand. You will be driving on the left-hand side of the road, a custom that goes back to the old days when travellers held the reins of their horse in their right hand and walked beside on the left edge of the road.

Get valid insurance before you leave if you're bringing your own car and remember that seatbelts are compulsory, front and back. Speed limits are in miles per hour: 30mph in built-up areas; 60mph on main roads; 70mph on motorways and dual carriageways. If you are stopped by the police, you can be asked to show your driving licence at a police station within five days. Familiarize yourself with the British Highway Code (available in newsagents) and take note of the strict drink-drive laws.

To hire a car in the UK you must be over 21 (sometimes 23, or even 25) and have at least one year's driving experience; a valid credit card is often required too. It is best to pre-book for cheaper deals and to guarantee a car. The big car-hire firms have branches in the major airports. Basic hire usually includes unlimited mileage and insurance (with an excess of up to £600 for any loss or damage). Prices vary, but as a guideline for a week's car rental the main companies ask around £150 if you book early. This price goes down if you use a small, local firm, but aftercare (breakdown service, replacement car) may be less reliable if you travel out of the local area.

Special Interest Holidays

Fishing Breaks, The Mill, Heathman Street, Nether Wallop, Stockbridge SO20 8EW, **t** (01264) 781988, *www.fishingbreaks.co.uk*. Guided sea trout, salmon and brown trout fly fishing in Devon.

HF Holidays, Catalyst House, 720 Centennial Court, Centennial Park, Elstree, Hertfordshire, WD6 3SY, **t** (020) 8732 1220, *www.hfholidays. co.uk*. Various themed walking tours, including garden tours of Devon and walks along the Southwest Coastal Path.

Livingstone Colbourne, Honeychurch, Northlew, Okehampton, Devon EX20 3NR, **t** (01409) 221939, *www.livingstonecolbourne. co.uk*. Tailor-made cultural tours of Devon and Cornwall for small groups, focusing on art, antiques and architecture.

National Surfing Centre, Newquay, Cornwall, **t** (01637) 850737, *www.nationalsurfing centre.co.uk*. Professional coaches run surf courses for beginners and improvers, as well as workshops for longboarders, shortboarders and bodyboarders April–Oct.

National Trust Holidays, PO Box 536, Melksham SN12 8SX, **t** 0870 458 4422, *www.nationaltrust. org.uk*. Holidays in historic homes and cottages across the region.

Naturetrek Ltd, Cheriton Mill, Cheriton, Alresford, Hampshire SO24 0NG, **t** (01962) 733051, *www.naturetrek.co.uk*. Various nature-themed holidays including eight days bird-watching on the Scilly Isles and 5-day tours of Cornish gardens.

Railtours Southwest, **t** (01752) 562009, *www.railtours-southwest.co.uk*. Train tours from Plymouth out into the Tamar Valley.

Road Trip, All Star Leisure (UK) Ltd, 27 Old Gloucester Road, London, WC1N 3XX, **t** (020) 8133 8375, *www.roadtrip.co.uk*. Various themed tours of the West Country, such as their 7-day 'Cream teas and Pasties' tours of Dorset, Devon and Cornwall.

Sherpa Expeditions, 131a Heston Road, Hounslow TW5 0RF, **t** (020) 8577 2717, *www.sherpaexpeditions.com*. Eight-day guided tours of the Cornish coastal path.

Car Rental Companies

Avis, **t** 0844 581 0147, *www.avis.co.uk*

Hertz, **t** 08708 44 88 44, *www.hertz.co.uk*

Alamo, **t** 0871 384 1086, *www.alamo.co.uk*

Thrifty, **t** (01494) 751 500, *www.thrifty.co.uk*

By Boat

It seems appropriate in such a proud seafaring region to spend at least some of your time exploring it by boat. Sea travel is also the cheapest way of reaching the principal offshore destinations of the Scilly Isles and Lundy Island. A few of the more interesting and picturesque boat trips available in the Southwest include:

Bath: Sightseeing boat trips up the River Avon (*see* p.82).

Bristol: Hop-on-hop-off water taxis exploring the city's industrial heritage. You can also take sightseeing cruises up the Avon Gorge from the city centre (*see* p.69).

Dartmouth: Ferry to Kingswear where you can climb aboard a steam railway (*see* p.132).

Exmouth: Boat trips up to Topsham, plus mackerel fishing trips (*see* p.126).

Looe: Trips to Looe Island Nature Reserve and shark-fishing out on the ocean (*see* p.174).

Penzance: Ferry service to the Isles of Scilly (*see* p.215).

Plymouth: Various local trips available around the harbour, the Naval Dockyard and to the Rame Peninsula, as well as passenger ferries to Spain and France (*see* p.142).

Salcombe: South Sands Ferry across the Kingsbridge Estuary to local beaches (*see* p.139).

Scilly Isles: Nature-spotting trips around the islands (*see* p.215).

Totnes: River cruises to Dartmouth, with add-on steam train rides available (*see* p.134).

Truro: Trips to Falmouth (*see* p.192).

By Bike

Arm yourself with an Ordnance Survey (OS) map and a puncture repair kit and head out into the region's network of bridlepaths, disused railway lines, forest tracks, country lanes and towpaths. Once out of the vacuum-pack of your car, you start to notice the small things, and soon you'll feel sorry for anyone travelling over 30 miles per hour. The National Cycle Network is the flagship project of the Bristol-based Sustrans, 2 Cathedral Square, College Green, Bristol, **t** (0117) 926 8893, *www.sustrans.org.uk*, a charity that promotes sustainable transport, and provides hundreds of miles of cycle routes in the Southwest and around the UK. About one-third is on paths free from motor traffic. Route maps are available from tourist information centres and cycle-hire shops, or can be downloaded direct from the website.

Where to Stay

Confine yourself to the mustier guesthouses and chain hotels lining every A-road and the Southwest seems a sad place. Seek out the abundance of charming places to stay and it immediately starts warming up. On offer are a variety of places, from medieval inns and rustic cottages buried in wisteria to white-painted Victorian seafront hotels, elegant Georgian townhouses, barns, chapels, castles, country pubs and farmhouses, and family homes full of clutter and cooking smells.

Of those approved by the Tourist Board, standards range from functional – 'here's your key, breakfast's at 8' – to gorgeous and luxurious. The board, in common with the AA and RAC, uses a 1–5 rating scheme: stars for hotels and diamonds for guesthouses, inns, farmhouses and bed and breakfasts. They slap gold and silver awards on anywhere outstanding. Small 5-diamond guesthouses do not offer the same service as 5-star hotels – don't expect liveried flunkies and 24-hour room service in your B&B. The rating system works well for hotels, hostels, camping and caravan sites, but less well for guesthouses and B&Bs because it rewards facilities to the detriment of charm. This partly explains the number of L-shaped bedrooms with the obligatory bathroom squeezed in the corner. Not all properties put themselves up for inspection.

Each section of this book will provide a list of recommended places to stay. All of them have something special, whether it is a warm welcome, unique architecture, the character of the rooms, the garden or proximity to the main tourist attractions – or all of the above. The worst of the anonymous chain hotels, creepy roadside motels and jaded B&Bs have been avoided, but not every place is brimming with delightful places to stay. In some instances the rum old establishments of the town have been avoided and a crop of lovely B&Bs, inns and farmhouses found in the surrounding countryside. In all cases, you will be spared the desire to hightail it back to the car or train station on first stepping through the front door. 'Friendly' is the first pre-requisite of the book.

Accommodation Price Categories

luxury: over £180
very expensive: £135–£180
expensive: £90–£135
moderate: £45–£90
budget: Under £45

Booking

There are large numbers of contract workers, sales people, visiting relatives, stand-up comedians and guidebook writers booking rooms all around the Southwest at all times of year. Always book in advance to avoid trouble or disappointment. It is a depressing business working your way down a dwindling list of phone numbers from the train or car and finding that each one in turn is full. If you exhaust the lists in this book, contact the tourist information centres, who will give you another clutch of phone numbers and often make a reservation for you, perhaps for a small fee. If all else fails, it is not bad manners to ask B&Bs for recommendations. You will soon find yourself being passed from one helpful voice to another, all demanding you call back if you don't have any luck; eventually you always do.

Prices

Prices in this book have been divided into five categories, from budget to luxury, with properties listed in descending price order, starting with the most expensive. Prices quoted are for a full-price double room with bath, where there is one. Hotels, as a rule, are overpriced throughout the country. What you pay for is often only distantly related to the quality of service you get in return. However, many hotels do deals out of season, midweek or at weekends, if you stay for more than one night or if dinner is included. Don't be put off by the rack rate; try subtle negotiation.

The luxury hotels are fabulous properties, including country houses, castles and swanky city-centre hotels with beautifully furnished public rooms and bedrooms with character. Some are set in gorgeous gardens, all have leisure facilities. The dining is generally superb and the service all you could wish for.

As for the expensive hotels, in most cases you will be won over by elegant rooms, high-quality food and attractive furnishings. Not always, though. To stay in the centre of town, you may be forced to pay these prices.

The moderate places include delightful properties with an eye for home comforts and charm, from Victorian townhouses, Georgian rectories and old stone farmhouses to quaint seaside B&Bs. Remarkably few places fall into the budget category, generally the smaller B&Bs in remote areas. The prices reflect a down-to-earth quality in their proprietors.

Accommodation Guides

VisitBritain (*www.visitbritain.co.uk*) publishes a range of brochures, mostly free, available from tourist information centres to help you find somewhere to stay. They also offer various guides to different types of accommodation on their website – family friendly, pet-friendly, green, budget etc. – and offer an accommodation booking service. You should also check out the accommodation section of the tourist board site for Southwest England (*www.visit-southwest.co.uk*).

B&Bs, Guesthouses, Farms and Inns

At the top end, where you might find a rambling country house with a walled garden or a mellow townhouse in a well-heeled provincial town, guest accommodation is close to hotel standard in its professionalism. The character of the smaller places, however, is determined by their owners, whose tastes, hobbies, interests, backgrounds, aspirations and housekeeping skills are all reflected in the décor, furnishings and atmosphere. If you want to know the real Southwest, stick to the diamond-graded properties as opposed to starred hotels. But be wary of five-diamond properties where the level of care is misplaced in gift-wrapped chocolates on pink satin pillow, and en suite hot tubs. In four-diamond places the comfort and care matches the informality of the service. Three-diamond houses might be a real treat – a beautiful old house with threadbare rugs – or merely well maintained with the right choice of breakfast cereals. Two- and one-diamond properties are clean and comfortable, and often take the form of delightful family homes, farmhouses or country pubs. You are unlikely to find en suite bedrooms, but at least your room will have four-square proportions.

Working farmhouses are always memorable and welcoming, and remember what it is to be truly hospitable, perhaps knocking up baked beans and toast with the children if you are too frazzled to go into town for dinner.

Renting a House or Cottage

If there are several of you, it is worth exploring an area from a rented cottage or house. They are often the most attractive places to stay in the most enticing countryside, from remote moorland houses, seaside cottages and moth-eaten rectories to converted windmills, castles and Victorian coastal fortresses. You can also enjoy the slower-paced domestic side of places: eating locally caught fish or cooking vegetables from the farmers' market, putting together picnics, reading the odd selection of books on the shelves and playing board games into the night.

Holiday Cottage Agencies

Classic Cottages, Leslie House, Lady Street, Helston, Cornwall, **t** (01326) 555555, *www.classic.co.uk*. Properties for rent in Somerset, Devon and Cornwall.

Coast and Country Cottages, Hannafords Landing, Island Street, Salcombe, Devon, **t** (01548) 843773, *www.coastandcountry.co.uk*. Self-catering cottages in South Devon.

Cornish Traditional Cottages, Blisland, Bodmin, Cornwall, **t** (01208) 821666, *www.corncott.com*. Properties in North Cornwall, South Cornwall, West Cornwall and the Roseland Peninsula.

Farm and Cottage Holidays, 5 The Quay, Bideford, Devon, **t** (01237) 459888, *www.holidaycottages.co.uk*. Properties across the region.

Helpful Holidays, Mill Street, Chagford, Devon, **t** (01647) 433593, *www.helpfulholidays.com*. Holiday cottages in Somerset, Devon and Cornwall.

Holiday Homes & Cottages Southwest, 28 Torwood Street, Torquay, Devon, **t** (01803) 299677, *www.swcottages.co.uk*. Properties in Devon and Cornwall.

Hoseasons, t 0844 847 1356, *www.hoseasons.co.uk*. One of the country's largest self-catering specialists, Hoseasons can offer properties throughout the region.

Youth Hostels and Camping Barns

The **YHA, t** (01629) 592700, *www.yha.org.uk*, has 30 hostels in the Southwest, ranging from 1960s city-centre blocks to rustic cottages, Georgian townhouses and coastal mansions. These are no-nonsense, cheap alternatives to guest accommodation for rugged outdoorsy types. The bedrooms and bathrooms are communal, divided only between the sexes. In some of them you cater for yourself, in others breakfast, dinner and packed lunches are available. One-year membership of the International Youth Hostel Federation (currently £15.95 for over-26s, £9.95 for under) entitles you to stay in YHA Hostels all over England and the world at reduced rates. There is no age limit for members in England, and only occasionally are you expected to pull your weigh with domestic chores. With your membership card you receive the *YHA Accommodation Guide*, which details all the hostels in England and Wales. You can take out membership in any YHA hostel, and get a bed on the same night. Hostels are cheap with discounts for under-18s and families. You don't have to provide your own bedding. However, note that children under five are not allowed to stay in the dormitories, and not all hostels have family rooms.

There are also five camping barns or 'stone tents' in the Southwest, including one at Mullacott Farm on Exmoor and one at Great Hound Tor in the wilds of Dartmoor. Although overseen by the YHA, these converted farm buildings are owned and operated by farmers. Communal dorms with bunk beds, basic showers and rudimentary cookers and fridges combine with remote rural locations to make these some of the more adventurous places to stay. You don't have to be a YHA member to stay, and dogs are often welcome.

Camping and Caravanning

There is no longer such a thing as a charming patch of free grass for you to pitch your tent without getting into trouble. Ask the farmer in advance of pitching your tent in his field. He may well be pleased to help you, and might even point you in the direction of clean water or fresh produce. It also saves a lot of nervousness about getting rumbled in the morning. Otherwise you might just as well book into a campsite where there are washing facilities and toilets. Campsites are graded by VisitBritain from one- to five-star according to the standard and range of services – showers, toilets and convenience stores rank high in the ratings. The VisitBritain website (*www.visit britain.co.uk*) has a dedicated section devoted to campsites, most of which can be booked online. The National Trust also operates camping and caravan sites which it lists on *www.nationaltrust.org.uk*. The Caravan Club (t 0800 328 6635, *www.caravanclub.co.uk*) has 35 campsites in the Southwest (10 in Somerset, 15 in Devon and 10 in Cornwall) for use by both members and non-members, with grass and all-weather pitches, waste disposal points, showers and laundry facilities.

Practical A–Z

06

Children

When you've exhausted beaches, walks and ruined castles, you'll be relieved to find that the Southwest's cultural attractions are peppered with interactive exhibits for children. Younger family members pay less almost everywhere, and you can often get family deals – but bring proof of age if your teenagers are hairy or tall. Hotels, pubs and restaurants have always been the sticking point, but things are improving, particularly since the smoking ban came into effect in 2007. Family pub-restaurants are increasing in number all the time, often segregating their bars and dining rooms to ensure that the innocence of under 18s is preserved and (more to the point) the law upheld. Many pub chains, such as Whitbread (who control the Brewer's Fayre and Beefeater brands) and Wetherspoon's, now actively trade on their child-friendliness, offering children's menus and play areas. However, some traditional pubs still take pride in excluding anyone who can't down a pint. Convivial family eating is not as customary in England as it is in Italy, Spain or Greece. For every restaurant that openly welcomes children with highchairs and smiles there will be another that barely tolerates the noise and mess, with pursed lips. Seaside resorts are the most accommodating, where you're most likely to find hotels providing cots, extra beds and bottle-warming facilities.

The website *www.familyholidaysouthwest. co.uk* provides details of family-related matters in the region – the location of public toilets, which beaches have lifeguards, lists of family-orientated attractions etc.

Countryside Code

• Guard against the risk of fire
• Fasten all gates.
• Keep dogs under close control.
• Keep to public footpaths across farmland, using gates and stiles to cross fences, hedges and walls.
• Leave livestock, crops and machinery alone.
• Take your litter home.
• Don't remove any wildlife, plants or trees.
• Don't make unnecessary noise.
• Don't leave valuables in your car.
• Don't take souvenirs of ancient monuments.

Electricity

The current is 240 volts AC, so you need a converter for US appliances. Wall sockets take uniquely British three-pin (square) fused plugs, so you will need a plug adaptor too. You can pick them up quite cheaply at airports, department stores and some chemists.

Embassies in the UK

All of the major embassies are located in London.

Australian High Commission, Australia House, Strand, London WC2B 4LA, **t** (020) 7379 4334, *www.australia.org.uk*.

Canada High Commission, 1 Grosvenor Square, London, W1K 4AB, **t** (020) 7258 6600, *www.canadainternational.gc.ca*.

Embassy of Ireland, 17 Grosvenor Place, London SW1X 7HR, **t** (020) 7235 2171, *www.embassyof ireland.co.uk*.

New Zealand High Commission, New Zealand House, 80 Haymarket, London, SW1Y 4TQ, **t** (020) 7930 8422, *www.nzembassy.com*.

US Embassy, 24 Grosvenor Square, London, W1A 1AE, **t** (020) 7499 9000, *www.usembassy.org.uk*.

Emergencies

The UK emergency telephone number is 999. An emergency operator will put you through to police, fire, ambulance, coastguard, mountain rescue or cave rescue (the last two via the police) as required. The European emergency number, 112, works in the UK too. Carry a mobile phone on long walks.

For vehicle breakdowns, check with your car hire firm if the roadside recovery policy is with the **AA** (emergency breakdown assistance: **t** 0800 88 77 66, from **mobiles t** 08457 887766, *www.theaa.com*) or the **RAC** (emergency breakdown assistance: **t** 08000 966 999, *www.rac.co.uk*). Call the rental company if you are going to need a new car.

Food and Drink

For more general information on the region's food and drink, *see* p.34.

In this book, prices quoted for a meal are for two courses (a main course and either a starter or dessert), not including drinks. We have divided prices into categories (*see* below). Many restaurants offer good-value set menus,

Restaurant Price Categories

Very expensive: cost no object

Expensive: £35-50

Moderate: £15-30

Budget: less than £15

especially at lunchtime. Always ask. Most restaurants open for lunch and dinner. Some stay open all day, especially at weekends.

Health and Insurance

If you injure yourself, you will be seen for free in a hospital Accident and Emergency department, but prepare for a long wait. If it's not urgent, ask your hotel to help you find a doctor. European nationals are eligible for free medical treatment it they have their European Health Insurance Card with them. Australians and New Zealanders may also benefit from reciprocal arrangements. To find out more about what you may be entitled to, go to *www.dh.gov.uk/en/Healthcare/Entitlements andcharges/OverseasVisitors/DH_836*.

Everyone else is advised to take out travel insurance, or check if you are covered by your credit card or home policy. All travellers will still need cover for baggage loss, cancellations and so on. Keep two copies of your policy in separate places, lest your luggage disappears, and hang on to any receipts.

Maps

Ordnance Survey has been producing small-scale accurate maps of Britain since the Napoleonic Wars, for defence purposes. Now the company publishes high-quality leisure maps. The Explorer 1:25,000 series (4cm to 1km or 2.5 inches to 1 mile) is the most detailed for walkers, off-road cyclists and horse riders. It shows places of interest, rights of way and camping sites. The Landranger 1:50,000 series is still small-scale, but not detailed enough to entirely depend upon for orienteering, say in a Dartmoor mist. Maps are available from their website (t 0845 456 0420, *http://leisure. ordnancesurvey.co.uk*). For the cities of the Southwest you'll need to invest in an individual A to Z, if you're looking to explore the backstreets, the paperback versions of which are available for less than £5, t (01732) 783422, *www.a-zmaps.co.uk*.

Media

Newspapers, Magazines & Listings

In addition to all the main daily national newspapers, the Southwest's cities and regions also support a network of local papers, usually published weekly and featuring a mixture of local-interest stories and national news. Some of the most widely read include the Cornwall-centred *Cornish Guardian*, *The Cornishman* and *The West Briton* as well as the more wide-reaching *Western Morning News*, which also covers Devon and Somerset. All are published by Devon and Cornwall Media (*www.thisiscornwall.co.uk*).

Somerset's two largest cities have their own papers. Bath is served by the weekly *Bath Chronicle* (*www.thisisbath.co.uk*), while Bristol's citizens get more regular updates via the daily *Bristol Evening Post* (*www.thisisbristol.co.uk*). *The Western Daily Press* is distributed in both cities.

Information on the latest Southwesterly trends in culture and food can be gleaned from the region's various glossy lifestyle magazines, including *Cornwall Today* (*www.cornwall-today.co.uk*) and *Devon Life* (*www.devonlife. co.uk*), while listings information is available from a wide variety of sources including the *Crackerjack* entertainment magazine, which comes with the Thursday edition of the *Bristol Evening Post*, the pull-out events guide from the monthly magazine, *Inside Cornwall* (*http://insidecornwall.co.uk*), and, perhaps the most comprehensive source, *What's On Southwest* (*www.whatsonsouthwest.co.uk*).

Radio

Each of the region's three counties has its own dedicated BBC station, as does the largest city, Bristol, splicing together national news and playlists with programs and phone-ins of more local appeal. The second biggest voice in the region is the commercial broadcaster, *Heart*, which has spent the past few years taking over many of the Southwest's formerly independent radio stations, and specializes in gentle, mainstream programming. There are now only a few independent broadcasters remaining.

Atlantic, 105–107 FM (*www.atlantic.fm*)

BBC Bristol, 94.9 FM & 104.6 FM (*http://news.bbc.co.uk/local/bristol/hi/tv_and_radio/*)

BBC Cornwall, 95.2 FM & 103.9 FM (*www.bbc.co.uk/cornwall/local_radio/*)

BBC Devon, 95.7 FM & 103.4 FM (*http://news.bbc.co.uk/local/devon/hi/tv_and_radio/*)

BBC Somerset, 95.5 FM & 1566 AM (*http://news.bbc.co.uk/local/somerset/hi/tv_and_radio/*)

Heart Bath, 103 FM (*www.heartbath.co.uk*)

Heart Bristol, 96.3 FM (*www.heartbristol.co.uk*)

Heart Exeter, 97 FM & 103 FM (*www.heart exeter.co.uk*)

Heart North Devon, 96.2 FM & 97.3 FM (*www.heartnorthdevon.co.uk*)

Heart Plymouth, 96.6 FM & 97 FM (*www.heart-plymouth.co.uk*)

Heart Somerset, 102.6 FM (*www.heartsom-erset.co.uk*)

Money and Banks

Currency

While the rest of Europe has been happily bartering with the euro for the best part of a decade, British euro-phobia means that the currency here still comes in pounds (sterling) and pence, with a hundred pennies to one pound. Coins come in denominations of 1p, 2p, 5p, 10p, 20p, 50p, £1 and £2, while notes are available in denominations of £5, £10, £20 and £50.

At the time of writing one US dollar will buy you 59p and one euro will buy you 87p. Put the other way round, one pound is worth 1.67 dollars and 1.14 euros, but of course foreign exchange rates fluctuate wildly. Shop around for the best rates in banks and bureaux de change. The worst rates tend to be offered in hotels, followed by bureaux de change in tourist areas, at airports and ferry terminals. Banks usually offer a slightly better rate. Always check the commission fee.

Cash and Credit Cards

If you are travelling from abroad, bring enough cash to get you to your first stop. Traveller's cheques remain the most secure means of carrying money around, but these days you can use credit and debit cards just about anywhere.

ATM machines abound in airports, towns and cities, allowing you to draw out money in local currency with your card. Some cards take a fee for the currency conversion. Visa and

Mastercard/Access are widely accepted in hotels, restaurants and shops. American Express and Diner's Club slightly less so. If the Sirrus or Maestro logo appears both on your card and the ATM machine, you can make international transactions from your home account. If you lose the credit card, a new one can be issued, but never quickly enough.

Banks

Opening hours are usually Mon–Fri 9am–4.30pm, although larger banks may stay open until 5pm and small-town banks may close at 3pm. Some banks open on Saturday mornings, but usually don't offer a full service.

Packing

Though it may enjoy a reputation as England's balmiest region, the Southwest's weather can be changeable, even in summer (in fact, especially in summer). Your best bet is to pack lots of layers, which can be peeled off should there be a heat wave or piled on when temperatures plummet. Bring a couple of jerseys even in summer. Jeans-weight trousers or skirts should do you all year, but you might want to pack shorts and T-shirts or a light dress in summer. A waterproof jacket is a year-round necessity. In winter you'll need a warm coat. Always pack at least two pairs of shoes, and make sure one is good for walking. You'll only need smart clothes if you plan to stay in very grand hotels and eat in the classiest of restaurants (even then, smart casual would do). Launderettes are everywhere, and the more upmarket hotels have their own laundry service, so it's easy to get cleaned up.

The only accessory worth packing is a pair of binoculars. They come in handy not only for spotting wildlife, particularly the dolphins, whales and basking sharks of the coastal waters, but also for reading road signs that you have passed in the car, saving you the trouble of reversing or getting out on a busy road.

Pets

You can bring a dog or cat into Britain from the USA, Canada and some European countries under the Pet Travel Scheme (PETS) without quarantine on certain approved airlines, sea and rail crossings providing they have been microchipped and vaccinated, and had a blood test at least six months before travelling. For more information contact the **Pet Travel**

Scheme Helpline (t 0870 241 1710, *www.defra.gov.uk*). Ask your airline about the specifics of pet transport. The majority of city hotels don't welcome pets, but attitudes are often more animal-tolerant in the countryside where some B&Bs do accommodate well-behaved dogs, who are also allowed in most pubs.

Post Offices

Under constant threat of privatization, and forced to make drastic savings, there's no doubt that the Royal Mail is currently feeling the pressure. These days it's a pleasant surprise if a first-class letter arrives the next day (once, this was the norm, and if it didn't come first post it would come with the now discontinued second post). Many rural post offices have closed down and those that remain can often be shabby with long queues. However, the service battles on in the face of competition from email and courier companies. Main post offices provide a dizzying array of services on top of letter and parcel post, including currency exchange and banking.

A first-class stamp currently costs 39p and is allowed six days' travel time before it is given up as lost. Special Delivery guarantees next-working-day delivery, but someone has to be in to sign for the parcel or it gets dumped at a depot miles away. Recorded delivery can take any number of days, as long as it's signed for. Delivery of letters or parcels to the USA, Canada, Australia and New Zealand by air mail takes about five days. You can get mail sent Poste Restante to any post office in the UK and pick it up with some form of ID.

Post offices are usually open Mon–Fri 9am–5.30pm, Sat 9am–12.30pm. Sub-post offices, which often sit at the back of corner shops, often close on Wed at 1pm, particularly in rural areas. For information about services, call t 08457 740740, *www.royalmail.com*.

Public Holidays

January: New Year's Day (1st)

March/April: Good Friday and Easter Monday

May: May Day (1st Mon); Spring Holiday (last Mon)

August: Late Summer Bank Holiday (last Mon)

December: Christmas Day (25th), Boxing Day (26th)

Shopping

Once upon a time, rural crafts relied on locally available raw materials. Devon was known for its pottery, the Somerset Levels for basket-making and Cornwall for its leather tanning. The demise of many traditional crafts caused by the Industrial Revolution was in part remedied by the middle-class artisans of the Arts and Crafts movement; these days every rural area supports a mixture of craftspeople. Two books might help in a quest for crafts: *Craftworkers Year Book* (£21.95, Write Angle Press, 16 Holm Oak Drive, Madeley, Crew CW3 9HR, t (01782) 750 986, a diary of craft fairs) and *Craft Galleries Guide* (£10, BCF Books, *www.bcfbooks.co.uk*) both of which have plenty of information relating to the Southwest.

For details of craft guilds and contemporary makers, contact The Craft Council Resource Centre (44a Pentonville Road, Islington, London N1 9BY, t (020) 7806 2500, *www.craftscouncil. org.uk*) the Rural Crafts Association (Heights Cottage, Brook Road, Wormley, Godalming, Surrey GU8 5UA, t (01428) 682292, *www.rural-craftsassociation.co.uk*), the Cornwall Crafts Association (Trelowarren, Mawgan-in-Meneage, Helston, Cornwall TR12 6AF, t (01326) 221 567, *www.cornwallcrafts.co.uk*) or the The Devon Guild of Craftsmen (Riverside Mill, Bovey Tracey, Devon TQ13 9AF, t (01626) 832223, *www.crafts.org.uk*).

For glass, try the famous Dartington Crystal in Torrington in North Devon, t (01805) 626262, *www.dartington.co.uk*, where you can watch demonstrations of glass-blowing at the visitor centre, or the Barbican Glass Centre in Plymouth (The Old Fish Market, The Barbican, PL1 2LS, t (01752) 224777).

The Southwest has been renowned for its pottery since the days of Bernard Leach's St Ives Pottery (*see* p.32) and the region is still home to a good number of small studios, many run by relatives or students of the great man. Two of the best are Muchelney Pottery in Muchelney, near Langport, t (01458) 250324, *www.johnleachpottery.co.uk*), and Springfield Pottery (88 Springfield, Hartland, Devon, EX39 6BG, t (01237) 441506, *www.springfield-pottery.com*).

Basket-making still goes on in the Somerset Levels around Bridgwater, where the willow beds provide the raw material. Coates Willows and Wetlands Centre in Stoke St Gregory, near

Taunton. **t** (01823) 490249, *www.englishwillow-baskets.co.uk*, sells wicker baskets and furniture.

It's also worth checking out the local craft produce for sale at the region's various covered pannier markets, such as those in Tavistock (*see* p.152), Barnstaple (*see* p.161), and Truro (*see* p.192).

Sports and Activities

On Land

Walking and Hiking

Walking rivals sunbathing for the title of the Southwest's most popular activity (and in winter there's no competition). The region boasts the country's longest footpath, the South West Coastal Path, which meanders for more than 600 miles around the perimeter of the entire peninsula from Minehead in Somerset to Poole Harbour in Dorset. Aurum Press (**t** (020) 7284 7160, *www.aurumpress.co.uk*) produce four guides which together cover the entirety of the route – Minehead to Padstow, Padstow to Falmouth, Falmouth to Exmouth and Exmouth to Poole – costing £12.99 each. The path intersects with various other walking routes, including the 102-mile-long Two Moors Way, linking Exmoor and Dartmoor. A guide to this route is available for £4.99 from The Two Moors Way Association (63 Higher Coombe Drive, Teignmouth, Devon TQ14 9NL, *www.twomoorsway.org.uk*). Further information is available from the Exmoor National Parks Authority (Exmoor House, Dulverton, Somerset, **t** (01398) 323665, *www.exmoor-nationalpark.gov.uk*) and the Dartmoor National Parks Authority (Parke, Bovey Tracey, Newton Abbot, Devon, **t** (01626) 832093, *www.dartmoor-npa.gov.uk*). You should also get in touch with the National Association of AONBs (**t** (01451) 862007, *www.aonb.org.uk*) who can furnish you with advice regarding walks within the three counties' nine 'Areas of Outstanding Natural Beauty'.

In the shape of Dartmoor, Exmoor and Bodmin Moor, the Southwest boasts some of the most forbidding expanses of wilderness in the country, and no major walk should be attempted without a decent map, such as those in the 1:25,000 Ordnance Survey Explorer series (*www.ordnancesurvey.co.uk*). *See* the relevant entries for the particular walking challenges posed by each moor. Local tourist information offices can provide leaflets listing local routes and regional highlights to explore, as well as contact details for local guides.

Bicycling

If two-wheel touring is your thing, then this may be your area. In a country not usually famed for its bicycle-friendliness, the Southwest is much more welcoming with a mazy network of routes, many running along former railway lines or canal towpaths that see little or no traffic. The ultimate challenge is provided by the West Country Way, a 250-mile cycling odyssey taking you all the way from Bristol to Padstow by way of the Mendips, the Somerset Levels, Exmoor and Bodmin Moor. If that sounds too daunting, you could aim a little lower with the 102-mile Devon Coast to Coast Route from Ilfracombe to Plymouth, three quarters of which is traffic free, the 30-mile Tarka Trail (*see* p.162–3) or the 13-mile-long Railway Path between Bristol and Bath (*www.bristolbathrailwaypath.org.uk*).

Details on all of the above, plus numerous other routes, are available from the region's principal cycling organization, Sustrans (2 Cathedral Square, College Green, Bristol, **t** (0117) 926 8893, *www.sustrans.org.uk*). A map of Dartmoor's main cycle routes can be ordered through the Dartmoor National Park Authority website (Parke, Bovey Tracey, Newton Abbot, Devon, **t** (01626) 832093, *www.dartmoor-npa.gov.uk*) while Exmoor for Off-Road Cyclists is available from *www.nationalparks.gov.uk* for £9.95.

Horseriding

Exmoor's and Dartmoor's resident populations of wild ponies pay testament to their equine friendliness. Both are crisscrossed by bridleways and boast numerous centres offering horse trekking across the moors, as well as more formal tuition for learner riders. For Exmoor, try the stables at Highercombe (Dulverton, Somerset, **t** (01398) 323451, *www.highercombe.co.uk*), for Dartmoor, try the Shilstone Rocks Riding Centre (**t** (01364) 621281; *www.dartmoorstables.com*). Otherwise contact the British Horse Society for a list of approved schools (**t** 0844 848 1666, *www.bhs.org.uk*).

On (and in) the Water

Surfing

Now that King Arthur is no longer riding out from his cliff-top fortresses to battle the Saxon invaders, the most extreme sport taking place on the coasts of North Devon and Cornwall is surfing. Improvements in wetsuit technology mean that it's available pretty much year round from towns and resorts including Croyde Bay, Bude and, most famously, Newquay, the country's premier surfing destination where you'll find plenty of outlets renting out boards for around £10 a day. For instruction on how to tame the big Atlantic rollers, contact the British Surfing Association (International Surfing Centre, Fistral Beach, **t** 01637 876474, *www.britsurf.co.uk*), which can put you in touch with one of their approved schools. Expect to pay around £25–30 for half a day's tuition. *See* p.190.

Kitesurfing and Windsurfing

The Dorset-based British Kitesurfing Association (Manor Barn, Stottingway Street, Uppway, Weymouth, **t** (01305) 813555, *www.britishkitesurfingassociation.co.uk*) is the body to get in touch with if you fancy skipping across the waves harnessed to a small c-shaped kite. Its more traditional cousin, windsurfing, is regarded as a 'sailing discipline', which brings it under the remit of the Royal Yachting Association, **t** (02380) 604 100, *www.rya.org.uk,* who can direct you to one of their approved training centres. Both sports are popular off of the windy shores of Exmouth (*see* p.126).

Canoeing & Kayaking

Taking your canoe for a hurtle down some Class II rapids, though undeniably exhilarating, can unfortunately take its toll on the environment, which is why it's only allowed between October and March these days. White-water kayaking is available on several of the region's rivers, including the River Exe on Exmoor, but the main challenge is provided by the River Dart on Dartmoor, where autumn rains send water hurtling at cascade velocity through its gorges. Contact the British Canoe Union (**t** 0845 370 9500, *www.bcu.org.uk*) for details of centres and courses. For those who prefer to experience their rivers at a more sedate pace, there are also plenty of smaller operators hiring out canoes year round for leisurely jaunts on the Southwest's calmer stretches of water, including Pulteney Cruisers in Bath on the River Avon (*see* p.82) and Canoe Adventures in Totnes which organizes 12-seater canoe trips along the lower reaches of the River Dart (*see* p.134).

Sailing

This is the activity that put the Southwest on the map, and indeed helped Southwesterners to map much of the New World during the great age of maritime exploration between the 16th and 18th centuries. Your ambitions will probably be a little bit more modest. Many of the region's main ports and coastal towns, including Dartmouth, Falmouth, Fowey, Plymouth and Salcombe, have centres offering tuition, starting at around £50 for a day aboard a small craft, and rising to many times that for experience of sailing something larger. The Royal Yachting Association (*see* above) can provide a list of places offering tuition in everything from dinghies and small-keel hulls to powerboats and multi-hulls.

Diving

With clear, warm waters, an abundance of sea life, not to mentions a treacherous coastline littered with shipwrecks, the Southwest is one of the country's very top dive spots. Prime submerged vistas are available offshore of Exmouth, the Isles of Scilly, which have more than 150 official dive sites, and Plymouth where in 2004 the National Marine Aquarium deliberately sank a wreck to act as the foundation for a new reef (*www.national-aquarium. co.uk/scylla-reef/*). For details of courses and rates, contact the British Sub Aqua Club, **t** (0151) 350 6200, *www.bsac.com*. Taster sessions start at around £25, rising to £200–300 for a two-day course.

Telephones and the Internet

As with the rest of the country, the Southwest's embrace of the internet grows ever tighter. Pretty much every service you might use in the region – from hotels and restaurants to tour guides and bike hire companies – will have their own website, and the number of Wi-Fi zones is growing all the time. Many hotels, hostels and cafés now offer access, often for free or for around £1–£2 an hour. You can find internet cafés in most major towns and cities, or failing that the local public library can usually help you out. If you bring your laptop from abroad, be sure to also invest in the appropriate adaptor (*see* p.54) and surge protector.

Now that mobile phones are ubiquitous, payphones are being phased out. If you have a mobile, see if you can replace your SIM card with a local pay-as-you-go card for your stay (or pay extortionate international call charges). Payphone calls cost a minimum of 40p for local calls, more for long-distance and international calls. Most phone booths accept cash, phonecards and credit/debit cards. Phonecards can be bought from any newsagent for £5, £10 or £20. Calls from hotel phones are always expensive.

Directory Enquiries: 118500, 118118 (calls can be expensive, from 90p a minute)

International Directory Enquires: 118505

Operator: 100

Emergency Services: 999 or 112

Time

Greenwich Mean Time (GMT) is the local time of the prime meridian or zero degrees longitude, which passes through Greenwich in London, and provides the standard time for the entire country, although it wasn't so long ago that England was carved into time zones with the Southwest's clocks set a few minutes behind those in the capital. British Summer Time runs from the end of March to the end of October: clocks are put forward one hour ahead of GMT to make the most of the summer daylight hours.

Tipping

If there is a relaxed etiquette for tipping in England, English people have yet to master it. You would normally tip about 10–15 percent of the price of the meal in a restaurant where there is table service and your waiter or waitress has been attentive. Taxi drivers, porters, hairdressers and tour guides might expect a little something, but don't feel obliged unless they are particularly deserving.

Somerset, Bristol and Bath

The region's two big cities make a neatly contrasting pair: aristocratic Bath, the epitome of refinement and Georgian (by way of Roman) elegance, and proletarian Bristol with its battered industrial aspects and vibrant big-city energy. Past these two urban hotspots, much of Somerset's countryside could be used to illustrate the dictionary definition of 'rolling'. The oh-so-English sounding hill ranges of the Mendips and the Quantocks provide plenty of undulating, view-filled (but none-too-taxing) walks, while the great wilds of Exmoor offer hikers a little more to get their crampons into. Somerset also does a mean line in craggy. The Mendips' limestone landscape is riddled with water-cut holes, caves and gorges, including the great rocky gash of Cheddar Gorge. At the centre of the county are the Somerset Levels, an area of low-lying wetlands, whose ancient peoples gave the county its modern name – Sumersata, the 'land of the summer people', a fitting description for this most sunny of regions.

07

Don't miss

⭐ **The wonders of the Industrial Age**
SS Great Britain, Bristol p.74

⭐ **Roman remains, and steamy roof-top bathing**
Bath p.81

⭐ **Meet the ancestors**
Cheddar Gorge p.99

⭐ **Feel the mystical power**
Glastonbury Tor p.103

⭐ **Steam through the landscape of the Romantic poets**
West Somerset Railway p.107

See map overleaf

20 km

10 miles

N

WALES

Bristol Channel

Bridgwater

Bay

Lynmouth

Lynton
Malmsmead
Oare
Porlock
Allerford
Minehead
Dunster
Watchet
East Quantoxhead
Kilve
Holford
Nether Stowey
Washford

Exmoor

Dunkery Hill

National

Cleave Abbey

West Somerset Railway

Quantock Hills

Park

Exford

Brendon Hills

A358

West Bagborough

Bishops Lydeard

Vale of Taunton Dean

Dulverton

A361

Taunton

A396

M5

ENGLAND

WALES

SOMERSET

DEVON

CORNWALL

A3

A30

Don't miss

⓵ SS Great Britain, Bristol **p.74**

⓶ Bath **p.81**

⓷ Cheddar Gorge **p.99**

⓸ Glastonbury Tor **p.103**

⓹ West Somerset Railway **p.107**

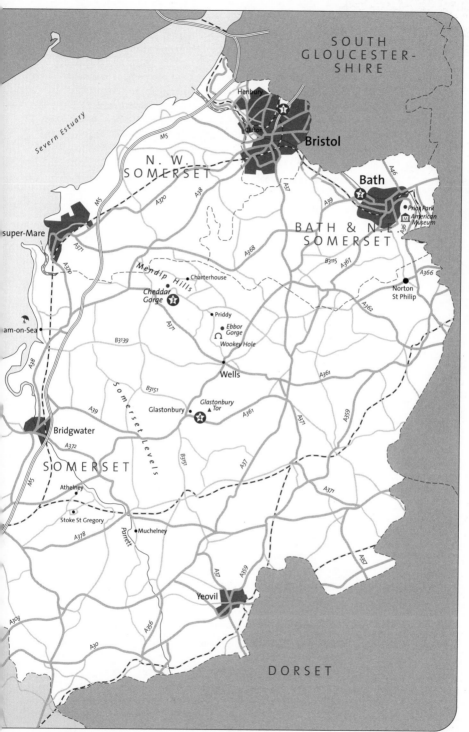

The borders are not set in (Bath) stone, but for many people Somerset marks the entry point to the West Country. It's an overwhelmingly pastoral county. Its biggest city, Bath, isn't that big at all, while nearby Bristol, which is at least properly city sized, has, perhaps in order to maintain the healthy countryside–urban ratio, been designated a separate county (albeit a rather small one). For the purposes of this chapter, however, it will be treated as an honorary Somersetonian. These two aside, the diminutive city of Wells, with its famed cathedral, and the mystical mecca of Glastonbury are the county's main representatives of urban sprawl.

Somerset has seen its fair share of history – perhaps most notably in Bath where the Romans left behind some of the country's most famous recreational ruins – and more than its fair share of myths and legends. As with much of the West Country, there are a number of places here claiming dubious allegiance to the legends of King Arthur, the best known of which is Cadbury Hill Fort, long cited as the location of Arthur's Camelot. Mystical, fantastical thinking is still very much present today, particularly at the country's supranatural capital, Glastonbury, with its streets filled with shops selling new-age paraphernalia: crystals instilled with healing powers, books of earnest astrological philosophizing etc. The town enjoys associations with both Christian and Arthurian legends, although it's perhaps best known these days for the music festival that takes place each year just outside of its confines, which has grown into one of the biggest and most prestigious in the world.

Somerset's coast is perhaps the least celebrated of the three Southwest counties. Its two main resorts, Weston-Super-Mare and Minehead, are not great ambassadors, being the sort of brash arcade, club and chippy affairs that could be found anywhere. There are prettier stretches, however, particular in the west along the wooded coast of Exmoor where you'll find the handsome towns of Porlock and Lynmouth.

Bristol

In its time Bristol has hit the heights and plumbed the depths. It's been England's second city, a thriving international trading hub and a centre of engineering innovation. But it's also seen the fall of its mercantile empire, the decline of its industries and its position as London's deputy usurped by younger, fitter contemporaries. Today it is once again back on top following a multi-million pound millennial makeover, which saw much sprucing and polishing and encouraged a spate of new openings – museums, restaurants, hotels etc. Following a period in the wilderness, the growth of the past decade seems to have restored the city's confidence and brought a smile back to its battered industrial visage.

Bristol and its environs make up one of England's smallest counties, a status the city has enjoyed since 1373, notwithstanding a brief intermission from 1974 to 1996 when it was incorporated into the now defunct County of Avon. When the countyship was awarded, it would have been a fitting recognition of the city's national standing. From the Middle Ages until superseded by the new giants of the Industrial

Revolution, Bristol was one of the country's pre-eminent cities. While it may have slipped down the national pecking order a bit in recent years, the city is still very much the big urban beast of the West Country – the one conurbation that feels properly metropolitan.

Of course, in terms of its tourist appeal, Bristol's muscular charms are rather overshadowed by the more graceful fancies of Bath just down the road. But then, being a proper working city rather than a museum piece, Bristol has always been too busy trying to make a living to put on the slap and try and cash in on its looks. Unlike Bath, with its exemplary record of self-preservation, Bristol's history has been one of constant reinvention – knocking down, rebuilding, overlaying, stripping back and re-erecting in order to take advantage of the next big thing, often with little concern for aesthetics. That's not to say that some fine architecture hasn't been created along the way, just that much of it has been swept away (or bombed into obliteration) with the passing years.

There have been some dark periods in recent decades. In the mid 1990s the eerie, brooding laments of local bands, including Portishead, Massive Attack and Tricky, seemed to provide the perfect soundtrack for the decaying city. What saved Bristol was what kept it going through all those turbulent centuries, the city's appreciation for the main chance and gift for rejuvenation. As the end of the Millennium approached, Bristol, along with dozens of other towns and cities around the country, took the opportunity (and the government's lottery money) to give itself a face-lift.

It proved remarkably successful. The grimy disused docks, for so long the visible reminder of the city's decline, were scrubbed, painted and renewed, and its warehouses are now home to flashy interactive museums, riverside apartment complexes and high-end restaurants and bars. The past ten years have also seen a corresponding growth in the city's media and technology industries, while Bristol's large student population ensures a thriving music scene and a varied and hectic nightlife. Today the soundtrack is a much happier one.

True, for all its successes, you'd still be hard pressed to find anyone willing to describe Bristol as a beautiful or particularly peaceful place – there are still far too many cars in the centre of town – but it is undeniably vibrant. If you spend a day or so exploring its confines, you will find that its functional city centre streets hide some wonderful examples of medieval and Georgian architecture, while those on its outskirts lead out to some glorious stretches of rolling countryside.

History

Trade gave Bristol its prosperity and status, and trade would take them away again. The first settlement, known as Brycgstow, was founded here by the Saxons in the early 11th century at the confluence of the rivers Frome and Avon – waterways that were to play a vital role in the city's development. Within a generation or so it had become established as one of the local region's main market towns and, in a foretaste of things to come, had started playing a prominent role in the local Saxon-Irish slave trade. The town continued to grow throughout the 12th century, acquiring a stone castle at the behest of the invading Normans – a sign of its increasing importance – and by the 13th century had become one of the country's most prosperous ports, by virtue of its navigable proximity to the Severn Estuary, just eight miles away along the narrow Avon Gorge. To further increase its trading opportunities the city undertook one of the most ambitious engineering projects of the Middle Ages, diverting the River Frome into an artificial channel – St Augustine's Reach – and building a new city centre dock. The ships poured in and Bristol soon found itself at the centre of an intricate European trading network, despatching English woollens to the continent and receiving olive oil, wine, dried fish and other goods in return. The importance of commerce to the town's fortunes is revealed in the surviving street names from that time – Corn Street, Wine Street etc. The great urban success story of the English Middle Ages, Bristol's growing importance would receive further confirmation with the award of county status in 1373.

'The greatest, the richest and the best port of trade in Great Britain, London only excepted'
Daniel Defoe

Bristol's upward ascent continued apace in the 16th and 17th centuries buoyed by transatlantic trade with the burgeoning New World markets. Indeed, one of the principal figures of North American discovery, **John Cabot**, set out from Bristol in 1497, funded by King Henry VII and wealthy Bristolian merchants. By the 1600s Bristol had cemented its position as one of the most important links in the triangular trade route between the Americas, Europe and Africa, its flourishing ports overseeing the comings and goings of a vast range of goods, including cocoa, sugar, cotton, tobacco and, unfortunately, human beings. The leading role played by Bristol in the transatlantic slave trade is one of the darkest aspects of its history.

The city's peak came in the early to mid 18th century when no less a figure than the great Whig parliamentarian, **Edmund Burke**, was briefly its MP. Flushed with wealth, the city's merchants proclaimed their new social status by creating grand mansions and town houses. Much of the fancy western suburb of Clifton was constructed on the proceeds of tobacco and slavery. It was, however, inevitable that the city's greatest era would precede its most dramatic decline.

As the 18th century gave way to the 19th, Bristol's status had already begun to slip. Liverpool had taken over as the country's main port, while industrialization would see Birmingham and Manchester's outgrow and out-earn their former West Country master. One of Bristol's main problems was the increase in shipping capacity. The great floating behemoths of the industrial age could no longer pass along the narrow, steep-sided Avon Gorge to reach the docks in the city centre. By the time new docks had been built outside of the city at Avonmouth and Portishead near the mouth of the Avon, the rot had set in.

But Bristol wasn't ready to throw in the towel just yet. In the mid 19th century it reinvented itself as a centre of engineering overseen by the high priest of the industrial age, **Isambard Kingdom Brunel**, who provided Bristol with some of its greatest engineering icons: the SS *Great Britain*, the Clifton Suspension Bridge and the terminus of the Great Western Railway. Although these were undoubtedly dazzling achievements, which briefly allowed the city to shine bright again on the

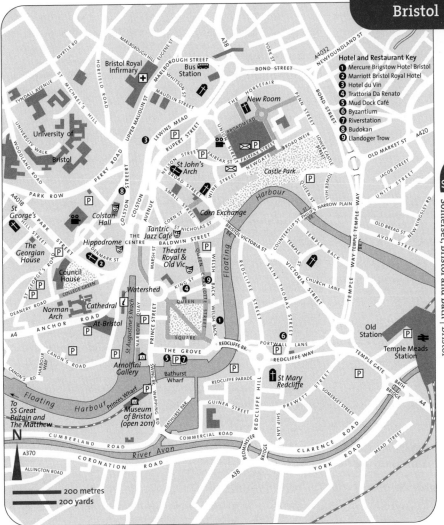

international stage, they were, in terms of the city's health, rages against the dying of the light rather than signals of a glorious rebirth.

At the turn of the 20th century, Bristol was firmly ensconced in provincial mediocrity. It was still a centre of manufacturing, but it was no longer a major player on the national stage. Unfortunately, it still had its head high enough above the parapet to be targeted by Nazi bombers in World War II – chiefly because of its role as a producer of military aircraft. Much of the centre of the city was destroyed in a series of brutal bombing raids. The subsequent rebuilding programmes of the 1950s and 60s involved lots of concrete, lots of height and lots of space for cars, but little care for beauty. For decades the best the city could do was keep its head down and keep going, which is what it did. In recent years, however, Bristol's fortunes have once again been on the up. Successful media (it's the home of the BBC Natural History Unit), computing and (until the crash) financial sectors have finally filled the yawning gaps left by the decline of manufacturing, while the Millennium makeover brought a bit of much needed spit and polish to Bristol's grimy surfaces and gave the whole city a burst of reinvigorating energy.

West of the Centre

From The Centre, it's a short walk up the hill to College Green, which boasts two neatly contrasting pieces of architecture. On one side is the gently curved and rather plain bulk of the city's 20th-century Council House, while on the other are the much more fussy pinnacles, arches and turrets of **Bristol Cathedral**. It was founded in mid 12th century, probably on the site of an earlier wooden church, and according to legend on the exact spot where St Augustine addressed local Celts during his 6th-century conversion of the country. Back then it was the rather simple church of the adjoining monastery. But, following the dissolution of the monasteries in the mid 16th century, which saw the abbey closed and the church redesignated as a cathedral, it grew into something grander.

Bristol Cathedral
College Green;
t (0117) 926 4879;
www.bristol-
cathedral.co.uk; open
8am–6pm daily; adm
free, but donations
appreciated

The building you see today is the result of numerous renovations, expansions and repair programmes, and comprises sections from various different ages, including the 12th century (the chapter house, abbot's house and abbot's gateway), the 13th century (the Elder Lady Chapel, notable for its carvings of what looks like monkeys playing bagpipes) and the 15th century (the choir – its misericords are the cathedral's must-see attraction, depicting bawdy scenes from the life of Reynard, the mischievous fox). Most of the current structure, however, including the nave and west towers, are 19th century, created as part of an attempt to restore the church to its original medieval design, a plan symptomatic of the contemporary fashion for all things medieval and Gothic.

From the outside the building looks very much like a like standard-issue Gothic cathedral, but the inside rather confounds expectations. Though the styling is obviously medieval, the structure looks anything but. The nave, choir and aisles are all the same height giving the cathedral's interior the appearance of a large hall rather than a church – a style known appropriately enough as 'hall church'.

From the cathedral, head up Park Street for five minutes until you reach, on your left, Great George Street. About halfway down at Number 7 is a restored sugar merchant's mansion, the **Georgian House**, which provides an intriguing glimpse into the role slavery played in the daily lives of the city's wealthier inhabitants. The house was built in the 1790s by John Pinney, a prominent sugar baron who accumulated a sizable fortune from his slave-worked plantations on the Caribbean island of Nevis. When Pinney returned to Bristol at the end of his life, he brought with him one of these slaves, whose name was Pero, to act as his personal valet. Pero's sisters, however, he left behind. Pero was eventually granted his freedom by Pinney while living in Bristol, but died not long after, aged 45.

Georgian House
7 Great George Street;
t (0117) 921 1362; open
Sat–Wed 10–5; adm free

Getting to and around Bristol

By Car

Bristol lies 122 miles west of London. The two cities are connected by the M4. To get to the city centre, leave the motorway at J19 and take the M32. The M5, linking the West Country with Birmingham, also passes Bristol.

By Train, Coach and Bus

There are direct train links from London (Paddington and Waterloo), Bath, Birmingham, Exeter and Oxford to Bristol Temple Meads Station, which lies around a mile southeast of the city centre. It's a 25-minute walk, or you can take a taxi or water taxi (*see* below). Contact National Rail Enquiries for train times.

The country's main coach operator, National Express, operates services from London (Victoria, Gatwick and Heathrow), Exeter, Oxford and Stratford-upon-Avon to Bristol Coach Station, which is located on Marlborough Street to the north of the city centre. Open Top Bus Tours, with live commentary are run by City Sightseeing Bristol from March to October and take in all the city's major sites, including Bristol Zoo Gardens, the City Museum and Art Gallery, the Broadmead Centre and the SS *Great Britain*. Fares are £1 per stop or £10 for an all-day hop on/off ticket (**t** 0870 444 0654, *www.bristolvisitor.co.uk*).

By Boat

Perhaps the most fun way to get around Bristol is to take a water taxi. The Bristol Ferry Boat Company (**t** (0117) 927 3416, *www.bristolferry.com*) operates a timetabled service 364 days a year, which stops off at various points in the city, including The Centre and the SS *Great Britain*. They can be caught from Temple Meads Station (turn left out of the station and follow the road round until you see the Temple Quay steps). Fares are £1.60: two-stop hop; £1.90: regular single; £3.30: return. The firm, which owns the Matthew, the replica of John Cabot's boat, also offers sightseeing cruises up the Avon Gorge, as do the Bristol Packet Company, **t** (0117) 926 8157, *www.bristolpacket.co.uk.*

By Bike and On Foot

Bikes can be hired from The Ferry Station on Narrow Quay (**t** (0117) 376 3942, *www.ferrystation.co.uk*). City Sightseeing Bristol organizes guided walks (**t** 0870 444 0654, *www.bristolvisitor.co.uk*).

Orientation

The largely pedestrianized square that marks the centre of town is known, rather handily, as **The Centre**. Once upon a time it was probably rather idyllic, back when it was part of the River Frome, the city's second river which used to arc its way through the town. The river now follows a subterranean course since being covered over in late 19th century. In the early 1900s, this area was Bristol's main tram hub, known as the Tram Centre, a name that was gradually abbreviated after the trams stopped running in 1939.

Following the Second World War, the square's purpose remained primarily traffic orientated, lying as it did at the centre of the city's fiercely congested inner ring road. It's been tamed a little of late. The ring road no longer forms a complete ring, with a section on Queen Square now closed to traffic and other parts pedestrianized and widened. Fountains were also added for the Millennium which slightly improved the overall aesthetic effect. Nonetheless, this is still a primarily utilitarian space, of most use as a central landmark from which to orientate yourself and for catching buses – nearly all of which seem to stop here. In the centre of The Centre stands a statue of Edmund Burke.

To the **southwest** of the Centre lie College Green and Bristol Cathedral, and beyond them up the hill the gentrified suburbs of Clifton.

To the **northwest** are the Corn Exchange and the heart of the old medieval town. Sites include Bristol Bridge, which once marked the confluence of Avon and Frome. Continuing northeast takes you to the main shopping district of Broadmead.

Southeast of The Centre is Queen Square, a grand 18th century development laid out by wealthy local merchants. It's been significantly renovated and restored in recent years.

South of The Centre is the restored quayside of St Augustine's Reach, originally part of the city's docks and floating harbour, which formed the epicentre of the city's millennial makeover. It's where all the latest bars, restaurants, hotels and attractions are located. You can also catch water taxis from here.

Temple Meads railway station lies a mile southeast of the centre and can also be reached via water taxi.

Most of the city's attractions would be within easy walking distance of The Centre if there weren't quite so many hills. As it is, some of the outlying sites – particularly those in Clifton – are within slightly-out-of-breath walking distance.

Today you can explore the mansion's four floors which are packed full of period furniture and decorations, from the cooking contraptions in the basement kitchen to the owner's cold-water plunge pool, book-lined libraries and spacious bedrooms. For the millennium a new footbridge in the city centre was named in honour of Pero (*see* p.72).

After touring the house, take a quick detour southwest to **Brandon Hill**, at the end of Great George Street, from where there are great views out over the city. Even better ones are offered from the top of the 105ft high red brick and Bath sandstone **Cabot's Tower**, built in 1987 to commemorate the 400th anniversary of John Cabot's journey of exploration to the Americas – hence the 'CCCC' cut into the tower's side. The winged figure atop the tower is apparently supposed to represent commerce. On a clear day you can see all the way to Wales from the top.

Cabot's Tower
open daily till dusk; adm free

If you retrace your steps to Park Street, continuing northwest will take you up to Queen's Road on the very outskirts of Clifton. In the 19th century this was the centre of an important artistic community, and since 1904 has been home to **Bristol's City Museum and Gallery**, which augments its good art collection – particularly strong on local Bristolian and West Country painters, with a few other Pre-Raphaelite and Impressionist choices – with displays on archaeology, British natural history (there's a freshwater aquarium), science and history. There's a particularly interesting display of maps showing how Bristol's appearance has been radically altered over the past 400 years. As is usually the case with collections assembled during the days of empire, the museum also boasts plenty of treasures from around the world, including a surprisingly fine collection of Chinese porcelain and a recently refurbished Egyptian gallery.

Bristol's City Museum and Gallery
Queen's Road; t (0117) 922 357; open daily 10–5; adm free

Northeast of the Centre

Heading northeast from the centre takes you into the city's commercial heart, both past and present. Corn Street and its environs – Broad Street, High Street, Wine Street – were the city's first market area, which grew up in the early medieval period when Bristol was first beginning to stretch its mercantile wings. The fine **Corn Exchange**, built in mid-18th century to a design by architect John Wood, shows how far the city came in the next few centuries, its exterior proclaiming Bristol's almost smug sense of economic self-importance. The carvings are supposed to represent the four corners of the Earth – or more exactly, Africa, America, Asia and Europe – with which Bristol, via her enormous trading route network, was linked. In front of the entrance are four bronze 17th-century trading tables, known locally as 'nails', from where the expression to 'pay on the nail' supposedly derives.

Heading northeast along Wine Street brings you to **Broadmead**, Bristol's main shopping area. Bombed heavily in the War, it's been site of some of the city's worst architectural outrages. Today it's home to a couple of modern, chain-store-filled shopping centres: the 1980s-built Galleries Shopping Centre, and Cabot Circus, which opened in late 2008. The latter was going to be called the Merchants Quarter, but changed its name to honour the city's most famous explorer following objections to the original name's connections with the slave trade. In the early modern period, Bristol's Society of Merchant Venturers was a prime´ mover in the slave trade, as it was in many other aspects of Bristolian life. Indeed the merchants were, ironically enough, also largely responsible for funding John Cabot's New World adventures. The area is exactly as you'd expect it to be, with one notable difference. This temple of mammon has within it one of the earliest examples of a more austere form of belief, England's first Methodist Chapel, the **New Room**, built in 1739, where the movement's founder, John Wesley, preached, often about the evils of slavery. Believers will no doubt see the chapel's near-miraculous survival, while all around it burned during Second World War, as proof of its divine approval.

South of Broadmead lies the riverside Castle Park where you can tour the few crumbling remains of the city's medieval fortress.

New Room
36 The Horsefair;
t (0117) 926 4740;
www.newroombristol.
org.uk; open Mon–Sat
10am–4pm; adm free,
but donations
appreciated

Southeast of the Centre

This is one of the city centre's more well-to-do areas, as exemplified by **Queen Square**, which was laid out in terribly tasteful style in the early 18th century to provide homes for Bristol's wealthy merchants. The architecture is as fine and elegant as the sources of the merchants' wealth were base and ugly. It's been restored in the past decade, with the once raging traffic cut significantly and its central park spruced up. At its centre lies an equestrian statue of William III.

Just north, on King Street, stands the **Old Vic**, the country's oldest working theatre, which opened in 1766, and is a veritable Georgian time capsule (*see* p.81). On this street look out also for the exceedingly salty **Llandoger Trow** pub (*see* p.80). Built in 1664, it boasts a couple of notable literary connections. It was here in the 18th century that Daniel Defoe reputedly met Alexander Selkirk, a sailor who spent four years marooned on an island, upon whom he would base his tale of Robinson Crusoe. Robert Louis Stevenson also found inspiration here in the 19th century, apparently modelling his descriptions of the *Admiral Benbow* in *Treasure Island* upon the pub. It's a fine Jacobean building, albeit maintained in a rather twee style. In case you're wondering, the name is reference to a type of flat-bottomed boat, the trow, made in the South Wales town of Llandoger.

Exiting the square's southeast corner takes you over Redcliffe Bridge to the south side of the Avon, a rather built-up area, where in amongst all the concrete is one of city's loveliest churches, **St Mary Redcliffe**. According to no less an authority than Elizabeth I, St Mary was once the 'most famous parish church in England', and 'fair' and 'good' to boot, although today it is a rather forgotten gem. The city's constant reshaping and reconstruction has played a part in its fall from prominence. Once upon a time the church stood on the quayside, proud and visible. Indeed it was considered a particularly holy site by the city's merchants who would make time to come here both before and after a hazardous sea journey to pray for protection from our Lady of Redcliffe. When they sailed back into port, the church's spire would be the first welcoming landmark they'd spot, providing assurance that they had returned home safely.

St Mary Redcliffe
t (0117) 929 1487;
www.stmaryredcliffe.co.
uk; open Mon–Sat
9am–5pm, Sun
8am–7.30pm

Following centuries of urban reconstruction, the church now lies away from the water at the centre of a busy roundabout amid oppressive-looking estates. Still, if you can ignore the rather low rent frame, the church itself still presents a pretty enough picture, set on a neat lawn with its light-coloured stone, busy Gothic decoration and tall spire.

Deriving its name from the nearby red-coloured sandstone cliffs, St Mary was begun in the 12th century and parts of the early structure remain, although most of what you see is 14th century, paid for by one William Canynges, a prominent local merchant who went on to become mayor of city (and the make-believe patron of a series of epic poems, see box, p.73). The importance placed on the church by the local seafaring community is shown in the interior details, including the four-foot-long whale bone by the entrance, presented by John Cabot as thanks for his safe return. A small modern replica of the boat in which he made his extraordinary journey, The Matthew, sits above the north porch door.

The interior is structurally Gothic and today rather solemn-looking, although in the early 18th century it was briefly decorated in an ostentatious Baroque fashion, paid for by a donation from Queen Anne. What colour there is in today's interior is found principally in the stained glass, some of which dates back to medieval times. Most, however, was smashed by Cromwell's troops in the Civil War and has been gradually replaced since the 1800s. A Hogarth triptych that once hung in the church can now be seen in the City Museum and Gallery.

The church boasts a celebrated organ, constructed in 1911 by the renowned firm Harrison & Harrison. It's a four manual, 71 stop version, which, according to the people who know about such things, is very impressive, but it is now in rather urgent need of repair. Donations are welcomed to try and raise the £800,000 required to fix it.

Continuing east takes you to Temple Meads Station, which stands guard over its diminutive forerunner, the **Old Station**, which is the world's oldest major railway terminus. Designed by Brunel in 1840, the building marked both the end of the first major stretch of the Great Western Railway, and the culmination of Brunel's first great railway project. Brunel put as much effort into making sure it looked just so as he had into making sure that it worked, giving it a country house-like facade, complete with castle-esque crenellations. If anything, however, he underestimated the extent to which his new railways would be embraced by the people. As train traffic to the region increased dramatically over subsequent decades, Brunel's terminus soon began to creak under the strain and was eventually replaced by a larger station with greater capacity. Brunel's building now hosts temporary exhibitions.

South of the Centre

Immediately south of The Centre, you'll find St Augustine's Reach, formerly part of the River Frome (which today flows under the city) and now the northernmost part of that floating harbour, the section of the river Avon enclosed within locks in the city centre so as to allow it to maintain a constant water level. Spanning the water just to the south is Pero's Bridge, a footbridge built for the millennium and named after a

Teenage Tricks – The Brief and Tragic Life of Thomas Chatterton

Of all the notable figures associated with the city one of the most intriguing is Thomas Chatterton who, in the late 18th century, achieved notoriety when he was revealed as the teenage forger behind a series of medieval poems. His early death in impoverished circumstances before his talent had been fully grasped by the public made him the leading poster boy of the nascent Romantic movement.

Thomas grew up a fairly privileged member of Bristolian society, his family having provided sextons for St Mary Redcliffe for nearly two centuries. Thomas' father held the post and, though he died a few months before Thomas' birth, the position passed to his uncle, Richard, which meant that the boy spent his early years immersed in church life. He grew up something of a prodigy, able to read and write from a young age, with a keen interest in music, heraldry, astronomy and particularly poetry. Apparently he expressed a desire to write almost as soon as he could talk and by the tender age of 12 had already had pieces published in the local *Bristol Journal*. Despite his early success, it seems Thomas felt his ambitions were being thwarted. Perhaps he had a piece of work rejected. Whatever the reason, it seems he took the decision to move away from presenting original works to creating forgeries.

Thomas spent a lot of time at the church, exploring its nooks and crannies and rooting around in drawers. It was during these explorations that he claimed to have made an astonishing find in some old oak chests in the muniments room above the north porch – a collection of 15th-century poems written on parchment by an unknown monk called Thomas Rowley. They were nothing of the sort.

In his teenage years, Thomas had become increasingly fascinated by medieval history, voraciously reading writers of the period, including Weever, Dugdale and Chaucer. It appears that, like many children, Chatterton spent much of his time living in a fantasy world – his imaginary period of choice being the Wars of the Roses. However, unlike other children, Chatterton had the ambition and literary talent to try – fantastical as it seems – to somehow create a sense of reality for his dreams.

His approach was meticulous. He used genuine medieval parchment (cut from the edge of legal documents), incorporated medieval jargon (probably lifted from John Kersey's *Dictionarium Anglo-Britannicum*) and drew fake heraldic drawings. He sent a fake verse history of the country, *Rowley's History of England* to Horace Walpole, the renowned writer and brother of the country's first Prime Minister, who believed the work to be genuine, emboldening Chatterton to create more 'Rowley' works.

Buoyed by his fake success, Chatterton now became determined to gain recognition for his own writings. He wrote furiously, submitting pieces to various journals of the day including the *Middlesex Journal*, *Hamilton's Town and Country Magazine* and *Freeholder's Magazine*. He was particularly taken with writing strident, and slightly naive, attacks against prominent political and religious figures of the Establishment, and in support of the radical politician John Wilkes. Moving to London where he took lodgings in Shoreditch, he enjoyed some success. However, perhaps as a result of his youth and inexperience, it appears he received little money for his efforts and soon began to regard his career as a failure, particularly after the rejection of another fabricated Rowley piece, the *Excelente Balade of Charitie*, by *Town and Country Magazine*.

Increasingly impoverished and despondent about his condition – as perhaps only a teenager can be – Thomas drank arsenic and killed himself three months before his 18th birthday.

At this stage, no one had discovered Chatterton's great deception. His death caused barely a ripple in the London literary scene where he was seen primarily as a minor writer of journal articles, and a 'transcriber' of a medieval text. In the decade after his death, however, more assiduous scholarship began to reveal problems with these transcribed works; namely that there appeared to be no other evidence that a monk called Rowley had ever existed or, as Chatterton purported, that the wealthy Bristol merchant William Canynges had acted as his patron. There could be only one conclusion – the works were forgeries. Which, of course, meant that the poems were Chatterton's own creations, and so began to be read on their own merits, rather than as items of historical curiosity. They proved to be of particular interest to the leading lights of the growing Romantic movement for their use of 'natural' imagery and rhythm. Furthermore, Chatterton's story – the radical politics, the undiscovered genius, the sensitive disposition, the tragic early death – ticked all the right boxes for the image-conscious Romantics (he would feature in poems by Wordsworth, Shelley and Coleridge), as it would in later decades for the Pre-Raphaelites, for whom the vision of the doomed poet looking wanly beautiful on his deathbed would become a favourite subject.

slave of a Bristolian merchant (see p.70). The central section can be raised to let ships pass through. The counterweight for the lifting device takes the form of a pair of horn-like structures, which look a bit like giant ear trumpets. Cross over the bridge to reach Bristol's main family attraction, **At-Bristol**. One of the main highlights of the city's millennium regeneration, the At-Bristol project saw disused harbour-side buildings – in this instance goods sheds and lead works – turned into a shiny new science and technology museum. It was an ambitious scheme comprising three parts: a hands-on science centre, Explore; a nature centre with an artificial rainforest and aquarium, Wildwalk; and an Imax cinema showing wildlife-themed 3D spectaculars called Wildscreen.

At-Bristol
Anchor Road,
Harbourside;
t 0845 345 1235;
www.at-bristol.org.uk;
open term time
Mon–Fri 10am–5pm, Sat
and Sun 10am–6pm;
adm £10.80

To begin with, At-Bristol was hailed as a big success, attracting high visitor numbers. But, in a microcosm of the history of the city, this initial promise proved ultimately unsustainable. After a few years fundraising efforts began to stall, leading to huge holes appearing in the budget, which the government declined to fill. In 2007, the most expensive parts of the scheme, Wildwalk and Wildscreen, closed their doors. However, plans to turn Wildwalk into an aquarium, and perhaps reopen the Imax, have been mooted, so the complex's status may well change during the lifetime of this book. Explore is still open and doing reasonably well. It's a highly interactive science centre aimed squarely at families, with exhibitions on the human brain, space travel, forces and flight, with lots of things to press, prod, turn and unravel.

Arnolfini
16 Narrow Quay;
t (0117) 917 2300;
www.arnolfini.org.uk;
open Tues–Sun
10am–6pm; adm free

Back across Pero's bridge and heading south, you reach the **Arnolfini**, a gallery dedicated to exploring the outer reaches of contemporary art and architecture. It offers a constantly changing programme of 'challenging' temporary exhibitions. It also puts on film screenings and concerts and has a great bookshop and café.

Across the Prince Street swing bridge to the south (which last swung in the 1930s) lies Prince's Wharf and a former transit shed which used to house the city's **Industrial Museum**, and which from 2011 will host a brand spanking new **Museum of Bristol**, built with help of a £11.3 million Heritage Lottery Fund grant.

SS *Great Britain*

The most potent reminder of the city's industrial heritage and engineering pedigree lies a ten-minute walk (or for preference a four-minute water taxi ride, see p.69 for details) west of here. Now sited in the original dry dock where it was built in the 1830s, following decades spent wandering the world's oceans, Brunel's **SS Great Britain** was the first iron-hulled propeller-driven ship built capable of travelling across oceans. It's still a splendid sight, but at the time of its launch in 1843, must have been simply awe-inspiring. Measuring 322ft (98m) long, it was the largest ship yet built, more than 100ft (30m) longer than its nearest rival.

⭐ **SS Great Britain**
t (0117) 926 0680;
www.ssgreatbritain.org;
open Nov–Dec
10am–4pm, Feb–March
10am–4.30pm,
April–Oct
10am–5.30pm; adm
£10.95, which allows
unlimited return visits
for 12 months, plus
access to the Matthew
and Dockyard Museum

In truth, her career never quite lived up to the wonder of her creation. Envisaged as a passenger liner, she was supposed to be the flagship of the Great Western Steamship Company, plying the glamour route between Bristol and New York. Brunel saw her as simply providing an international extension to his domestic travel network: customers arriving at London would travel by first class trains along his Great

John Cabot and the Age of Discovery

There must have been something in the Genoese water in the late 15th century that gave people a love of adventure and discovery, a wanderlust writ large. Columbus, of course, perhaps the world's most famous explorer, has been Genoa's most celebrated son ever since he became the first European (at least since the Vikings some 500 years earlier) to reach the Americas, when he arrived in the Caribbean in 1492. Just five years later, he would be followed by his fellow Genoese native, Giovanni Caboto, who became the first European to land on the mainland of North America. That Caboto is more usually remembered by the Anglicized version of his name, John Cabot, is simply because his trip was financed by the English king (and Bristolian merchants) rather than Spain. Indeed Henry VII had been on the verge of financing Columbus when Spain stepped in.

As with Columbus before him, Cabot's purpose was not the discovery of new countries but to undertake the first, but by no means the last, major attempt to locate the fabled northwest passage, which people believed would offer a quicker route to Asia, thereby greatly improving trade links, and, more importantly, vastly increasing the wealth of whichever country controlled it.

Despite the potential riches on offer, Cabot failed to convince either Spain or Portugal, the two great exploratory nations of the time, to finance him. The recent feats of Bartholomeu Dias, who had successfully rounded the southern tip of Africa, in the process opening up a new Asian trade route for Portugal, had made the passage's discovery much less pressing. Instead Cabot received the backing of the English king who was no doubt feeling threatened by the discoveries being made by his European rivals.

The Genoese adventurer set out from Bristol in 1497 with just one small boat, the *Matthew*, bound for failure, at least in his stated task. His attempt to find the passage would be thwarted by the small matter of a great and still unknown continent sitting in the way, the discovery of which would ultimately bring riches greater than any trade route. Making landfall around six weeks after departure somewhere on the American coast – possibly at Newfoundland, although no one is really sure – which he confidently asserted to be part of the Eastern shore of Asia, Cabot spent the next month mapping the coast. He then returned home without treasure or cargo or knowledge of a new Asian express route, but with maps that were at least significantly more accurate than those he left with. His achievements, though in truth modest, were enough to have him hailed as a hero upon his return – he was made an admiral and awarded a pension of £20. He didn't have long to enjoy his triumph, however, and was never able to capitalize upon, or even really understand, his discovery. The next year he undertook a more ambitious second journey, this time with five ships, but was never heard of again. Whether he made it back to the Americas or was lost at sea has never been established.

Western Railway, alighting at his Bristol station where they would be ferried to his ocean-going ship and onwards to America. In the event, the *Great Britain* proved too big for Bristol's docks, so the route was changed to Liverpool–New York. It would be just the first of many problems to beset the ship. She ran aground in 1846 and had to be refloated, but at a cost which effectively bankrupted her owners, leading to her being sold and put to work on the less glamorous and much more gruelling Liverpool-Melbourne route, laden with emigrants (up to 900 per crossing) hoping to make a new life in Australia. Other postings followed, each a down grading, as she was superseded by larger, faster craft. She served as a troop ship in the Crimean War (1853–56), before in 1881 being turned into a coal transporter. A fire in 1886 almost completely gutted her and she was turned into a floating coal container instead, moored off the Falkland Islands. The engineering wonder of its age, which had circumnavigated the globe 26 times, was eventually abandoned and left to the elements. In 1969, however, she was rescued and returned to Bristol. Since then she's undergone near permanent renovation. Much of her interior has been restored, including the very fine dining rooms, and you can visit the engine room and admire the ship's huge bright red propeller.

Adjacent, when not out on the water, and included in the price of your ticket, is a replica of the **Matthew** , the 15th-century ship on which the Anglicized Genoese explorer John Cabot became the first European to sail to the North American mainland in 1497. The vessel is surprisingly small, just 78 feet (23.7m) long, and staffed by volunteers who often indulge in a bit of fiddle di di role play, if you're into that sort of thing. Cruises around the harbour are offered from March to September.

Matthew
t (0117) 927 6868;
www.matthew.co.uk

Clifton

Located northwest of Bristol proper, and reachable via a stiff 20-minute walk, or a five minute bus ride, from the centre, Clifton has maintained its position as the city's most well-to-do suburb since the late 18th century. Like a relative from a poor family made good, it has a bit of an aloof, detached air to it as if it's slightly ashamed of its connections to its grubbier, more working-class sibling.

The attractions here are all rather refined – the elegant Georgian and Regency architecture of Victoria Square, Caledonian Place and Royal York Crescent, and its collection of upmarket boutiques and shops. It does also boast its own engineering heritage, albeit, in the shape of **Clifton Suspension Bridge**. Built to a design of Brunel, the bridge is often held up as one of his crowning achievements. But, its design aside, Brunel had almost nothing to do with its construction, and indeed died before it was finished. But then, Clifton was always a very different project to the ones the great man would become used to working on in his later career. Unlike his railways and ships, which seemed to be demanded by the march of progress, born in the crucible of the Industrial Revolution, Clifton was more of a sort of aristocratic whim, a giant Georgian folly, which probably goes some way to explaining why it would take nigh on a century from inception to completion.

There was, after all, no great need for a bridge in this position. It wasn't linking up a popular land route or replacing a ferry service. Somebody just thought it might look nice, that somebody being a local wine merchant, William Vick, who in 1784 left £1000 in his will for the construction of a bridge across the Avon Gorge from Clifton Down to Leigh Woods. The clause, which stated that the money should be left until the interest had built it up to £10,000 showed that not even Vick thought the bridge was a particularly pressing concern.

Fast-forward 45 years to 1829 and Vick's bequest had still only reached £8000, which at contemporary prices would have bought about a tenth of a bridge. However, by this time Vick's idea had begun to win popular favour, prompting the government to put up the rest of the money for its construction (to be recouped through tolls) and to organize a competition for its design. This was to be overseen by a committee headed by Thomas Telford, the designer of the Menai Suspension Bridge, which in 1826 had linked Wales with Anglesey for the first time. In the event, and to no one's great surprise, Telford rejected all the submitted designs, including one by the then 25-year-old Brunel, claiming that the bridge should be designed by a true expert in the field, i.e. himself.

The young Brunel, however, showing the dogged tenacity that would characterize his later career, persuaded the rest of the committee to back his design. Soon Brunel may have wished that he hadn't argued quite so eloquently. The project was undermined by setbacks from the start. Riots in Bristol, prompted by parliament's rejection of the Reform Bill, delayed the bridge's construction for five years, and then in 1843, with just the towers built in rough stone, the money ran out. And that was pretty much how the situation remained at the time of Brunel's death in 1859. The following year, his former colleagues at the Institution of Civil Engineers decided to raise the funds to complete the bridge so as to commemorate the great man's achievements. They used parts from the recently demolished Brunel-built Hungerford Suspension Bridge, and a slightly revised design, which ironically did away with the Egyptian styling. The bridge was finally finished in 1864. Its 702ft span, supported by massive iron chains, sits 250ft above the River Avon and is still in use today. An estimated four million vehicles a year pass over it.

The bridge also has an unwanted reputation as a suicide hot spot. More than 100 people have jumped to their deaths from here. As a result, the site is fitted with plaques advertising the contact details of the Samaritans. But even this rather unsavoury aspect has provided at least one charming story. When the broken-hearted Sarah Ann Henley, aged just 22, jumped in 1885, her voluminous petticoats acted as a parachute, gently depositing her in the river mud below. She thought better of making a second attempt and lived to be 85.

Clifton Bridge Interpretation Centre
t (0117) 974 4664; www.clifton-suspension-bridge.org.uk; open daily 10am–5pm; adm free

The bridge is easy to reach from the centre of Clifton on foot and is free to walk across. You can find out more at the **Clifton Bridge Interpretation Centre**, which lies adjacent to the Leigh Woods end,

Engineering Bristol's Future: Isambard Kingdom Brunel

Brunel (1806–59) was not Bristolian by birth (he was born in Portsmouth to a French father), nor were his great engineering endeavours solely located here, but his name will forever be associated with the West Country city, a place for which he had an obvious and deep fondness, and a place which he helped as much as anyone to rise to the challenge of the industrial age.

Following an early life spent studying in France and working at his father's (himself a renowned engineer) side, on projects that would include the creation of the first tunnel beneath the River Thames, Brunel's association with Bristol began when he was commissioned to design a new bridge over the River Avon. Although the plan initially foundered through lack of funds (*see* above), subsequent local schemes fared significantly better. In 1837 he launched the SS *Great Western* from the city, the first trans-Atlantic passenger steamship, and at the time the largest ship in the world, which was followed in 1843 by the even larger SS *Great Britain*, which today can be seen in dry dock on Bristol's waterfront (*see* p.74). Brunel would also spend years linking Bristol with London via the creation of the Great Western Railway –118 miles of tracks, tunnels, viaducts and stations that represented the world's then most advanced railway connection and the very cutting edge of Victorian technology.

In addition to his Bristol projects his third, and greatest, ship the SS *Great Eastern*, a vast iron behemoth capable of carrying 4,000 passengers around the world without refuelling, was built in London because Bristol's docks were not quite mighty enough to cope. What links many of Brunel's engineering accomplishments is that they were so often the superlative examples in their field. His tunnels were the longest, his ships the biggest, his bridges the tallest – in almost all instances the result of solving difficulties believed insurmountable by previous engineers.

where you can see the design for the rather ugly Gothic bridge Telford preferred. The centre can arrange guided tours.

Good views of the bridge and gorge are available from nearby Durdham Down. Here the **Clifton Observatory** occupies an 18th-century former snuff mill where, a century later, a local artist installed a camera obscura, still in operation today. The observatory also provides access to **St Vincent's Cave**, offering views out over the gorge.

Bristol Zoo

Bristol Zoo
Guthrie Road;
t (0117) 974 7399;
www.bristolzoo.org.uk;
open summer
9am–5.30pm, winter
9am–5pm; adm £12.50

Outside town, but easily reachable via the 8 or 9 bus from the Centre or via train from Temple Meads Station – it's a ten-minute walk from Clifton Down Station – this is one of the country's best big city zoos. It's home to gorillas, lions, monkeys, penguins and seals, plus plenty of smaller critters in the aquarium, reptile house and Moonlight World. As tends to be the way with modern menageries, Bristol is heavy on interaction and family fun, the highlights being a tropical bird house and parrot-feeding experience, the butterfly forest, gorilla world and monkey jungle – where you can walk through the lemur enclosure. There are also regular talks and animal demonstrations. Parents and grandparents of a certain age will remember this as the setting for Johnny Morris' weekly tales of grumbling camels and chattering lemurs in the TV programme *Animal Magic*.

Around Bristol

Avon Valley Railway
t (0117) 932 5538;
www.avonvalleyrailway.
org; open Apr–Oct every
Sun; there are additional
midweek services in Aug

Just off the A431, midway between Bristol and Bath, the **Avon Valley Railway** offers steam-train rides most Sundays between April and October along a short two-mile stretch of the former Midland Railway line.

Although the trains aren't quite so picturesque as the Avon, the **Severn Beach Railway** operates on one of the prettiest lines in the West Country between Temple Meads Station and Severn Beach. It makes a fine way to take in the sights of the Avon Gorge, visit Clifton or walk the sea wall. Trains are operated by First Great Western.

Bristol's northern suburb of Henbury is the site of the **Blaise Castle House Museum**, an 18th-century Gothic-revival mansion that now provides a home to a small museum of social history. There's a recreated Victorian schoolroom as well as model trains, toy soldiers and dolls, and it's surrounded by 162 acres of park and woodland – a good family day out.

ⓘ **Bristol**
Bristol Visitor
Information Centre,
Anchor Rd;
t (0117) 926 0767;
http://visitbristol.co.uk

⭐ Hotel Du Vin >>

Festivals in Bristol

During the **Bristol International Balloon Fiesta**, held on the second weekend in August, countless hot-air balloons take to the Bristolian skies. It's held at the Ashton Court Estate, an 850-acre historic mansion on the western outskirts of the city. Entry is free, car parking is £7 per car (*www.bristolfiesta.co.uk*).

Where to Stay in Bristol

Bristol's accommodation options have greatly improved over the past decade with swish new places opening up around the restored docks.

Very Expensive

Hotel Du Vin, The Sugar House, Narrow Lewins Mead; **t** (0117) 925 5577; *www.hotelduvin.com*. One of the town's most successful industrial renovations, the Du Vin occupies a collection of restored 18th-century sugar warehouses on the old docks. The owners have resisted the temptation to prettify the hotel too much, the rough and ready texture of the exterior contrasting neatly with the high spec facilities within. The large rooms come with big beds, leather chairs, claw foot baths, hifi and Wi-Fi. There's also a good **bistro**.

Expensive

Arnos Manor Hotel, 470 Bath Road, Arnos Vale; **t** (0117) 9711461; *www. arnosmanorhotel.co.uk*. In the suburb of Arnos Vale, this feels a world away from the hubbub of the centre. Occupying a fine-looking 18th-century manor house, the hotel does have a bit of a corporate feel to it, an inevitable side effect of its predominantly business-orientated clientele. Still it's very comfortable and, if you're willing to pay top dollar, very luxurious – the best rooms come with spa baths. The glass-roofed **restaurant** is of a very high standard.

Berkeley Square Hotel, 15 Berkeley Square, Clifton; **t** (0117) 925 4000; *www.cliftonhotels.com*. Outside it's a quintessential Georgian townhouse – reserved, quietly elegant and enjoying a prime location on one of Clifton's loveliest squares. Inside it's as stylish and designery with lots of unusual décor. Plenty of extras – free fruit, newspapers, wifi, DVD players, decanters of sherry plus access to the next-door private member's club, The Square – make this pretty good value.

Best Western Victoria Square, Victoria Square, Clifton; **t** (0117) 973 9058; *www.vicsquare.com*. On a leafy Clifton square near the university, the Victoria offers a superior standard of chain comfort. All 41 rooms are light and airy with decent-sized bathrooms and wireless internet. There's also a reasonable restaurant, but no lift.

Marriott Bristol Royal Hotel, College Green; **t** (0117) 9255 100; *www. marriott.co.uk*. If, having seen its sturdy exterior, you're hoping to immerse yourself in Victoriana, you may be a tad disappointed. Although the hotel first opened in 1863, the interior is very much of the times:

comfortable, convenient and well equipped, but lacking the charm of the grandiose facade. With 242 rooms, most with queen-size beds and large TVs, this is still one of the city's largest establishments, located next to Bristol Cathedral in the heart of the city.

Mercure Brigstow Hotel Bristol, Welsh Back 5–7; **t** (0117) 929 1030; *www. mercure.com*. Very much an exemplar of the 'new Bristol' this smart four-star harbour-side hotel is one of the city's swishest choices, its rather mundane exterior notwithstanding. Rooms are large, sleek and stylishly minimal – all whites, woods and subtle lighting. The superior rooms have balconies with harbour views.

Moderate

The Rodney, 4 Rodney Place, Clifton; **t** (0117) 973 5422; *www.cliftonhotels. com*. Now spruced and refurbished, this hotel makes a fittingly smart and moderately priced member of the Clifton Hotels Group, who also operate the Berkeley Square. Rooms do vary in size rather, so check what you're getting. There's also a good **restaurant**, No.4 (*see* p.80).

Downlands House, 33 Henleaze Gardens, Henleaze; **t** (0117) 962 1639; *www.downlandshouse.com*. A way out of the city centre on the edge of Dirdham Downs, this Victorian semi is a comfortable, reasonably priced B&B.

Eating Out in Bristol

Dining is something Bristol does pretty well with a good selection of cuisines on offer at competitive prices. The main dining areas are King Street, Corn Street and around the harbour.

Moderate

Byzantium, 2 Portwall Lane; **t** (0117) 922 1883; *www.byzantium.co.uk*. A touch of balmy North Africa in blustery Bristol, Byzantium's interior, which occupies a former Victorian warehouse, is decked out in full-on Moroccan style. The food is equally exotic. For a sample, try the starter lantern – 6 small starters on a two-tier lantern for £6.50. Mains are a not exactly bargain at £14.95–£18.95. Belly dancing evenings are also staged.

⭐ Primrose Café >

Hotel du Vin Bistro, The Sugar House, Narrow Lewins Mead; **t** (0117) 925 5577; *www.hotelduvin.com*. Top-notch dining in one of the city's best modern hotels. The dining room is elegant, the French-inspired menu a cut above and the prices not too outlandish (*mains £13.50–18.95*). Excellent and extensive wine list.

Number 4, 4 Rodney Place, Clifton; **t** (0117) 973 5422; *www.numberfour restaurant.co.uk*. A revamped restaurant for a revamped hotel, No.4 is a great improvement, serving up decent Anglo-French cooking in a wood-panelled Georgian interior. Light meals are available at the bar and there's a nice garden for summer evening dining. They offer a two-course set menu for £12.99.

Primrose Café, 1 Clifton Arcade, Boyces Avenue, Clifton; **t** (0117) 946 6577; *www.primrosecafe.co.uk*. Something of a Clifton stalwart, this snug little place by Clifton Arcade is a café and local meeting spot during the day, before transforming into a restaurant at night, serving a British and Mediterranean influenced menu. A member of the 'slow food movement', it offers a set two-course menu for £14.95.

Riverstation, The Grove; **t** (0117) 914 4434; *www.riverstation.co.uk*. The name refers to the building's previous incarnation as a police station, and it enjoys a prime position on the harbour with views of the docks and St Mary Redcliffe. Downstairs is a deli counter, while upstairs is a bar, serving reasonably priced bar meals, and a more expensive sit-down restaurant offering a Mediterranean influence menu. They offer a 2-course lunch for £9.50. Otherwise mains are £12–18.

Trattoria Da Renato, 19 King St; **t** (0117) 929 8291. Near the Old Vic, this is a theatre-goer's favourite, offering very reasonably priced Italian fare. The walls are adorned with pictures of notable actors who have trodden the boards at Bristol. The management also operate a pizzeria and bar, **La Taverna dell' Artista** at No.33 King St.

Budget

Browns, 38 Queens Road, Clifton; **t** (0117) 930 4777; *www.browns-restaur ants.co.uk*. Housed in an attractive 19th-century building, modelled on the Doge's palace in Venice, Bristol's branch of the popular British chain is one of the city's more atmospheric options, with a lively bar and an adjoining restaurant serving bistro-style food.

Budokan, 31 Colston Street; **t** (0117) 914 1488; *www.budokan.co.uk*. A superior Pan-Asian affair offering a variety of Malaysian, Indonesia, Singaporean and Japanese choices cooked up quickly in an open kitchen and served at long communal tables. From 12–2.30pm and 5.30–7pm Mon–Sat they offer a 'Rapid Refuel Menu' when you can get a main, a side dish and a bowl of rice or noodles for a very reasonable £7.50. A second branch operates in Clifton at Whiteladies Rd.

Llandoger Trow, King Street; **t** 0870 990 6424. Decent pub grub served in this historic Jacobean pub once reputedly frequented by Daniel Defoe. Good range of beers on tap (*see* also p.71).

Mud Dock Café, 40 The Grove; **t** (0117) 934 9734; *www.mud-dock.com*. This real biking aficionado's bike shop also has, incongruously enough, a top floor café-restaurant where you can stock up on tasty carb-heavy fare – sausage and mash, burgers, steaks etc. – before getting back in the saddle. They offer a very good-value lunch menu for £5 (main course and a drink) and a 2-course evening menu for £10.95. *Closed Sun & Mon eve.*

Entertainment and Nightlife in Bristol

Live Music

St George's Bristol, Great George Street; **t** 0845 40 24 001; *www.st georgesbristol.co.uk*. Nationally renowned concert hall just outside the city centre that lays on a prestigious year-round programme of classical, jazz, blues and world music concerts. Lunchtime performances at 1pm, evening performances at 8pm.

Tantric Jazz Café, 39-41 St Nicholas Street; **t** (0117) 940 2304; *www.tantric-jazz.co.uk*. Live jazz five nights a week in this rather snugly sized, but extremely popular, café-bar, where the music presumably lasts all night but never quite reaches a crescendo. Resident band Tantra are joined by a succession of guests throughout each week. It's open Tues–Sat 6pm– 3am. It's free Tues–Thurs, but costs £3 Fri & Sat (or £13 with two tapas).

Victoria Rooms, Queens Road; **t** (0117) 331 4040. Now part of the University of Bristol, this grand neoclassical venue opened in the 1840s as a concert hall and quickly became one of the West Country's pre-eminent venues. Largely gutted by a 1934 fire, the building was for a while the headquarters of the university union before being turned back into a concert hall in 1996. It now stages regular free recitals by students.

Theatre

The Bristol Hippodrome, St Augustines Parade; **t** (0117) 302 333; *www.bristolhippodrome.org.uk*. The main Bristol venue for family-friendly shows of the Cirque de Soleil, Mama Mia!, High School Musical, Dancing on Ice type. Seats 3,000.

The Bristol Old Vic, King Street; **t** (0117) 987 7877; *www.bristololdvic.org.uk* Redolent of theatrical history, the Bristol Old Vic is Britain's oldest working theatre, having first raised its curtain way back in 1766. Today it comprises two stages: the main 650-seat Theatre Royal where major works, both modern and classical, are put on; and the more modest 140-seat Studio Theatre which stages more experimental fare. The theatre will be closed from 2010 to 2012 for refurbishment during which time all shows will be staged at other venues around Bristol.

Cinemas

The Arnolfini, 16 Narrow Quay; **t** (0117) 917 2300; *www.arnolfini.org.uk*. The city's prime modern art and architecture venue also stages events and film screenings.

The Watershed, 1 Canon's Road, Harbourside; **t** (0117) 927 6444; *www.watershed.co.uk*. Arthouse cinema and media venue next to the boats on St Augustine's Reach.

Bath

 Bath

It's been held up as an ideal of English aristocratic gentility and tasteful architectural preening for more than 300 years now, and there's little sign of its influence or popularity waning. Bath's elegant streets – where every building, from the most modest townhouse to the most boastful mansion, has been carefully designed, arranged and colour-coded to achieve perfect architectural harmony – attract hundreds of thousands of tourists every year. The city is, there's no denying it, an out-and-out tourist trap and yet, such is its snooty genius, it somehow manages to give the impression that it's not.

Visually the main influences are, of course, Roman and Georgian, and for many people (and the majority of tour groups) Bath's charms can be boiled down to just a handful of attractions – the Roman Baths, the 18th century architecture of John Woods (father and son), and the various locations associated with Jane Austen, chief among them the Pump Room. There's a bit more to the city than that, however. Bath rewards some dedicated time spent exploring its confines. Sure, you could get the essence of tourist Bath in a couple of hours (and many tourists do), particularly as the Roman Baths, the Pump Room and Bath Abbey are all located within a few metres of each other. But you'd be missing out. Queen Square, the Royal Crescent and Pulteney Bridge may take the headlines, but this is a city almost overburdened with architectural treats, not to mention great swathes of parkland. Indeed

Getting to and around Bath

By Car

Bath is ten miles south of J18 of the M4 and 12 miles southeast of Bristol on the A4 and the A36. Note that parking can be tricky in Bath. You may be better off using the park-and-ride facilities at Lansdown, just north of the city (signposted from the A46 and the A420), Newbridge (A4) and Old Down (A367). Double-decker buses will leave you in Queen's Square in the city centre, and provide you with panoramic views of the area as they negotiate the city's steep outlying hills.

By Train and Coach

It takes 60–90 minutes to reach Bath by train from London (Paddington). Services also arrive from Bristol, Salisbury and Portsmouth. All arrive at the station on Manvers Street.

National Express services arrive from London, Bristol, Salisbury, Portsmouth, Oxford and Stratford-upon-Avon, stopping at the bus station in Manvers Street.

Walking Tours

Free walking tours taking in all of Bath's major sites depart from the Abbey Church Yard every day at 10.30am. There are also additional tours Mon–Fri & Sun at 2pm, and on Sat at 7pm. Lead by the Mayor of Bath Honorary Guides, the tours last around two hours. No pre-booking is required. Other tours include a 'Bizarre Bath' tour which leaves from the Huntsman Inn on North Passage daily at 8pm Apr–Sept (t (01225) 335124; : *www.bizarrebath.co.uk*; adm £8), a 'Ghost Walk', which leaves from the Garricks Head pub next to the Theatre Royal on Sawclose at 8pm from Thurs–Sat throughout the year (t (01225) 350512; *www.ghostwalksofbath.co.uk*; adm £7), and a Jane Austen Tour leading you past the various sites associated her novels and sojourn in the city, which leave from the Abbey Church Yard all year, Sat–Sun and Bank Hols at 11am. There are additional tours in July–Aug at 6pm (t (01225) 443000; : *www.janeausten.co.uk*; adm £4.50).

Bus Tours

The Bath Bus Company offers open-top bus tours of all the main sights. Tours last 45 minutes with around 20 stops, including one outside Bath Abbey (t (01225) 330444; *www.bathbuscompany.com*; adm £11).

Boat Tours

Several companies operate boat trips from Pulteney Bridge, including Pulteney Cruisers, who offer 1-hour cruises down the Avon Valley to Bathampton (t (01225) 312900, *www.bathboating.com*; adm £8). Alternatively the Bath Boating Station hires out punts, canoes and skiffs for £7 an hour, or £16 per day (Forester Road, t (01225) 312900, *www.bathboating.co.uk*).

Unesco was so loath to pick a single highlight they gave up in the end and simply designated the entire city a World Heritage Site.

Still, don't go thinking it's all going to be perfect – the crowds and the traffic can be intense; the attitude of restaurant and bar staff a touch on the superior side and the hills will test your sightseeing resolve – but it's still one of the finest city experiences the country can offer.

History

The city's history does not, as is generally presumed, begin with the Romans. There is evidence that local Celtic tribes had settled here long before the Romans turned up, drawn by what has been attracting visitors ever since, the country's only hot (as in 'above body temperature') volcanic spring. Still, the Romans certainly left their mark, creating a large town known as Aquae Sulis (in honour of the spring and a local Celtic goddess, Sulis) filled with fine buildings, not the least of which was the grand bathing complex itself. What had so charmed the Romans, however, failed to elicit much interest from their successors, the Saxons, following the collapse of the Western Roman Empire in the 5th century

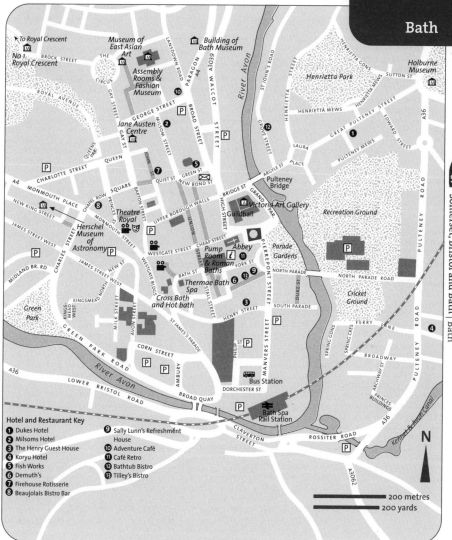

Hotel and Restaurant Key

1. Dukes Hotel
2. Milsoms Hotel
3. The Henry Guest House
4. Koryu Hotel
5. Fish Works
6. Demuth's
7. Firehouse Rotisserie
8. Beaujolais Bistro Bar
9. Sally Lunn's Refreshment House
10. Adventure Café
11. Café Retro
12. Bathtub Bistro
13. Tilley's Bistro

200 metres
200 yards

N

AD. The Germanic tribes had no culture of bathing, and the town was abandoned and left to decay over the ensuing centuries.

A revival of sorts took place following Alfred the Great's defeat of the Vikings in 878, when the town was rebuilt according to a grid plan. In the 10th century a monastery was erected in the centre, which was replaced by an enormous Norman cathedral, which was itself replaced by a slightly smaller abbey in the 15th century, which still stands. The town enjoyed modest success during this period as a centre of wool trading, but its loss of the local bishopric to its mini-sized rival of Wells showed how low its stock had fallen.

Bath's path to its current regional ascendancy began in the early 18th century when Georgian England suddenly became fixated with the curative properties of spa water, and none were deemed to be of more curative value than those gurgling out of the ground at the then rather down-at-heel West Country town. It was these Georgian health-seekers who oversaw Bath's spectacular rise from the gutter to the parlour, who were responsible for the town's most elegant architecture, who rediscovered and restored the Roman Baths, and who turned the Pump Room into one of the country's most fashionable meeting places – somewhere you might come across Jane Austen scribbling a quick note or Gainsborough indulging in an idle doodle.

That's not to say that England's architects and patrons arrived with any clear scheme worked out for the city. Indeed Bath's architectural uniformity is all the more remarkable when you consider that it was constructed according to no particular plan, but rather in fits and starts as the will – and more importantly the money – came and went. In truth, Bath's cohesion is something of a colour-coded illusion, due in large part to the dominance of a particular type of honey-hued stone. This was used, not because of a coincidence of taste, but because Ralph Allen, the owner of the Combe Down quarry, just outside the city, had the foresight to build a railway to transport his stones to the town, making them the cheapest and most convenient. Prime users of these stones, and the main architectural stars of the day, were John Wood the Elder (1704–54) and John Wood the Younger (1728–81) who between them were responsible for many of the city's finest terraces and crescents. The town's heady social interplay, meanwhile, was overseen by the famous dandy, Richard 'Beau' Nash, who became a 'master of ceremonies' (or 'events organizer' in modern parlance) at the city's endless social engagements, for which he drew up a strict code of etiquette.

And that, many visitors could be forgiven for thinking, was clearly that as far as Bath's progress went. Certainly any time traveller from Georgian England would find great swaths of the city still much as they left it. Bath's subsequent history has been more about preservation than reformation, but then you can hardly argue with the results. And there have been periods during the past couple of centuries when the city has fallen briefly out of fashion – and its usually sky-high house prices and rents have momentarily fallen – but Bath has always been content to sit and bide its time rather than attempt any radical remodelling, safe in the knowledge that the spotlight will in due course return.

Bath Centre

Abbey Church Yard is the site of the Roman Baths, the Pump Room and Bath Abbey – the entrances to which are just a few metres away from each other. This small square marks the most obvious point at which to begin your tour of the city.

Roman Baths Museum

Roman Baths Museum
*Abbey Church Yard;
t (01225) 477785;
www.romanbaths.co.uk;
Nov–Feb 9.30–5.30,
Mar–June and Sept–Oct
9–6; July–Aug
9am–10pm (last
admission 1hr before
closing); adm £11.00*

Whether stationed in Britain or Gaul or Asia or Africa, the Romans liked their environments to be as familiar as possible, which meant always building their towns according to the same plan, with a grid of streets, a forum (town square), a basilica (town hall), a theatre (or amphitheatre), a temple and, completing the set, a bath house (known as a thermae). To the Romans, bathing was more than just a means of getting clean, although cleanliness was a prized value, it was an important social experience. The Roman bathhouse was the equivalent of the modern pub or café. It was an informal meeting place, somewhere for people to chat and gossip about the day's events. However, when the Western Roman Empire collapsed in the 5th century AD, these bathhouses went out of fashion. The invading Germanic tribes had little need for such fancies and most were either destroyed or left to decay. Intriguingly, the Ottoman successors to the Eastern Roman Empire were much more taken with the idea of bathing and continued the practice. Hammams – or Turkish baths – are the direct descendants of Roman public baths.

Following the Roman departure, the bathhouse in Bath was built over and forgotten about until the early 18th century when workmen stumbled upon part of it by accident when digging in the centre of town. The rest of the complex was uncovered over the next century and, following some careful restoration (and a little bit of recreation), reopened to the public, whereupon it became one of the region's most popular attractions.

The baths, which look a little like a cross between an ancient temple and a modern swimming pool, have survived remarkably well and wandering through them today you can, at a pinch, imagine what it must have been like in Roman times, full of chattering, gossiping locals.

On arrival, you are given a self-paced audioguide, which will lead you through the complex and adjoining museum to the hot, bubbling spring itself. It's still going strong, churning out 250,000 gallons of water every day at a constant temperature of 116°F (47°C) – the bubbles you see are a result of escaping gas rather than the heat. The Romans channelled this water into a whole range of different baths: a large hot bath, a number of small tepid pools and treatment baths as well as a cold, circular plunge pool into which bathers would jump after their hot dips to freshen up. There were also steam rooms and saunas heated by underfloor hypocausts (the Roman version of central heating). Today, you can see the remnants of all these facilities, although only the main bath and plunge pool still contain water, which you should on no account drink – it flows along lead pipes laid down by Roman engineers.

In Roman times, the source of the spring was marked by a shrine to the goddess Sulis Minerva, where people would come to worship and throw curses written on sheets of lead into the water. You can see examples of these requests for supernatural intervention at the museum (most seem to have been inspired by petty vendettas and disputes between neighbours) along with a bust of the goddess herself. This tradition continues today at the plunge pool, which is littered with coins tossed in by visitors for luck. The museum also contains various models and dioramas showing what the complex would have looked like 1,600 years ago, as well as a number of mosaics and a collection of everyday Romano-British objects, such as coins and hairpins.

Pump Room

Pump Room
Abbey Church Yard;
t (01225) 444477;
www.romanbaths.co.uk;
open morning coffee
9.30–12; lunch 12–2.30;
afternoon tea 2.30–5

Built between 1789–99, this grand neoclassical dining room, adorned with portraits and sculptures of 18th century celebrities – including Robert Walpole, Britain's first Prime Minister, Ralph Allen, the Bath stone king, and Beau Nash, Bath's Mr Party – was the hub of the city's social life during the Georgian and Regency periods. Jane Austen set several scenes from her novels here, making it a must-see stop on any Austen-themed itinerary. Still a functioning – and very fancy – tea room and restaurant where diners are still serenaded by a classical trio (cello, violin and piano), as in Georgian times, its main interest for the casual visitor is the ornate fountain dispensing hot, steaming water, straight from the spa's source. You can sup with the Romans across 2,000 years with a cupful if you want, although do note that, while the water may contain 43 minerals, they don't seem to combine particularly well, as it tastes absolutely disgusting – which presumably means it's very good for you.

Jane Austen Centre

Jane Austen Centre
40 Gay Street;
t (01225) 443000;
www.janeausten.co.uk;
open mid-Mar–June
and Sep–Oct daily
9.45–5.30; July–Aug
Sun–Wed 9.45–5.30,
Thurs–Sat 9.45–7;
Nov–March Sun–Fri
11–4.30, Sat 9.45–5.30

No.40 Gay Street, near where Austen once lived, is now the city's **Jane Austen Centre**, which can provide all the background detail on Austen's time in Bath (*see* box opposite), and has displays of period costumes as well as a Regency-themed tea room. Austen-themed walking tours of the city – which leave from the Abbey Churchyard – can be booked through the centre, and perhaps offer the best insight into the writer's world, the city having changed so little visually since that time. Many of the locations mentioned in her books survive.

Bath Abbey

Bath Abbey
Abbey Church Yard;
t (01225) 422462;
www.bathabbey.org;
open Apr–Oct Mon–Sat
9–6, Sun 1–2.30 and
4.30–5.30; Nov–Mar
Mon–Sat 9–4.30, Sun
1–2.30 & 4.30–5.30;
adm free (donation
suggested)

When workmen began constructing a new church for Bath's Benedictine monastery in 1499, they couldn't have realized that it would represent pretty much the last hurrah of Catholic church building in England. Four decades later, with work nearing completion, the city's monks found themselves the unwitting victims of a religious revolution when Henry VIII's thwarted wedding plans caused him to wrest control of England's churches away from the Pope in Rome and establish an independent Church of England. A new Protestant rule was established, the most significant aspect of which was, as far as the residents of Bath were concerned, the dissolution of the country's monasteries. In 1539, the abbey and its church were surrendered to the agents of Henry VIII, who quickly removed anything of value to fill Henry's war coffers for his campaigns against the French. Gutted and plundered, the abbey lay abandoned until 1574 when Elizabeth I ordered restoration work to begin, this time with the intention of turning the building into a more modest parish church. It was completed in 1616 and, aside from a few 19th-century additions – notably the fan vaulting in the nave – is largely the structure you see now.

The abbey is the third major church to stand on this spot. The original seventh-century Saxon church, which hosted the coronation of Edgar, the

Jane Austen's Bath

No other author or literary figure is as closely associated with Bath as Jane Austen, and yet her attitude towards the city that inspired so many of the scenes in her novels could be described as at best ambivalent, and at times downright hostile. Born in 1775, Austen grew up in a rectory in the small rural village of Steventon in Hampshire. She visited Bath twice in the 1790s, staying first at No.1 The Paragon and then at 13 Queen Square, and it's clear that the city initially met with her approval. She describes Queen's Square House thus: 'we are exceedingly pleased with the house. It is far more cheerful than the Paragon, and the prospect from the drawing room, at which I now write, is rather picturesque.'

However, as fond as Jane was to visit the place, her father's decision to move the family home there in 1801 seems to have caused her considerable disquiet. What had seemed novel and fun on a brief visit now seemed wearisome and distracting when experienced on a permanent basis. She quickly tired of the endless social whirl, which she found got in the way of her writing. 'Do you know, I get so immoderately sick of Bath,' she wrote in *Northanger Abbey*.

Furthermore, the constant moving from one dwelling to another can hardly have helped the writing process, with the family living in four separate properties during their five-year stay: at 4 Sydney Place in Bathwick on the east side of the River Avon, at 27 Green Park Mansion, which overlooks the city's main park, at 25 Gay Street, which links Queen Square with the Circus, and finally, following her father's death, in a modest dwelling in Trim Street. During those five years Austen produced nothing of note, beyond a few revisions to earlier works, and in 1806, she finally upped sticks and went to live with her mother, sister and brother in Southampton, where she was able to restart her literary endeavours almost immediately.

With the city behind her, she found that its social scene provided excellent fodder for her tales of upper class life. All but one of her novels – *Pride and Prejudice* – feature scenes set in the city, while two, *Northanger Abbey* and *Persuasion*, have it as their main setting.

first king of England, in 973, was replaced by a huge Norman structure in the 12th century, measuring 301ft (92 m) long, following the transfer of the local bishopric from Wells to Bath in 1090. When the bishop's seat was moved back again in 1245, the loss of status (and funds) caused the great church to fall into a state of severe disrepair, prompting its replacement with the current structure at the end of the 15th century.

According to legend (first recorded at least a hundred years after the fact), when the local bishop, Oliver King, travelled from Wells to Bath to visit the church in the late 15th century, its shocking state prompted a vision in which he saw angels climbing a ladder up to heaven. It was taken to be a divine instruction to have the church rebuilt, and the prophetic ladders and angels were incorporated into the design of the west front – still clearly visible today. Inside, the church's windows, which account for some 60 per cent of the wall space, make the interior very bright, and led to it being known as the 'Lantern of the West'. The east window is divided into 56 stained glass scenes from the life of Christ. Other highlights include a small museum, the **Bath Abbey Heritage Vaults Museum**, on the abbey's southern side, which details the building's history, and the tombs and memorials of prominent locals, including Beau Nash (*see* p.84), the 19th century social philosopher, Thomas Malthus, and the inventor of shorthand, Isaac Pitman.

Thermae Bath Spa

Thermae Bath Spa
The Hetling Pump Room, Hot Bath Street; t 0844 888 0844; www.thermaebathspa. com; open New Royal Bath 9am–10pm (last entry 7.30pm); Cross Bath 10am–8pm (last entry 6.30pm); adm 2-hour spa session £22, 4-hour spa session £32, full day spa session £52

The strict building regulations, which are supposed to ensure that every new building in Bath is constructed in a style in keeping with its elegant surrounds, were clearly relaxed when the **Thermae Bath Spa** submitted its blueprints to the council just after the Millennium.

Compared to its Georgian and medieval neighbours, the city's new spa couldn't be more modern and out of place. Though plenty of Bath stone was clearly used in the building's construction – one of the requirements for all new projects – most of it lies submerged beneath a shiny veneer of plate glass and stainless steel.

To say the building has not won universal favour with the locals would be a bit of an understatement, but the justification for the spa is not its controversial exterior, but what goes on inside where the city's volcanic spring water has been harnessed to its best effect in almost 1600 years. Just like its Roman predecessor, today's spa, which is divided into two sections – the New Royal Bath and the Cross Bath – offers visitors the chance to bathe in a number of volcanically heated baths, sweat themselves silly in steam rooms and cool off in plunge pools. They also have the opportunity to indulge in a range of new treatments that were not available to the Romans – body cocoons, watsu massages and kraxa stoves (explained as 'traditional Alpine hay chambers', which doesn't really explain much). The highlight, however, is most definitely the open-air roof-top pool where you can sit in steamy luxury admiring the views out over Bath. A visitor centre provides an overview of spa life in Bath through the ages via a 30-minute audiovisual presentation.

Pulteney Bridge and the River

From the Abbey Church Yard, the High Street heads north for around a hundred metres or so before connecting with Bridge Street, which leads east down to the river. Just to the north, on Northgate Street, is the city's **Postal Museum**. This jaunty, privately run collection is located just around the corner from where the world's first postage stamp, the Penny Black, was sent affixed to a letter on May 2, 1840. Within its rather snug confines are lively displays tracing the history of written communication from clay mail to email, with emphasis on the development of Britain's post.

Postal Museum
27 Northgate Street;
t (01225) 460333;
www.bathpostal
museum.co.uk; open
11–5; adm £3.50

Back down on Bridge Street, you'll find the city's premier art collection, the **Victoria Art Gallery**, which contains paintings, drawings and sculptures from the 16th century to the present day, including works by such illustrious local names as Thomas Gainsborough, Walter Sickert and Thomas Baker. There's also a collection of Georgian political cartoons and a plaster replica of the Parthenon friezes/Elgin marbles (depending on what side of the 'give them back/keep them' debate you're on).

Victoria Art Gallery
Bridge Street;
t (01225) 477233;
www.victoriagal.org.uk;
open Tues–Sat 10–5, Sun
1.30–5; adm free

Continuing east you reach the graceful, if rather truncated span of **Pulteney Bridge**. With shops lining both sides of its three-arch span, it looks like a mini Georgian version of the Ponte Vecchio, which is more or less what it is, having been designed by Robert Adam following a trip to Florence. Though its graceful neoclassical styling was greatly admired upon its completion in 1773, the bridge seems to have been regarded as something of a work in progress over the next century or so as it underwent a succession of minor adaptations – part of its south side was even destroyed in the early 20th century to facilitate a road-widening scheme. Thankfully, its designation as a Grade I listed building later in the century put an end to any further structural meddling. Today it is as fine and neat a bridge as you'll find anywhere. Sightseeing boat trips along the River Avon are available nearby (*see* p.82).

The bridge was funded by William Pulteney, who saw it as just the first stage of his grand scheme to turn the country estate of Bathwick on the east side of the River Avon, across from Bath, into a new town which would one day rival its more illustrious neighbour. As things turned out, only the bridge's continuation, Great Pulteney Street, was completed before funds ran out. Bathwick is now merely a suburb of Bath.

Great Pulteney Street leads to one of the Georgian era's most celebrated hotels, the Sydney, which today provides a home to the **Holburne Museum of Art** – or at least it will do once refurbishment work is completed in 2010. It's based on the collection of William Holburne, a native of the city who became a local pint-sized hero during the Napoleonic Wars when he served aboard HMS *Orion* during the Battle of Trafalgar aged just 12. Later in life he returned to Bath where he inherited a baronetcy and set about gathering together works of art with a magpie-like enthusiasm. When the museum reopens, expect plenty of old masters, silver, ceramics, sculptures etc.

Holburne Museum of Art
Great Pulteney Street;
t (01225) 466669;
www.bath.ac.uk/
holburne/futur

The Heart of Georgian Bath

Any tour of Georgian Bath should begin at the era's first great development, **Queen Square**, which was laid out by John Wood the Elder from 1728 onwards. With the square's elegant use of space – which involved creating elegant neoclassical facades, behind which town-houses were crammed into terraces so as to maximize their interior dimensions – Wood set the city's architectural template for the rest of the century. These houses were marketed squarely at Georgian society's wealthiest members who would rent them while 'taking the waters'.

Just west of Queen Square on New King Street is an example of a much more modest townhouse, which was the former home of one of the 18th century's greatest astronomers, William Herschel. In 1781, Herschel became the first person in modern history to observe a new planet when he spotted Uranus through a self-made telescope, making it also the first planet to be found using a telescope. Indeed, Herschel was quite a pioneer of telescopic development, building a series of ever larger models (over 400 in total), culminating in a huge 40ft (12m) long specimen, although in the event this would prove too cumbersome to be of any great use. He was assisted in his studies by his sister, Caroline, herself a renowned astronomer, who discovered several comets and was responsible for collating and cataloguing much of the known astronomical data of the time. Today the house is the **Herschel Museum of Astronomy**. Within, the domestic quarters have been furnished in period detail – look out for the music room where William, who was also a noted composer, played the organ – and you can see examples of the couple's scientific equipment, including a replica of the telescope through which Herschel made his momentous discovery and a brass orrery, showing Uranus, but not Neptune, which was not discovered until the next century.

Herschel Museum of Astronomy
19 New King Street;
t (01225) 446865;
www.bath-
preservation-
trust.org.uk; open
Feb–Dec Mon, Tues,
Thurs, Fri 1–5pm,
Sat–Sun 11–5; adm £4

To the north Gay Street links Queen Square with Wood the Elder's other great project, the **Circus**, widely regarded as his masterpiece. Sadly, Wood never lived to see it, passing away just a few months after the first stones were laid in 1755, and it was left to his son to complete. When finished in 1766, the circle of graceful Palladian-style houses soon became the most desirable address in town, attracting some renowned residents, including David Livingstone, Clive of India and Thomas Gainsborough. Split into three equal-sided sections, the Circus originally surrounded a paved area, which covered a reservoir that provided the crescent's homes with water. It was turned into a park in the early 19th century when the homes were connected to the general mains. As with most of Bath's Georgian architecture, the Circus takes its cue from classical Italy. Apparently, Wood envisaged it as a sort of back-to-front Colosseum, with the facade on the inside rather than the outside.

Just northeast, rather hidden away in a Georgian townhouse on Bennett Street (and thus often rather overlooked) is the city's **Museum of East Asian Art**, which boasts a collection of nearly 2,000 objects including ceramics, jade jewellery and bronze sculptures, garnered from Southeast Asian destinations and dating from 5,000 BC to the present.

A few steps further east, still on Bennett Street, are the **Assembly Rooms**, a purpose-built neoclassical entertainment centre with a temple-esque facade, which was designed in 1771 by the younger John Woods working in close collaboration with the city's chief social events organizer, Beau Nash. Together with the Pump Room it lay at the very heart of Georgian and Regency upper-class social life. Today it still hosts social functions (although these tend to be private affairs, for which the entry requirements are based on cash, not class). Fittingly, for a place that was once so concerned with keeping up appearances, its basement is now home to the city's **Fashion Museum**, a constantly changing display of modes of dress, featuring mannequins dressed in original costumes from the 16th to the 21st centuries.

To the northeast of the Assembly Rooms is an area known as the Paragon where, in a slightly strange-looking Gothic-Georgian chapel, you'll find the rather fun **Building of Bath Museum**. This has exhibits detailing the various different stages of the city's construction – Celtic, Roman, Saxon, Medieval, Tudor etc. – focusing in particular on the classical styles that so influenced the city's Georgian architects. The centrepiece is the huge scale model of the city, with every street and building beautifully rendered in miniature detail. Note that it operates fairly restricted opening hours.

Heading back west, Brock Street links the **Circus** with the **Royal Crescent**, perhaps the stateliest and most imposing of all Bath's stately and imposing crescents. Designed by John Wood the Younger and laid out from 1767 onwards, the crescent's columned grandeur is neatly complemented by its setting, with the sweeping arc of houses set in front of a rolling sea of grass, which provides great views out over the town. **No.1 Royal Crescent**, the first house to be built, is today a sort of Georgian show home, decked out in luxurious contemporary style. You

Museum of East Asian Art
12 Bennett Street;
t (01225) 464640;
www.meaa.org.uk;
open Tues–Sat 10–5, Sun
12–5, last admission
4.30; adm

Fashion Museum
formerly the Museum
of Costume; Bennett
Street; t (01225) 477173;
www.museumofcostume
.co.uk; open daily
March–Oct 10.30–6,
Nov–Feb 10.30–5; last
entrance 1 hr before
closing; adm £7.00 or
£14.50 combined ticket
with the Roman Baths

Building of Bath Museum
The Countess of
Huntingdon's Chapel, The
Vineyards; t (01225)
333895; www.bath-
preservation-trust.org.uk;
open Apr–Oct 10.30–5,
last admission 4.30;
Nov–Mar by prior
arrangement only

No.1 Royal Crescent
t (01225) 428126;
www.bath-preservation-
trust.org.uk; open
Tues–Sun 10.30–5; adm

can tour the dining room, gentlemen's study, lady's bedroom and below stairs kitchen, all staffed by appropriately costumed guides.

Just west of the Crescent, on Royal Avenue, is **Royal Victoria Park**, the city's main open, grassy space and site of the annual Bath Festival (*see below*). It contains an aviary, botanical gardens and a café.

Around Bath

Prior Park

Prior Park
Ralph Allen Drive;
t (01225) 833422;
www.nationaltrust.org.
uk/main/w-priorpark;
open Feb–Oct Mon and
Wed–Sun 11–5.30,
Nov–Jan Sat and Sun
11–dusk; adm £5.25

Ralph Allen was one of 18th-century Bath's most remarkable men, making not one, but two enormous fortunes from his local business dealings. Beginning his career as a humble postal clerk in the early 18th century, he rose to become Bath's Postmaster General and would go on to reform the national postal system. His most significant contributions were to stop the time-consuming practice of sending cross-country mail via London, and instigating a 'signed for' system that prevented postal delivery boys from carrying impromptu unpaid for items on their routes. His success brought him great wealth, which he used to buy the Combe Down Quarries, with which he made an even larger one. The neatly hewn honey-coloured blocks produced by the quarry became the material of choice for Bath's 18th-century building boom.

At the height of his success he had this mansion built – out of Combe Down stone, obviously – on a hill about a mile south of Bath, positioned so that he could gaze out over the city whose appearance he had so influenced. Its design was the result of an illustrious collaboration between Allen, John Wood and the poet, Alexander Pope. The 28-acre gardens were later landscaped by Capability Brown, and are today the principal draw, offering great views and containing a Palladian Bridge (one of just four left in the world). The building is now a school.

American Museum

American
Museum
Claverton Manor;
t (01225) 460503;
www.americanmuseum
.org; open Mar–Nov
Tues–Sun 12–5;
adm £8

Located two miles east of Bath off the A36, this is the only museum in the country devoted solely to the American way of life. Its 18 rooms have been decorated and furnished to look like historic house interiors, while in the grounds there's a replica of George Washington's garden at Mount Vernon, a teepee, a colonial herb garden and an American arboretum. Various events are held throughout the year, including a Native American Weekend, a Civil War Weekend and, of course, Independence Day celebrations, as well as occasional open-air film shows.

Festivals in Bath

Bath hosts two prestigious annual cultural events. Its **Music Festival** (*www.bathmusicfest.org.uk*), which specializes in jazz, classical and world music, has being going for over 50 years. It takes place in mid-May when events are staged at venues across Bath, including the Pump Rooms, Assembly Rooms and Bath Abbey.

The **Literature Festival** (*www.bathlit fest.org.uk*) is a newer, and rather more small-scale affair, taking the form of book-readings, workshops, debates and talks in March.

Bath Festivals Box Office, 2 Church Street Abbey; **t** (01225) 462231.

(i) **Bath**
Abbey Chambers,
Abbey Church Yard
t 0906 711 2000 (50p a
minute) or from
overseas 0844 847 5257;
www.visitbath.co.uk;
open June–Sep
Mon–Sat 9.30–6, Sun
10–4; Oct–May
Mon–Sat 9.30–5, Sun
10–4

(★) **The Royal**
Crescent >

Where to Stay in Bath

With so much of the city's accommodation occupying Georgian buildings, hotel operators are faced with a clear choice – to go period and antique, or modern and stripped down. Until recently the majority went for the former, but the latter style is becoming increasingly popular as hotels move away from swag curtains, gilt frames, Regency prints and dark-wood furniture towards a more contemporary light and bright look. Room rates are quite high, whichever approach has been taken.

Very Expensive

The Queensberry Hotel, 4-7 Russell Street, Lower Lansdown, t (01225) 447928, *www.thequeensberry.co.uk*. A very fine choice, occupying no fewer than six Georgian townhouses. The façade says 'Old Bath', but the interior is decidedly modern, its large bright rooms decorated in a minimal fashion with stylish furniture and fresh flowers. The terrace garden is home to the Olive Tree **restaurant**, one of Bath's best (*see* p.93).

The Royal Crescent, 16 Royal Crescent; t (01225) 823333; *www.royalcrescent. co.uk*. The top choice, enjoying Bath's most celebrated address, slap bang in the middle of its finest Georgian terrace, the Royal is as sumptuous and luxurious as you could hope for with huge bedrooms filled with antique furniture, and public rooms casually adorned with paintings by Gainsborough and Reynolds. The rooms are spread out between the two Grade I listed buildings and re-stored coach houses in the garden, where you'll also find the hotel's spa, the Bath House, and its fine **restau-rant**, set in a former dower house.

Expensive

Dukes Hotel, Great Pulteney Street; t (01225) 787960; *www.dukesbath.co. uk*. Set in a Grade I listed house, Dukes has been decorated in a fashion so resolutely Georgian it could almost be the set of a TV period drama. Everything is plush and thickly carpeted and heavily draped. Rooms are large with high ceilings and the **restaurant**, the Cavendish, serves good modern British cuisine and leads out to a peaceful patio garden.

Paradise House, 86-88 Holloway; t (01225) 317723; *www.paradise-house.co.uk*. The views out over the city are definitely worth the thigh-burning trek it takes to reach this hill top B&B. Set in an 18th-century villa, the rooms have been decorated in a style perhaps best described as Georgian-lite – bright and modern with light streaming in from the large windows, but with plenty of period touches, such as open fireplaces, roll-top baths and flower prints. Breakfast is served in a large rose-filled garden.

Moderate

Meadowland, Bloomfield Park; t (01225) 311079; *www.meadowland bath.co.uk*. Be sure to book in advance before attempting the 20-minute uphill walk to Meadowland as it has just three bedrooms, which book up quickly in high season. And with good reason. The rooms, which occupy a 19th-century house are large and beautifully furnished, the garden peaceful and the owners friendly and knowledgeable.

Milsoms, 24 Milsom Street; t (01225) 750 128; *www.milsomshotel. co.uk/bath.php*. Right in the heart of the city, just a few minutes' walk from all the main attractions, this is chic, boutiquey and rather luxurious – think geometric black and white décor, leather armchairs, roll-top baths – but very reasonably priced. It's also got a great fish **restaurant**, Loch Fyne.

The Henry Guest House, 6 Henry Street, Bath; t (01225) 424052; *www. thehenry.com*. Formerly the best bargain in town, this has been revamped in recent years. The rooms have been given a lick of paint, new beds and furniture, and, in the biggest departure from the past, now all have private shower rooms. Prices have consequently risen. Still, it's very well situated, near the abbey, and the owners are helpful and friendly.

The Koryu, 7 Pulteney Gardens, t (01225) 337642, email *japanesekoryu@aol.com*. Run by a lovely Japanese lady, the Koryu offers something a bit different from the chintzy Georgian norm. The rooms, though small, are bright and appropriately shiny (the hotel's name means 'sunshine' in Japanese) and have new bathrooms and tea and coffee-making facilities. The East Asian influence is clear in much of the décor. Extremely charming.

Budget
Bath YHA, Bathwick Hill; **t** 0845 371 9303; www.yha.org.uk. If you haven't quite got the cash to pamper yourself at one of the city's five-star Georgian time capsules, you can get a taste of what you're missing at Bath's very fine youth hostel. Located about a mile from the centre, the stately Italianate mansion boasts all the requisite architectural features – high ceilings, stone staircases, moulded plasterwork etc. – but a rather basic standard of accommodation with rather cramped dorms (£15.95 per bed). Still there are great views from the garden and plenty of facilities, including internet access and bike hire. Some double rooms available.

★ Beaujolais Bistro Bar >>

★ Olive Tree Restaurant >

Eating Out in Bath

Very Expensive
Olive Tree Restaurant, Queensbury Hotel, 4-7 Russell Street, Lower Lansdown, **t** (01225) 447928, www.thequeensberry.co.uk. One of the city's most celebrated and chic restaurants in one of the city's most celebrated and chic hotels. Great modern British cooking. The two-course lunch menu is £16. Otherwise mains are £15–20.

Expensive
FishWorks, 6 Green Street, Bath BA1 2JY; **t** (01225) 448707; www.fishworks.co.uk. The original branch of an excellent four-strong chain, this combined fishmongers-restaurant serves a wide variety of fresh fish and seafood (both raw and cooked). It's not cheap – with mains costing £14.50–19 – but it is good.
Pump Room, Abbey Church Yard; **t** (01225) 444477; www.romanbaths.co.uk. The ultimate Jane Austen dining experience, the Pump Room, the epicentre of Georgian society, is as much a tourist attraction as it is a restaurant. But it's not a bad restaurant, serving coffee and cakes in the morning, meals at lunch and cream teas in the afternoon – all to the tinkling accompaniment of a classical trio. Open 9–5 only.

Moderate
Adventure Café, George Street, 5 Princes Building; **t** (01225) 462038. Friendly little café that does a neat range of sandwiches and salads.
Bathtub Bistro, 2 Grove Street; Pulteney Bridge; **t** (01225) 460593. Tardis-like place with a much bigger interior than you might expect from the outside. The food is reasonable and reasonably priced and there's a good wine list.
Beaujolais Bistro Bar, 5 Chapel Row; **t** (01225) 423417; www.beaujolaisbath.co.uk. Hugely popular French place with a dedicated local following, which means you're best off booking in advance. The key selling points are the top-quality traditional cooking (roast rack of lamb, confit of barbary duck, steak tartare), a big bright dining room adorned with modern art, a lovely walled garden and a great wine list. Mains £13–17 or you can get a two-course dinner for £16.95.
Cafe Retro, 18 York Street, **t** (01225) 339347; www.caferetro.co.uk. Cool, cutely decorated and very friendly café close to the abbey, the Retro offers great burgers and sandwiches.
Demuth's, North Parade Passage, off Abbey Green; **t** (01225) 446059; www.demuths.co.uk. Bath's top vegetarian choice, Demuth's open kitchen cooks up a range of inventive meat-free dishes that take their inspiration from all over the world: falafels, beetroot blinis, lasagne, Middle Eastern platters etc. It is fairly pricey (mains £12.50–14.95), but the quality is high and they do offer an 'early bird' two-course dinner for £14.50 6–7pm.
Firehouse Rotisserie, 2 John Street; **t** (01225) 482070; www.firehouserotisserie.co.uk. A taste of sun-baked California, the Firehouse offers a more authentic experience than you might think. Huge, brick-fired pizzas (£9.95–11.95) and grilled meats (half chicken £11.95, slow-roasted pork £13.95) are the menu mainstays. It has a pleasant wooden dining room.
Sally Lunn's Refreshment House, North Parade Passage; **t** (01225) 461 634; www.sallylunns.co.uk. The eponymous Ms Lunn was a French Huguenot refugee who came to

England in 1680 to escape religious persecution and found work in a baker's where she invented a bun – actually, to modern tastes, more a sort of bread – that took 17th-century England by storm. Occupying what is reputedly the oldest building in Bath, the establishment that today bears her name comprises a tea shop – where you can try said bun, still baked by hand according to Sally's recipe – an ultra-traditional English restaurant (mains £8–11) and a museum where you can see Sally's original kitchen.

The Walrus and the Carpenter, 28 Barton Street; t (01225) 314864; *www.walrusandcarpenter.com*. A cutesy place, all window boxes, posters and gingham tablecloths, serving some excellent beef burgers, some other meaty offerings (kebabs, curries) and a large range of vegetarian choices.

Budget

Tilley's Bistro, 3 North Parade Passage, Bath BA1 1NX; t (01225) 484200; *www.tilleysbistro.co.uk*. Good value, charming bistro that takes a sort of tapas approach to French cuisine, serving up a range of small and medium-sized dishes to share £6–9. They also offer a 2-course lunch menu for £11.50 and a pre-theatre menu for £10 from 6–7pm.

Eating Out Around Bath

If driving, there are a some excellent antique pubs within easy reach.

The George Inn, High Street, Norton St. Philip; t (01373) 834224; *www.the georgeinn-nsp.co.uk* (*moderate–expensive*). Around six miles southeast of Bath. Having been in business for over 700 years, this is one of the oldest continuously operated pubs in the country. Notable visitors over the years have included Samuel Pepys and the Duke of Monmouth who briefly used it as his headquarters following his failed rebellion (*see p.106*). It occupies a terribly picturesque half-timbered house within which hearty English fare (venison, duck, Beef Wellington; all mains £13.95) is served in a fine oak dining room.

The Packhorse Inn, Southstoke; t (01225) 832060; *www.packhorseinn.com*; (*moderate*). A comparative whippersnapper, having first opened its doors as recently as the 1650s, this is a ten-minute drive east of Bath, it enjoys a lovely country setting. The food is mainly traditional hearty pub staples made with local ingredients – lamb chops, crab cakes etc. – but with a few foreign influences thrown in, such as their pork and chorizo burger. Mains are £10–12.95.

Entertainment and Nightlife in Bath

Theatre Royal, Sawclose; t (01225) 448844; *www.theatreroyal.org.uk*. First opened in 1803, Bath's main theatrical venue is still going strong, staging a year-round programme of drama, comedy, ballet and more.

Wells and the Mendips
Wells

Wells' city status comes not as a result of its size or importance – it's the smallest city in England, after all, with a population of just over 10,000, and not even particularly influential to the people who live there – but by virtue of its glorious cathedral and associated bishopric. That's not to say it's a complete urban nonentity. When Wells was first made a city, back in 1205, it was something of a major player in these parts. A prosperous little town it had, following centuries of to-ing and fro-ing, once again found itself in the ascendant in its ongoing rivalry with Bath for regional spiritual supremacy, having recently been re-established as the seat of the local bishop, enabling it to build a new cathedral.

The trouble is, 800 years later, not much has changed. While Bath has grown and sprawled into the great Georgian theme park it is today, Wells remains a prosperous little town, or as Henry James put it, 'a cathedral with a city gathered at the base'. However, while Wells may never have got the hang of urban sprawl – it never even grew big enough to warrant its own train station – the most important and enduring symbol of its status, the bishopric, remains. His title may be the Bishop of Bath and Wells, but Wells is where he resides and, so long as he remains, Wells will continue to be counted as a city.

Today Wells is pretty and quaint and provincially quiet with a charming core of medieval streets and buildings. Though there's not a great deal to do, it boasts plenty of inns and restaurants and makes a good base for exploring the nearby Mendip Hills.

The Town and Cathedral

The centre of town is the **marketplace**, most of which was laid out in the 15th century. It is bordered by quaint-looking shops and on one side has two medieval stone gateways. The one on the right, the **Bishop's Eye**, leads into the grounds of the Bishop's Palace, while the other, **Pennyless Porch**, takes you through to the cathedral. As the name suggests, the latter gateway was an authorized begging spot where the poor could entreat those heading to the cathedral for charity. Other notable features include a conduit where water from the spring that first drew settlers here still flows, and, a more modern touch, a plaque commemorating the world long jump record set by Mary Rand, a native of the city, at the 1964 Olympics. Markets take place twice weekly on the square.

Passing through Pennyless Porch takes you into the cathedral green and the city's pride and joy, its 13th century **cathedral**, built of a light brown, sandy stone, which on sunny days contrasts neatly against the surrounding blue skies and green lawns. At first glance, its famed west front may not be quite as magnificent as you might expect. With two rather truncated towers, it has a rather stunted aspect as if the builders gave up before it was finished. But then, the glory lies not in the structure, but in the details, and particularly the serried columns of carved figures that fill the front, peeking out of almost every alcove. At one stage there were as more than 400, but many are now missing or in the cathedral museum, while those that remain have suffered a good deal of damage over the centuries.

In the centre, at the top, commanding all, is Christ flanked by angels, while below ranks of apostles, saints, bishops and kings swarm in hierarchical order. When originally carved, the sculptures would have been painted in gaudy colours and stood in red alcoves, which must have been rather startling. Their current unpainted state seems much more in keeping with the building's stately visage.

Inside there are plenty more carvings, particularly on the capitals which depict narrative scenes, the most notable of which shows thieves scrumping in an orchard. More figures can be found in the north transept where there's a charming **mechanical clock** dating back to 1390, making it one of the world's oldest. Its face, which is divided into 24 hours, demonstrates the then pre-Copernican world-view, showing the

cathedral
Cathedral Green;
t (01749) 674483,
www.wellscathedral.org
.uk; open April–Sept 7–7,
Oct–Mar 7–6; adm free,
£5.50 donation
requested

Somerset, Bristol and Bath | Wells and the Mendips: Wells

07

Getting to and around Wells

If travelling **by car,** take the M5, leaving at J22, then head north on the A38 towards Cheddar and Wookey Hole, before joining the A371 to Wells. Those arriving **by train** will find there is no train station in Wells, but regular bus services link the city with Bristol Temple Meads and Bath Spa stations.

Sun and Moon orbiting a stationary Earth. Above, a seated mechanical figure known as Jack Blandifer marks each quarter hour by kicking two bells with his heels. On the hour he strikes another bell with a hammer, which is the cue for jousting knights to appear on horseback and chase each other around a castle. The clock has been restored many times, but the face is more or less the medieval original. However, its (still working) original mechanism is in the Science Museum in London.

The interior's most notable features are the great **scissor arches** in the nave, which look like one giant arch set upside down on top of another. They were built in the early 14th century when the cathedral's stonework was found to be cracking under the weight of the central tower. To the north a smoothly worn stairway leads out to the octagonal **Chapter House**, which has elaborate fan vaulting. The Choir aisles contain a number of craggy old tombs, while at the far east end of the church is the **Lady Chapel**, which has five large stained glass windows (some of glass dates back to 14th century) topped by an intricate star vault.

Back outside, the north side of **Cathedral Green** is taken up by a row of 17th and 18th century houses, one of which, the old chancellor's house, is now the town's **museum.** Founded by Herbert Ernest Balch, the renowned caver and discoverer of Wookey Hole in the early 20th century (*see* p.99), it holds an interesting set of displays in old cabinets related to both the cathedral and the local area, including carvings from the front of the cathedral and remains of the area's prehistoric inhabitants, including flint tools, a bear skull and an ichthyosaur.

museum
8 Cathedral Green;
t (01749) 673477;
www.wellsmuseum.org.
uk; open Easter–Oct
Mon–Sat 11–5, Sun 11–4;
Oct–Easter daily 11–4;
adm £3

In the northeast corner of the green, an arch leads through to **Vicars' Close**, a charming cobbled row of 14th-century cottages built for members of the clergy – who have occupied by them ever since, making it one of the oldest continuously used medieval streets in the world. One of the houses is now a holiday home and can be rented out by the week by members of the public (*see* p.97).

The close was supposed to be a self-contained community, separated from Wells, so as to prevent the clergy from succumbing to the temptations of the wild city. The clergymen remained within the close at all times unless summoned by a bell, whereupon they ran directly from the close to the cathedral over a bridge, so as to avoid coming into contact with Wells' dissolute ways (things were clearly different back then).

On the south side of the cathedral, protected by high walls, is the Bishop's Palace and Gardens. Entrance is via a combination of the old world and the new, through the cathedral shop and then over a drawbridge. Alternatively, you can gain access via the Bishop's Eye arch on Market Place.

Far from being the serene dwelling of the region's spiritual leader, the palace has a rather militaristic bearing, the result of tensions between the bishop and local burghers in the 15th century. Fearing attacks by the locals, the bishop had the palace surrounded by a high wall and moat, and, just to show he took the threat seriously, had a chute added to the portcullis for pouring boiling oil onto any potential assailants.

The gardens are rather tranquil in comparison, and contain the three natural wells from which the city got its name. You can also tour some of the interior rooms, including the Bishop's Chapel and the remains of the Great Hall, which was ruined following the Reformation.

(i) Wells
Wells TIC, Market Place; t (01749) 672552; www.wellstourism.com; open April and Oct Mon–Sat 10–5, Sun 10–4; May–Sept Mon–Sat 9–5, Sun 10–4; Nov–Mar Mon–Sat 10–4.

(★) Vicars' Close Holiday House >>

Market Days in Wells

Two weekly markets take place: a general market on Saturday, and a farmer's market on Wednesday.

Where to Stay in Wells

Luxury
Swan Hotel, Sadler Street; t (01749) 836300; *www.swanhotelwells.co.uk*. Forty nine bedrooms, suites and apartments spread throughout a restored medieval posthouse. It's a Best Western, but in place of the usual bland chain stylings come period furnishings – antique furniture, wood panelling and heritage wallpaper. It boasts a good **restaurant**, the Garden Room.

Expensive
Beryl, top of Hawkers Lane; t (01749) 678738; *www.beryl-wells.co.uk*. A rather grand B&B a mile outside the city set in a Gothic revival mansion, built in the early 19th century by a pupil of Pugin and surrounded by 13 acres of gardens and woodland. The interior is thick with antique clutter and all of the ten richly decorated rooms have views (either of the gardens or the cathedral).

The Crown at Wells, Market Place; t (01749) 673457, *www.crownatwells. co.uk*. This 15th-century building has 15 en suite rooms of varying sizes and shapes (four with four-poster beds) and a decent **restaurant**, Anton's, overlooking the market place.

Moderate
Canon Grange, Cathedral Green; t (01749) 671800; *www.canongrange. co.uk*. The hotel's 1970s pebble-dashed exterior provides quite a contrast with the cathedral's grand facade just across the green. Inside it's a more tasteful story with period furniture

and exposed beams. A great location and pretty reasonably priced.

Infield House, 36 Portway; t (01749) 670 989; *www.infieldhouse.co.uk*. A 10-minute walk from the centre, near an area of woodland, this charming and very reasonably priced Victorian town-house has just three bedrooms, all with original fireplaces, coffee-making facilities, TVs and free Wi-Fi. Two have showers, the other a large bath.

The Ancient Gate House Hotel, 20 Sadler Street, t (01749) 672029; *www. ancientgatehouse.co.uk*. The former west gatehouse of the old cathedral wall, this is a hugely atmospheric place – think stone staircases, wood panelling, plenty of medieval-style touches and views of Cathedral Green. It also has a good Italian restaurant, **Rugalino**. If full, try its sister hotel, the White Hart, opposite.

Budget
Vicars' Close Holiday House, Wells Cathedral Office, Chain Gate, Cathedral Green; t (01749) 674483; *www.wellscathedral.org.uk*. Holiday in a piece of history at this property in Vicars' Close, the oldest continuously occupied street in Europe. Built to accommodate the cathedral clergy, the house has two doubles, one twin and one single bedroom and is great for a large group or family. *Min. stay three nights.*

Eating Out in Wells

Café Romna, 13 Sadler Street; t (01749) 670240; *www.caferomna.co.uk* (*moderate*). The name is a touch misleading, this is actually a very good Bangladeshi restaurant serving traditional spicy dishes – plus a few modern 'fusion' concoctions – in a bright modern setting.

Fountain Inn & Boxer Restaurant, 1 St. Thomas Street; **t** (01749) 672317; *www. thefountaininn.co.uk* (*moderate*). The downstairs of this 16th century building is a decent traditional pub while upstairs is an award winning English restaurant. Main £7.95–£15.50.

(★) **Goodfellows >**

Goodfellows, 5 Sadler Street; **t** (01749) 673866; *www.goodfellowswells.co.uk*; (*moderate–expensive*). One of the town's top choices for both snacks and meals, this three-in-one venture comprises a patisserie, a café and a very well-to-do fish restaurant. Expect local ingredients and French recipes. Offers a two-course lunch for £10. *Closed dinner Sun–Tues.*

Old Spot, 12 Sadler Street, **t** (01749) 689099 (*moderate*). Highly regarded Bistro that's been wowing the locals (and critics) since it opened a couple of years ago. The food is French inspired and made using the best local ingredients.

Slab House Inn, West Horrington; **t** (01749) 840310; *www.slabhouseinn. co.uk* (*moderate*). This ancient pub's first foray into serving the good people of Wells was a rather grim experience. In the 14th century, at the height of the Black Death, a three-mile quarantine zone was placed around the city. In order to keep its inhabitants alive, local farmers placed food on a slab (hence the name) here for survivors to come and collect. Today it's a much jollier affair serving hearty English grub – rack of lamb, roast beef etc. The kitchen is overseen by renowned chef, Brian Turner.

The Mendip Hills

The gently tumbling hills of the Mendips sit sandwiched between Wells and the north Somerset coast covering an area of some 77 sq miles (200 sq km). Much of the Mendip plateau is underpinned by easily eroded limestone, which combined with England's famously damp climate has created a landscape pockmarked by water-cut features – holes, caves, gorges etc. – including some truly spectacular formations, such as the Wookey Hole Caves and Cheddar Gorge. These have become major, and often very busy, tourist attractions. That's not to say that this area boasts an overly dramatic geography. Taken as a whole, the Mendips could hardly be described as wilderness. Most of its expanses are given over to agriculture. Nor are its peaks particularly challenging. The highest, Black Down, stands just 1069 ft (326 m) high. Only the surrounding landscape, and particularly the Somerset Levels at the hills' southern end, one of lowest areas in the entire country, make it stand out. Still, there's plenty of good walking here and the area does boasts its harsher, more rugged corners, particularly at the top of the plateau, an exposed windy spot where weather can be severe.

The uplands were first settled by the Romans who dug out lead and zinc mines. Mining continued in the area until the early 20th century near the villages of Priddy and Charterhouse. At the latter you can see the scruffy remains of ancient lead mines in a nature reserve, home to a range of local wildlife.

Mendip AONB
*Charterhouse Centre,
Blagdon;
t (01761) 462338;
www.mendiphills.org.uk*

The **Mendip AONB** (Area of Outstanding Natural Beauty) Office can provide 'Walk Cards' detailing local routes and beauty spots, such as Chew Valley Lake, a prime haunt for wildfowl, the wooded ravine of Ebbor Gorge, and Blackdown . The routes can also be downloaded.

Bear in mind that the Mendip villages are rather remote and the accommodation options somewhat limited. You'd be more comfortable basing yourself in one of the towns on the southern edge of the hills: Wells (*see* p.97), Cheddar, Shepton Mallett or Axbridge.

Wookey Hole Caves

Just outside Wells (ten minutes on the no. 670 bus) these sinister, water-cut underground caverns, full of dark tunnels, eerie lakes and mysterious flickering shadows, had been known to locals for centuries when Herbert Balch began an in-depth excavation of their inner reaches in 1914. In the 18th century they had even provided inspiration to the poets Coleridge and Pope, the latter of whom indulged in the peculiar practice of shooting down stalactites (which he used to decorate his home, of course). But the presumption was that they had always been uninhabited. Balch proved otherwise, discovering evidence of human habitation going back to prehistoric times and continuing right through the Roman occupation and into the early Middle Ages. Indeed, with the caves at a constant and eminently habitable temperature of 11°C, the real mystery was why people stopped living here.

Today, the caves can be visited only as part of a guided tour. It's a kitschy old trip, the whole complex having been augmented with models and lighting effects. The guides tend to focus less on the history and archaeology of the place and more on the myths and legends associated with it, taking great pleasure in regaling visitors with tales of the Witch of Wookey, who is supposed to inhabit the cave's dark inner recesses. In fact, the witch is nothing more than a sinister-shaped stalagmite, made menacing by a bit of fancy lighting. It's a fascinating journey, nonetheless, particularly when you get to the underground river, the Axe, responsible for carving out the caves and which has also been cleverly lighted so that it seems to glimmer a bright crystal blue.

The cave now forms part of a veritable family entertainment complex. Nearby stands a Victorian paper mill, which holds a display on the history of paper-making and is still churning out sheets of rag paper by hand, a vintage fairground with carousels, a maze of mirrors and slot machines, and a 'Dinosaur Valley' with life-size model dinosaurs.

Cheddar Gorge & Show Caves

This three-mile long rent in the ground may look like a steep cliff valley, but it is perhaps best described as a huge outdoor cave, formed when a water-cut cavern roof collapsed thousands of years ago. Although it can easily be viewed by car, or from one of the open-top tour buses that trundle up and down the B3135 road running through the centre of the gorge, it's well worth stopping every now and then in order to wander along some of the signposted walks. The views can be spectacular, particularly from the lookout tower at the top of Jacob's Ladder, a 274-step stairway cut into the side of the gorge – you can see all the way to Glastonbury Tor. As you ascend, you'll see boards pointing out the age of the various rocks – they get younger as you climb higher – and the type of creatures that would have existed on the Earth at that time.

Heading in the other direction, you can also visit the Cheddar Showcaves, which consist of three enormous caverns beneath the gorge, two of which, **Gough's Cave** and **Cox's Cave**, are natural, while the third, **Pavey's Cave**, is man-made. You can explore a good deal of these vast cathedral-like structures, full of stalactites and stalagmites, glistening pools and flickering shadows, at leisure, although you will need a guide to go into the very deepest caves. Pavey's Cave has been turned into a cheesy dark walk fantasy adventure called 'The Crystal Quest' and is lined with models of goblins, dragons and witches. Of more interest is the small museum housing the 9,000-year-old remains of Cheddar Man – the oldest complete skeleton found in the UK – whose DNA has, remarkably enough, been found to closely correspond to that of local residents.

As one of the country's great natural wonders, Cheddar Gorge is understandably hugely popular, and you should expect crowds and rampant commercialism to be a significant part of your experience here, particularly in summer. But for all the potential discomfort, the gorge's towering majesty makes it all worthwhile.

Where to Stay and Eat in the Mendips

(i) **Mendips**
*Cheddar Gorge,
t (01934) 744071; open
Easter–Oct daily
10am–5pm, Nov–Easter
Sun 11am–4pm.*

Glencot House, Glencot Lane, t (01749) 677160, www.glencothouse.co.uk (*very expensive–luxury*). Terribly fancy mock Jacobian place built in the 19th century by the owner of the Wookey Hole Paper Mill set in 18 acres of grounds bordering the River Exe. Inside it's an antiquey affair with chandeliers, stuffed peacocks, ornate fireplaces, oak and walnut panelling and 13 very fancy bedrooms (with LCD TVs and Wi-Fi). The very grand **restaurant** overlooks the river.

Harptree Court, East Harptree; t (01761) 221729; www.harptreecourt. co.uk (*expensive*). One of the Mendips' finest choices, this Georgian country house makes its guests feel snug, secluded and very pampered. There are just three rooms – all of a good size with great views and TVs and DVD players.

The New Inn, Priddy Green, Priddy; t (01749) 676465; www.newinnpriddy. co.uk (*budget–moderate*). Back when this first opened in the 17th century it no doubt lived up to its name. Enjoying a rather remote setting in Priddy, this welcomes a steady stream of walkers with a range of ales and reasonable pub grub. There are also a few basically furnished rooms to rent.

Wookey Hole Inn, Wookey Hole; t (01749) 676677; www.wookeyholeinn. com (*moderate*). A superior gastro pub en route to its namesake cavern, about three miles outside of Wells. From the front, it is mock-Tudor and very traditional looking, but inside it is anything but, with Belgian beers and a Mediterranean-inspired menu. There's a nice garden at the rear as well as five large rooms to rent.

Weston-super-Mare

Somerset's larger coastal resorts tend to be rather functional purveyors of the classic British seaside holiday. **Weston-super-Mare** is a very traditional type of a place, notwithstanding its Latin name, which was coined in the early 19th century in a vain attempt to gain the resort upmarket kudos. Today this pretension has an almost mocking quality to it. This is not a fancy town. It's a place of piers and pedalos and bouncy castles, of donkey rides on the beach and ice creams on the promenade, of arcades and saucy postcards.

North Somerset Museum
*Burlington Street;
t (01934) 621028;
www.n-somerset. gov.uk;
open Mon–Sat 10–4.30;
adm*

The town's main formal attraction is the **North Somerset Museum**, which specializes in historic interiors – including a 19th-century chemist, dentist and cottage – and also has a large collection of ancient toys and dolls. Just outside town is the **Helicopter Museum**, which has more than 50 helicopters and autogyra on display.

Helicopter Museum
*The Heliport; Locking Moor Road;
t (01934) 635227;
www.helicoptermuseum. co.uk; open Apr–Oct Wed–Sun 10–5.30 (last admission 4.30), Nov–Mar 10–4.30, last admission 3.30; open everyday during Easter and summer school hols;
adm £5.50*

Somerset Levels

In the centre of the county, between the Mendip Hills to the northeast, and the Quantocks to the southwest, lies one of the flattest areas in the country, known as the Somerset Levels, encompassing some 160,000 acres. It's divided into two main regions: the North Somerset Levels, which sit on a bed of clay just inland from Weston-super-Mare about six metres above sea level, and the peat-based Mid-Somerset Levels, which lie south of the Polden Hills and in places can be as low as six metres below sea level at high tide.

It's a wet, boggy area, waterlogged for much of the year, making transport and building extremely difficult. But, owing to the extreme fertility of the soil, and an abundance of wildlife – particularly wildfowl – it has attracted settlers since ancient times. Indeed, the local people's use of the rich grassland here as summer pasture may well have given rise to county's name – 'summersatta', the 'land of the summer people'.

Remains of several Iron Age lake villages have been found. In 1970 the sodden ground even yielded up wooden planks from a causeway built above the wetlands almost 6,000 years ago, and now known as the **Sweet Track** after its discoverer, Ray Sweet. Tree-ring dating has placed the track's construction fairly precisely to the winter of 3807–3806 BC, making it one of the oldest known roads in the world. It originally stretched for over a mile and much of it remains *in situ*.

In the 9th century Alfred the Great reputedly hid out amid the remote moors and bogs at the abbey of **Athelney**, while he made plans for the reconquest of Wessex from the Vikings. The famous Alfred Jewel, a beautifully carved piece of gold, quartz and enamel, bearing the legend 'aelfred mec heht gewyrcan' ('Alfred ordered me made') was found just four miles north of the town. A replica can be seen in the church at North Petherton (the original is in the Ashmolean Museum in Oxford). A route, known as the Alfred and the Levels Line, links many of the region's main sites, including Athelney Abbey, Glastonbury and the Willows and Wetlands Visitor Centre in Taunton. The Levels also form part of the 50-mile-long **River Parrett Walking Trail**, which follows the River Parrett from its source in Dorset to its estuary on the Somerset coast.

The trail passes through the village of **Muchelney** on the banks of the Parrett. The name means 'great island'. 'Ey', the Old English for Island, features in many local names (Athelney means 'Island of Princes'), as villages tended to be founded on the Level's few small areas of raised land, or islands, amid the surrounding sea of flatter bogs and marshes.

Today Muchelney is small and picturesque. The abbey founded here by King Athelstan in 939 was largely destroyed six centuries later in the Reformation. It never grew particularly big or rich, but the monks who lived here certainly made themselves comfortable. In 1335 they were even chastised by the Bishop of Shrewsbury for their lack of asceticism and self-sacrifice – he accused them of living comfortable lives in large beds, with plenty of food and travelling by horseback rather than on foot, contrary to strict monastic practice. You can still see the ruins of the Benedictine abbey, even though most of its stones were carted off to build the nearby town following the dissolution, as well as an early Tudor house that served as the monks' lodgings and which still boasts its original roof, fireplace and stained glass. The highlight is the thatched two-storey monk's toilet – the only one of its kind in Britain.

Muchelney Pottery

t (01458) 250324;
www.johnleachpottery.
co.uk; open Mon–Sat
9–1 and 2–5

These days the village is also known for the earthy, rustic looking **Muchelney Pottery** of John Leach, the grandson of Bernard Leach, the so-called 'father' of British studio pottery, who set up a renowned potting studio in St Ives in the 1920s where he created 'utilitarian' pieces heavily influenced by the designs of Hong Kong and Japan (*see* p.206).

Though in this day and age much given over to agriculture, the Levels still support a great deal of wild flora and fauna, and are an important feeding ground for wildfowl, including swans, curlews, redshanks, teal and skylarks (who themselves form an important food source for the region's various birds of prey including peregrine falcons and marsh harriers).

Glastonbury

Glastonbury has more myths and legends associated with it than almost anywhere else in the country. If there's a tale doing the rounds, epic in scope and ideally with some supernatural element to it, chances are it will have the small Somerset town as one of its main settings.

According to the stories, Jesus Christ is supposed to have visited the area early in his life in the company of his great-uncle Joseph of Arimathea – an episode that is strangely omitted from the Bible, although it did inspire William Blake to compose the opening lines of *Jerusalem*: '*And did those feet in ancient time, Walk upon England's mountains green?, And was the holy lamb of God, On England's pleasant pastures seen?*'

Following the crucifixion, Joseph is then believed to have returned to Glastonbury carrying with him the Holy Grail, a goblet filled with the Messiah's blood, and to have founded England's first Christian church, later to become Glastonbury Abbey. Centuries after, while his knights hunted the Holy Grail, a mortally wounded King Arthur sailed to Glastonbury to die. Glastonbury was once an island in a vast inland lake and thus has been identified by some as the mythical Isle of Avalon. The bodies of Arthur and his queen, Guinevere, supposedly lie under the ruins of Glastonbury Abbey. Needless to say, there is absolutely no evidence for any of these claims – although that doesn't mean they're not true. There's something strange about Glastonbury, something that seems to inspire myth-makers, that makes people want to believe important events must have happened here. Lately, it has become the capital for a vague sort of spiritualism, attracting hordes of New Agers, modern pagans and shamen, who come to absorb the famed 'positive energy' of its mythical sites and then, often as not, open a shop on its high street selling mystical knick-knacks.

Getting to and around Glastonbury

By road, Glastonbury is 135 miles west of London via the M3, the A303 and the A361. It can also be reached via Bristol and the M5. Leave at junction 23 and follow the A39.

The nearest **train** station to Glastonbury is Castle Cary (on the London Paddington to Plymouth line), a taxi fare from here costs £25. National Express run daily **coaches** from London and there are good bus links from Bristol, Bath and Wells.

Considering its fame, Glastonbury is surprisingly small. Its main sights, the great bulk of the tor (the big hill just ouside the town) aside, can all be found on or around the short High Street, which is lined with new-age shops, vegetarian cafés, spiritualist bookshops and crystal boutiques. Just to the south are the ruins of **Glastonbury Abbey**. Stretching for an impressive 581ft, this was once England's longest church. However, if it does indeed mark the spot where local legend insists the country's first church was built in the 1st century AD, then the original must have been a much smaller affair as no remains have ever been found. The first definitively documented church was erected here in the 7th century under the Saxon King Ine, and soon grew into an important and prestigious site. So important, in fact, that Edgar, the first king of a united England, was buried here in the 10th century. The Saxon church was replaced by a Norman construction, only a few parts of which – most notably the Lady Chapel – survive. Rebuilt in the late 12th century, following a devastating fire, the church's final chapter came in the mid-16th century when Henry VIII had it destroyed as part of the dissolution of the monasteries. The last abbot was hung, drawn and quartered on top of Glastonbury Tor. You can see a model of the abbey in the visitor centre showing how it would have looked in its prime as well as the 'graves' of Arthur and Guinevere. Look out too for the holy thorn trees in the grounds, said to be descended from one that magically grew from a staff stuck in the ground by Joseph of Arimathea.

Glastonbury Abbey
Abbey Gatehouse, Magdalene Street; t (01458) 831631; www.glastonburyabbey. com; open daily Feb 10–5, March 10–5.30, Apr–May 9.30–6, June–Sept 9–6, Oct 9.30–5, Nov–Jan 10–4.30; adm £5

The edge of the abbey grounds is occupied by the charming **Somerset Rural Life Museum**, where you can watch (and occasionally take part in) a range of traditional rural crafts: cheese-making, cider-pressing, peat digging etc. Note the old-fashioned three-seat toilet, which enabled the well-bonded family to relieve themselves together.

Somerset Rural Life Museum
Abbey Farm, Chilkwell Street; t (01458) 831197; www.somerset.gov.uk; open Tues–Fri 10–5

Just south of the abbey, in the public gardens on Wellhouse Lane at the foot of the Tor, stands the **Chalice Well** where Joseph of Arimathea supposedly hid the Holy Grail. The legend probably arose as a result of the peculiar reddish water produced by the well. Not surprisingly, various healing properties have been attributed to the water. Take a drink as it pours out of the lion's head spout and put these claims to the test.

Chalice Well
t (01458) 831154; www.chalicewell.org.uk Apr–Oct 10–5.30, Nov–Mar 10–4; adm

 Glastonbury Tor

From here it's a 20-minute walk to the top of **Glastonbury Tor**, the great conical grass hill that looms over the town (the name comes from the Celtic word for hill). Some 520ft (160m) tall, and topped by the ruins of a medieval church, which collapsed following a landslide in the 13th century, it's one of the West Country's most distinctive sights. It is a steep climb to the top but well worth it for the views out over the town below and along the Vale of Avalon.

07 Somerset, Bristol and Bath | Glastonbury

ⓘ Glastonbury
9 High Street, The Tribunal
t *(01458) 832954, www.glastonburytic. co.uk.* Open summer daily 10am–5pm, winter daily 10am–4pm.

Glastonbury Festival

The great 3-day music festival – perhaps the biggest and most prestigious of the summer – is, unless you're attending the event, not a great time to visit, as the place will be swarming. For all the details contact **Glastonbury Festival Office**, 28 Northload Street, Glastonbury; **t** (01458) 834596; *www.glastonbury festivals.co.uk.*

Where to Stay & Eat in Glastonbury

Considering the huge number of people who come here each year, Glastonbury boasts a small selection of decent accommodation options.
Number Three, 3 Magdalene Street; **t** (01458) 832129; *www.numberthree. co.uk* (*expensive*). Right at the heart of things, next to the abbey, this is one of the better choices with five good-sized, nicely decorated rooms in a Georgian townhouse, and a pretty walled garden with abbey views.
Hawthorns Hotel, 8 Northload Street; **t** (01458) 831255; *www.hawthorns hotel.com* (*moderate*). Deservedly popular pub restaurant specializing in curries – they do a good value lunchtime curry buffet. There are also a couple of rooms for rent (*moderate*).

Rainbows End, 17a High Street; **t** (01458) 833896 (*moderate*). The archetypal Glasto café – all cushions, plants and beads, and serving a very good vegetarian/vegan menu: vegetable chilli, lasagne, quiche etc. It's tiny and popular, so arrive early.
The George and Pilgrim, 1 High Street; **t** (01458) 831146; *www.relaxinnz.co.uk* (*moderate*). 15th-century stone inn originally constructed to service pilgrims visiting the abbey and now catering for a more new-age type of disciple. The 14 rooms are turned out in a nice antique style. Decent pub grub is served in the restaurant.
Tordown, 5 Ashwell Lane; **t** (01458) 832287; *www.tordown.com* (*moderate*). A very Glastonbury sort of a place on the lower slopes of the Tor offering reika massage, a hydro-therapy spa and ear candling. Oh, and rooms, each themed on a different crystal. They're of a decent size and have such worldly pleasures as TVs, tea-making facilities and stereos.
Glastonbury Backpackers, 4 Market Place; **t** (01458) 833353; *www.glaston burybackpackers.com* (*budget*). Low-rent favourite housed in a former coaching inn offering a wide range of facilities, including a bar, a TV lounge, a kitchen, internet access and parking. Doubles (£40) are available as well as dorms (from £14 per bunk). No curfew.

Taunton and the Quantocks

Taunton, the county town of Somerset, is the largest, best-equipped and most obvious base for exploring the Quantocks. The town sits on the edge of the Quantocks in the Vale of Taunton, nestled between the Brendon and Blackdown Hills. It's an intensively agricultural region and Taunton lies at the centre of a major cider- and scrumpy-producing region. It is also the site of a major local cattle market. Taunton is a pleasant enough place with a few decent accommodation and eating options, but probably wouldn't detain you long were it not for its location. With the **castle** and **Somerset County Museum** currently closed for renovation, the town's chief attraction is its sandstone church, **St Mary Magdalene**, one of the largest examples of a type of late Gothic architecture known as perpendicular, a style characterized by an emphasis on its vertical elements, particularly its long narrow windows. It was built in the early Tudor period on the site of a 12th-century original, and in the late 18th century boasted the poet Coleridge as one

Getting to and around Taunton and the Quantocks

Taunton lies 5 miles from the M5. Leave at Junction 25. For those arriving by **train**, daily intercity trains link the city with London (Paddington) and many other major cities, including Bristol, Birmingham, Derby, York and Newcastle. The West Somerset Railway (*see* p.107) traverses the west side of the Quantocks between Bishops Lydeard and Minehead, via Watchet and Dunster. The round trip takes three hours. National Express **coaches** leave for Taunton from London Victoria daily.

of its preachers. The church underwent a revamp in the 19th century: its 163ft tower rebuilt and new statues and stained glass added.

The town has a few other attractive historic buildings, notably the Georgian houses and shops of Bath Place and the Georgian Market House.

You could try **Bridgwater** as an alternative Quantock base, which is just as convenient but perhaps has even less immediate appeal than Taunton. Much of the town is modern and rather ugly, although there are still some fine buildings in its centre, notably the red brick **St Mary's Church** with its distinctive multi-sided spire, which was built piecemeal between the 12th and 15th centuries, and then largely remodelled during the Victorian era.

St Mary's Church
Saint Mary Street;
t (01278) 424972;
www.saintmaryschurch
bridgwater.org.uk

Quiet and provincial now, just over three centuries ago Bridgwater had a ringside seat at history in the making, for it was at Sedgemoor, three miles outside of town, that the Duke of Monmouth's ill-advised, ill-equipped and ill-prepared rebellion was brought to a bloody end by the royal artillery of James II (*see* p.xxx). The story of the battle is retold at the town's **Blake Museum**, as is that of Robert Blake, a local hero of the Civil War who served on the parliamentary side and later became a commander in the British Navy fighting successful campaigns against the Ottomans, the Dutch and the Spanish.

Blake Museum
Blake Street,
t (01278) 456127;
www.blakemuseum.
org.uk

The Quantocks

It's poet-inspiring stuff, this narrow range of gently undulating sandstone hills, stretching for around 15 miles from the Vale of Taunton to the Bristol Channel on the western edge of the Somerset Levels. Both Coleridge and Wordsworth, two of the leading lights of the Romantic Movement, wrote some of their best works here following sturdy walks along its rambling paths. Their meanderings, which often took place in the dead of night, attracted the attention and suspicion of the locals, some of whom thought the poets might be spies. Officers were even despatched from London to observe their movements, but in the end concluded that the poets were just a bit odd.

For Coleridge the region proved particularly fecund, inspiring two of his most celebrated epics: *Kubla Khan* and *The Rime of the Ancient Mariner*. Since 2005, visitors have been able to follow the **Coleridge Way**, which traces a 36-mile course from Coleridge Cottage in the village of Nether Stowey to Porlock, to see if they can become similarly stimulated.

Coleridge Way
www.coleridgeway.co.
uk for more
information and to
download maps and
route details

The Quantocks offers a variety of landscapes to explore, from the beech woodland of its northern and eastern slopes, which are home to herds of red deer and provide good views of the Bristol Channel and Exmoor, to the rolling moorland of its more westerly reaches, the whole

The Monmouth Rebellion

When James Scott, the Duke of Monmouth, landed at Lyme Regis on 11 June 1685, he was on a mission of conquest. The illegitimate son of Charles II, he had come to take what he believed to be rightfully his – the Crown of England. As a fervent Protestant he had objected to the succession of his uncle, the Catholic James II, to the throne, the first non-Protestant to rule the country since Mary I in 1558. Indeed in the early 1680s he had tried to pass a bill through parliament changing the succession in his own favour. When this failed, he exiled himself to The Hague, where he plotted and schemed with his supporters.

Monmouth's plan was simple, but rather hopeful. He would land with a small force – in the event just 82 men – and begin a march towards London, on which he expected to be largely unopposed. He believed that such was the country's antipathy towards the Catholic king that the locals would flock to his side, and by the time he reached the capital he would be marching at the head of an impromptu army many thousands strong. At the same moment, a similar popular uprising was due to being in Scotland, led by Archibald Campbell, the 9th Earl of Argyll.

Monmouth's optimism was not entirely misplaced. Anti-Catholicism was entrenched, and there were many opposed to the papist king. Just three years later James II would be chased from the country and replaced by William III, and the Protestant succession enshrined in law as part of the Glorious Revolution (see p.128). And Monmouth was himself a popular figure, having served with distinction in the British army in the 1670s, but in the event, it seems, just not quite popular enough. Monmouth's rebellion came just a little too early for the country – public dissatisfaction with James had not yet grown to a level where enough of the country's ruling classes were willing to see him deposed.

Still, to begin with, things went well. Upon disembarking at Lyme Regis, Monmouth's force was immediately swelled by some 300 locals who rallied to the Duke's side bearing whatever arms they could find – leading to events being nicknamed the 'Pitchfork Rebellion'. He marched west into Somerset to try and drum up more support, which duly arrived. Some 6,000 flocked to his cause, which emboldened Monmouth to have himself crowned king at Taunton on 20 June. This, however, would prove to be the high point of the rebellion. In the next few weeks his ships were captured by the Royal Navy, preventing any chance of escape; attempts to take Bristol, then the country's second largest city, failed; and the Scottish rebellion never materialized. Just a fortnight into his campaign, Monmouth found himself on the retreat and his support haemorrhaging. His rag tag army was defeated at the Battle of Sedgemoor on 6 July – the last major battle on British soil. He escaped but was found and captured days later, hiding in a ditch.

It was at this point that Monmouth's hitherto brave and determined rebel demeanour deserted him. He pleaded with James for mercy and even tried to convince the king that he had converted to Catholicism, but to no avail. He was put to death by the famously inexpert executioner, Jack Ketch, who reportedly took at least half dozen swipes at the would-be-king's neck before eventually finishing the job with his knife.

The rebel leader's supporters fared little better. A series of trials, known as Bloody Assizes saw more than 300 people hung, drawn and quartered, and many more transported to the West Indies.

But James II was unable to use this victory to shore up his position. Indeed the bloodthirsty nature of the reprisals engendered great resentment. Just a few years later he would be usurped in a coup d'état by the ruling classes. His heirs would become the 'pretenders', the kings across the water who would spend the best part of the next century trying, unsuccessfully, to reverse the events of the Glorious Revolution.

region scored by a network of ancient paths and track ways. Though marginally higher than the Mendips, and fairly challenging in places, none of the range's peaks exceed 1,300ft (400m). The Quantocks are, however, rather less cultivated than the eastern range, which gives them a more unkempt, feral appearance.

One of the most popular starting points for walks is the Lydeard Hill car park, just off the A358, near the second highest point in the range, from where you can enjoy walks past heather-clad hills to the highest, Wills Neck (1,260ft/384m). There are great views from the top out over the hills and beyond to Exmoor, Dartmoor and the Brecon Beacons.

West Somerset Railway

⭐ **West Somerset Railway**
The Railway Station, Minehead;
t (01643) 704996;
www.west-somerset-railway.co.uk; open all year round, but days and times vary, check in advance; adm £14

One of most pleasant ways to explore region is aboard the **West Somerset Railway**, a preserved steam line offering chuffingly picturesque tours. The 20-mile-long line starts four miles outside Taunton at Bishops Lydeard, a pretty village with a renowned 15th-century perpendicular church, and then heads north along the Quantocks' western reaches, stopping off at various quaint thatched villages en route, before tacking west along the coast to its final destination – the resort of Minehead on the border of Exmoor.

The first stop, **Crowcombe**, with its thatched buildings made of the region's distinctive red sandstone and single shop serving a population of 500, is perhaps the archetypal Quantock village. Just south, Combe Florey is even smaller, with just 250 residents but no less than 24 listed buildings, including an Elizabethan gatehouse. It also boasts a couple of famous literary connections. In the early 19th century the village's rector was the celebrated wit, Sydney Smith, and today you can see the 18th-century rectory where he lived. As proud as the village is of the association, it appears that Smith's view of life in the bucolic town was less than fulsome. He described country living as 'a kind of healthy grave', preferring a convivial, sociable metropolitan existence.

The great novelist Evelyn Waugh moved here with his family in 1956 and stayed until his death ten years later. He is buried along with his wife in a private plot next to the village church. His son, the journalist Auberon Waugh, is also buried nearby.

Nether Stowey

Inland, on the northern edge of the hills, about eight miles west of Bridgwater, the little village of Nether Stowey was, for a brief period in the late 18th century, one of the centres of the literary universe. In 1797, the 25-year-old Samuel Taylor Coleridge moved to the village from Bristol – he reportedly walked all the way – to set up home with his wife, Sarah. Soon after, his friend William Wordsworth, and his sister Dorothy, rented Alfoxton Park, a country house, just three miles away. Together the two pairs went for long country walks during which they discussed literature and ruminated on the themes of day.

In 1798 they collaborated on *The Lyrical Ballads*, nearly always referred to as the 'manifesto for romanticism', a collection of poems that showcased the major themes of the movement: egalitarian politics, anti-rationalism, an emphasis on aesthetics, the appreciation of natural beauty, and above all, the value and importance of emotional experience. It was a hugely influential work. Most of it was Wordsworth's, although it was Coleridge's *The Rime of the Ancient Mariner* that attracted the most attention.

Coleridge also wrote one of his other most celebrated poems here, *Kubla Khan*, which describes the creation of a magnificent palace by the 13th-century Mongol Emperor, and contains one of most famous opening couplets in English literararure:

'In Xanadu did Kubla Khan
A stately pleasure-dome decree'

In the event the poem wouldn't be published till 1816. Although Coleridge claimed it was composed at Nether Stowey following an opium-induced dream, it was never completed as the poet was interrupted, mid stanza, by a 'man from Porlock' (a nearby town, *see* p.112), and when he returned to work found that inspiration had deserted him. The poem was put aside and forgotten for two decades. The phrase, a 'man from Porlock', has since entered the language to mean any unwanted interruption. Coleridge would never again be so prolific.

cottage
*35 Lime Street;
t (01278) 732662;
www.nationaltrust.org.
uk/main/w-vh/w-
visits/w-findaplace/w-
coleridgecottage/; open
Apr–Sep Thur–Sun 2–5,
last entry 4.30; adm
£3.90*

You can visit his bright pink **cottage** which is now in the care of the National Trust. A rather modest abode, it's adorned with a few authentic items, including his gilt and ebony inkstand, letters and his regimental sword (dating from his brief period of service in the Royal Dragoons in which he served under the assumed name, Silas Tomkyn Comberbache). From the cottage you can follow the Coleridge Way past various places related to the poet, and through the countryside that so inspired him to Porlock on the coast, some 36 miles away. One of easiest sections is a three-mile walk to Holford where you can see (albeit unfortunately only from the perimeter fence) **Alfoxton Park** where Wordsworth lived.

Watchet

The next biggest coastal town west of Weston-super-Mare, Watchet, at the mouth of the Washford River, is a pleasant enough place that tries hard to make a modern living from the remnants of its past. In the 10th century it was one of the most important towns in the Kingdom of Wessex, it had its own mint, and was considered wealthy enough to be raided by Vikings. Later, as its status waned, its inhabitants indulging in a variety of commercial activities, including fishing, grain milling, cloth manufacturing and dyeing – the name of the town apparently derives from the blue watchet dye made from lias rocks in the local cliffs. In the 17th century no less a figure than Charles I had a coat made of Watchet blue, which must have been a great source of pride, although the fact that he wore it to his execution may have slightly taken the edge off it.

In the 1800s the harbour expanded and Watchet became a successful commercial port and fishing town, with a celebrated shipbuilding yard and a paper mill. The lighthouse on the pier dates from this time. As the region became increasingly industrialized, so a railway line was built to bring iron ore from the Brendon Hills to the harbour where it was loaded onto boats and shipped around the country. A passenger line was also built in the late 19th century opening the town up to the wider world.

All these industries have now faded but some of the infrastructure remains, now often as not turned into visitor attractions: the passenger railway closed in 1971 and today forms part of a sightseeing line; the harbour, which closed to commercial traffic in the 1990s, has become a marina for pleasure craft; the route of the mineral line is now a walking route, while many of the town's former fishermen's cottages are souvenir shops. Indeed, tourism is now the town's principal source of revenue. To this end it makes great play of its Coleridge associations. It was a visit to Watchet that supposedly inspired *The Rime of the Ancient Mariner*. Since 2003 a statue of the mariner holding the accursed albatross has stood next to the harbour.

The Orchard Squad

Mention 'Somerset' in a word association game with someone from England and the chances are that 'cider' will be one of their top responses. The county is the fermented apple drink's spiritual home, supporting 25 cider producers, including the largest plant in Europe, operated by Gaymers, the firm responsible for such well known brands as Blackthorn, Olde English and that 80s yuppy favourite, Babycham. But there's trouble brewing in Somerset's orchard. In 2009, having conducted research into the nation's cider-drinking habits, Gaymers discovered what they saw as a significant disparity between the tastes of West Country cider drinkers, and those of people in the rest of the country. In order to find some common ground, Gaymers made a bold decision – they were going to change the recipe of their bestselling brand, Blackthorn, to make it sweeter and, according to the official advertising blurb, 'mellower'. They were also going to lower the drink's alcohol content from 5% to 4.7%. By taking the edge off Blackthorn's famed dryness, which their research showed put off many drinkers, Gaymers believed they would boost Blackthorn's popularity beyond its West Country heartland, allowing them to increase the drink's market share against its main rival. Crucially, they also believed they could do this without alienating their core base. In this last regard they were singularly mistaken. Though Gaymers took pains to stress the drink's strong local ties the changes caused an absolute furore in the West Country, particularly in Somerset. What Gaymers saw as minor improving tweaks, cider stalwarts regarded as betrayals that had ruined their beloved drink. Worst of all, they believed these changes had been made in order to satisfy that least educated of all palates – the Londoner's. They saw the Blackthorn revamp as nothing less than pandering to the country's metropolitan élite. They accused Gaymers of taking a drink that was proud to be strong, robust and as dry as a sidewinder's belly and cynically transforming it into something little better than an alcopop (or, ever worse, a version of Strongbow).

But, unlike an evening spent on the Blackthorn, the anti-change brigade weren't going to take this affront to their drinking dignity lying down, and made their feelings known to the Gaymers' board in the strongest terms they could think of. They registered their protests using techniques both modern: setting up Facebook pressure groups demanding that Gaymers go back to using the old recipe – and traditional: defacing the 'Black is Back' relaunch posters so that they proclaimed the rather less celebratory message, 'Black is Crap'.

Unfortunately for the protestors, money talks. Although Gaymers seemed surprised by the vehemence of the protests (they issued a statement saying they 'disappointed' with the West Country campaign), they pronounced themselves generally happy with the revamp, as it had, after all, resulted in the hoped-for rise in sales in the rest of country. Ultimately, protests and pressure groups will never be a match for profit, and it seems that, unless Gaymers commit a dramatic volte-face, or Blackthorn suffers a sudden dip in popularity, the cider hardcore will have to content themselves with slowly supping the last remaining barrels of old-recipe Blackthorn stored in remote Somerset pub cellars.

The esplanade also boasts a statue erected in honour of one of the town's most famous inhabitants, Jack Short, who spent more than 40 years at sea, and in the 1860s helped to run the American Civil War blockade, which earned him the nickname 'Yankee Jack'. During all those years at sea he gained a reputation for his powerful singing voice, which he used to belt out traditional sea shanties, several of which were recorded during the early 20th century by Cecil Sharp, a collector of folk songs. After he retired, Jack continued to make full use of his voice in his role as town crier. He died in 1933 aged 94.

Watchet Museum
Market Street;
t (01984) 631 209

Small Boat Museum
www.wbm.org.uk;
open Tues–Sun 2–4

You can find out more about the town's maritime, industrial and social history at the small **Watchet Museum**, which is housed in a former market house. The town's other museum, the **Small Boat Museum**, is dedicated to the rather specific craft of making flatner boats, small flat-bottomed boasts exclusive to Somerset. Both are staffed by volunteers. The town holds a popular carnival (*www.watchetcarnival.org.uk*) in July.

(i) **Bridgwater**
King Square;
t (01278) 436438.; open
Mon–Fri 9–5

(i) **Watchet**
8 The Esplanade,
t (01984) 633344

(★) **Farmer's Inn** >

Where to Stay and Eat in Taunton and the Quantocks

The Castle Hotel, Castle Green, Taunton, t (01823) 272671, *www.the-castle-hotel.com* (*very expensive*). Top-class hotel which incorporates part of the medieval castle's east gate, and offers a high standard of hospitality. It also boasts an excellent **restaurant** where Gary Rhodes earned his first Michelin star and a less formal **brasserie**.

Farmer's Inn, Higher West Hatch, t (01823) 480480, *www.farmersinn westhatch.co.uk* (*moderate–expensive*). Four miles east of Taunton, this is a charming place that has just the right balance of rustic touches and modern conveniences. The five large bedrooms are luxuriously decorated with great views of the Somerset Levels. Apparently it's only one of only 19 hotels in the country to have been awarded five stars by the English Tourist Board. The food is an equally enticing mixture of rustic and modern and it's very decently priced.

Bashfords Farmhouse, West Bagborough, t (01823) 432015, *www.bashfordsfarmhouse.co.uk* (*moderate*). Delightful 18th-century farmhouse with three cheerful piney bedrooms (two doubles and a twin). Hearty breakfasts served and even heartier dinners by arrangement.

Esplanade House, The Esplanade, Watchet, t (01984) 633444, *www. esplanade-house.co.uk* (*moderate*). A former Georgian farmhouse on the harbour with a walled garden and three pretty bedrooms with window seats. Welcoming hosts.

Rising Sun, West Bagborough, t (01823) 432575, *www.risingsuninn. info* (*moderate*). The picture of an old-fashioned pub, but it's all brand new and very smart since a refurb a few years back. Food is the main emphasis with a great selection of bar meals and dinners (sausages and onion gravy, Cornish cod in beer batter). There are also two reasonably-priced upstairs bedrooms. *Closed Mon.*

Thai Jasmine, 49 East Reach, t (01823) 256688, *www.thaijasmine.co.uk* (*moderate*). Good quality Thai food.

The Corner House Hotel, Park Street, t (01823) 284683, *www.corner-house. co.uk* (*moderate*). Medium-sized hotel in a turreted Victorian building, 500 yards from the town centre with 28 business-ish rooms and a **bistro**, 4DQ, serving local Somerset produce.

The Sanctuary, Middle Street, t (01823) 257788, *www.sanctuarywinebar.co.uk* (*moderate*). Wine bar and candle-lit restaurant downstairs, brighter dining room and roof terrace upstairs. Warm salads, hearty breads and daily fresh Brixham fish. Mains £15–19.

Tilbury Farm, West Bagborough, t (01823) 432391 (*moderate*). Up on the windswept slopes, this rough golden stone 17th-century farmhouse surrounded by 20 acres is the highest B&B in Somerset. The three bedrooms are furnished with rush matting and pine and offer views over the Vale of Taunton Deane towards the Brendon Hills. There are walks from the back garden onto the Quantocks ridge. The day begins with an Aga-cooked organic breakfast.

Chantry Tea Gardens, Sea Lane, Kilve, t (01278) 741457 (*budget*). Offering a warm welcome, next to the ruins of a medieval chantry and a pebble's throw from the sea. Delicious cream teas and ploughman's.

Blue Ball, Triscombe, Bishops Lydeard, t (01984) 618242 (*budget*). Traditional thatched pub with inglenook and beams. Strong emphasis on food, with a small but well-sourced menu, usually featuring a number of fish choices. Good range of ales at the bar.

The Star Inn, Mill Lane, Watchet, t (01984) 631367 (*budget*). A popular refreshment stop for passengers on the West Somerset Railway, this serves a good choice of beers and generously portioned, if slightly pricey, bar meals: fresh cod and chips, sausage and mash, steak and kidney pudding etc. In summer you can drink in the beer garden.

The Corner House, Market Street, Watchet, t (01984) 631251 (*budget*). Decent café serving quiches, soups and warm filled rolls.

Sally Edwards, The Crescent, t (01823) 326793 (*budget*). Lovely café offering tea and coffee, home-made pastries, Somerset apple cake and ciabattas.

Exmoor National Park

Covering an area of 267 square miles split between Somerset and Devon, including 34 miles of coast, Exmoor is Dartmoor's smaller tamer, lusher sibling. Underpinned by soft sandstone rather than unyielding granite, it's seen much of its landscape altered and reshaped by people over the centuries. Parts have been drained and re-sown with thick grasses, and much is given over to agriculture, although there are still some wild, windswept parts left at its margins. It's a great place for walking and biking, although be aware that you'll be tackling some fairly steep climbs. It can feel remote in places, but as it's a mere 21 miles wide and just 12 miles north to south, your chances of getting lost or in serious danger are much less than on Dartmoor.

A good base for exploring Exmoor is the market town of **Dulverton** on the southern edge of the moors, from where you can take a four-mile walk along a wooded valley to the Tarr Steps, a prehistoric bridge (known as a 'clapper bridge') made of 17 granite slabs, each weighing 1–2 tonnes, that were laid across the 180ft span of River Barle in c.1000 BC.

About seven miles north, almost at the very centre of the moor, on the banks of the River Exe, **Exford** is surrounded by some delightful wooded countryside. It's a sleepy little place with a long history of hunting – up until the imposition of the hunting ban in 2004 at least. From here you can begin the thigh-burning ascent to the top of Dunkery Beacon, which at 519m is the highest point on Exmoor (and Somerset).

The region's tourist offices can provide details of themed **walks**, some of which are aimed at discovering the region's wildlife. The moor is inhabited by herds of free-roaming deer, the largest concentration in the country, who have lived here since prehistoric times, as well as badgers, buzzards, merlins and ravens. Nature walks across Exmoor are organized by the **Exmoor Falconry and Animal Farm** near Porlock. Other routes have literary associations. You can go for a Doone Walk, on the lookout for scenes featured in R. D. Blackmore's 19th century classic, *Lorna Doone*, which was set at the time of the Monmouth Rebellion (*see* p.106) or walk part of the Tarka Trail, the route described by Henry Williamson in his book *Tarka the Otter*. Only a short section of the trail actually passes through Exmoor but it's as much as you're likely to cover. The full trail, along the banks of the Rivers Taw and Torridge and down into Dartmoor, is over 180 miles long. A railway line, known as the 'Tarka Line', runs for 39 scenic miles between Barnstaple and Exeter (*see* pp.162–3).

Exmoor Falconry and Animal Farm
*West Lynch Farm, Allerford;
t (01643) 862816;
www.exmoor-falconry.
co.uk; open daily
10am–5pm*

The Exmoor Coast

Perhaps the most rewarding walking in Exmoor is along its shore, which boasts the highest coastal cliffs in England (some are over 800 feet high) and the longest stretch of naturally wooded coastline in the British Isles. The approach to the moor's shore along the coastal road from the Quantocks is the same as that taken by Cromwell's men on their march to Dunster Castle during the Civil War, and later, in a rather less militaristic fashion, by Coleridge and Wordsworth during one of their innumerable inspiring nature walks.

Getting to and around Exmoor

There is a circular moorland **bus** between Minehead Peak and Porlock, via Dunster and Wheddon Cross and Exford (Easter–Sept weekends only, July–Aug also Tues and Thurs). For information call **t** (01823) 251140. First Somerset and Dorset, **t** (01823) 272 033; *www.firstgroup.com,* also runs a seasonal bus service along the coast from Taunton (summer daily, winter weekends only) to Lynton via Butlins Minehead, Bishops Lydeard, Watchet, Dunster and Porlock. First North Devon, **t** (01271) 376524, runs a year-round bus service from Butlins Minehead (daily) to Lynton via Porlock/Lynmouth. For timetable enquiries, contact Traveline (**t** 0871 2002233).

You come first to **Dunster**, a charming town that today supports less than a thousand inhabitants who live in picturesque, red stone, thatched cottages. An important wood-exporting town in medieval times, it has in the modern age become a rather sleepy, albeit very charming, place overlooked by the slumbering bulk of its castle, which, though begun in the 11th century, was almost entirely remodelled in the 19th. Its other main sights include the church of St George's, which boasts the longest rood screen in the country, a 17th-century covered yarn market and, around half a mile away, a beach lined with zealously protected beach cabins. Re-enactments of Civil War battles are staged here in summer.

Four miles northwest the resort of **Minehead** is a very knees-up sort of a place, full of fish and chip shops, tearooms and places selling rock, inflatables and buckets and spades. But then, as the site of Britain's first Butlins Holiday Camp (still going strong), it could be regarded as the very capital of knees-up Britain. There are gentler, more traditional pleasures here too, including a Hobby Horse fertility dance in May, the lovely chuffing steam train rides of the West Somerset Railway (Minehead is the line's terminus *see* p.107) and the great rolling, grassy expanses and wooded coastline of Exmoor, which lie just beyond its borders.

Eight miles west of Minehead, the road reaches the pretty town of **Porlock**, set at the foot of a wooded cliff, which provides a great thatched-cottaged base for exploring the moors and coast. Walks lead out from here up to the top of the 1,300ft Porlock Hill and the 1,700ft Dunkery Beacon, the highest point on the moor.

Past Porlock, Somerset turns into Devon as the road reaches **Lynton**. Perched on a steep wooded gorge where the West Lyn River meets the sea, Lynton is one of the most photogenic resorts in Devon, linked to its handsome harbourside sibling, Lynmouth, some 185 metres below it, by a

The Southwest Coastal Path

Minehead marks the start of the Southwest Coastal Path, Britain's longest national trail, which stretches for around 600 miles all the way around the perimeter of the southwest peninsula to Studland Bay in Dorset. En route it passes through and past some great scenery: high cliffs, rolling hills, picturesque villages and surf-battered beaches. The path is no modern invention but is rather based on the routes patrolled by the region's coastguards in centuries past as they tried to protect the coast against smuggling. Charged with inspecting every cave and inlet on coast, they beat out a path that hugs tightly to the shoreline, establishing a series of coastguard cottages along the route for their use. Many still stand today, although they have largely been adapted for different purposes.

It takes around two weeks to do the whole thing, walking at a brisk pace for eight hours a day. The Southwest Coastal Path Association, **t** (01752) 896237; *www.swcp.org.uk* can provide details of short itineraries, plus accommodation recommendations. It recommends late spring or early autumn as the best times to undertake the walk.

water-operated Victorian cliff railway. A terrible flood here in 1952 killed 34 people – you can see a memorial on the harbourside. The Tarka Trail passes through both towns, as does the **Two Moors Way** linking Exmoor and Dartmoor, while just outside Lynton lies the beautiful Gly Lyn Gorge. The towns share three beaches, the best of which is the sand and shingle Lee Bay Beach, which offers access to the famous Valley of Rocks, a great natural bowl surrounded by rocky outcrops.

ⓘ **Exmoor National Park Visitor Centres**
www.exmoor-nationalpark.gov.uk

ⓘ **Dulverton**
7–9 Fore Street,
t *(01398) 323841*

ⓘ **Porlock**
The Old School, West End, High Street,
t *(01643) 863150,*
www.porlock.co.uk;

ⓘ **Dunster**
Dunster Steep,
t *(01643) 821835*

⭐ **Spears Cross Hotel >>**

Tourist Information

The Exmoor Visitor is published in March with a calendar of events for the whole year, guided walks and lists of places to stay. The best walker's map is the Ordnance Survey, Outdoor Leisure 9, Exmoor 1:25,000.

Where to Stay and Eat on Exmoor

Dulverton

The Crown Hotel, Exford, t (01643) 831554, *www.crownhotelexmoor.co.uk* (*expensive*). Attractive coaching inn in the heart of Exmoor's hunting countryside. Rifles and foxes' heads adorn the walls, and the fire blazes away in winter. Great **restaurant** too.

Highercombe, 2–3 miles north of Dulverton, t (01398) 323451, *www.higher combe.co.uk* (*moderate*). Restored Georgian hunting lodge and farmhouse with large bedrooms and delightful flower gardens. There is also a three-bedroom self-catering cottage. The farm also runs a stable.

The Lion Hotel, 2 Bank Square, Dulverton, t (01398) 324437, *www.lion hoteldulverton.com* (*moderate*). Traditional 19th-century coaching hotel with a friendly bar, 13 good-sized bedrooms and a decent **restaurant**.

Town Mills, High Street, Dulverton, t (01398) 323124, *www.townmillsdulver ton.co.uk* (*moderate*). Handsome creeper-clad Georgian B&B, minutes walk from Dulverton, offering pretty, fresh-looking bedrooms and Wi-Fi.

Lewis's Tea Rooms, 13 High Street, Dulverton, t (01398) 323850, *www. lewisexmoortearooms.co.uk* (*budget*). Delightfully old-fashioned tearoom with a log fire and a table laden with cakes, jam and honey. Loose leaf tea served by the pot. Lunches include Welsh rarebit or ham and eggs.

Exford

The Exmoor White Horse Inn, Exford, t (01643) 831229, *www.exmoor-whitehorse.co.uk* (*expensive–very expensive*). 16th-century coaching inn beside the River Exe with 26 bedrooms, a traditional **restaurant** and a good locals' bar.

Dunster

Dunster Water Mill, 7 Mill Land, t (01643) 821759, *www.dunsterwater mill.co.uk* (*moderate*). 18th-century mill with two simple bedrooms, a tearoom and garden. Guests have free access to the castle grounds.

Hathaways of Dunster, 6–8 West Street, t (01643) 821725 (*moderate*). An intimate candle-lit restaurant with a menu of fresh Weston Bay fish and Somerset pork with cider-apple sauce.

Spears Cross Hotel, 1 West Street, t (01643) 821439, *www.spearscross-bed-and-breakfast.co.uk* (*moderate*). You'll get a warm welcome in this small, snug B&B with three bedrooms, a fireplace in the guests' lounge and oak-panelled rooms. The terraced garden dotted with model houses was created by hotel's original owner.

Stags Head, 10 West Street, t (01643) 821229 (*budget*). Snug, friendly pub serving local beers including Exmoor Ale, and bar meals.

The Yarn Market Hotel, High Street, t (01643) 821425, *www.yarnmarket hotel.co.uk* (*moderate*). Some of the 25 bright bedrooms overlook the ancient market cross; two get a glimpse of the castle. The **restaurant** has character.

Porlock

The Oaks Hotel, Porlock, t (01643) 862265, *www.oakshotel.co.uk* (*very expensive*). Pretty Edwardian country house hotel off the main Minehead–Lynton road with eight comfortable rooms. It has a gentle, period feel and terrific views towards Porlock Weir.

⭐ The Rising Sun
Hotel >>

The Anchor Hotel, Porlock Weir, t (01643) 862753 (*expensive*). Victorian hotel with 14 big, bright double bedrooms, most with views over the harbour. Another six rooms are available in the pub next door.

Exmoor Falconry and Animal Farm, West Lynch Farm, Allerford, Porlock, t (01643) 862816, *www.exmoor-falconry.co.uk* (*moderate*). Pretty yellow 15th-century farmhouse with ancient beams and a garden. Cream teas and home-made cakes.

Seapoint, Upway, Redway, Porlock, t (01643) 862 289, *www.seapoint.co.uk* (*moderate*). In a quiet spot above the village, just behind the Ship Inn, Seapoint is a large Edwardian house with four attractive bedrooms and a beautiful guest lounge; fireplace and window seat overlooking the bar.

Silcombe Farm, Culbone, t (01643) 862248 (*moderate*). Lovely, clean Victorian farmhouse with pretty gardens on the edge of Silcombe Combe, offering amazing views over the Bristol Channel. Three bedrooms and Aga-cooked breakfasts.

The Castle Hotel, High Street, West Porlock, t (01643) 862504, *www.castle porlock.co.uk* (*moderate*). Small hotel with firm beds and an inviting bar offering meals (*budget*).

West Porlock House, West Porlock, t (01643) 862880 (*moderate*). Half of a handsome 1920s manor house in wooded hillside above Porlock Bay with an overgrown garden full of azaleas and rhododendrons. Five charming bedrooms, most with sea views. *Open Mar–Oct only*.

Ash Farm, Porlock, t (01643) 862414 (*budget*). Take the Lynmouth road out of Porlock, and turn off after four miles towards Yeanor. This homely farmhouse above Culbone Combe in the midst of some of the region's best walking countryside is where Coleridge wrote 'Kubla Khan'.

The Ship Inn, High Street, Porlock, t (01643) 862507, *www.shipinnporlock. co.uk* (*budget*). Atmospheric thatched pub with snug bar, where Southey wrote an abysmal sonnet during one of his walks. Serves ploughman's lunches and has five en suite bedrooms (*moderate*).

Lynmouth and Lynton

Hewitt's Hotel, North Walk, Lynton, t (01598) 752293, *www.hewittshotel.co. uk* (*very expensive*). Rambling 19th-century house overlooking Lynmouth Bay. From the grand hall, an oak staircase sweeps up past a Burne-Jones stained-glass window.

Lynton Cottage Hotel, North Walk, Lynton, t (01598) 752342, *www.lynton-cottage.co.uk* (*expensive*). Cream-painted 19th-century hotel with grandstand views over the bay. Elegant double flight of stairs leads up to 17 bedrooms. There's also a decent **restaurant** (*open eves only*).

The Rising Sun Hotel, Harbour Lights, Lynmouth Street, Lynmouth, t (01598) 753223, *www.risingsunlynmouth.co.uk* (*expensive*). Thatched 14th-century smugglers' inn with a terraced garden and 16 comfortable bedrooms, including a detached cottage where the poet Shelley honeymooned with his teenage bride in 1812. You can eat lunch at the bar, or dinner in the oak-panelled **restaurant**. Traditional English/French dishes.

Le Bistro, 7 Watersmeet Road, Lynmouth t (01598) 753302, *www.le bistrolynmouth.co.uk* (*moderate*). Traditional English menu of fish and game.

Riverside Cottage, Riverside Road, Lynmouth, t (01598) 752390, *www. riversidecottage.co.uk* (*moderate*). Cheerful townhouse with six bedrooms. *Closed Dec–Jan*.

Southcliffe, 34 Lee Road, Lynton, t (01598) 753328, *www.southcliffe.co. uk* (*moderate*). Gothic resort architecture, five minutes' walk from the funicular. Clean and welcoming with home-cooked meals.

The Crown Hotel, Market Street, Lynton, t (01598) 752253, *www. crownhotellynton.co.uk* (*moderate*). Traditional old town hotel with 12 bedrooms and a pleasant atmosphere. Snooker room, reading room, bar and restaurant. Friendly. Good food.

Hunter's Inn, Heddon Valley, Parracombe, t (01598) 763230, *www. thehuntersinn.net* (*budget*). Large Victorian Swiss-style chalet at the top of Heddon Valley, 15 minutes' drive from Lynton. A good place for a cup of tea, a pint, or hot and cold food.

Devon

Devon is like a giant photo album, filled with yellowing snapshots of England's past, all mounted on glossy, modern pages. Walking the lonely, brooding heart of Dartmoor can be a primeval experience, but step outside of its granite borders and you'll find vigorous, dynamic cities and great shrieking fun-filled resorts. Plymouth's post-war suburbs protect a harbour where you'll be transported back to the maritime age of Elizabeth I when the salty sea dogs Raleigh and Drake were plundering new worlds, while at Exeter you can trace the remains of the country's Roman past and revel in the glory of its medieval cathedral architecture, before succumbing to the modern temptations of its quayside bars and restaurants. In other words, Devon's backward, yokel-ish reputation is a macguffin. It's as modern as they come, but has had the foresight to keep those parts of its past worth preserving preserved – if only England's other counties could say the same.

08

Don't miss

1 A medieval masons' masterpiece.
St Peter's Cathedral, Exeter p.181

2 Steam trains and riverboat rides.
Dartmouth p.130

3 A modernist rural revolution
Dartington Hall p.135

4 Sun on the sands
Salcombe p.138

5 Tors, mires and horse-trekking
Dartmoor p.148

See map overleaf

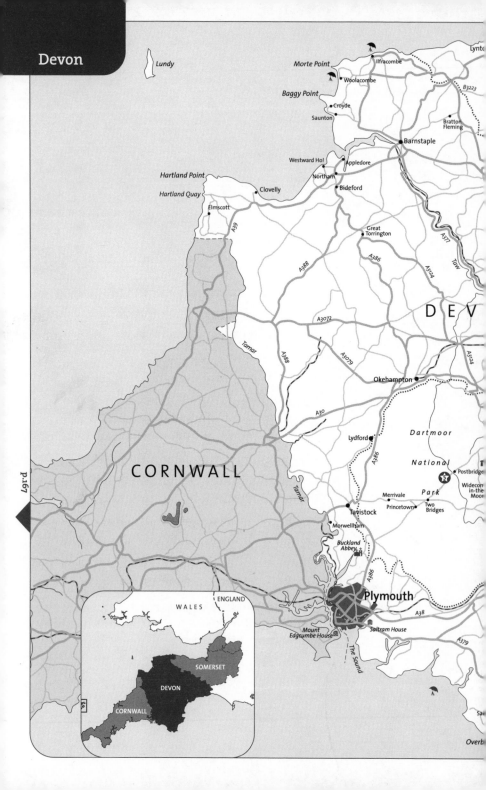

Lundy

Lynt

Morte Point
Ilfracombe
Woolacombe
B3223
Baggy Point
Croyde
Bratton
Saunton
Fleming

Barnstaple

Westward Ho!
Appledore
Hartland Point
Northam
Hartland Quay
Clovelly
Bideford
Elmscott
A39

Great
Torrington
A386
A377
A388
Taw
A3124

D E V

A3072
A3079
A388

A3124

A30
Okehampton

Tamar

Dartmoor

Lydford
National
Postbridge

A386
Park
Widecon
in-the
Merrivale
Moor
CORNWALL
Princetown
Two
Bridges

Tamar

Tavistock
Morwellham
Buckland
Abbey

Plymouth
A38

Saltram House
WALES
ENGLAND

A386
Mount
Edgcumbe House

The Sound
A379

SOMERSET
Overb
DEVON

CORNWALL

Sa

SOMERSET

A361

A396

A361

A3072

A377

Exe

A396

M5

A30

A373

A375

A35

A30

Exeter

A30

Ottery
St Mary

B3180

A3052

A3052

Seaton

A358

A38

A379

A376

Topsham

Sidmouth

Beer

tonhampstead

Powderham Castle

B3178

Lyme Bay

A382

Bovey Tracey

Budleigh Salterton

ytor

A380

Exmouth

A38

A381

Dawlish

Newton
Abbot

A380

Teignmouth

uckfastleigh

Babbacombe

Cockington

Torquay

A385

Tor Bay

tnes

Paignton

Brixham

Dartmouth

Stoke Fleming

Ley
Nature
ve

Blackpool Sands

A379

Start Bay

South Hallands

Start Point

Don't miss

① St Peter's Cathedral, Exeter **p.118**

② Dartmouth **p.130**

③ Dartington Hall **p.135**

④ Salcombe **p.138**

⑤ Dartmoor **p.148**

N

40 km

20 miles

Exeter

Exeter is Devon's largest town and main transport hub. Its cathedral and guildhall aside, much of the centre is modern and generic, but the city has got character, with a thriving university which helps to give it a lively, youthful ambience. Most of the town's attractions are grouped around the pedestrianized High Street, making it easily navigable on foot. Well stocked with shops and restaurants, Exeter also makes a good base for exploring Dartmoor and for boat trips along the River Exe.

Two thousand years ago the city was a small, Celtic settlement made of a few basic huts. Despite its lowly status, the Romans clearly saw something they liked, making it one of their main army camps and subsequently building it up into one of the most important towns in the whole country, known by the rather tongue-twisting name of Isca Dumnoniorum. When the Romans left in the early 5th century AD, the town was passed from owner to owner – the Britons were kicked out by the Saxons, who were kicked out by the Vikings, who were kicked out by another lot of Vikings – before being recaptured by Alfred the Great in the 10th century. Alfred ordered a massive rebuilding programme and by the time of the Norman Conquest it was once again the Southwest's dominant town – it took William the Conqueror two whole months to break through its walls – and continued to grow throughout the medieval period when it became an important trading port. Although much of its medieval core was destroyed in the Second World War, parts of old Exeter do remain, including the original Roman street plan, the medieval Guildhall (still in use), some picturesque Tudor houses, a few parts of the old Roman wall, and the vast 750-year-old cathedral.

To find the city at its most vibrant, come in June when the Exeter Festival, a celebration of music, theatre and fireworks, is in full swing.

Note that the **Royal Albert Memorial Museum and Art Gallery** will be closed for the next few years while it undergoes a £10 million revamp.

Royal Albert Memorial Museum & Art Gallery
Queen Street
t (01392) 665858;
www.exeter.gov.uk/ramm

St Peter's Cathedral & Cathedral Close

⭐ **St Peter's Cathedral & Cathedral Close**
Cathedral Close;
t (01392) 255573;
www.exeter-cathedral.org.uk; open Mon–Sat 9.30–5; adm £5; free 45-minute tours given daily Apr–Oct 11am and 2.30pm Mon–Fri, 11am on Sat and 4pm Sun

Looming down over Exeter's low-rise skyline, the medieval cathedral has been the city's main visitor attraction for well over 700 years. Its origins go back further than that, however. The very first religious structure was probably erected here by the Saxons in the 5th century, although it would take the Normans to give it some proper solidity, erecting a stone church in the early 12th century. This was expanded (by about a third) and largely remodelled in an ornate Gothic style in the 13th and 14th centuries.

The entrance is in the west front, which is guarded by a triple row of stone figures, which comprise one of the largest collections of 14th-century sculptures in the country. Beyond, the cathedral's interior is a mixture of fine, soaring architecture and strange, almost incongruous curios. The first thing that will strike you will no doubt be the Gothic fan vaulting soaring atop the nave for 319ft – like an 'avenue of palms' or a succession of enormous spidery hands. It is linked by some 400 carved bosses (the knobs at the intersection of the vaults), painted in gilt and bright colours. The great swooping ceiling appears delicate and intricate

Map labels:

St David's Station
University of Exeter Bill Douglass Centre
BONHAY ROAD
A377
B3183
ST DAVID'S HILL
NEW NORTH ROAD
HOWELL ROAD
HOWELL ROAD
BLACKALL ROAD
LONGBROOK STREET
SIDWELL STREET
B3212
HELE ROAD
NEW NORTH ROAD
RICHMOND ROAD
QUEEN STREET
Central Station
Rougemont Gardens
Castle (Crown Court)
City Wall
NEW NORTH ROAD
SIDWELL STREET
WESTERN WAY
CLIFTON ROAD
Royal Albert Museum
Exeter Phoenix
Entrance to Underground Passages
PARIS STREET
P
Bus Station
HEAVITREE ROAD
B3183
P
PAUL STREET
Guildhall
BARTHOLOMEW ST WEST
NORTH STREET
HIGH STREET
PRINCESSHAY
Civic Centre
City Wall
BARNFIELD RD
SOUTHERNHAY EAST
SOUTHERNHAY WEST
WESTERN WAY
COLLEGE ROAD
River Exe
BONHAY ROAD
MARY ARCHES ST
St Nicholas's Priory
Wall
BARTHOLOMEW STREET
FORE STREET
SOUTH STREET
CATHEDRAL YARD
CATHEDRAL CLOSE
Exeter Cathedral
PRESTON STREET
MAGDALEN STREET
MAGDALEN ROAD
WESTERN RD
OKEHAMPTON STREET
BULLER RD
BULLER ROAD
B3212
A377
NORTH BR
SOUTH BR
EDMUND ST
NORTH ST
COMMERCIAL ROAD
WESTERN WAY
Wall
City
P
Custom House
Quay House Visitor Centre
HOLLOWAY STREET
RADFORD ROAD
A3015
THE QUAY
River Exe
HAVEN ROAD
P
N
A3015

250 metres
250 yards

Hotel and Restaurant Key
1 Abode Exeter Hotel
2 Michael Caines
3 The Well House
4 St Olaves Court Hotel
5 The Townhouse
6 Brazz
7 Thai Orchid
8 Ganges

in a way that several tonnes worth of stonework have no real right to be. The largest of its type anywhere in the world, the vaulting was created during the 14th century Gothic revamp – a quite astonishing piece of engineering.

Other spectacular features worth hunting out include, the 60ft-high medieval oak canopy rearing over the bishop's throne like some sinister wooden rocket (again the tallest of its kind in the country); the 13th century misericords, the oldest existing set in the country (which mostly depict animals, both real and fantastical); and the Great East Window which boasts some of its original 14th-century stained glass. The glass in the Great West Window was destroyed in the Second World War.

There are also plenty of smaller curios to look out for, including the flag that Captain Scott took to the North Pole, the rather gruesome-looking 16th-century stone cadaver tomb of 19-year-old Rachel O'Brien, who was burnt alive when her dress caught fire in 1800 (both are in the north choir aisle) and a 15th-century astronomical clock in the north transept, which shows the earth – represented by a golden ball – being circled by a Moon and a fleur-de-lys representing the Sun. It still works,

Getting to and around Exeter

By Car, Train or Bus

Exeter is 170 miles from London, 75 miles from Bristol and 45 miles from Plymouth and can be reached via the M5 (leave at junction 30), the A38 and the A30. Services arrive at its two **train** stations, Exeter Central and Exeter St David's (which is just outside the city centre), from London Waterloo, London Paddington, Bristol and Salisbury. The **bus** station is on Paris Street. There are regular National Express **coach** services to Exeter from London Victoria, Bristol and Salisbury.

Guided Walks

Free guided **walks** provided by Exeter Council in the company of a 'red coat' guide leave from Cathedral Yard throughout the year. As well as tours taking in all the principal sights of the city, the red coats also offer seasonal port tours (which start outside Quay House) as well as a number of popular themed tours – 'Ghosts and Legends' etc., and a unique torchlight tour of the city's catacombs.

albeit using a 19th-century electric movement rather than the original mechanical one.

Keep an eye out too for the Dog Whipper's room where in the Middle Ages one of the vergers would periodically emerge to chase away stray animals that had crept into church, a more common occurrence in medieval times. It's located beneath the Minstrel's Gallery where a band of carved angels playing medieval musical instruments is depicted.

Finally see if you can pick out the the 'green man'– an ancient pagan symbol showing a foliage-sprouting face representing spring and rebirth which, though entirely un-Christian, has found its way into the decoration of many West Country churches.

The **Cathedral Close**, filled with fine timber-framed and Georgian buildings, now housing to well-to-do shops, restaurants and hotels, is the place to hang out on a sunny day, with a picnic.

Guildhall

Guildhall
High Street,
t (01392) 665500,
www.exeter.gov.uk.

Exeter's 14th-century guildhall is the oldest municipal building still in use in the country. That very fact can make it rather tricky to visit as it's often closed for official business, and there are no set opening times. However, outside of civic functions, it is free to look inside at its fine Tudor wood panelling.

Rougement Gardens and City Walls

The landscaped gardens are one of the city's finest open spaces, and also contain the patchy remains of the city's Norman castle. These can be found surrounding a Georgian mansion built on the old motte, which is now used as city's crown court. The gardens also provide good views of some of the best-preserved sections of Exeter's city walls, parts of which are 2,000 years old. There's a particularly impressive section with bastions on Southernhay – it can be fascinating picking out the different layers of construction: Roman, medieval, civil war etc. For more information pick up a 'City Wall' trail leaflet from the tourist office.

Bill Douglass Centre

Bill Douglass
Centre
Old Library, University
of Exeter, Prince of
Wales Road;
t (01392) 264321;
Mon–Fri 10–4; adm free

A 15-minute walk from the city centre on the University of Exeter campus, this is a fun little film museum, telling the history of moving pictures from shadow puppets to Hollywood musicals, and from 'what the butler saw' machines to Blu Ray. The centrepiece is a vast collection of film-related memorabilia and ephemera – posters, models, lunchboxes, magazines, soaps, programmes, playing cards, toys etc.

Exeter Quayside

Exeter Quayside
Quay House Visitor
Centre, The Quay;
t (01392) 271611; open
April–Oct daily 10–5pm,
Nov–March Sat–Sun
11–4; adm free

Exeter's quays once bustled with activity inspired by a thriving wool trade. Now, as with so many other quayside areas where trade has long since dried up, they have been transformed into a sort of arts-cum-leisure complex. The red stone warehouses and customs buildings have been turned into souvenir shops, cafés, craft centres and pubs, while the **Quay House** itself is now a heritage centre, where you can find out about the city's history through a range of exhibits and audiovisual presentations.

In summer, this is one of the city's most pleasant areas, particularly on weekends when jazz bands entertain the passing crowds. There's a 'slow food' market on the third Saturday of each month.

Exeter Underground Passages

Exeter
Underground
Passages
Romangate Passage,
High Street; t (01392)
665887; open June–Sept
Mon–Sat 9.30–5.30, Sun
10.30–4; Oct–May
Tues–Fri 11.30–5.30, Sat
10.30–5.30, Sun 11.30–4
(1st tour half hour after
opening, last tour 1hr
before closing); adm
£4.90

These narrow, winding subterranean passageways were constructed in the 13th century as a means of bringing water into the city. Today, you can explore the clammy network as part of a guided tour. You begin with an introductory exhibition and video presentation before donning your hard hat and heading into the gloomy vaults to hear tales of smuggling, disease and ghosts. Bring a sturdy pair of waterproof shoes.

Around Exeter

Powderham Castle

Powderham Castle
Kenton,
t (01626) 890243;
www.powderham.co.uk;
open Apr–Oct 11–4.30
(until 5.30 during
summer holidays); adm
£8.95

The family seat of the Earl of Devon, this much-restored medieval castle set in an ancient deer park is near Kenton, about five miles south of Exeter on the A379, and linked by frequent buses. Tours of the grand state rooms, filled with lots of fine 18th-century furniture, take place every half hour or so throughout the day. Children will enjoy the grounds which contain a petting zoo (known as the Secret Garden and housed in the original Victorian walled garden), and a play area.

Topsham

From Exeter, it's a short train journey down the estuary to Topsham, a handsome old seafaring town. This was Exeter's port from Roman times onwards. In the late 13th century, the Countess of Devonshire built a weir upriver of Topsham to cut off trade to Exeter; four centuries later Exeter built a canal parallel to the river to bypass it. Its colourful Dutch gabled houses along the strand reflect trading links with the Low Countries.

(i) **Exeter**
Civic Centre, Paris Street, t (01392) 265700 www.exeter.gov.uk; open Mon–Sat 9am–5pm, and Sun July–Aug 9am–4pm

(★) **Michael Caines**
>>

(★) **The Townhouse** >

Festivals in Exeter

Exeter Arts Festival, t (01392) 265200, *www.exeter.gov.uk*, takes place over two weeks in July. The repertoire includes music and drama, with celebrity guests.

Where to Stay in Exeter

St Olaves Court Hotel, Mary Arches Street, **t** (01392) 217736, *www.olaves. co.uk* (*expensive*). Medium-sized, family-run Georgian townhouse hotel with a walled garden, decanters of sherry in the 15 very stylish bedrooms, and a high-class intimate **restaurant**.

Abode Exeter, Cathedral Yard, **t** (01392) 319955, *www.abodehotels.co.uk* (*moderate–expensive*). Formerly the Royal Clarence, this is a very swish 56-bedroom four-star hotel opposite the cathedral whose classy restaurant and café bar are a franchise of Michael Caines (*see below*).

The Townhouse, 54 St David's Hill, **t** (01392) 494994, *www.townhouse exeter.co.uk* (*moderate*). Set in a creeper-clad Edwardian house, this jolly little B&B is just a three-minute walk from the city centre. Its rooms, all named after literary characters, are stylishly minimal and very reasonably priced. Good breakfasts.

Exeter YHA Hostel, Mount Wear House, 47 Countess Wear Road, **t** 0845 371 9516, *www.yha.org.uk* (*budget*). Exeter's cheapest accommodation is in a 17th-century house a 10-minute bus ride from the centre. It boasts all the usual hostel basics – dorms sleeping 4–8, a couple of private rooms, kitchen, games room, lounge, laundry facilities etc. – as well as a pretty garden.

Eating Out in Exeter

In the summer, Exeter Quayside is the place to go for a drink, especially at the weekend when there are often street performers and jazz bands on hand to entertain the crowds. The lawns around the cathedral are a good spot for a picnic on a sunny day. Somewhat pricey supplies can be picked up from Michael Caines' well-stocked delicatessen (*see below*).

Michael Caines, Abode Exeter, Cathedral Yard, **t** (01392) 319955, *www. abodehotels.co.uk* (*moderate–expensive*). This hotel restaurant provides a very stylish setting for upmarket, modern French cooking, including honeyed duck or calf's liver with sage. The slightly cheaper café-bar serves bistro-style food. There's also a delicatessen.

Brazz, 10–12 Palace Gate, **t** (01392) 252525 (*moderate*). Lively, modern place to eat, one of a small West Country chain, offering a hearty brasserie menu (fishcakes, steak and chips etc) served by upbeat staff.

Thai Orchid, Cathedral Yard, **t** (01392) 214215, *www.thaiorchidrestaurant. co.uk* (*moderate*). Elegant, friendly Thai restaurant (Exeter's first when it opened in 1995) housed in a 16th-century stonemason's cottage and serving spicy Southeast Asian staples such as Tom Yum soup, phad thai and green chicken curry, as well as exotic fresh fruit salads. Takeaway service available. *Close Sat lunch and Sun.*

The Well House, Cathedral Yard, **t** (01392) 223611, *www.michaelcaines. com/taverns/exeter* (*moderate*). This revamped tavern, with its black-stained planks and contemporary leather and wicker furniture, forms yet another part of Michael Caines' burgeoning empire. It serves a wide range of West Country real ales and the bar meals come direct from Mr Caines' celebrated kitchen. Popular dishes include the 'Well House Pye' – a steak pie with ale gravy £8.50.

Ganges, 156 Fore Street, **t** (01392) 272630, *www.thegangesrestaurant. com* (*budget–moderate*). A very decent Indian restaurant with a wide range of dishes (starters £3–5, mains £6–12), including plenty of choices for vegetarians. Students get a 10% discount. Takeaways available.

Phoenix Café-Bar, Bradninch Place, Gandy Street, **t** (01392) 667080, *www.exeterphoenix.org.uk* (*budget*). The arts centre's (*see below*) bar offers a decent menu and a nice minimally arty space to hang out. *Closed Sun eve.*

Eating out in Topsham

La Petite Maison, 35 Fore Street,
t (01392) 873660, *www.lapetitemaison.co.uk* (*expensive*). This small, stylish, family-run restaurant behind an old shop front serves up a top-quality menu of English/French dishes, such as lamb infused with rosemary and red wine, all home-made on the premises, including the petit-fours and bread. Two courses for £28.95. *Closed Sun and Mon, summer lunch only.*

The Bridge Inn, t (01392) 873862, *www.cheffers.co.uk/bridge. html* (*budget*). A 16th-century former maltings above the River Clyst with a huge range of real ales and river views from the bar and garden. It serves ploughman's, pasties, sandwiches and soups at lunch and from 6–8pm.

Entertainment in Exeter

Exeter Phoenix Arts Centre, Bradninch Place, Gandy Street, t (01392) 667080, *www.exeterphoenix.org.uk*. Drama, comedy, dance, theatre, spoken word, film and visual arts performances, including touring productions.

The Exeter Northcott Theatre, Stocker Road, t (01392) 493493, *www.exeternorthcott.co.uk*. Stages a year-round programme of drama, classical music recitals, comedy and children's performances, as well as a month of Shakespeare in Rougemont Gardens from July to August.

The South Devon Coast

Today the resorts of South Devon are among the best known and most visited in the country. Those around Torbay – Torquay, Paignton and Brixham – are sometimes known collectively as the English Riviera. But 250 years ago these were just simple low-key fishing villages. The principal travellers of the era – the upper classes – rarely holidayed in England, instead taking themselves off on cultural jaunts to the continent. However, the French Revolution and subsequent Napoleonic Wars changed all that, effectively shutting down the continent to leisure travel from 1789 to 1815.

Denied a winter season abroad, the aristocracy began searching for a domestic alternative. The South Devon towns' relatively mild climate – at least when compared with the rest of the country – got them the nod. Soon they were catering to an influx of moneyed indolents looking to promenade along the front in the latest fashions and 'take the waters'. Sidmouth, Dawlish and Teignmouth all experienced a burst of genteel-inspired growth – the latter was so popular it was dubbed by an Exeter newspaper the 'Montpelier of England'.

However, following Napoleon's defeat at Waterloo, the continental resorts reopened and South Devon became less appealing.

A bit of quick rebranding was needed to prevent the resorts from slipping back into obscurity. The Devon towns began to promote the health benefits of their sea air and water (the colder and more bracing the better). Soon the resorts were thriving once more as popular and profitable winter health retreats for consumptive gentility. The middle and lower classes joined them following the coming of the railways in the mid-1800s, prompting the great British seaside holiday boom.

Getting to and around the South Devon coast

Beer: Beer lies just west of the Dorset border, off the A3052 and B3174.

Sidmouth: Sidmouth is on the South Devon coast between Exmouth and Beer. Take the A375 from the A3052 and follow the signs. There are good **bus** links with Exeter.

Exmouth: Exmouth is on Devon's southern coast about 15 miles north of Torbay. Follow the signs along the A377 or A376. Good **rail** links with Exeter.

Torquay: Torquay, the main Torbay resort, has good links with Exeter, 20 miles north. By **car**, follow the signs from the M5 – Torquay is off the A380. **Trains** from Exeter arrive at Torquay via Newton Abbot and run along the coast to Paignton. The X46 **coach** runs hourly between Exeter and Torquay.

Paignton: Two miles west of Torquay, Paignton also has good links with Exeter. To arrive in style, board the **Paignton and Dartmouth Steam Railway** at Kingswear (*see* p.129).

Brixham: Situated five miles southwest of Torquay, a 15-minute bus ride from Paignton, Brixham also has good road, rail (change train at Paignton) and bus links (direct) with Exeter. Follow the signs from the M5.

Beer

Lying at the east end of Devon's coast, Beer never fully succumbed to the region's 19th-century holiday boom. As a result it is today still a proper working fishing village (and there aren't too many of those around here) with a sideline in lace-making (local workshops supplied the lace for Queen Victoria's wedding dress) and a picturesque, low-key charm – all bobbing boats, colourful cottages, crab pots and nets laid out to dry on the harbourside. It's built around a small cove backed by chalk cliffs. These are filled with a riddly network of caves that in the 18th and 19th centuries provided popular hiding places for local smugglers. Indeed, the taking of illicit booty seems to be a particularly popular practice around here. In 2007, just a few miles west of town, the container ship, MSC *Napoli*, ran aground, spilling much of its contents onto the shore and prompting a horde of bounty hunters to descend from all parts of the country to claim the assorted bottles of wine, packets of shampoo and even BMW motorbikes that washed up. Technically it was not illegal for these items to be taken – but it was for the people taking them not to declare them (which very few did). In the end the police were forced to invoke special powers to close the beach.

Beer boasts just a handful of very low-key attractions. The real appeal here is the relaxed lifestyle – strolling the shingle beach and eating in quirky little fish restaurants. You can tour the vaulted caves of the **Beer Quarry Caves**, where stone has been extracted since Roman times, to see the smugglers' hideaways and hear tales of their adventures. Jack Rattenbury apparently became a noted celebrity in these parts, nicknamed the 'Rob Roy of the West' by repeatedly evading capture by the authorities. You can also learn how the caves acted as refuges for persecuted Catholics following the Reformation and try and spot some of the hundreds of bats who are the caverns' principal modern inhabitants.

The **Beer Heritage Centre** by the beach has displays on the local fishing industry and sea life, with an aquarium containing starfish and anemones.

Children will enjoy the **Pecorama Pleasure Gardens**, a gentle, train-themed park with flower gardens, a model railway exhibition and a

Beer Quarry Caves
Quarry Lane;
t (01297) 625830;
www.beerquarrycaves.com; open daily Apr–Oct, tour times vary; adm £6

Beer Heritage Centre
intermittent opening times; adm free

Pecorama Pleasure Gardens
Underleys,
t (01297) 21542;
www.peco-uk.com/ Pecorama/Pecorama.htm; open Sun–Fri 10–5.30, Sat 10–1; adm

miniature steam engine. Incidentally, the town's name is derived from the Saxon word for wood, 'bearu' and not the modern word for ale.

Sidmouth

Sidmouth was one of the main beneficiaries of the enforced continental holiday ban of the late 18th and early 19th centuries when it briefly became the leading resort on this stretch of coast. Unfortunately, it proved less adept than its neighbours at reinvention and went into a steep decline following the resumption of European travel – the upside of which is that it has retained much of the handsome Georgian and Regency architecture built during the Napoleonic holiday bubble, which has been razed in many other resorts. Today its front is lined with dozens of listed buildings, sat beneath imposing red sandstone cliffs.

The pace of life in Sidmouth is as stately as a galleon. The rougher edges of Torbay's resorts have here been smoothed to a fine finish. This is a place for elegant promenades along the front and afternoon cream teas, not arcades, bargain burgers and candyfloss.

For a little excitement, try the **Vintage Toy Train Shop and Museum**, which has a large display of metal and mechanical toys from the period 1925–40, including a number of Hornby train engines and Dinky cars. Or pick up a bag of carrots and head off to **The Donkey Sanctuary** at Slade Hall Farm. Home to hundreds of old, sick or retired animals living an idyllic existence in acres of beautiful countryside, this is the largest donkey sanctuary in the world, funded by a level of yearly donations that would make most charities green with envy (it seems the British really do love their donkeys). In addition to its equine inhabitants, the sanctuary can also offer walks and nature trails, including one through a nearby nature reserve down to the South Devon coast.

Every summer the resort's peace and quiet is ever so slightly disturbed by the earnest murmurings of the **Sidmouth International Folk Festival**, which consists of eight days of music, dance, concerts and craft fairs.

Budleigh Salterton, about eight miles west along the coast, offers more of the same, albeit of an even less lively nature (if you can imagine such a thing), while inland **Ottery St Mary** has a fine church, St Mary's, which looks a bit like a miniature version of Exeter's with its own fine 14th-century fan vaulting and medieval mechanical clock.

Exmouth

Exmouth, at the mouth of the River Exe, offers a range of pleasures – some modern, some of a more ancient vintage. The town marks the far end of the **Jurassic Coast**, the stretch of coastal sedimentary rocks that has proved such a fertile ground for fossil hunters over the years. A chisel and a bit of patience are all that's usually required to turn up the preserved remains of some ancient organism.

For something a little more lively, you could try your hand at **wind-and kite-surfing** which have become hugely popular offshore activities in recent decades, the town's exposed position providing the perfect blustery conditions for the sport. As with many of the towns along this stretch of coast, Exmouth first came to prominence in the late 18th and

Vintage Toy Train Shop and Museum
Devonshire House, All Saints Road;
t (01395) 512588; open Mon–Sat 10–5

The Donkey Sanctuary
t (01395) 578222; http://drupal.thedonkey sanctuary.org.uk; open daily 9–dusk

Sidmouth International Folk Festival
www.sidmouthfolk week.co.uk

Edge Watersports
3 The Royal Avenue; t (01395) 222551 www.edgewater sports.com

Great Exmouth Model Railway
Queens Drive;
t (01395) 278383;
www.exmouthmodelrail
way.co.uk; summer daily
10–3, winter Sat & Sun
10–3; adm £2.25

boat trips
t (01395) 222144,
www.stuartline
cruises.co.uk

Jurassic Coast Diving
The Royal Avenue;
t (01395) 268090;
www.jcdiving.co.uk

A La Ronde
Summer Lane;
t (01395) 265514;
www.nationaltrust.org.uk
Mar–Nov Sat–Wed 11–5;
adm £6.60

World of Country Life
Sandy Bay;
t (01395) 274533,
www.worldofcountry
life.co.uk; open Apr–Oct
10–dusk; adm £9.85

Dawlish Warren Nature Reserve
t (01626) 863980;
www.dawlish
warren.co.uk

early 19th centuries when it seemed to become the resort of choice for women caught up in love triangles: the Duke of York's (as in 'grand old') mistress lived here, as did Lady Nelson and Lady Byron. Today the town is stretched out behind a long, sandy beach and a lively harbour surrounded by cafés and tourist shops. The **Great Exmouth Model Railway**, one of the world's longest model railways, can be found on the seafront. In summer, **boat trips** are offered from the harbour to Topsham, and mackerel-fishing trips depart from the beach. It's also one of the few places on this coast where you can go diving. Try **Jurassic Coast Diving**.

Exmouth's most intriguing attraction can be found on the edge of the town. **A La Ronde**, a bizarre 16-sided, multi-windowed house, was constructed in the late 18th century to display the assorted curios, curiosities and keepsakes accumulated by two spinster cousins during a ten-year 'grand tour' of the continent. The interior is hand-decorated in bizarre fashion with seashells, seaweed, feathers and coloured sand.

A mile southeast of Exmouth is the **World of Country Life**, a 40-acre family fun park with a petting zoo, bird of prey displays and a safari ride through llama and deer paddocks. Further southwest along the coast, and reachable by water taxi from Exmouth Marina is the **Dawlish Warren Nature Reserve**. Set on the southern banks of the Exe estuary and made up of a variety of landscapes (including dunes, marshes and mud flats), the reserve provides the region's premier nesting site for wildfowl, in particular wading birds. There are guided nature walks in summer.

To the south of the reserve, set beneath red sandstone cliffs, is **Dawlish** itself, a rather old-fashioned town that's had a not wholly successful modern face-lift, its picturesque cottages now joined by a range of typically generic seaside attractions, including amusement arcades, children's playgrounds and a pitch n' putt course. The main beach, which is made up of sand and shingle with some rock pools, is over one and a half miles long and the proud possessor of a European Blue Flag. The small, faded, but bustling and lively resort of **Teignmouth** lies a few miles south.

Tor Bay and the English Riviera

The 'English Riviera' is the section of Devon coastline stretching around Tor Bay, comprising the resorts of Brixham, Paignton and Torquay. Though these resorts are nominally separate entities, the coast has become so built up over recent decades – particularly between Torquay and Paignton – that they do now rather bleed into one another to form a seamless holiday whole (or hole, depending on your point of view). The region's nickname is not entirely fanciful. Thanks to a happy combination of sunshine (on average, the bay enjoys more hours per day than anywhere else in the country), the warming effects of the Gulf Stream and a secluded location away from the worst Atlantic storms, the climate here can, at times, be practically balmy. But this is still England, so it can also be very rainy and cold, even at the height of summer. And it's not exactly steeped in glamour, as anyone who has been to the French or Italian equivalents will testify. Starlets, Russian billionaires' yachts and glittery film festivals are all rather thin on the ground.

It's a Mystery – Torquay's Queen of crime

According to the official records, Torbay and its environs have always had a rather low crime rate, although you wouldn't believe it from a quick perusal of the works of the area's most celebrated literary daughter, Dame Agatha Christie, full as they are of the most diabolically cunning murders. Christie was born in Torquay in 1890 and apparently expressed an ambition to become a writer at a tender age, getting her first piece published when just 11 years old. However, what attracted her to crime writing in particular is a mystery. There is certainly little in her background to suggest a reason. It is thought that time spent as a nurse working in the pharmacy of the Red Cross Hospital in Torquay Town Hall during the First World War gave her the intimate knowledge of poisons she would use to do away with so many in her books.

Her first novel was published in 1920, but it would be another six years before Christie's career really took off with the release of *The Murder of Roger Ackroyd*, the cunning plot twist of which (spoiler alert: the narrator is the murderer) made it an instant smash. For the next fifty years she churned out the tales, including 75 novels and 33 plays. Almost all are elaborately plotted whodunits set in upper and upper-middle class society and tend to proceed according to a set template: a murder victim is discovered, a detective is summoned to investigate and gradually the murderer is revealed, usually at a gathering of all the main suspects. Most novels feature one or other of her two most famous creations: the priggish Belgian detective, Hercule Poirot, and Miss Marple, the elderly sleuthing spinster.

Her extraordinary popularity has made her the third best-selling author of all time, behind only God (for the Bible) and William Shakespeare, and the world's most translated author. Her play, *The Mousetrap*, is the longest running of all time, still showing nightly at the Ambassadors Theatre in London after more than 23,000 performances.

There was one mystery created by Christie, however, that was never satisfactorily solved. When her husband embarked on an affair in 1926 and asked for a divorce, she disappeared for ten days, prompting a national outcry. She was eventually found in a hotel in Harrogate where she had checked in under the name of her husband's mistress, Nancy Neele. At the time speculation was rife as to whether the disappearance had been a publicity stunt, the result of a nervous breakdown or – the most fantastical theory and the one that would sit best in her novels – an attempt by Christie to fake her own death and frame her husband for the murder. After the event Christie claimed amnesia, stating that she couldn't remember what had happened.

Her subsequent marriage to the archaeologist Max Mallowan proved much happier. Christie once joked that all women would be better off marrying archaeologists as they would be regarded as more valuable and beautiful the older they got.

Torquay's museum has a good display of Christie memorabilia. However, for a fascinating glimpse into her life, pay a visit to Greenway, her holiday home just outside Brixham, which boasts fantastic rolling gardens (albeit no stabbed librarians in the flower beds). You can also take guided tours of the house which was opened to public for first time by the National Trust in 2009. Christie described it as the 'loveliest place in the world'. In 2009 notebooks containing four unpublished stories were discovered here (Greenway Road, Galmpton; t (01803) 842382; *www.nationaltrust.org.uk*; March–Oct Wed–Sun 10.30–5, also open Tues summer hols; adm £8.20).

Torquay

Torquay is both an exotic alternative to traditional English resorts and a traditional English resort. For every promenade lined with palm trees (they're actually the rather unromantic-sounding New Zealand Cabbage Trees but they look similar), there's a parade of cheap cafés; for every expensive boutique, there's a tacky souvenir shop, and for every modern luxury hotel, there's a crusty old Basil Fawlty-esque hotel.

The town's focal point is the harbour surrounded by shops and restaurants and framed by huge limestone cliffs. At night, the whole of the waterfront is lit up with coloured lights. The main beaches, out of a choice of no less than 20, are the sandy **Abbey Sands**, where you can hire pedalos and boats, the rock and shingle **Anstey's Cove**, and the

The Glorious Revolution – The Future's Orange

In the winter of 1688 William of Orange invaded England at the invitation of prominent English nobles unhappy with their autocratic Catholic King James II. William landed at Brixham with 500 boats – a force four times bigger than the Spanish Armada – carrying 14,000 troops, clearly intent on taking the Crown by force. At the head of the procession that marched to London were 200 English cavalry, 200 Africans from the Dutch colonies, 200 Laplanders, 300 Swiss, 500 volunteers drawn from Anglo-Scottish regiments and banners proclaiming the motto 'for the Protestant religion and liberties in England'. Then came the Dutch army. Dutch stadtholder William called himself 'William of Orange' – Orange being a tiny independent sovereignty in France – better to play the part of an independent Protestant sovereign prince at the head of an international liberation force coming to rescue England from a Catholic tyrant. It worked. James fled the country and William ascended the throne with his consort, Mary, without a shot having been fired.

Babbacombe Model Village
Hampton Avenue;
t (01803) 315315;
www.babbacombemodel
village.co.uk; open
Nov–Feb 10–3.30, Mar and
Oct 10–4, Apr–May
10–4.30, June–Aug
10–9.30, Sept 10–9; adm

Bygones
Fore Street, Marychurch;
t (01803) 316874;
www.bygones.co.uk; open
Nov–Jan 10–4, Feb–March
10–5, April–Oct 10–6; adm

Kent's Cavern Showcaves
The Caves, Wellswood;
t (01803) 215136;
www.kents-cavern.co.uk;
open 10–4.30; adm £8.50

Living Coasts
Beacon Quay, Torquay;
t (01803) 202470;
www.livingcoasts.org.uk;
open daily 10–6; adm
£6.75

pebble and sand **Medfleet Beach**. However, the best beach in the area is probably at **Babbacombe**, about two miles from Torquay harbour on the Babbacombe Road. Follow the signs, park up where you can, and then hop aboard the funicular railway, which will take you down to the sand and shingle beach. Note, that owing to the high iron content in the surrounding rocks, many of Torbay's beaches have a reddish hue which can, in wet weather, stain light-coloured clothing.

The resort boasts a number of family attractions. At **Babbacombe Model Village** you can wander past an array of miniature landmarks from across the globe including Stonehenge and the Statue of Liberty. There are four acres of 1:12-scale models to explore, featuring thatched villages, Tudor and Georgian buildings, a celebrity banquet, a 1,200-feet model railway and even a nudist beach, all enhanced by sound and lighting effects and touch-screen computer boards. Cheesy but fun.

Bygones is a replica Victorian street with an ironmonger's, a grocer's, a forge and a sweetshop, as well as a reconstructed First World War trench, a 1950s shopping arcade and a giant model railway.

There are stalactites and stalagmites galore in **Kent's Cavern Showcaves**, a well-presented, albeit rather eerie, archaeological site. Guided tours take you deep into the heart of the complex, where you can see illuminated dioramas showing how prehistoric cave-dwellers used to live. In July and August you can take spooky evening tours by candlelight.

Another family-friendly attraction, **Living Coasts** is a coastal zoo to the east of the harbour where you can watch penguins, puffins and seals swimming underwater and walk beneath free-flying birds in a huge aviary. The café has one of the best views in Torquay.

Paignton

A quieter, slightly less touristy version of Torquay, Paignton has much the same look as its neighbour without quite the same gloss. Its harbour is smaller and filled with working fishing boats and besides its four sandy beaches, the main attractions are the pier (with all the usual arcades, rides, cafés and restaurants) and the Zoo. There's also the outdoor **QuayWest Waterpark** on the seafront with various slides, chutes and pools where the water is heated to a constant 80°F, just along the coast at Goodrington Sands. The pleasant thatched village of **Cockington**, surrounded by over 180 acres of gardens, lies on coast back towards Torquay.

QuayWest Waterpark
Goodrington Sands;
t (01803) 555550;
www.quaywest.co.uk;
open May, July and Aug
10–6, June and Sept
11–5; adm £10.95

Paignton and Dartmouth Steam Railway
Queen's Park Station, Torbay Road; t (01803) 555872; www.paignton-steamrailway.co.uk; open April–Oct, plus 'Santa Specials' in Dec; adm train only £9, train and ferry £11, train, ferry and riverboat £17.50

Paignton Zoo Environmental Park
Totnes Road; t (01803) 697500; www.paigntonzoo. org.uk; open summer daily 10–6; winter daily 10–dusk; adm £11.35

Paignton and Dartmouth Steam Railway offers seven-mile steam train rides along the Torbay coast and up the River Dart estuary to Kingswear, where you can catch a ferry to Dartmouth and then, if you're still in a sightseeing mood, a riverboat up the River Dart to Totnes.

Paignton Zoo Environmental Park is a conservation-conscious zoo where the animals – of whom there are over 1,200, including gorillas, orangutans, giraffes, tigers, lions, crocodiles and elephants – live in carefully designed 'themed' enclosures: 'Wetland', 'Forest', 'Savannah', 'Desert' etc., in which they are encouraged to act in as natural a way as possible. For instance, rather than have their meals simply handed to them, the lizards and birds of the desert zone have to root out worms stuffed into an artificial termite mound. Information boards emphasize the important conservation work carried out by the zoo – in 2009, one of the zoo's rare Sumatran tigers gave birth to four cubs. There's a full programme of keeper talks and feeding displays.

Brixham

Brixham is first and foremost a working town, not a tourist resort, with a gritty, hard-bitten edge to it that comes as a refreshing change to the tourist-orientated commerce of the rest of the bay. Brixham's economy is still largely dependent on the daily catch from the fishing boats in the harbour. With around 140 small boats and 40 big trawlers harvesting the local waters, this is still the UK's third largest fishing port. You can buy fresh fish all along the quayside, which is also popular with local artists who set up here in their droves in summer to capture the picturesque scenes as the fishing fleet goes about its business.

Golden Hinde
The Quay; t 08700 118700; open daily 10–6; adm £5.50

The **Golden Hinde**, a reconstruction of the surprisingly small 16th-century ship on which Sir Francis Drake became the first Briton to sail around the world, stands by the harbour. It's open to visitors in summer when you can tour its tiny rooms and decks. You'll also find a statue on the harbour commemorating William of Orange's landing here in 1688 on his mission to seize the English throne (*see* p.128).

Brixham Heritage Museum
The Old Police Station, New Road; t (01803) 856267; www.brixhamheritage. org.uk; open Feb–Oct Tues–Fri 10–4, Sat 10–1; adm £2

Back from the water's edge, Brixham is a very pretty town of colourful houses that seem to occupy every square inch of hillside. The small **Brixham Heritage Museum**, housed in an old police station, can fill you in on the town's maritime history, with displays on smuggling, defences during Napoleonic Wars and the lives of local trawlermen.

Brixham has three attractive sand and shingle beaches, including **Shoalstone Beach**, which has a seawater swimming pool.

(i) **Beer**
Nearest tourist office in Seaton, just west along the coast, Harbour Road Car Park, t (01297) 21660, www.seatontic.com

Where to Stay and Eat on the South Devon Coast

Sidmouth

The Hotel Riviera, The Esplanade, t (01395) 515201, *www.hotelriviera.co.uk* (*luxury*). Behind iron railings and potted palm trees, this is Sidmouth's most attractive seafront hotel, with traces of its former Georgian elegance in its 27 bedrooms.

The Belmont Hotel, The Esplanade, t (01395) 512555, *www.brend-hotels.co. uk/ TheBelmont* (*very expensive– luxury*). One of an attractive group of red-brick Regency and Georgian buildings around the cricket field, in period décor. Very stylish.

The Victoria Hotel, The Esplanade, t (01395) 512651, *www.brend-hotels.co. uk/TheVictoria* (*very expensive*). Sibling of the Belmont, its sunny lounge is

(i) **Sidmouth**
Ham Lane,
t *(01395) 516441,*
www.visitsidmouth.co.uk

(i) **Exmouth**
Alexandra Terrace
t *(01395) 222299,*
www.exmouthguide.co.uk

(i) **Torquay**
Vaughan Parade,
t *(01803) 211211,*

(i) **Paignton**
Apollo Cinema
Complex, The Esplanade,
t *(01803) 211211*

(i) **Brixham**
The Old Market House,
The Quay, **t** *(01803) 211211,*

(★) **The Osborne**
Hotel >

decorated with old prints of Sidmouth. It boasts an indoor and outdoor pool and a putting green.
The Royal Glen Hotel, Glen Road, **t** (01395) 513221, *www.royalglenhotel.co.uk* (*expensive*). Old-fashioned Regency hotel, 100 yards back from the Esplanade. Baby Queen Victoria spent her first Christmas here in 1819 with the Duke of Kent, who later died here. Plenty of classy touches, including an indoor pool.

Clock Tower Tea Room, Connaught House, Peak Hill Rd, **t** (01395) 512477 (*budget*). An attractive mock castle and clock tower with walled gardens, this serves tea, coffee, sandwiches, cakes and cream teas, as well as hot dishes such as lasagne.

Torquay

The Osborne Hotel, Hesketh Crescent, **t** (01803) 213311, *www.osborne-torquay.co.uk* (*very expensive*). This lies on the sea with perfect views, around the corner and over the hill from Torquay harbour, 10 minutes' walk into town. With two **restaurants** – a brasserie and an à la carte (*moderate*).

Barceló Torquay Imperial Hotel, Park Hill Road, **t** (01803) 294301, *www.barcelo-hotels.co.uk* (*moderate-expensive*). This grand Victorian survivor was recently bought out by the Barceló chain. Offers all-inclusive packages – accommodation, all meals and drinks for £499 for five days per person. Its wealth of facilities include two **restaurants**, two pools and tennis and squash courts.

Number 7 Fish Bistro, Beacon Terrace, **t** (01803) 295055, *www.no7-fish.com* (*moderate*). Smallish, family-run

seafood bistro with simple, bright décor and fresh fish on the menu. *Open lunch all year Wed–Sat, dinner winter Tues–Sat, summer daily.*

Brixham

The Quayside Hotel, King Street, **t** (01803) 855751, *www.quaysidehotel.co.uk* (*expensive*). Friendly terracotta-painted hotel in six 18th-century fishermen's cottages with 29 bedrooms and an excellent seafood restaurant. Lunches in the bar, evening meals in the restaurant.

The Poop Deck, 14 The Quay, **t** (01803) 858681, *www.poopdeckrestaurant.com* (*budget–moderate*). One of several long-established restaurants around the quay specializing in locally caught seafood, including lobster, mullet and mussels, served in an informal bistro style.

Entertainment on the South Devon Coast

Babbacombe Theatre, Cary Point, Babbacombe Down, **t** (01803) 328385. Small, old-fashioned variety theatre, two miles outside of Torquay up the Babbacombe Road from the harbour.

The Princess Theatre, Torbay Road, Torquay, **t** (01803) 290288, *www.princesstheatre.org.uk*. Large modern theatre (1500 seats) hosting touring productions of West End musicals, glitzy operas, popular ballets and mainstream drama. Two or three weeks a year Torbay's local amateur groups put on shows. Large bar and **restaurant**. The 'summer show' starts in February and ends in October, then the Christmas variety show begins.

Dartmouth

(2) **Dartmouth**

Royal Britannia
Naval College
t *(01803) 832141,*
www.royalnavy.mod.uk

There's no denying it, Dartmouth is a beauty. Set on a wide, gleaming estuary, encased in a bowl of verdant hills, with a harbour bobbing with boats – everything from yachts and trawlers to rowboats and even the occasional liner – it has views that have graced a thousand postcards. Its charming, narrow streets, where naval cadets stride stiffly in crisp and polished uniforms, weave their way up a wooded hillside. You can see the cadets' renowned school, the **Royal Britannia Naval College**, with its distinctive red-brick clocktower from

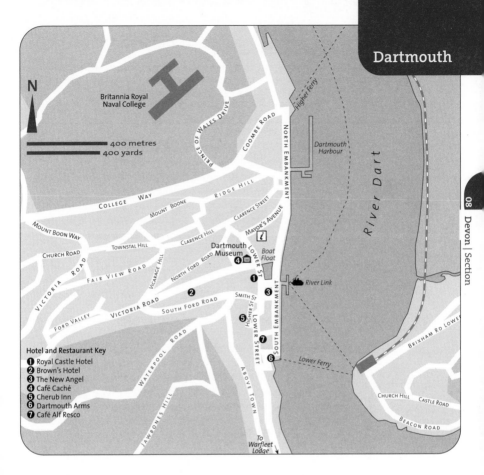

Hotel and Restaurant Key

1 Royal Castle Hotel
2 Brown's Hotel
3 The New Angel
4 Café Caché
5 Cherub Inn
6 Dartmouth Arms
7 Café Alf Resco

most points of the town. Built in the late 19th century, its long, thin shape was intended by the architect Sir Aston Webb to be reminiscent of a ship in sail. A highly prestigious academy, it has been attended by every male heir to the throne in the 20th and 21st centuries. Tours are available in the Easter and summer holidays.

The town's seafront is a long, gleaming line of Victorian buildings built on land reclaimed from a tidal creek. Along its length kiosks advertise sightseeing boat trips up the river Dart (*see* below). Look out for the Boat Float marina about halfway down, which is linked to the estuary by a tunnel running under the embankment. Just behind stands **Butterwalk**, a row of charmingly warped and wonky-looking 17th-century houses built by a wealthy Newfoundlound merchant. One of the houses contains the **Dartmouth Museum** , which retells the town's salty history with plenty of nautical paraphernalia and an exhibition of model boats.

There are few other formal attractions, but it's a great place to wander and explore, with its narrow lanes filled with elegantly carved facades and tumbling flower boxes, behind which lies a quirky

Dartmouth Museum

The Butterwalk,
t (01803) 832923,
www.devonmuseums.
net/dartmouth,
open year round
10am–3/4/4.30pm
depending on season
Mon–Sat; adm £1.50

Getting to and around Dartmouth

If you are coming to Dartmouth by **car** from Torquay you will have to finish the journey on the **car ferry** over the River Dart from Kingswear, or go inland via Totnes. The nearest **railway** station is Totnes, which links up with mainline services from London Paddington and Bristol. Regular **buses** run from Totnes to Dartmouth. If you catch a train to Torquay, you can continue by steam train and then the ferry over the Dart.

Dartmouth Castle
*t (01803) 833588;
www.english-
heritage.org.uk; open
Apr–Jun and Sept daily
10–5, Jul–Aug daily
10–6, Oct 10–4,
Nov–Mar Sat and Sun
10–4; adm £4.20*

collection of craft shops, upmarket boutiques and fancy restaurants. If you fancy stretching your legs, you can walk south along the river to Bayard's Cove where in 1620 the *Mayflower* and *Speedwell* stopped off for repairs en route to Plymouth, and ultimately America. Alternatively, you could take the ferry (every 15 mins, £1.20) from South Embankment to **Dartmouth Castle**, a well-preserved 14th-century fortress standing guard at the mouth of the Dart Estuary, around a mile southeast of town. It's fun to tour its battlements and there are good walks in the surrounding woods.

Boat Trips

ferry
*t 0781 8001108;
www.dartmouth
dittishamferry.co.uk;
open 10–5 every half
hour; £7 return*

**Dartmouth Boat
Hire Centre**
*t (01803) 834600;
www.dartmouth-boat-
hire.co.uk; from £30 p.h.*

Greenway Ferry
*t 0845 489 0418;
www.greenwayferry.
co.uk; adm £6*

River Link
*t (01803) 834488;
www.pdsr.co.uk; daily
Apr–Oct; journey 1 1/2
hours; adm boat only
£10; train only £9, train
and ferry £11, train, ferry
and riverboat £17.50*

⭐ **The New
Angel >>**

There are plenty of options, from the **ferry** that links Dartmouth with the little town of Dittisham across the river to hiring a self-drive motorboat or chartering a skippered yacht for a little impromptu exploration in local waters from **Dartmouth Boat Hire Centre** at the North Embankment. The **Greenway Ferry** links the town with Greenway, the sumptuous holiday home and gardens of Agatha Christie (*see* box, p.127). However, the most pleasant choice is to take a cruise up the river Dart to Totnes and back with **River Link**, whose boats line up at the South Embankment. It's also possible to do a combined river and steam train journey to Paignton (*see* p.129).

Festivals in Dartmouth

The Port of Dartmouth Regatta,
*t (01803) 834912, www.dartmouth
regatta.co.uk*. Takes place over three days including the last Friday in August, but there are activities all week including a fair, displays by the Red Arrows, market stalls along the Embankment and the Regatta Ball in Coronation Park.

The **Dart Music Festival** (*www.dart
musicfestival.co.uk*) takes place over three days in May, with a variety of music including rock, salsa, classical, flamenco and pop tribute acts. The main venues are pubs and gardens.

Where to Stay and Eat in Dartmouth

The Royal Castle Hotel, 11 The Quay, *t (01803) 833033, www.royalcastle.co. uk* (*very expensive*). An inn since the 17th century, the Royal Castle is much older than the Victorian castle façade. It boasts a cosy flagstone bar, design-er bedrooms and a good seafood **restaurant** overlooking the river.

The New Angel, 2 South Embankment, *t (01803) 839425, www.thenewangel. co.uk* (*expensive*). Run by celebrity chef, John Burton Race, this glass-fronted restaurant overlooking the estuary serves classic Michelin-starred French/English cuisine, including 'hand-dived' Start Bay scallops, poached Dartmouth lobster and line-caught sea bass.

(i) **Dartmouth**
The Engine House,
Mayors Avenue,
t (01803) 834224,
www.discoverdartmouth.
com; open Mon–Sat
9.30–5, Easter–Sept also
Sun 10am–4pm

Browns Hotel Dartmouth, 27–29 Victoria Rd, **t** (01803) 832572, *www.brownshoteldartmouth.co.uk* (*moderate–expensive*). Comfortable, recently renovated townhouse hotel with stylish décor and a decent Mediterranean restaurant and bar.

Café Caché, 24 Duke Street, **t** (01803) 833804 (*moderate*). Zingy Mediterannean-style restaurant and café serving lunches and dinners of smoked prawns and spicy baby squid and rice. *Closed Sun in winter.*

The Cherub Inn, Higher Street, **t** (01803) 832571, *http://the-cherub. co.uk* (*moderate*).Beamy old pub, dating back to the 14th century, with tiny windows and little fire-lit rooms. Eat in the upstairs restaurant or at the bar from a menu including venison and locally caught scallops.

The Ship in Dock Inn, Ridge Hill, **t** (01803) 839614, *http://theshipindock inn.co.uk* (*moderate*). On the corner of Coronation Park, about 50 yards from the centre, looking out over the River Dart, the Ship in Dock is friendly with a snug bar and five small rooms.

Warfleet Lodge, Warfleet Road, **t** (01803) 834352 (*moderate*). Victorian-Gothic house set above the road behind battlements. It used to belong to Sir Charles Freake, who moved in royal circles and once had Prince Edward VII to stay. Dark wood panelling, a grand staircase and gargoyles on the posts. Three lovely big bedrooms and views over the river. It's a ten-minute walk into town.

Dartmouth Arms, Bayards Cove, **t** (01803) 832903, *www.dartmouth arms inn.co.uk* (*budget–moderate*). Delightful old pub on the water's edge, backed up against a great retaining wall. It's particularly popular with young naval officers, and serves great home-made pizzas (*£5.80–9*).

Café Alf Resco, Lower Street, **t** (01803) 835880, *www.cafealfresco.co.uk* (*budget*). Murals and burning torches enliven the patio of this ever popular 'fusion café'. Big breakfasts, good coffee and grilled open sandwiches. It also offers a self-catering apartment above the café (*moderate*).

Totnes

About 12 miles inland of Dartmouth, on the banks of the River Dart, Totnes has a long-established reputation for eco-friendliness. The town also has a bit of a love affair going on with the Elizabethan era, probably as a result of its architectural heritage. Founded in the Middle Ages, Totnes still has many well-maintained 16th-century buildings remaining in an atmospheric part of town known as the Narrows. The **museum** is housed in a four-storey Elizabethan merchant's house. Displays range from an exhibition on life in Elizabethan times, with period furniture, costumes, and even toys, to a room devoted to the inventor and local resident Charles Babbage, who created the world's first mechanical adding machine, a sort of proto-computer. The nearby **Devonshire Collection of Period Costume**, which also occupies a 16th-century building, holds a constantly changing collection of antique clothes, including a number of Tudor items. During the summer, some Tuesday market stallholders even don Elizabethan dress to entertain tourists.

museum
70 Fore Street;
t (01803) 863821; open
Easter–Oct Mon–Fri
10.30–5; adm £2

Devonshire
Collection of
Period Costume
Bogan House, 43 High
Street, t (01803) 862857;
open March–Oct
Tues–Fri 11–5; adm £2

Other attractions include an 11th-century guildhall (still in use), where you can visit the former medieval jail cells and courtroom.

There are plenty of interesting places within easy reach of the town. Dartmoor and the English Riviera are just a few miles away, and

Getting to and around Totnes

By Car, Train or Coach

Totnes is 6 miles from Torbay on the A361, and 24 miles southwest of Exeter via the A38 Plymouth road and the A384, which leads into town. There are good **rail** links with Plymouth and Exeter, as well as London Paddington. The South Devon Railway Trust also operates a seasonal steam train between Totnes and Buckfastleigh which jogs along 7 1/2 miles of the River Dart between Totnes and Buckfastleight (*see* p.136).

National Express **coaches** from Exeter and London stop here, as do local buses from Exeter

By Boat

River Link operates the River Dart ferry between Totnes and Dartmouth. A round robin ticket takes you to Dartmouth by **ferry** but gives you a choice of route back: via the foot ferry to Kingswear, catching a steam train from Kingswear to Paignton (*see* p.129) and returning to Totnes on an open-top double decker sightseeing bus, stopping off, if you want, at Agatha Christie's Greenway Gardens, opposite Dittisham on the north bank of the River Dart. Once you've bought your ticket, you can start your journey at any point; t (01803) 834488; *www.pdsr.co.uk*; daily Apr–Oct; adm boat only £10; train only £9, train and ferry £11, train, ferry and riverboat £17.50.

Canoe Adventures
t (01803) 865301;
www.canoeadventures.
co.uk; April–Oct; from £19

Totnes provides numerous ways of exploring the **River Dart**: in a 12-seater canoe with **Canoe Adventures**; aboard a River Link sightseeing boat (*see* above), or along the riverbanks aboard one of the steam trains of the South Devon Railway (*see* p.136), which runs from Totnes through seven miles of delightful Dart Valley countryside to the **Buckfast Butterflies and Dartmoor Otter Sanctuary**. Otter feeding times are 11.30am, 2pm, 4pm.

Buckfast Butterflies
and Dartmoor
Otter Sanctuary
The Station,
Buckfastleigh,
t (01364) 642916,
www.ottersandbutterflies
.co.uk, open daily
10am–5p,; adm £7.25,
joint ticket with South
Devon Railway, £15.40

Berry Pomeroy Castle

Said to be the most haunted castle in England (but then, aren't they all?), Berry Pomeroy lies in ruins atop a wooded crag close to the River Dart around 2.5 miles east of Totnes off the A385. The building itself is a combination of a medieval castle and a Tudor mansion. When Edward Seymour, brother of Jane Seymour, third wife of Henry VIII, bought it in the mid-16th century from Sir Thomas de Pomeroy – the first Duke of Somerset and the Lord Protector during the reign of Edward VI – the castle had already been home to 19 generations of de Pomeroys. That's a lot of potential ghosts.

Berry Pomeroy
Castle
t (01803) 866618;
www.english-
heritage.org.uk; open
daily Apr–June & Sept
10–5, July–Aug 10–6; Oct
10–4; adm £4.20

In the late 16th and early 17th centuries, the building was greatly expanded as the Seymours attempted to turn it into the grandest house in all Devon. They failed. In fact by end of the 1600s it had been abandoned, and most of contents stripped out. Today it's an atmospheric place with plenty of space for picnics. Events, including medieval tournaments, are organized here in summer.

Totnes Castle

Totnes Castle
Castle Street;
t (01803) 864406;
www.english-heritage.
org.uk; open Apr–June &
Sept daily 10–5, July–Aug
daily 10–6; Oct daily
10–4; adm £3

Sat like a giant stone crown atop a steep (practically vertical in places) man-made hill, the Norman castle keep offers great views over the town, and is well worth an hour or so's clambering time. It was erected shortly after the Norman Conquest, but abandoned after the Civil War. Most of the current structure is the result of a 13th-century renovation. Medieval themed events – cooking, music, mask-making etc. – are put on here throughout the year.

Dartington Hall

⭐ Dartington
Hall
*2 miles northwest of
Totnes, on the A385, and
just off the A38,*
t (01803) 847070
www.dartington.org

This large country house on the outskirts of Totnes, which contains medieval, Tudor, Georgian and 20th-century elements, may look peaceful, serene and, above all, traditionally English, but for a few decades in the mid-20th century it was the epicentre of an extraordinary social experi-ment, the aim of which was nothing less than a reinvention of artistic, industrial, educational and rural practices in Britain – no mean agenda.

The people behind this ambitious scheme were Leonard and Dorothy Elmhirst. He came from a well-to-do landowning family in Yorkshire. She was one of America's wealthiest women, thanks to a fortune inherited from her famed financier father William C. Whitney. Together they embarked on a programme of 'rural reconstruction', based on ideas formulated by Leonard during time spent working in rural India. They bought the, then derelict, medieval Dartington Hall to act as their headquarters and template for their plans. In essence their big idea was to put rural living back at heart of British society. Cities, they felt, had taken over, and yet in their opinion many of the most important aspects of society – including the arts, industry and education – flourished better in a rural setting than an urban one. At Dartington they would attempt to redress the balance by creating a synthesis of traditional rural crafts and modern production methods (not to mention modernist aesthetics). They revitalized the estate, planting orchards and wood-lands, and setting up a farm employing the latest farming techniques – such as a new-fangled method of artificial insemination imported from Russia. They built a sawmill, a textile mill, a cider-making plant and a pottery studio. They started a building company, which soon became the largest in the southwest, and established a charity which funded arts festivals and music schools. Perhaps most notably, they founded a school employing ultra-modern teaching methods, where 'natural' creativity was encouraged and formal lessons frowned upon. The venture attracted support from many of the leading artistic lights of the day, including Barbara Hepworth (who sent her children to the school), the modernist architect William Lescaze, and the potter Bernard Leach.

The school was initially a great success (the painter Lucien Freud is one of its more celebrated alumni), but as time went on began to adopt a more conservative, traditional ethos, contrary to its original remit, just at the time when mainstream state-sponsored education was becoming more progressive. The more it moved away from its progressive mandate, the less popular it became. Pupil numbers dwindled and in 1987 it was forced to close its doors. Many of the other businesses set up by the couple also foundered as time went on, most winding up after the couple's death (she in 1968, he in 1974). The Dartington College of Arts proved more successful but is too due to close in 2010 and merge with the University of Falmouth. However, the Dartington Hall Charity continues to operate and fund causes, including the Dartington International Summer School and the Dartington Arts Centre which stages a full programme of arts events throughout the year.

Parts of the estate are open to the public today, including the lavish gardens, which were landscaped by the renowned architect, Beatrix Ferrand (under the instruction of Dorothy Elmhirst), and contain sculptures by Henry Moore. The first part of the complex you come to is the former **Dartington Cider Press Centre**, now a complex of 12 shops and two restaurants housed in a group of 16th- and 17th-century buildings. The shops sell a diverse (and very Dartington) range of goods, including aromatherapy oils, kitchenware, books, toys, sweets, plants and local cheeses. From the centre head up the A384, turn right at the church and follow the signs for **High Cross House**. Built in 1932, this ultra-modern building, all gleaming rectangles of blue and white set in a lush, green country setting, pretty much symbolizes what the Elmhirsts were all about. It was designed to provide accommodation for Dartington School's headmaster and today is home to the Elmhirsts' art collection, which includes works by such renowned British artists as Ben and Winifred Nicholson, Alfred Wallis and Christopher Wood.

Further along the drive is the bathetic sight of Dartington Hall itself. The one-time beacon of social radicalism and progressive politics now enjoys a slightly less revolutionary role as a hotel, conference centre and restaurant.

Dartington Cider Press Centre
t (01803) 847500; www.dartingtoncider press.co.uk; open Mon–Sat 9.30–5.30; Sun 10.30–4.30; adm free

High Cross House
t (01803) 864114; www.dartingtonarchive .org.uk; open May–Sept Tues–Fri 2–4.30, also 10.30–12.30 school hols; adm £3.50

South Devon Railway

Also known as the 'Primrose Line', this offers seven-mile steam train rides alongside the otherwise inaccessible banks of the River Dart between Totnes and Buckfastleigh. It is one of the best railways in the country for observing and encountering animals, with herons, swans and kingfishers all living on or around the river and a nationally renowned otter and butterfly sanctuary at Buckfastleigh (*see* p.134).

South Devon Railway
Buckfastleigh Station, t 0845 345 1466; www.southdevonrailway. org; open most days from Apr–Oct; Santa Specials Dec; adm £9.90

ⓘ **Totnes**
The Town Mill, Coronation Road, t (01803) 863168, www.totnesinformation. co.uk; open Apr–Oct Mon–Fri 9.30–5, Sat 10–4, Nov–March Mon–Fri 10–4, Sat 10–1

Markets in Totnes

There is an old-fashioned market in the Civic Square on Friday and Saturday, selling organic produce and a farmer's market is held every fourth Saturday in the Civic Hall. The small Elizabethan Market takes place May–Sept on Tuesdays in the Civic Square, selling home-made wares.

Festivals and Events in Totnes

Intriguing events that take place in Totnes include the **August Orange Race**, organized by the Elizabethan Society, commemorating a visit to the town by Francis Drake when, apparently, he presented a local boy with an orange (then a rare and exotic treat). The **October Raft Race** takes place on the first Sunday of the month when home-made craft race down a nine-mile stretch of river between Buckfastleigh and Totnes.

Way With Words, a ten-day literature festival, takes place at Dartington Hall in mid-July, featuring 200 speakers – writers, actors, politicians and celebrities – and more than 100 events. It's particularly strong on non-fiction. For more information, call t (01803) 867373, *www.wayswithwords.co.uk*.

The **International Summer School and Music Festival**, lasting five weeks, follows on from the literature festival at Dartington and features a number of high-calibre classical, jazz and rock concerts, t (01803) 847070, *www.dart ington.org/summer-school*.

Where to Stay and Eat in Totnes

The Royal Seven Stars Hotel, The Plains, t (01803) 862125, *www.royal sevenstars.co.uk (expensive)*. The Seven Stars occupies a 17th-century coaching inn – its glassed-over flagstone yard serves as the reception area – within which are 16 snazzily decorated en suite bedrooms and a decent restaurant.

King William IV, 45 Fore Street, **t** (01803) 866689, *www.kingwilliam theiv.co.uk* (*moderate*). A handsome bow-fronted pub serving sturdy, workmanlike fare with five, simple clean bedrooms, all en suite with TVs and tea-making facilities.

Sharpham, Sharpham Estate, **t** (01803) 732203, *www.sharpham.com* (*moderate*). Vineyard and dairy a 3-mile walk south of Totnes, offering talks, tastings and a fabulous café serving locally sourced organic fare (asparagus, red pepper & Sharpham Brie tarts, organic char-griddled salmon with dill crème fraiche etc.) and an al fresco dining area with views out over the River Dart.

The Elbow Room, North Street, **t** (01803) 863480, *www.theelbowroom totnes.co.uk* (*moderate*). A centuries-old barn conversion B&B in a cluster of townhouses at the foot of Totnes Castle with two attractive bedrooms and a lovely first-floor lounge decorated with wooden elephants, as well as a self-contained apartment with two bedrooms, a kitchen and views out over the town.

The Old Forge, Seymour Place, **t** (01803) 862174, *www.oldforgetotnes. com* (*moderate*). Old stone building dating back to the 15th century with a cobbled yard and ten lovely bedrooms. Breakfast is served in a conservatory adjoining the garden at the rear. Very friendly owners and decently priced.

Grey's Tea Shop, 96 High Street, **t** (01803) 866369 (*budget*). Traditional tearoom with a lovely, enticing window display. Inside you're confronted with a wonderful selection of cakes (all made fresh on the premises), teas and coffees, as well as light lunch options.

Ticklemore Fish Shop, 10 Ticklemore Street, **t** (01803) 867805 (*budget*). Seafood sandwiches, a pot of cockles, a seafood cocktail or fresh peeled prawns. Produce arrives fresh daily from Brixham and Plymouth harbourside making it a great staple for self-caterers.

Willow Vegetarian Garden Restaurant, 87 High Street, **t** (01803) 862605, *www. restaurant-guide.com* (*budget*). Hugely popular vegetarian café with a sunny garden and a notice board plastered with details of every sort of holistic happening. Menu favourites include falafel, and mushroom crumble. Regular live music.

Entertainment in Totnes

The Barn, Dartington Hall, **t** (01803) 847070, *www.dartington.org/arts*. The Barn Theatre and Cinema hosts numerous concerts, art installations and events, including Dartington International Summer School Concerts, and the Totnes Short Film Festival.

(★) Willow Vegetarian Garden Restaurant >>

(★) The Old Forge >

South to Salcombe

South of Torbay and Dartmouth the coastline is generally much less developed than its northern counterpart. The A379 coastal road is one of the most spectacular in the region, climbing its way over high cliffs and through rolling fields. Leaving Dartmouth, you soon find yourself at **Start Bay**, which begins at Stoke Fleming and continues for another ten miles to Start Point. Just south of Stoke Fleming is one of the area's most spectacular beaches, **Blackpool Sands**. A crescent of clean, white, soft sand hemmed in by thick woods, the beach has an almost tropical island feel to it (in summer at least). Widely acknowledged as one of Devon's most beautiful beaches, it is also officially one of the cleanest, and has the European Blue Flag to prove it. Unfortunately, although it may once have been secluded and unspoilt, its reputation has grown in recent years and in summer it can get rather crowded. Windsurfing lessons are offered between May and September.

Getting to Salcombe

Salcombe is on the South Devon coast on the A381 and linked by regular **buses** to Kingsbridge and Plymouth.

Continuing south, the road hugs the coastline only as far as Torcross before heading inland to some charming rural towns and villages, such as Kingsbridge, a cheery market town. South of here you can reach the coast by car via a series of narrow interconnecting lanes or, if walking (the most scenic option), along the coastal path. En route you'll pass a number of interesting sights, including the abandoned houses of **South Hallands**, a ghostly Mary-Celeste village perched on the clifftops. Until the early 20th century this was a bustling and successful fishing village. However, a savage storm in 1917 destroyed most of the town, ripping the houses apart and washing them out to sea. Its effects were exacerbated by the local building industry having dredging the beach just before, removing a vital protective barrier. Thankfully none of the residents were killed. You're free to explore amid the ghostly ruins – there's a display showing what the town looked like before the disaster.

Slapton Ley National Nature Reserve
t (01548) 580466; www.slnnr.org.uk

The three-mile-long Slapton Sands, which despite its name is actually rather pebbly, occupies the central stretch of Start Bay, behind which lies **Slapton Ley National Nature Reserve**. Set around the region's largest lake, it provides an important nesting and feeding site for wildfowl. Guided walks are offered from the Field Study Centre. The sands were used in the Second World War as a training site during preparations for the Normandy landings. At Torcross there's a memorial to 749 American soldiers killed by U-boats during the exercises.

At the southern end of Start Bay is one of the county's most isolated **lighthouses**, which stands peering out into the lonely sea at the end of a mile-long peninsula. You can visit to get a sense of the remote life led here by lighthouse keepers before automation in 1993.

Salcombe & Around

⭐ **Salcombe**

Salcombe is like a miniature Dartmouth. There's not much of it, just a few waterside lanes and a small village hugging the steep hillside, but what's there is refined and elegant. Its upmarket boutiques and fancy restaurants pay testament to the huge influx of wealthy inhabitants who have settled here in recent years. In a particular blow to the town's winter economy, a significant proportion of these are second-home inhabitants. In one recent survey, Salcombe was estimated to have the highest property prices in the country after London and Poole.

Maritime Museum
Council Hall, Market Street; open Easter–Oct daily 10.30–12.30 and 2.30–4.30

Back in the 19th century, when Salcombe was still a proper working port, its boatyards turned out fishing vessels and super-fast schooners for the Atlantic fruit trade – they needed to be speedy to get the fruit back before it spoiled. The town's small **Maritime Museum** relates the history of its seafaring past with plenty of model boats, pictures of historic ships and finds recovered from local shipwrecks. Today, the few yards that remain are almost exclusively involved in the leisure sailing industry, servicing the yachts of the town's summer smart set. Fore

Salcombe Boat Hire
11 Clifton Place;
t (01548) 844475;
www.salcombeboat
hire.co.uk

Whitestrand Boat
Hire
Strand Court
Whitestrand Quay;
t (01548) 843818;
www.whitestrand
boathire.co.uk

South Sands
Sailing
South Sands Beach;
t (01548) 843451;
www.southsands
sailing.co.uk

Overbecks
Sharpitor;
t (01548) 842893;
www.nationaltrust.
org.uk; open Nov–Feb
Mon–Fri 11–5, Mar–June
& Sep–Oct Mon–Wed &
Sat–Sun 11–5, July–Aug
daily 11–5; adm £6.40

Street, running parallel to the front, is the place to hire yourself a yacht – and indeed get yourself kitted out in yachting clothes.

If you fancy taking to the water in something more modest, you can rent a small fibreglass motorboat for £25 an hour from **Salcombe Boat Hire** or **Whitestrand Boat Hire**. If even these are beyond your means, you may have to settle for catching the South Sands Ferry across the Kingsbridge Estuary to the fine beaches of South Sands, which costs just £5. The ferry runs every half hour and takes around 20 minutes. The small boat is guided to shore by a mechanized platform known as a 'sea tractor'. At the beach, **South Sands Sailing** offers instruction and equipment hire for surfing, catamaran sailing and sea kayaking.

Another ferry journey – this one lasting just five minutes – will take you from Ferry Steps on Fore Street to East Portlemouth where there are a string of pristine sandy beaches and coves, including Sunny Cove, Mill Bay, Cable Cove, Small's Cove and Fisherman's Cove.

There's lots of good **walking** in the wooded estuary surrounding Salcombe. One of the best, and easiest, routes is Snape Walk, which takes you on a two-mile meander around Batson Creek and down into the Kingsbridge Estuary. The Bolt Head Coastal walk is a bit more challenging, taking a dramatic and rather more intense route which passes **Overbecks** and Sharp Tor. The former was the Edwardian home of Otto Overbeck, an eccentric scientist, inventor and incorrigible collector. His home is filled with all manner of odd things: stuffed animals, dolls, and various strange musical instruments, including a Victorian polyphon, a sort of musical box that plays tunes according to a pattern of holes punched into a metal disc. Pride of place goes to a very strange device called the Rejuvenator, an invention of Overbecks that could, according to his rather outlandish claims, cure a staggering range of ailments via the administration of electric shocks. Perhaps most amazingly, the device made Overbecks a small fortune. The house, which the museum shares with the local YHA, is set in seven acres of lovely luxuriant gardens perched on cliffs overlooking the estuary. The tourist board can provide maps for both routes.

The coast **west of Salcombe** is among the most unspoilt anywhere in Devon. Its high cliffs, isolated sandy coves and tiny villages make it a great area for a leisurely drive. **Bantham**, about five miles west, has in recent years become a popular surfing destination owing to its exposed position and consistent breaks. However, it's still relatively undeveloped which means you'll probably get the beach more or less to yourself. Accommodation is available here and in the nearby villages of Hope Cove and Bigbury on Sea (*see* below).

Where to Stay around Salcombe

⭐ Burgh Island ›

Burgh Island, Bigbury-on-Sea, t (01548) 810514, *www.burghisland.com* (*luxury*). In the 1920s the smart set weekended in this glistening white Art Deco hotel on Burgh island, just west of Plymouth. Noël Coward and friends danced the Charleston in evening dress under the peacock dome of the Palm Court. Other guests included Lord Mountbatten, Edward and Mrs Simpson and Agatha Christie, who wrote *Evil under the Sun* and *And Then There were None* on the island, which also provided the settings. At low tide the island is joined to the mainland by a narrow strip of sand; at high tide, guests are ferried to and from the

(i) **Salcombe**

Council Hall, Market Street, t (01548) 843927, www.salcombeinformation.co.uk. Open summer daily 10am–5pm, winter Mon–Sat 10.30am–4pm.

(★) The Winking Prawn >>

mainland by a sea tractor. Today it offers 21 terribly stylish rooms, including 14 suites, a great **restaurant** (which aims to source 80% of its ingredients from within a 20 mile radius), a games room (with full-size billiard table), a gym and pub.

The Marine Hotel, Cliff Road, t (01548) 844444, *www.marinehotelsalcombe.com* (*very expensive*). Top class, very Salcombe hotel right on the water's edge – huge 1960s lounge with big windows and a grand piano, 53 well-equipped stylish bedrooms, a spa and pool and a rather fancy **restaurant**.

The Tides Reach Hotel, South Sands, t (01548) 843466, *www.tidesreach.com* (*expensive–very expensive*). Reachable either via a 20-minute walk from town or from the ferry, this graceful hotel is set right on the beach. The 35 rooms are comfortable, if a little generically furnished. Those at the front have great sea views. There's also a spa, an indoor pool and a good fish and seafood **restaurant**.

Ria View, Devon Road, t 07767 665321, *www.salcombebandb.co.uk* (*moderate*). A simple, friendly B&B near the front with great views over the town and water and three stylishly decorated bedrooms (two with sea views, one with garden view). *Min. stay 2 nights.*

YHA Salcombe, Sharpitor, t 0845 371 9341, *www.yha.org.uk* (*budget*). Salcombe's YHA enjoys a fantastic setting in the Edwardian property of Overbecks, overlooking the house's beautiful National Trust-maintained gardens. It's a good choice for outdoor types with the beach and coastal path in easy reach. Diners are served in the wood-panelled dining room. Dorm beds from £15.95.

Eating Out in Salcombe

Moderate

Restaurant 42, Fore Street, t (01548) 843408. This looks the part, with its tasteful, oak-floored dining room and lounge with leather sofas, and a sunny terrace with teak furniture and parasols. The food is also top quality Modern English fare with plenty of seafood choices and some delicious West Country bouillabaisse.

The Galley Restaurant, 5 Fore Street, t (01548) 842828, *www.thegalleyrestaurant.co.uk*. Excellent, freshly caught, locally sourced seafood meals: River Exe mussels, Salcombe lobster, Plymouth plaice, Brixham scallops etc. Ask for a window table.

The Victoria Inn, Fore Street, t (01548) 842604, *www.victoriainn-salcombe.co.uk*. Snug, traditional pub adorned with pictures of yachts and Queen Victoria, that's gone a bit gastro of late, now serving an expertly prepared range of lunches (cod and chips £9.95), open sandwiches (Salcombe white crabmeat £8.95), cream teas and evening meals (shellfish chowder £9.95, pork belly with grilled apple £12.95). A barbecue is served every night in summer.

Budget

Catch 55, 55 Fore Street, t (01548) 842646. Seasonal bistro serving fillet steak, burgers and pasta and a wide range of fish and seafood, including mussels, scallops, lobster and monkfish.

The Ferry Inn, Fore St, t (01548) 844000. In a prime position by the ferry, this pub has stunning views and provides an ideal spot for some idyllic outdoor eating. Good food includes local fresh fish and crab sandwiches. It's also a good place just to sit with a beer or a glass of wine watching the world drift by.

Fortescue Inn, Union St, t (01548) 842868. Good, timeless old pub near the water. It's very popular and can get very crowded, which gives it a bit of a boisterous atmosphere. Also serves a decent, simple food menu.

The Winking Prawn, North Sands, t (01548) 842 326, *www.winkingprawn.co.uk*. Relaxed waterside brasserie seemingly decorated with bits and bobs washed up on the beach. The cooking is simple and fresh tasting. From 10am–4pm you can order from a range of sandwiches and simple seafood choices, after which they serve their barbecue menu for £15.95: king prawns, cajun spiced salmon, 8 oz rib steak, fillet of chicken, halloumi cheese, accompanied by salad, new potatoes and dips, and followed by ice cream.

Plymouth

Little of interest may ever have taken place in Plymouth itself, but people are forever leaving it, to do exciting things. An important naval base for much of its history, most stories about Plymouth begin with someone setting sail away from it. In 1588, Sir Francis Drake set out from Plymouth to engage the Spanish Armada in battle (he won, having first finished his game of bowls on the Hoe, of course) and, in 1620, this was where 102 pilgrims reboarded a ship called the *Mayflower* with the intention of starting a new life in the then vast empty wilderness of North America. The ship had originally set sail from Southampton but had to stop off at Plymouth for repairs. It was anchored just in front of where the aquarium stands today. In the 18th century, Plymouth provided the base for Captain Cook's numerous journeys of discovery (to Australia, the South Seas and Antarctica) and, in the early 19th century, was the main departure point for ships transporting convicts to the penal colonies of Australia. In 1831, a young naturalist named Charles Darwin boarded the *Beagle* as part of an expedition to chart the South American coastline. It was the only foreign trip Darwin ever took, yet the discoveries he made completely changed the way we view the world.

Thanks to the attention of the Luftwaffe in the Second World War, little evidence of Plymouth's historic past survives and most of the town is of a post-war vintage, and divided into zones – a commercial zone, a civic zone, a hotel zone etc. – at the behest of some over-zealous 1950s city planners. Their desire to see the city reborn as a sort of modern interpretation of the Georgian masterpieces of John Nash the Younger saw plenty of Bath stone used, if little of their predecessors' flair. Archaic exceptions include the **Barbican**, a carefully preserved section of old buildings and narrow part-cobbled streets near the harbour and an Elizabethan captain's cottage.

Plymouth's most picturesque spot is its famous **Hoe**, the landscaped area in front of the Sound, the great basin of water formed by the combined estuaries of the Plym, Tavy and Tamar rivers. It is dotted with numerous memorials (to Drake, to the defeat of the Armada, to the airmen of the Second World War and to the Navy) and has a recon-structed red and white lighthouse, Smeaton's Tower, which you can climb for good views out over the water – it stood on Eddystone Rocks, about 20km south, until moved here in 1877. The tower overlooks Tinside Pool, a restored and rather elegant 1930s lido, which is open for bracing bathing between May and September. The domed building here, Plymouth Dome, used to hold an interactive exhibition on the city, but is currently closed. The Hoe is also the site of the city's Royal

Royal Citadel
*t (01752) 773346;
open May–Sept Tues
and Thurs guided
tours only;
adm £3.50*

Citadel, an imposing fortress built in 1666 to defend the town against a possible Dutch invasion, which has been in constant use by the military ever since. Today it is home to 29 Commando Regiment. According to local legend, the fortress's guns have special mountings, which allows them to be pointed both out to sea and towards the town itself, a precaution arising from Plymouth's rebellious reputation – it was the only town in the Southwest to be held by parliamentary forces during the Civil War. Guided tours are offered in summer.

Getting to and around Plymouth

By Car

Plymouth is 46 miles southwest of Exeter and 211 miles from London, off the A38.

By Train/Coach

There are direct **train** links with London, Exeter, Bristol and Penzance.

The **Tamar Valley Line** (t 08457 000 125, *www.firstgreatwestern.co.uk*), a 14-mile scenic branch line on the east bank of the River Tamar, passes Plymouth's dockyard and Brunel's bridge and then crosses the Tamar on the Calstock Viaduct into Cornwall heading toward the old mining village of Gunnislake. You can combine a short section with a walk (*www.carfreedaysout.com*). Calstock is a good place to break the journey; you can walk a mile uphill to Cotehele House through woods from the station. First Great Western sell a Tamar Valley Line Ranger Ticket which allows you to hop on and off the train as many times as you want during a single day for £4.40.

National Express **coaches** run a frequent service from Bristol and London Victoria.

By Boat

Passenger ferries to Spain and France depart from Millbay Docks on Grand Parade.

From Stonehouse you can get the Cremyll foot ferry, t (01752) 822105, *www.tamarcruising.com*, to Mount Edgcumbe House (*see* p.145). It is a good walk along the coastal path to the pretty villages of Kingsand and Cawsand, from where you can catch a ferry back to Plymouth. For other boat trips, *see* p.144.

The Barbican

The Barbican, originally a small fort built to protect the harbour in 14th century, is today the name used to describe the whole waterside area from Hoe Street to Lamby Hill, which makes up the antique core of this otherwise rather modern city. Its narrow cobbled streets are lined with Tudor and Jacobean buildings, many now turned into shops, cafés and bars. On West Pier, you can see the Mayflower Steps (not the actual steps, but ones in the same position) and a plaque commemorating the pioneers' journey in 1620. Other plaques pay tribute to some of the other remarkable voyages to have departed from here, including Captain Cook's voyage to Australia and Humphrey Gilbert's founding of the first American colony in the name of Elizabeth I in 1583.

National Marine Aquarium

*National Marine Aquarium
Rope Walk, Coxside;
t (01752) 600301;
www.national-aquarium.co.uk; open
Apr–Sept daily 10–6;
Oct–Mar daily 10–5; adm*

Built at a cost of some £15 million, next to city's fish market, this has one of the country's best aquatic displays with a freshwater pool, a British coastal pool, a tropical pool, a huge Atlantic reef tank, a shark theatre, Europe's largest collection of seahorses and a Discovery Pool where you can stroke some long-suffering rays. Daily talks and presentations on sharks and rock-pool rambles are given and you can watch divers descend into the Deep Reef to feed hundreds of fish by hand. The aquarium café overlooks the Barbican and Plymouth Sound.

Plymouth Gin Distillery

*Plymouth Gin Distillery
Black Friars Distillery;
60 Southside St;
t (01752) 665292;
www.plymouthgin.com;
open Mon–Sat
10.30–4.30, Sun
11.30–3.30; adm £6*

In the mid-18th century gin was by far the most popular alcoholic drink in Britain, its sales fare outstripping those of beer. There were more than 7,000 gin shops in London alone where consumption of the spirit was blamed for outbreaks of lawlessness and public debauchery,

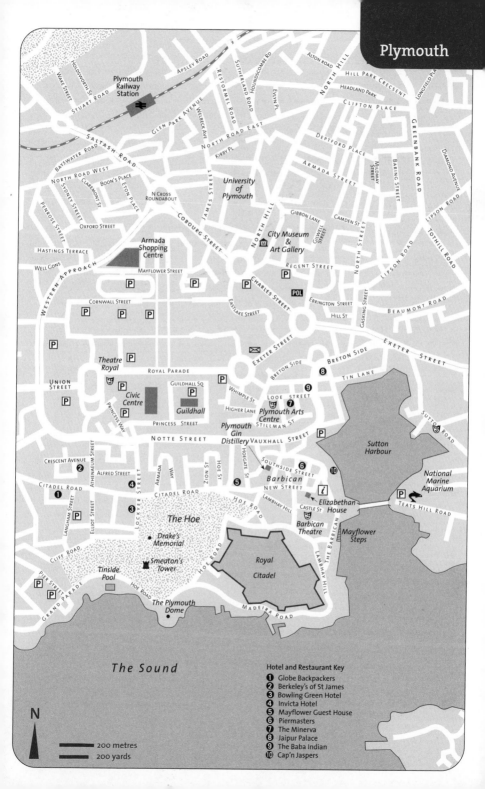

leading the government to tighten the laws governing its production and sale. This distillery, which opened in 1793 in a former Dominican monastery (known as the Black Friars Distillery), helped take the drink's repuation in a more upmarket direction, aided by the Royal Navy who set sail around world from Plymouth with cupboards full of the stuff.

From mother's ruin, the drink is now so highly thought of that Plymouth Gin has been given special protected geographical status, like champagne or Parma ham, which means it can only be made in Plymouth. You can take a tour past the stills to see the potent brew being created from seven ingredients (or 'botanicals' as the promotional blurb insists on calling them) and then test the results in the bar.

City Museum and Art Gallery

City Museum and Art Gallery
Drake Circus;
t (01752) 304774;
www.plymouth.gov.
uk/museumpcmag.htm;
open Tues–Fri 10–5.30,
Sat 10–5; adm free

The museum has displays on natural history, archaeology, world cultures and local history, the last focusing, as you'd expect, on the city's long maritime tradition. The art collection contains works by some of the city's most famous painters, including the first president of the Royal Academy, Joshua Reynolds, and that modern chronicler of the city's raucous pub life, Beryl Cook (*see* box opposite).

Elizabethan House
32 New Street, The
Barbican; t (01752)
304774; open Tues–Sat
10–5; adm

The museum also operates a couple of historic houses in the city: the **Elizabethan House**, which is furnished in the style of a 16th-century sea captain; and the **Merchant's House**, which was the 17th-century home to three of the city's mayors, and is today filled with a mishmash of historical curios: 19th-century painted shop front signs, an ancient doll's house, a ducking stool and a recreated Victorian chemist.

Merchant's House
33 St Andrew Street;
t (01752) 304774; open
Tues–Sat 10–5; adm £2

Cawsand Ferry
t (01752) 822784;
www.cawsandferry.com;
4 sailings daily 10.30am,
noon, 2.30pm & 4pm;
adm £4

Boat Trips

There's plenty of choice as you'd expect for a city with such a rich boating tradition. You can follow the first 1000th part of the Plymouth pilgrims' journey by setting sail from the Mayflower Steps on the **Cawsand Ferry** which chugs across Plymouth Sound to the Rame Peninsula, to visit former smuggling villages, Kingsand and Cawsand.

Sound Cruising
Phoenix wharf,
Madeira Road, Barbican;
t (01752) 408590;
www.soundcruising.com;
7 cruises daily 10.45–3.30;
adm £5

Alternatively, you could take a cruise with **Sound Cruising** to look at the warships of Plymouth's naval dockyard.

Around Plymouth

Buckland Abbey

Buckland Abbey
Yelverton;
t (01822) 853607
www.nationaltrust.org.uk
open Feb, Mar & Nov
Fri–Sun 11–5, March–June
& Sept–Oct Mon–Wed &
Fri–Sun 10.30–5.30,
July–Aug daily 10.30–5.30;
adm £7.40

Six miles north of Plymouth stands **Buckland Abbey**, a former monastery that was Sir Francis Drake's home from 1582, the year he became Mayor of Plymouth, until his death in 1596. It remained in the Drake family until 1946 and is today filled with Drake memorabilia, including the famous 'Drake's Drum', which is said to start beating whenever the country is under threat. Tours of the house and its extensive grounds are provided by guides in Tudor costume.

Mount Edgecumbe House

To reach Mount Edgcumbe, take the Cremyll foot ferry from Admiral's Hard in Stonehouse. Richard Edgcumbe moved his main family seat from

The Fat Lady Paints

These days, most of the Barbican's traditional pubs have been updated and refurbished; their antique clutter and stained, faded carpets stripped out and replaced with light, minimal décor. One pub that has so far resisted the lure of the modern world is the Dolphin. Its rough edges remain proudly, defiantly unsmoothed – a description that extends both to the clientele and the décor. Had you visited the pub on a Friday or Saturday night a few years back, you may well have seen an elderly couple sat by the door – the man with a pint of beer, the lady with a gin and tonic – happily taking in the atmosphere. Every once in a while the woman might have pulled out a card to quickly sketch something down, but otherwise there was nothing especially remarkable about them. The woman was Beryl Cook, perhaps the country's foremost painter of the baroque extremes of pub life, who came here with her husband almost every day for around 30 years until her death in 2008 to observe, enjoy and report.

The Dolphin and other bawdy pubs of its ilk, and the characters who drank, danced and caroused there, were the grist for Cook's paintings. Hers was a sort of folk art, recording and reproducing the social life of the city in its most exuberant and extreme forms. Her ladies were always leggy and large, squeezed into tiny dresses that strained at the seams. Her men were leering, lecherous show-offs, roaming the room armed with a wink and pinch, roaring with raucous laughter and leaping into ill-advised jigs.

Cook recorded them all in celebratory, life-affirming representations. She loved pub culture – ladies out on the pull, lads on the lash, and sought to eulogize their exploits in her gaudy saucy postcard style.

Everyone was rendered larger than life. 'I do think large is gorgeous' Cook said, also claiming that making her subjects as big as possible covered up more of the background, which she was less interested in painting. She even showed herself looking fat in self-portraits, although she was anything but.

Born in 1926 in Epsom, Surrey, Cook came to painting late in life. Indeed, she didn't pick up a brush for the first time until nearly forty and wouldn't sell her first painting until ten years later. She left school at 14, and had a succession of jobs, including a brief stint in World War II as a showgirl. In 1946 she married her childhood friend, John, and four years later they emigrated to Zimbabwe. It was here that John bought his wife a child's oil painting kit and she began to paint. She didn't take up the hobby in earnest, however, until the mid-1960s by which time they'd returned to England to run a B&B in Plymouth.

Using slabs of wood she found lying around – old doors, driftwood etc. – as her canvasses, she began to create her colourful, cacophonous creations based on her nights at the local pub. She hung them on the walls of the boarding house – ostensibly because it was cheaper than buying 'formal' decorations – where they soon began to attract the attention, and admiration, of guests. Bernard Samuels, the then director of Plymouth Arts Centre, persuaded the shy artist to put on an exhibition. It was an instant success, gaining national press coverage and leading to another, bigger exhibition at the Portal Gallery in London.

Its success allowed her to close the B&B – though the couple continued to live there – and concentrate full time on painting. Though Cook soon became one of the country's most successful and best-loved artists, she was never entirely comfortable with her success or status, always referring to herself as a 'maker of pictures' rather than an artist.

You can see examples of her work on display in the town museum and in the gallery on Southside Street. However, if you really want to get a glimpse into Cook's world, you could always pay a visit to the Dolphin itself to see her favourite subjects in action on a raucous Saturday night: 14 The Barbican, t (01752) 660876.

Mount Edgcumbe House
Cremyll, Torpoint; t (01752) 822236; www.mountedgcumbe. gov.uk; open, house: Apr–Sept Sun–Thurs 11am–4.30pm; park: daily 8am–dusk; adm £3

Cotehele House to the mouth of the estuary in 1553. His new house was supposed to have been so beautiful that the Spanish Duke of Medina Sidonia, who lead the Spanish Armada in 1588, wanted to live there after the conquest. The Spaniard didn't get it, but it was destroyed by an incendiary bomb in the Second World War. Completely rebuilt in the 1950s, **Mount Edgcumbe House** looks like a Tudor mansion, but is not; many pieces of old furniture and paintings survived, however, and are on display. The real attraction is the country park, from which you can follow the Southwest Coastal Path to the old smuggling villages of Kingsand and Cawsand at the end of the Rame Peninsula.

El Draque

Your opinion of Sir Francis Drake probably has a lot to do with where you were brought up. To the English he has always been portrayed as the greatest sea adventurer of all time, a yo-ho-hoing, global-circumnavigating, Armada-bashing hero of the Elizabethan age. Not only has his legend never faded, but at times it has taken on a near-mythic quality. The Spanish, on the other hand, view him quite differently. Drake may have won many battles for the English and brought his country much wealth. The trouble is, most of it was stolen from Spain. As such 'El Draque' has always been regarded there as little better than a pirate and a thief; a skilled thief admittedly, for whose capture the King of Spain was once willing to put up a reward of 20,000 ducats (£4 million in modern money), but a thief nonetheless.

Unusually for the time, Drake was a self-made man. Born in around 1540, the son of a humble Devon farmer, he began his nautical career aged just 13 as an apprentice on a small ship sailing between the North Sea ports. He showed such ability that when his captain died, he left his ship to Drake, then aged just 20. Less than a decade later, he was recognized as one of the best sailors of the age, bringing him to the attention of Queen Elizabeth I, who was on the lookout for recruits for her 'secret war' with Spain.

England and Spain had long been vying for control of the American continents, discovered less than a century before. Elizabeth had no desire to start a full-scale war with Spain, she just wanted to increase her influence over – and her share of wealth coming from – the New World, whilst simultaneously reducing that of her great continental rival. With the tacit approval of the Crown, Drake began attacking Spanish ships along the Central and South American coasts. Just as fast as the Spanish could loot the wealth of the Americas' indigenous populations, Drake would loot it back off them. So successful were these raids that, according to legend, on one occassion his ship was so overladen with looted booty that it almost sank.

Drake also did his fair share of adventuring. He was the first Englishman to set eyes on the Pacific and the first to sail all the way around the world aboard his trusty ship, the *Golden Hinde*, feats which saw him receive a hero's welcome upon his return to Plymouth in 1580, where he was knighted.

By 1587, Philip II, the king of Spain, had had enough of Drake's privateering. Just two years earlier, the Englishman had wreaked so much havoc in Spain's West Indian territories that the Bank of Spain went bankrupt. Philip ordered a fleet or 'Armada' be built with the intention of invading and capturing England. Drake's typically bold reaction was to sail into Cadiz harbour and set fire to the fleet, an event which became known as the 'singeing of the King of Spain's beard'. The next year, with the Spanish ships rebuilt and sailing towards England, Drake led the fight in the Channel, deliberately setting fire to English ships and then sailing them into the midst of the Spanish fleet where they caused panic, forcing the Spanish ships to retreat to deeper waters where they were caught in a storm, the 'Protestant Wind', and destroyed.

Drake's status leapt from hero to legend, fêted by the masses who bought souvenirs of his likeness by the thousand. By 1590 Drake was a very wealthy man, with a large house, Buckland Abbey, on the outskirts of Plymouth, and could have retired into a very easy private life. But he just couldn't let it lie and in the mid-1590s led yet another expedition against Spain's West Indian territories. This time, however, his luck finally ran out. He contracted a tropical fever and died. He was buried at sea in the Caribbean on 28 January 1596. Today a statue of Drake, looking suitably heroic, stands on Plymouth Hoe.

Saltram House

Saltram House

Plympton, Plymouth;
t (01752) 333500;
www.nationaltrust.org.
uk/main/w-saltram;
open Easter–Oct
Sun–Thurs house
12.30pm–6pm; kitchen,
garden and gallery
11am–6pm; adm £8.25

Saltram House is to the east of Plymouth (and just south of the A38) on the edge of the tidal estuary of the Plym. This large mid-18th-century mansion was partly built by Robert Adam for John and Lady Catherine Parker around the remains of a group of Tudor and Stuart buildings. The rooms display all the original contents, including carved gilt-wood furniture by Chippendale, a dozen portraits by Reynolds (who was born in Plymton St Maurice and often visited the house), Axminster carpets and Chinese wallpapers. The Victorian garden was laid out by the 3rd Earl, with exotic ornamental trees. The deer park was landscaped in the 18th century with vistas and follies. You can walk down the valley to Blaxton Quay, along the estuary to Saltram Point and back across the park.

Festivals and Events in Plymouth

The British Fireworks Festival (*www.britishfireworks.co.uk*) takes place over two days at the beginning of August, best viewed from the Hoe, which is also the venue for other events throughout the year, including car shows and concerts.

On alternate years, the **Royal Dockyard** (signposted off the A38) opens its doors to the public on August Bank Holiday.

Where to Stay in Plymouth

Expensive
The Duke of Cornwall Hotel, Millbay Road, t (01752) 275850, *www.theduke ofcornwallhotel.com*. Magnificent Victorian-Gothic hotel west of the Hoe with 72 'individually styled' en suite bedrooms and a good **restaurant** on the ground floor.

Moderate
Berkeley's of St. James, 4 St James Place East, The Hoe, t (01752) 221654, *www.onthehoe.co.uk*. Clean, brightly decorated and supremely friendly B&B close to the Hoe and a couple of minute's walk from the Barbican. The slightly chintzy rooms are of a good size and well equipped, and they serve up a mean full English.

Bowling Green Hotel, 9–10 Osborne Place, Lockyer Street, The Hoe, t (01752) 209090, *www.thebowlinggreen plymouth.com*. A lovely place to stay overlooking the Hoe (and the famous bowling green) boasting 12 pleasant bedrooms and a friendly atmosphere. A full English breakfast is included.

Invicta Hotel, 11–12 Osborne Place, Lockyer Street, The Hoe, t (01752) 664997, *www.invictahotel.co.uk*. Attractive family-run hotel with period-style décor in its 23 rooms. Oblique views of the Hoe are available from the front rooms. It's very clean and friendly. Prices are reasonable.

Mayflower Guest House, 209 Citadel Road East, The Hoe, t (01752) 667496, *www.mayflowerguesthouse.co.uk*. Friendly basic place to stay with smallish bedrooms, two minutes' walk from the Hoe. Doubles from £52.

ⓘ Plymouth
*Island House, 9 The Barbican
t (01752) 306330
www.plymouth.gov.uk;
open summer Mon–Sat
9am–5pm, winter
Mon–Fri 9am–5pm, Sat
10am–4pm*

★ Bowling Green Hotel >

Eating Out in Plymouth

Moderate
Piermasters, 33 Southside Street, The Barbican, t (01752) 229345, *www.piermastersrestaurant.com*. Popular rustic-style seafood restaurant on two floors of a tall Victorian townhouse. Fillet of salmon or moules marinières for lunch (two courses for £10), parma ham and sage-wrapped monkfish followed by a selection of Devon cheeses for dinner. Also be sure to check out the daily specials board. Pre-theatre menu available 5–7pm at £12.95.

Budget
Cap'n Jaspers, Whitehouse Pier, Barbican, t (01752) 262444, *http://capn -jaspers.co.uk*. A real Plymouth Institution, on the Barbican's waterfront, this is a very superior fast-food place serving a huge range of reasonably priced burgers and hot dogs, including the infamous half yarder (two jumbo sausages in a baguette for £3.85). Lots of quirky décor and seating by the water.

Jaipur Palace, 146 Vauxhall Street, t (01752) 252918. This regional outpost of a London original is one of the town's better Indians with some sizzling spicy choices and helpful staff. Takeaway service available.

The Minerva, 1 Looe Street, t (01752) 223047. Old-fashioned locals' pub near the Plymouth Arts Centre with exposed wooden beams and decorated with old photos and fishing paraphernalia. Lots of real ales.

Entertainment and Nightlife in Plymouth

It is probably best to avoid the drinking holes of Union Street on Friday and Saturday nights, when it gets pretty rowdy.

Plymouth Arts Centre, 38 Looe Street, t (01752) 206114, *www.plymoutharts centre.org*. Exhibition space and arthouse cinema with daily screenings at 6pm and 8pm. There's also a good **café**, the Green Room, offering plenty of vegetarian choices. You can get a cinema ticket and main course from the café for £10.

The Barbican Theatre, Castle Street, **t** (01752) 267131, *www.barbicantheatre. co.uk*. An old 18th-century seamen's club which hosts small-scale touring productions of dance, drama and comedy. The theatre bar puts on live comedy, cabaret and music on Friday and Saturday evenings.

The Theatre Royal, Royal Parade, **t** (01752) 668282, *www.theatreroyal. com*. The largest theatre in the southwest hosts a popular repertoire of large-scale musicals, drama, ballet and opera (mainly touring productions).

Dartmoor National Park

⭐ Dartmoor
National Park

This vast 365-square-mile swathe of moorland is the largest remaining area of wilderness in southern England. Indeed, the term 'moor' doesn't begin to do justice to the vast variety of landscapes to be found here: great expanses of grassland interspersed with thick, muddy bogs and heather-clad hills, isolated villages seemingly little changed since the Middle Ages, fast-flowing rivers and tiny streams curling around craggy contours, small copses of oak in sheltered valleys, ancient stone clapper bridges and murky ponds, prehistoric ruins, deep, dark gorges and, of course, tors, the granite monoliths that are Dartmoor's most famous feature. You'll see them everywhere punctuating the skyline, their silhouettes weathered by thousands of years of wind and rain into fantastical shapes. Dartmoor is a wondrous place, but also a forbidding and rather daunting one. Anyone familiar with its reputation will be wary of its dangers, particularly the soggy moss bogs, or mires, which lie at the bottom of the peat valleys and have snared many a disorientated walker in their gloopy embrace.

The moor may not be as old as the Devonian lowlands around it, but is a good deal more menacing. Its bogs, cleaves and danger areas shroud it in a deep, dark unsettling mystery. From the gentle Devon farmland you are suddenly up on the moor, surrounded by a heathery wilderness of grass beaten flat by the howling wind. The weather on the high moor can close in suddenly; the mist, in particular, is perilous to walkers. The tors of the plateau, far from providing useful guiding landmarks, can exacerbate the sense of confusion, as the author of *A Gentleman's Walking Tour of Dartmoor* commented in 1864: 'To a stranger on the moor, the country round seems almost exactly alike; there are tors in every direction, and with very little apparent difference between them, too. The whole country round consists of moorland hill-and-dale; you toil over one hill and down the other side, cross a brook (just like the one at the foot of the last hill), and then up another steep ascent, and on looking round, you seem to be pretty much where you were about an hour before'.

Around the fringes of the granite dome, you may breathe a sigh of relief as you return to scattered villages, enclosed farmland, and deep wooded gorges where the rivers Dart, Tavy, Teign and Plym tumble off the top.

If you've arrived without suitable hiking gear and a good map, or are not overly confident of your orientating ability, it's probably best to explore Dartmoor either from the safety of a car, following the A382, the B3212 or the B3357, stopping off here and there for a few short strolls, or as part of an organized **horse-trekking tour**. Try the **Shilstone Rocks Riding Centre**, which offers treks for all abilities from around £20 an hour.

Shilstone Rocks
Riding Centre
*t (01364) 621281;
www.dartmoor
stables.com*

Getting to and around Dartmoor

By Car

The fast A38 Plymouth–Exeter road skirts the southern and eastern edges of the moor, with views of the big hills and turn-offs to the moorland villages. The western peripheral road (A386) between Plymouth and Okehampton is virtually a moorland road, and particularly atmospheric between Tavistock and Okehampton. But the trans-moor roads are the best: the B3357 and B3212, which cross at Two Bridges.

By Train/Bus

See p.136 for details of the South Devon **Railway**, a steam line running between Totnes and Buckfastleigh. Sunday, when there are regular **bus** services, is the best day to get around the moor by bus. The no.82 Transmoor Link crisscrosses the moors between Plymouth and Exeter, stopping at all the beauty spots including Moretonhampstead, Postbridge and Princetown. Buy your ticket on the bus and hop on and off as you choose. For more information, contact First Group, t 0845 600 1420; www.firstgroup.com/ukbus/southwest/devon/home.

On Foot

The Abbots' Way runs from Buckfastleigh to Tavistock through southern Dartmoor via Princetown, Nuns Cross Farm and Merrivale. The Two Moors Way stretches for more than 100 miles from Ivybridge on Dartmoor to Lynmouth on Exmoor cutting right across both moors. There are several other long-distance walking trails, including the West Devon Way, Two Castles Trail and Dartmoor Way.

In summer the Dartmoor National Park Authority runs two or three guided walks daily. You can also download audio-guide walks from their website, www.dartmoor-npa.gov.uk

Orientation

The high moor is carved into three sections – north, south and east – by the main moorland roads. The B3357 runs east-west across the moor between Tavistock and Dartmeet, where it unravels into a tangle of lanes. The B3212 runs from Moretonhampstead into the northeast to Yelverton in the southwest. Where the two roads cross, at Princetown, is the heart of the moor – marked by an infamous prison (even if these days it accommodates mainly white-collar criminals). The high moor is so bleak that most tourists head for the honeypots near the roads: Becka Falls (a commercialized nightmare); the reservoirs (particularly Burrator); Bovey Tracey's Guild of Craftsmen; Lydford Gorge; the clapper bridge at Postbridge and Haytor.

The Dartmoor National Park Authority

Bovey Tracey, Newton Abbot;
t (01626) 832093;
www.dartmoor-npa.gov.uk

The Dartmoor National Park Authority organizes walks and activities across the moors and you can download free audio walks from their website.

It is perhaps surprising that somewhere so harsh shows so much evidence of human activity: the moor was more populous 5,000 years ago than it is today. Bronze Age villages such as Grimspound were built on the lower slopes, and the dead were buried in monumental stone tombs called cists and cairns incorporating standing stones. These prehistoric monuments make useful landmarks, as do the area's industrial remains. Over the last thousand years, Dartmoor has been one of Europe's major sources of tin and copper. Its 19th-century granite quarries supplied stone for several of the country's most iconic constructions, including London Bridge, the British Museum, Nelson's Column and the Plymouth Breakwater. Today the moor is littered with the relics of quarries, tin workings, tramways, mills and tinners' cottages. Medieval tinners once 'tin-streamed' the river beds – digging out tin ore and working their way upstream to the metal's source. The tin was then smelted and taxed in the stannary ('tin-working') towns of Tavistock, Ashburton, Plympton and Chagford, which grew rich on it. The 19th-century copper boom brought more metallic prosperity to the western fringes around the Tamar Valley and Mary Tavy mines.

Walking

The open moor is treacherous, so most walks follow landmarks – tors, stone monuments, industrial ruins, river valleys, and man-made watercourses called leats. Parts of the moor are army firing ranges; red flags on prominent hilltops indicate when the ranges are in use. For longer walks, you need an Ordnance Survey map (at least 1:25,000), a compass, a basic idea of orientation, wet- and cold-weather clothes, and proper walking shoes or boots. The Dartmoor mist can descend fast, deadening sound, and, in winter, roads and trails are often obliterated by snow. But there are good walks even for the casual wanderer.

Eastern Fringes

East Dartmoor is the most densely populated part of the moor, speckled with villages along the Teign and Bovey rivers and their tributaries. **Buckfastleigh**, just off the busy A38 at the southwestern foot of the moor, was a thriving mill town in 1900, and is now enjoying a modest regeneration based around the **Valiant Soldier**, a fossilized 1950s pub on the High Street. One day in 1965 the widowed landlady went a bit Miss Havisham, locking the front door, disappearing into an upstairs bedroom and never coming out again. The poor old thing declined behind closed curtains until passing away in 1996. It's a sad story but the pub has been preserved intact, down to the old money in the cash till.

Valiant Soldier
79 Fore Street,
t (01364) 64452; open
Wed–Sun noon–4.30pm

Buckfast Abbey

In summer a special bus runs from Buckfastleigh to **Buckfast Abbey**, a Roman Catholic monastery of about 40 Benedictine monks who are joined each year by around half a million visitors. The huge complex, comprising a church, shops and a restaurant, stands on the site of a 12th-century Cistercian monastery which was abandoned in the mid-16th century. A new contingent of monks didn't arrive until 1882, in response to an advert in the Catholic newspaper, *The Tablet* – the French Government had just thrown them out of their monastery near Avignon and they were looking for a new home. It took the monks 31 years (1907–38) to build their church, which they completed entirely unaided, four monks working at a time, cutting and dressing the stone by hand and using wooden scaffolding lashed together with ropes. The medieval-style grey limestone church is imposing but, being unsoftened by time and use, has a slightly unreal look to it. A few of the original monastic buildings survive, including the old south gate (now a retreat centre) and guesthouse (now the bookshop). In the early 19th century a wealthy miller flattened the rest of the ruins and built himself a neogothic mansion and mill, where there is now a shop selling monastic produce, including candles, honey and Buckfast Tonic Wine.

Buckfast Abbey
t (01364) 645550;
www.buckfast.org.uk;
open Wed 9am–6pm, Fri
10am–6pm, Sun
noon–6pm; shops
Mon–Fri 9.30am–5pm,
Sun noon–5pm

Bovey Tracey & Around

Bovey Tracey, a busy little market town on the eastern edge of Dartmoor, is home to the showrooms of the **Devon Guild of Craftsmen**. The guild was set up in 1955 by a small group of local craftsmen,

Devon Guild of Craftsmen
Riverside Mill,
t (01626) 832223;
www.crafts.org.uk; open
daily 10am–5.30pm

including Bovey potter David Leach (son of the great Bernard Leach) to promote the best regional crafts. In 1986 the guild bought the Victorian riverside mill and converted it into a gallery and craft shop, stacked with furniture, ceramics, glass, clothes, wood and metalwork.

The B3387 climbs about 300 yards out of Bovey Tracey onto the east moor. Here the great twin **Haytor Rocks** sit plumply above the landscape, providing classic easy-to-climb Dartmoor scenery. From the top, some 1500ft up, you can see all the way across Devon to the coast.

Becky Falls Woodland Park
Manaton, Newton Abbot; t (01647) 221259; www.beckyfalls.com; open mid Feb–mid Nov 10am–5pm; adm £6.50–6.95

A couple of miles north lies the **Becky Falls Woodland Park**, a 25-acre private woodland estate in which waterfalls tumble gently over huge granite rocks. It's a particularly good choice for families with animal encounter sessions and pony rides offered in the summer holidays.

Back on the B3387, heading west, you reach the grey stone market town of **Widecombe-in-the-Moor**, made famous by the folk song 'Widecombe Fair', which hugs the hillside beneath its 240ft-high church tower. The fair still takes place on the second Tuesday, although you're guaranteed to see crowds wandering around the old market square looking for it at weekends.

North of Bovey Tracey the A382 goes to **Lustleigh**, a pretty village with a famous 15th-century thatched pub, the Cleave Inn, on the edge of the dramatic Lustleigh Cleave (cliff), which was carved out by the River Bovey. There's a lovely five-mile walk along the top of the cleave to **Hunter's Tor**, a jumble of smoothly eroded, overhanging rocks.

Moretonhampstead, a handsome, albeit rather down-at-heel, market town with some fine old buildings – including late medieval coaching inns and a Victorian library – is on the edge of the high moor at a big junction of minor roads. It is believed that Sir Edwin Landseer Lutyens, the great architect of the British Raj in India, was responsible for the town's neo-Georgian bank, now the elegant Lion Gallery, specializing in equestrian art. Two miles west of town is another of the area's prime family attractions, the **Dartmoor Miniature Pony and Animal Farm**, where children can meet and stroke a range of diminutive equine inhabitants including Shetland ponies, miniature donkeys and, by way of contrast, a shire horse. There is also an adventure playground, an indoor assault course and lakeside nature trails.

Dartmoor Miniature Pony and Animal Farm
Wormhill Farm; t (01647) 432400; www.miniaturepony centre.com; open Apr–Oct 10.30–4.30; adm £6.95

As you enter **Chagford** off the moor, you are squeezed down its narrow lanes into the small, sloping town square. This old stannary town, on the lower slopes of the moors above the River Teign, is one of the prettiest on Dartmoor, bustling with creaky pubs and old-fashioned shops. It was a popular Victorian centre for expeditions onto the moor and is still a convenient starting point for walks to the moor's very first and famously inaccessible letterbox at Cranmere Pool (*see* p.153) and the **Grey Wethers**, a pair of prehistoric stone circles, each measuring more than 100ft in diameter, set on a grassy plateau.

Castle Drogo
t (01647) 433 306; www.nationaltrust.org. uk/main/w-castledrogo; open Mar–Oct daily 11am–4pm, Dec–Feb Sat & Sun 11am–4pm

In the northwest corner of Dartmoor, **Drewsteignton** is a typical old Dartmoor village on a windy hill with a square of painted houses and an excellent pub. It takes its name from Drogò de Teign, the Norman baron who owned the parish in the 12th century. A few miles south, **Castle Drogo** sits loftily preening on a crag 853ft above the Teign Gorge. Despite its pretensions and portcullises, this is not medieval and has nothing to do with Drogo de Teign. It was built between 1911 and 1930 by Edwin Lutyens for the millionaire tea merchant Julius Drewe and has been dubbed 'the last castle built in England'. The rooms were styled in the manner of different periods: the drawing room 18th century, the dining room Jacobean etc. Lutyens even fitted it with a lift and a telephone (state-of-the-art luxuries for the time) and also laid out the granite structure of the formal terraced gardens to the northeast. There is a good walk along the Teign Gorge from Castle Drogo to Fingle Bridge.

Western Fringes

Between Tavistock and Okehampton the A386 skirts the north moor, the most inhospitable part of Dartmoor and almost entirely incorporated within three MOD firing ranges. Only experienced walkers are advised to venture here. The presence of red flags means that live firing is in progress and that you should not enter the area. White flags mean that it is (in theory at least) safe to enter. Live firing usually only occurs in the winter months.

Okehampton

Museum of Dartmoor Life
*3 West Street;
t (01837) 52295;
www.museumofdartmo
or life.eclipse.co.uk;
open Mon–Sat
10.15–4.30;
adm £3*

Two Museum Trail to the Finch Foundry
*t (01837) 840046;
www.nationaltrust.org.
uk/main/w-
finchfoundry; open
Mar–Nov Mon &
Wed–Sun 11am–5pm;
adm £4.20*

Okehampton is a busy market town, cut off from the moor by the busy A30. South of the road is some of the bleakest, boggiest moorland and the 2,037ft high High Willhays, the highest point on Dartmoor (and, indeed, the whole of Southern England). For the daring, there's a six-mile walk between Yes Tor, High Willhays, Dinger Tor and East Mill Tor that sticks largely to military roads. Just outside Okehampton is a ruined medieval castle overlooking the West Okement River. On West Street, the **Museum of Dartmoor Life** tells the social history of the moor. There's a pleasant, hilly five-mile walk known as the **Two Museum Trail to the Finch Foundry** at Sticklepath. Pick up the leaflet 'Okehampton Countryside Walks East' in town.

Tavistock

museum
*Court Gate,
Bedford Square;
t (01822) 612546;
www.tavistockhistory.ik.
com; Mar–Oct Tues–Sat
11am–3pm; free*

Tavistock is easily reached off the A386 periphery road and the B3357 moor road, and offers lots of places to stay. It's an old-fashioned market town with hand-painted shop signs and a Victorian market stacked with local cheeses, bread and fresh produce. The town grew up around the 10th-century Benedictine abbey. In the early Middle Ages it became one of four stannary towns built around the edge of the moor, where tin was smelted and taxed. Tavistock's glory days came in the 19th-century copper boom, when one of the biggest copper lodes in the world was discovered between the Tavy and Tamar valleys. The Devon Great Consuls copper mine became the richest copper mine ever, its shares rising from £1 to £800 in a single year. The seventh Duke of Bedford owned the mineral rights and became hugely wealthy. Visit the market on Bedford Square (closed Mon) for Devon cheeses. There's a small **museum**, run by the local history society, devoted to local history and two statues: one of the duke, the other of Sir Francis Drake, born down the road in Crowndale.

Letterboxing

Although you may not at first be able to spot them, Dartmoor is littered with thousands of 'letterboxes'. These are not remote outposts of the postal service but rather visitor books hidden in tree stumps and under rocks, which together form a sort of informal treasure hunt. Each box comes attached with an ink pad and stamp with which 'letterboxers' stamp their record books before heading off in search of the next box. The aim is to collect as many stamps as possible. Collect 100 of these stamps and you qualify to join the exclusive '100 Club'. The practice began in the mid-19th century with a box at Cranmere Pool, then regarded as one of the wildest and most inaccessible places on the moors, and now has thousands of (often quite obsessive) devotees. *www.dartmoorletterboxing.org*.

Morwellham Quay
t (01822) 832766;
www.morwellham-
quay.co.uk; open
Easter–Oct daily
10am–5pm; adm £9.50

Six miles south of Tavistock, at the highest point of navigation on the River Tamar, **Morwellham Quay** was the port of the west Dartmoor tin and copper mines. Its fortunes took off when the Tavistock Canal was opened in 1816, anticipating the opening of the mine in 1844. The decline of the mine, coinciding with the arrival of the railway line, marginalized Morwellham into obscurity. Since 1969 it has been restored and turned into a popular industrial attraction: costumed staff work the old equipment; tram rides take you into the George and Charlotte copper mine; restored buildings include the fully licensed Ship Inn, and a salvaged ketch called the *Garlandstone* in the Devon Great Consuls docks.

Lydford Gorge

The dramatic and wooded Lydford Gorge is one of the 'natural wonders' of Dartmoor. It has been a tourist attraction since the 18th century when the fashion for the picturesque attracted travel writers and painters. From the village of Lydford it's a three-mile walk along the River Lyd past the **Devil's Cauldron**, a series of foaming whirlpools, and various potholes to the 90-ft high **White Lady Waterfall** and back. **Lydford** itself, now a handful of roadside cottages, was once a centre of stannary and forest law. The courts were held in the 12th-century keep of the castle. One prisoner, Richard Strode, was locked up without trial, even though he was MP for Plymouth, for objecting that the waste products of the tinners were choking the estuary at Plympton and obstructing fishing boats. In the churchyard, right of the church door is the charming epitaph of George Routleigh, watchmaker, who died 'aged 57, wound up, in the hopes of being taken in hand by his maker and of being thoroughly cleaned, repaired and set agoing in the world to come'.

From the Dartmoor Inn at the Lydford Junction of the A386 you can walk into the rock-strewn Tavy Cleave to Willsworthy Bridge. Another good walk is from the Mary Tavy Inn into Tavy Cleave and around Ger Tor to Deadlake Foot and Hare Tor.

The Heart of Dartmoor

The B3357 between Tavistock and Princetown climbs onto the high moor. Check your petrol gauge before you set out. To either side are the rugged outlines of tors: to the north Cox Tor, Great Staple Tor and Middle Staple Tor; to the south Feather Tor, Pew Tor, Vixen Tor and King's Tor. The road continues to **Merrivale**, a gentle valley (with a good pub – the

Dartmoor Inn) where a group of prehistoric stone monuments stand near old quarries and tin mines. It's a fairly gentle two-mile walk to the standing stones from the Four Winds car park. Two rows of Bronze Age granite stone stumps form an avenue 600 ft long. A cairn (a man-made pile of stones) on the line of the southern row is thought to mark the burial place of an important person; about 20 yards beyond that is a cist, an enormous slab of granite with a chamber underneath used for burying the dead. A hundred or so feet southwest is a small Bronze Age cairn circle. Further southwest again is a monumental Neolithic stone circle. From Merrivale the road runs on to Princetown and Two Bridges.

Princetown straddles the crossroads on top of the moor, HM Dartmoor Prison at its heart. Built in the early 19th century to hold prisoners of the Napoleonic Wars, Dartmoor is today a Category C jail holding non-violent offenders. Near the prison gates is the Prison Museum which has a display of items confiscated from prisoners, such as a tattoo gun made out of a biro. The **High Moorland Visitors' Centre** was built in 1809 as a barracks for prison officers, later becoming the Duchy Hotel where Sir Arthur Conan Doyle wrote *The Hound of the Baskervilles*. A five-mile walk takes you along the old railway line to Foggintor Quarries.

High Moorland Visitors' Centre
Tavistock Road;
t (01822) 890414;
www.dartmoor-npa.
gov.uk/vi-highmoorland
centre; open Easter–Oct
daily 10–5, Nov–Easter
daily 10–4

Foxtor Mire, or the Great Grimpen Mire

Foxtor Mire was the moorland inspiration for the Great Grimpen Mire in Conan Doyle's *The Hound of the Baskervilles*, with fictional Baskerville Hall on the site of Whiteworks cottages, facing across the mire to Fox Tor (High Tor in the book). Seldon, the escaped convict, made signals across the mire to Barrymore in the Hall, from Fox Tor. A treacherous mire path leads between Whiteworks and Fox Tor – it's not as dangerous as Conan Doyle suggests, but do try to avoid the bright green patches if you want to avoid an impromptu and very muddy dip. Below Fox Tor you can see a cross known as Childe's Tomb, which commemorates a 14th-century huntsmen called Amyas or Ordulf Childe who got lost in a blizzard, killed his horse and slept inside it for warmth, but died anyway in the snow. He was laid in the Bronze Age cist beneath the cross.

'That is the great Grimpen Mire', said he. 'A false step yonder means death to man or beast.'
The Hound of the Baskervilles, Sir Arthur Conan Doyle

Two Bridges

On top of the moor, at the crossing of the B3212 and B3357, the pub at Two Bridges is a cheerful place to break your journey. You could go up to the top of Crockern Tor, just off the B3212 Postbridge road where the stannary parliament met in the 15th century – such was the influence of tin mining in the area that the mining community had its own legislative body, separate from the British Parliament, which exercised executive authority in Devon and Cornwall until the 18th century. You can still see the seats cut into the rock. Some of the most popular Dart Valley walks begin further along the B3357 at Dartmeet, where the East and West Dart rivers converge amid terrific scenery (with a shop and a café).

Postbridge

Along the B3212 northeast from Two Bridges to Moretonhampstead the moor looks darker than ever. Postbridge, in the fertile valley of the East Dart, alleviates the gloom. It's a popular base for the central moor.

Day-trippers come to see the medieval clapper bridge on its granite pillars above the Dart. There are plenty of good walks starting here too.

The **Warren House Inn** sits high up on the lonely road in the middle of nowhere. It's a Dartmoor legend, where there's always a cosy fire blazing. From here it's three miles across the moor to **Grimspound**, a well-preserved Bronze Age settlement of 24 huts in an enclosure on the north slope of Hambledon. Although it looks defensive, with its massive paved entrance and 6ft-high walls, it was almost certainly a farming village. The thresholds are the most evocative detail.

ⓘ **High Moorland Visitor Centre**
Tavistock Road, Princetown, t (01822) 890414, www.dartmoor-npa.gov.uk; open Easter–Oct daily 10–5, Nov–Easter daily 10–4

ⓘ **Postbridge**
Main car park on the B3212, t (01822) 880272

ⓘ **Haytor**
Lower car park on the B3387, 3 miles west of Bovey Tracey, t (01364) 661520

ⓘ **Okehampton**
Museum Courtyard, 3, West Street, t (01837) 53020, www.okehampton devon.co.uk

ⓘ **Ashburton**
Town Hall, t (01364) 653426, www.ashburton.org

ⓘ **Bovey Tracey**
The Lower Car Park, Station Road, t (01626) 832047

ⓘ **Moretonhampstead**
New Street, t (01647) 440043, www.moreton hampstead.com

★ **Gidleigh Park Hotel >>**

Firing Ranges on Dartmoor

The Ministry of Defence ranges at Okehampton, Merrivale and Willsworthy, in the northwest of Dartmoor, are often closed to walkers for live firing. Call **t** (01837) 650010 or go to *www.dartmoor-ranges.co.uk* to find out if the ranges are safe. The boundaries are clearly marked on Ordnance Survey maps and on the ground with red and white posts.

Markets on Dartmoor

Tavistock's historic charter market takes place on Fridays in the purpose-built Victorian Pannier Market, offering a mixture of food, clothing and Women's Institute stalls. On Tues–Thurs and Saturday you will usually find stalls selling bric-a-brac and craftwork, **t** (01822) 611003; *www.tavistockpanniermarket.co.uk*.

Tours of Dartmoor

Spirit of Adventure, Powder Mills, Princetown, **t** (01822) 880277, *www.spirit-of-adventure.com*. Organizes climbing, abseiling, cycling, kayaking and orienteering activities for groups and individuals. Book in advance.

Where to Stay and Eat on Dartmoor

East Dartmoor

The Edgemoor, Haytor Road, Bovey Tracey, **t** (01626) 832466, *www.edge moor.co.uk* (*expensive*). Less than a mile out of Bovey Tracey on the Widecombe road, this attractive ivy-clad former 19th-century school caters for well-heeled tourists who like their comforts. An excellent **restaurant**.

Great Sloncombe Farm, Moretonhampstead (off the A382 from Chagford), **t** (01647) 440595, *www.greatsloncombefarm.co.uk* (*moderate*). This B&B accommodation occupies a 13th-century Dartmoor farmhouse set amid a busy working farm of Aberdeen Angus beef cattle. The three cottage bedrooms have patchwork quilts and lovely views, the guest lounge has a cosy wood-burning stove and there's a warm and friendly atmosphere throughout. Perhaps best of all, breakfast is served using the farm's own eggs and organically grown vegetables.

Great Wooston Farm, Mardon Down (2 miles north of Moretonhampstead), **t** (01647) 440367, *www.greatwoostonfarm.com* (*moderate*). Three pretty en suite old-fashioned bedrooms occupy this large 1900 farmhouse, all with LCD TVs and tea and coffee-making facilities. The B&B has a wonderful rural feel to it and offers access to walks along the Teign Valley. The room rate includes a full English breakfast.

The Cleave Inn, Lustleigh, **t** (01647) 277223, *www.thecleaveinn.co.uk* (*moderate*).Pleasant village pub dating back to the 15th century, offering good-quality food. It's a member of the 'slow food movement'.

Chagford

Gidleigh Park Hotel, **t** (01647) 432367, *www.gidleigh.com* (*luxury*). Gabled, 1929 mock-Tudor house two miles out of Chagford, surrounded by woodland. From a porch filled with golfing umbrellas, lawns sweep away to an 18-hole putting course. The lounge and bar overlook the gardens, and some of the best food in the southwest is served in two small dining rooms

ⓘ **Tavistock**
Town Hall, Bedford Square, **t** *(01822) 612938, www.dartmoor-npa.gov.uk; open Mon, Tues, Fri & Sat 10am–4pm*

⭐ **Parford Well** >

(lunch: *moderate*, dinner: *expensive*). If you're on a restricted budget, you could just have a cream tea.

22 Mill Street, 22 Mill Street, *www. 22millst.com* (*expensive*). Small, glass-fronted restaurant offering a quality but expensive European menu (2 courses for £36) and a couple of rustic looking rooms for hire with large beds, leather sofas, flat-screen TVs, Egyptian cotton sheets and more.

Mill End Hotel, **t** (01647) 432282, *www.millendhotel.com* (*expensive*). This 18th-century former mill house beside the River Teign has been a hotel for more than 70 years, boasting several cosy lounges and 15 old English-style bedrooms. The high-quality **restaurant** offers modern English dishes (with a twist).

The Globe Inn, 9 High Street, **t** (01647) 433485, *www.globeinnchagford.co.uk* (*moderate*). Just off the main square, offering home-made pies at the bar, a dining room serving locally-sourced produce, fires in winter and, upstairs, 7 comfortable en suite rooms.

Parford Well, Parford Well, Sandy Park, (1.5 miles from Chagford in the direction of Drewsteignton), **t** (01647) 433353, *www.parfordwell.co.uk* (*moderate*). Beautiful modern B&B furnished with old pine furniture offering three bedrooms, all overlooking a lovely walled garden. The owners claim that 'only God makes a better breakfast'.

The Three Crowns Hotel, High Street, **t** (01647) 433444, *www.chagford-accom.co.uk* (*budget*). This has 22 rooms, some with four-poster beds, spread out through a 13th-century building. The very inn-ish bar serves a good selection of meals and the dining room does reasonably priced à la carte and set meal options.

Moretonhampstead

The White Hart Hotel, The Square, **t** (01647) 441340, *www.whitehart dartmoor.co.uk* (*expensive*). The White Hart is a handsome, old-fashioned town centre hotel with a cosy friendly bar offering good standard pub grub. Ask for a room in the main building.

The Drewe Arms, The Square, **t** (01647) 281224, *www.thedrewearms.co.uk* (*moderate*). A cosy 17th-century

thatched inn with wooden floor-boards, long bench seats, wood panelling, old photos adorning the walls and a small coal fire. It serves great food, like hock of ham, belly pork and homity pie, as well as real ale through a hatch. There are also three large rooms for £80 a night.

Buckfastleigh

The Singing Kettle, 54 Fore St, **t** (01364) 642383 (*budget*). Old-fashioned tea shop – serves excellent breakfasts, morning coffee, lunches, best of all, afternoon tea in bone china teapots and cups (£2 a pot).

The White Hart, Plymouth Road, **t** (01364) 642337 (*budget*). Traditional and rather quiet 400-year-old pub serving a range of real ales and draught cider.

Lydford

Lydford Country House, Lydford, **t** (01822) 820347, *www.lydfordcountry house.co.uk* (*moderate*). The Dartmoor artist William Widgery built this country house in 1880 which he lived in for the next ten years. (In 1887 he erected the large granite cross on the top of Brat Tor to commemorate Queen Victoria's Golden Jubilee). Today it offers 11 comfortable bedrooms and a self-catering apartment for reasonable rates, an Italian **restaurant**, riding stables and a large sitting room adorned with ornaments over the fire place and some of Widgery's Dartmoor paintings. Coffee, light lunches and cream teas are served in the conservatory or on the lawn.

The Castle Inn, Lydford, **t** (01822) 820241, *www.castleinnlydford.co.uk* (*moderate*). A short walk from Lydford Gorge, the Castle Inn has eight en suite bedrooms with window seats and patchwork throws. One balconied double overlooks Lydford Castle. The restaurant is furnished with high-backed wooden settles. Bar meals include ploughman's lunch and bubble and squeak, while the restaurant menu features lots of hearty game and fish options.

The Dartmoor Inn, Lydford, **t** 01822 820221, *www.dartmoorinn.com* (*moderate*). Top-notch gastro pub on the main Tavistock-Okehampton road, a mile from Lydford village. The elegant, almost Scandinavian looking bar and dining areas have high-backed settles and a log-burning stove. The menu is packed with posh pub classics: farmhouse sausages with onion gravy and mash, steak sandwiches etc. In the evening there is a traditional country-inn menu. There are also three bedrooms to rent (*expensive*).

Tavistock

★ Horn of Plenty >

Horn of Plenty, Gulworthy (3 miles west of Tavistock in the direction of Gunnislake), **t** (01822) 832528, *www.thehornofplenty.co.uk* (*expensive–luxury*). This Georgian country house hotel overlooking the Tamar Valley was originally built for the captain of the Duke of Bedford's mines, and is now home to ludicrously luxurious bedrooms and a Michelin-starred conservatory restaurant (lunch *moderate*, dinner *expensive*) offering delicious, high-quality fusion cooking and grand countryside views.

The Bedford Hotel, Plymouth Road, **t** (01822) 613221, *www.bedford-hotel. co.uk* (*very expensive*). Imposing Victorian-Gothic hotel on the town square with 29 bedrooms and traces of its former elegance. Morning coffee and light lunches are served in the Duke's Bar where the grand piano is played on Friday/Saturday evenings.

Browns Hotel, 80 West Street, **t** (01822) 618686, *www.brownsdevon. com* (*expensive–very expensive*). The sister property of 22 Mill Street, Browns is a welcoming Victorian coaching inn occupying the site of an even older hostelry, with comfortable bedrooms. The conservatory, which spills out into a pretty garden, is a pleasant setting for a light lunch.

Higher Rowe Farm, Horndon, **t** (01822) 810816, *www.hrowesfarm.co.uk* (*moderate*). A rough stone track leads to this 17th-century longhouse B&B with a friendly atmosphere and a yard full of animals. It has three rooms looking out over the moor.

★ Cherrybrook
Hotel >>

Mallard's Guest House, 48 Plymouth Road, **t** (01822) 615171, *mallardsof tavistock.co.uk* (*moderate*). Family-run guesthouse in the centre of town overlooking the park, set in a Grade II listed Victorian townhouse.

Peter Tavy Inn, Peter Tavy, **t** (01822) 810348, *www.petertavyinn.com* (*moderate*). The pub staples served in the flagstoned bar of this 15th-century inn include hearty dishes of eggs and ham, traditional Devonshire cheese ploughman's, bread and butter pudding and chocolate tart.

Hele Farm, Gulworthy, **t** (01822) 833084, *www.dartmoorbb.co.uk* (*budget– moderate*). Two en-suite bedrooms and two self-catering units in an 18th-century Grade II listed farmhouse standing at the centre of an organic dairy farm. Surrounded by woodland, this provides a great introduction to country living.

Duke's Coffee House, 8–11 The Market, **t** (01822) 613718 (*budget*). Small coffee shop serving good coffee and snack lunches. On a warm day you can sit outside and watch the market bustle.

The Coffee Mill, 44 Brook street, **t** (01822) 612092 (*budget*). All-day breakfasts and simple lunches at decent prices. *Closed Sun.*

The Elephant's Nest, Horndon, **t** (01822) 810273, *www.elephantsnest. co.uk* (*budget*). An excellent pub – just one of three to have featured in every edition of the Good Pub Guide – serving a wide range of local ales, scrumpy cider and snacks. To find it, follow the signs from the A386.

The Heart of the Moor

Two Bridges Hotel, Princetown, **t** (01822) 890581, *www.twobridges. co.uk* (*very expensive*). The superior sister to Tavistock's Bedford Hotel, this slate-roofed country-house hotel at the junction of four transmoor roads looks out at the West Dart River and to the tors beyond Princetown. It's an elegant Victorian sort of place with stuffed birds in cases, leather sofas and four-poster and brass beds. Afternoon tea is served in the lounge.

Cherrybrook Hotel, Two Bridges, **t** (01822) 880260, *www.thecherry brook.co.uk* (*expensive*). Enjoying a terribly picturesque setting surrounded by small fields and hemmed in by drystone walls, this former early 19th-century farmhouse set in 3 1/2 acres has seven simply furnished bedrooms and a cosy lounge and bar with a log-burning stove. You can opt for B&B or pay a little extra to enjoy the evening meals prepared using local produce, which feature delicious desserts such as steamed syrup pudding and Devon cheeses. Wistman's Wood is a 20-minute walk away.

Lydgate House Hotel, Postbridge, t (01822) 880209, *www.lydgatehouse. co.uk* (*expensive*). Cream-painted Victorian country house on a steep wooded valleyside of the East Dart River with smashing views down the valley. Its seven bedrooms are nicely furnished in period style. The delicious home-cooked meals are for guests only, but anyone can stop off here for cream teas with scones and strawberry jam or light lunches.

Duchy Guest House, Tavistock Road, Princetown, t (01822) 890552 (*moderate*) A Victorian house looking out over the moor a rope's throw from Dartmoor Prison. It's very friendly with three cheerful bedrooms.

East Dart Hotel, Postbridge, t (01822) 880213, *www.eastdart.co.uk* (*moderate*). A 19th-century coaching inn and former temperance inn less than 100 yards from the river. It's got a country sports vibe with a Hunts-

⭐ Warren House Inn >>

man's Bar adorned with fox heads and friezes of hunting scenes, where decent pub meals are served. There are also comfortable bedrooms.

The Plume of Feathers, Princetown, t (01822) 890240, *www.theplumeof feathers.co.uk* (*budget*). With its log fire in the bar, worn flagstones and sign creaking in the wind, the Plume, housed in Princetown's oldest building (1785), is a very Dartmoor sort of a place. It offers a range of accommodation options, including private rooms, dormitories and camping space. The bar serves topical pints such as Jail Ale and Dartmoor IPA.

Warren House Inn, t (01822) 880208, *www.warrenhouseinn.co.uk* (*budget*). Standing alone on the remote Postbridge to Moretonhampstead road, miles from anywhere, the Warren makes a welcome refuge for tired, cold hikers with a fire that's supposedly been kept burning since 1945. It's particularly cosy when the weather closes in with a comfy bar where hearty local fare, such as steak and ale pie is served.

The North Devon Coast

With its rocky headlands raked by the full force of the Atlantic, North Devon has some of the most dramatic coastal scenery in Britain, with small coastal settlements at the mouths of steep wooded combes. Charles Kingsley in *Westward Ho!* describes these combes as 'like no other English scenery. Each has its upright walls, inland of rich oak wood, nearer the sea of dark green furze, then of smooth turf, then of weird black cliffs which range out right and left into the deep sea, in castles, spires and wings of jagged iron stone.' Writing in the 1920s, Henry Williamson, author of *Tarka the Otter*, was equally effusive about the inland scenery. Try to avoid built-up Barnstaple Bay and the resorts of Westward Ho! if you can.

Ilfracombe and Around

The most popular resort on the North Devon coast, **Ilfracombe**, lies on the northern headland of Barnstaple Bay and is a terribly English affair with a whiff of boiled cabbage and stewed tea about it. It's built on the steep sides of a combe above a sheltered river harbour, with no seafront as such. Its beaches are reached through tunnels blasted in the rock at the foot of massive grey cliffs. It offers all the usual stuff for families, its principal clientele: sandy (if rather grey) beaches, a harbour filled with

Getting to and around Ilfracombe

Ilfracombe is on the North Devon coast, 5 miles from Barnstaple. Take the A39 and the A361. Woolacombe is located around five miles southwest. Take the A361 south, then the B3343 and follow the signs. You'll need a car to get around too, unless you plan to walk or cycle.

bobbing boats, a rock-carved lido filled with bobbing children, a small aquarium and plenty of candyfloss, rock and fish n' chips. The least-crowded beaches lie away from the town itself towards **Woolacombe**, which also has a number of very decent hotels.

If not here with your family, you probably won't want to linger long, but the town can be used as a base for exploring Lundy Island and there are several good coastal walks in the vicinity. For one of the best, park in the harbour and climb Lantern Hill to the romantic 13th-century stone chapel with its sea light on top. The views are fabulous.

Watermouth Castle
Berrynarbor,
t (01271) 867474,
www.watermouth
castle.com; open
Easter–Oct daily 10–4,
later Jul–Aug; adm
adults £12, children £10,
under 3s free

From the headland to the west of town you can join the zigzagging Torrs Walk to Lee Bay, three miles west, dominated by the Lee Bay Hotel and its fuchsia-filled gardens.

If you do have the children with you, you might want to pay a visit to the 19th-century **Watermouth Castle**, three miles east of town, which has been turned into a sort of fairytale grotto for children, inhabited by numerous plastic gnomes, trolls and goblins. There are also fairground rides, slides and swings.

Lundy Island

Lundy Island
Lundy Shore Office
The Quay, Bideford,
t (01271) 863636,
www.lundyisland.co.uk

This lonely island, three miles long and half a mile wide, has a dozen inhabitants, no shops and no roads. It's popular with breeding seabirds, including puffins (Lundy is Old Norse for puffin) and oystercatchers, as well as seals, while great 25ft-long basking sharks are often spotted off its coast during July and August. On the south and west side are rugged grey cliffs, on the east side steep, grassy slopes; in between it's flat and green. Habitation is in the south, around St Helena's Church, Marisco

Rock Pools

'It is not very much use coming to Ilfracombe unless you have some little taste for natural history' wrote a visitor in 1867. 'Socially it is everything here. You are hardly fit to live unless you know something about anemones. Nearly every house has got its aquarium.'

Lacking royal patronage or the endorsement of leading physicians, the remote North Devon coast failed to attract early holidaymakers. Instead it appealed to a few upper-class travellers who followed writers like Wordsworth and Coleridge, searching for the picturesque. Mainstream popularity came later, when Charles Kingley's *Westward Ho!* (1854) and Richard Blackmore's *Lorna Doone (1869)* made the North Devon coast a place of romantic adventure. At around the same time a series of books entitled *A Naturalist's Rambles on the Devon Coast, Seaside Pleasures* and *Land and Sea* turned Ilfracombe into the home of the new amateur science of marine biology – one of the more enduring seaside pursuits invented by Victorian holiday-makers hungry for self-improvement. The author of these books, Philip Gosse, can be credited with the discovery of the rock pool. He set in motion an invasion of the coast by enthusiastic collectors who observed, sketched and, of course, cleaned out all the living organisms left behind in the tidal pools. Nowadays Gosse is perhaps best remembered as the father of the poet, Edmund.

23 properties
*all owned by the
Landmark Trust,
t (01628) 825925,
www.landmark
trust.org.uk*

Tavern and the jetty. The island's ship, MS *Oldenburg*, takes less than two hours from Bideford (sailings all year round), Ilfracombe and Clovelly (summer only), four or five times a week in summer, less often in winter. You can go on a day trip or stay in one of **23 properties**, including a cottage, a lighthouse, a schoolhouse and a medieval castle .

Morte Point to the Taw

South of Ilfracombe, Morte Point heralds west-facing sandy beaches, good for swimming and suring. The rollers come straight into two-mile **Morte Bay** between rocky headlands. The small resort town of **Woolacombe** is full of hotels. Just around the headland is **Barricane Beach**, famous for the Caribbean shells washed here by strong Atlantic current. **Putsborough** shelters behind the long arm of the Baggy Point headland. You can walk along the beach from Woolacombe, or drive down narrow lanes. Croyde straggles along the coast road on the other side of Baggy Point. It's a big surfing centre. **Croyde Bay** is wonderful with rich yellow sand. The café above the beach has a webcam focused on the waves, so internet surfers can decide whether to come and surf for real. **Saunton** has a four-mile beach backed by the grassy dunes of Braunton Barrows. The beach is popular with longboarders.

Where To Stay and Eat on the North Devon Coast

(i) **Ilfracombe**
*The Landmark Theatre,
The Seafront,
t (01271) 863001,
www.visitilfracombe.
co.uk; open summer daily
10–5.30, winter 10–5*

(i) **Woolacombe**
*The Esplanade,
t (01271) 870553,
www.woolacombe
tourism.co.uk; open
summer Mon–Sat 10–5,
winter Mon–Sat 10–1*

★ **Woolacombe
Bay Hotel >>**

★ **The Quay >**

Ilfracombe

Most of Ilfracombe seems to put out a B&B sign in the summer, particularly along Brannocks Road. The nicest places are on Torr Park Road, half way down the Torrs.
Norbury House Hotel, Torrs Park , t (01271) 863888, *www.norburyhouse. co.uk (moderate)*. Surprisingly stylish B&B in a pretty part of town with views over the town to sea and eight smart bedrooms.
The Orchard, Lee Bay, t (01271) 867212, *www.theorchardlee.co.uk (moderate)* In the quiet one-pub town of Lee, three miles from Ilfracombe over the Torrs, this 17th-century converted barn has three brightly-coloured comfortable bedrooms. The friendly owners will pick you up after a long walk and you can throw your wet clothes into the drier. It's five minutes down to the beach and just thirty seconds to the Grampus Inn, which does bar meals.
The Quay, 11 The Quay, t (01271) 868090, *www.11thequay.co.uk (moderate)*. Owned by the one-man

art movement, Damien Hirst, this offers some of Ilfracombe's very finest dining. Downstairs is a very swanky bar and terrace (sandwiches and nibbles £5–8), while upstairs is an even swankier restaurant with views out over the water. The menu features upmarket takes on seaside specials, such as lobster and chips (no sharks in formaldehyde, unfortunately; mains £14.95–17.95). The walls are adorned with Mr Hirst's artworks.

Woolacombe

The Watersmeet Hotel, Mortehoe, t (01271) 870333, *www.watersmeethotel. co.uk (very expensive–luxury)*. Medium-sized, cream-painted hotel set on the hills above a small cove near Woolacombe, with a spa, an indoor pool, a heated outdoor pool and grass tennis courts. The dining room has white linen and panoramic sea views and offers good locally-sourced cuisine, while the bedrooms are airy and pleasant with coordinated fabrics.
Woolacombe Bay Hotel, Woolacombe, t (01271) 870388, *www.woolacombe-bay-hotel.co.uk (very expensive–luxury)*. This hotel resembles a Disney town nestling beneath the downs

with gables, chimneys and timber-work set amid rolling greenery just back from the beach. It's a substantial place with 65 bedrooms, two pools, two restaurants, a spa, tennis courts and a putting green. It's particularly good for families organizing a range of activities for children and offering a crèche for 0–5 year olds.

Croyde

Combas Farm, Putsborough, **t** (01271) 890398, *www.combasfarm.co.uk* (*budget–moderate*). Pretty white-painted 17th-century farmhouse in a colourful garden in a secluded valley, near Baggy Point, a mile from Putsborough Sands with four comfortable rooms to stay in. Good hearty breakfast and very reasonable rates.

Entertainment on the North Devon Coast

Landmark Theatre and Cinema, Seafront, Wilder Road, Ilfracombe **t** (01271) 865655, *www.northdevon theatres.org.uk*. Built in the 1990s, and resembling a sandcastle, the Landmark's unusual architectural style caused a bit of a fracas when it opened – but, like it or loathe it, it has nonetheless become a cultural beacon (and a recognizable landmark) on the North Devon Coast. One upturned bucket holds the auditorium (which doubles up as a theatre and a cinema). The repertoire includes good touring companies and old-time music hall performances. Arthouse films are shown Thurs–Sat if nothing else is on. There's an airy café-bar. It's the sister venue of the Queen's Theatre in Barnstaple.

Devon | The North Devon Coast: Barnstaple Bay

Barnstaple Bay

The ports of Barnstaple Bay caught the Atlantic trade in the 17th century, then cod, herring and mackerel until the 18th century, and local trade after that. Now the ports are dead. Barnstaple and Bideford are the main towns, at the lowest crossings of the rivers Taw and Torridge. The coastal footpath and road divert inland here; you may want to skip the estuary en route to the spectacular landscape north and south.

The large market town of **Barnstaple** is particularly worth visiting on market day (almost every day). The **Pannier Market**, built in 1885, leads out into Butcher's Row, a lovely street of small shops. On Friday, the main market day, the market hall fills up with more than 300 stalls selling locally-produced goodies, including cream, butter, chickens and pies and a wealth of fruit and vegetables. Saturday is a commercial market, with a hotchpotch of stalls selling shoes, clothes, groceries, tools and kitchenware. Tuesday is plants and flowers and Wednesday bric-a-brac.

The town has two museums. In the square next to the bridge, the **Museum of Barnstaple and North Devon** exhibits local slipware; the 1900s pottery of the Branhams factory is particularly interesting. Beside the old quayside, in an attractive Queen Anne building (once a merchant's meeting place), the **Heritage Centre** can tell you about the town's maritime history.

Bideford is a smaller version of Barnstaple. Its charm is its location on the steep valley side of the Torridge River. Climb up Bridge Street to the handsome Pannier Market (where there's not much to buy, unfortunately). The quayside still looks the part, with boats and cranes and the

Museum of Barnstaple and North Devon
The Square; **t** *(01271) 346747; www.devonmuseums. net; open Mon–Sat 9.30–5; adm free*

Heritage Centre
Queen Anne's Walk, **t** *(01271) 373003; open April–Oct Tues–Sat 10.30am–5.30pm, Nov–March Tues–Fri 10.30am–5pm, Sat 10.30pm–3.30pm; adm £3.50*

Getting to and around Barnstaple Bay

Barnstaple can be reached via the A39 and A361. Local buses link it to Exeter and Plymouth, and there are also National Express **coach** services from London, Bristol and Birmingham.

From Exeter St Davids, the **Tarka Line train** runs to Barnstaple in just over an hour, 12–14 times a day. The railway station is on the south side of the river, half a mile from the centre.

You can hire a **bike** in the station at Tarka Trail Cycle Hire, **t** (01271) 324202, *www.tarkabikes.co.uk*, £10.50 per day). The Tarka Trail heads north and south from Barnstaple. If you are heading north to Bideford, you'll spend the first two miles negotiating the town (on cycle lanes). If you go south towards Instow you'll head straight out into the countryside, from where you can continue to Great Torrington and Petrocstow, the end of the Tarka Trail. You can also hire bikes at Bideford Bicycle Hire (Torrington Street; **t** (01237) 424123; *www.bidefordbicycle hire.co.uk*; £10.50 a day).

Burton Art Gallery and Museum
Kingsley Road,
t *(01237) 471455,*
www.burtonart gallery.co.uk; open Mon–Fri 10am–5pm, Sun 11am–4pm

24-arched Long Bridge spanning the wide river. The **Burton Art Gallery and Museum** by the river has an excellent collection of Fishley slipware, including harvest jugs with yellow glazes decorated with sgraffito (scratched) words and leaves, or childish figures, and is also home to the town's tourist office. The downstairs galleries host contemporary art exhibitions. There is a craft shop and café too. Just off the Quay, up Rope Walk, is **Bideford Pottery**, a traditional pottery which makes sgraffito-decorated slipware pots, including harvest jugs.

The North Devon Potteries

North Devon has been a pottery centre since the Middle Ages. The traditional manufacturing style is either earthenware (low-fired rustic clay pots) or slipware (earthenware that has been dipped in a solution of water and clay and decorated). The main potteries were at Barnstaple and Bideford, where they exploited the rich seam of red earthenware clay at Fremington and the supply of wood in the river valleys to fire kilns. A huge export trade flourished in Wales, Ireland and America (where the 17th-century slipware pots are not major archaeological prizes). For collectors, there are three important periods. First, the late 18th century, when elaborate harvest pitchers, unique to this area, were made on commission for wealthy families; these now fetch thousands of pounds at auction and are filling the display cases of the V&A and Fitzwilliam museums, as well as the Burton in Bideford. In the mid-19th century there was a revival of slipware manufacturing, which was sustained until the early 20th century in the work of the Fishley family. From the early 1800s until the First World War four generations of Fishleys worked in the same rural pottery in Fremington; their work is now also exhibited in museums all over the country. After the Industrial Revolution, the pottery industry moved north to Stoke-on-Trent, near the coalfields; the clay still came from Devon, but the North Devon families could no longer compete with businessmen like Josiah Wedgwood. So the third period was characterized by a reaction against the industrialization of pottery in the north. In the 20th century a number of renowned craft potters set up workshops in North Devon to be near the materials, and for the way of life. Important potters such as Michael Leach, Clive Bowen, Svend Bayer and Sandy Brown moved to the area. Some of their workshops can still be visited today.

Clive Bowen trained with Michael Leach and set up his pottery in Shebbear in 1971 (**Shebbear Pottery**, Shebbear, Beaworthy, **t** (01409) 281 271). He is one of the best of his generation of potters, producing wood-fired Fremington clay tableware. Svend Bayer, who was trained by Michael Cardrew, has a workshop two miles out of Sheepwash on the Torrington Road (Duckpool Cottage, Sheepwash, Beaworthy, **t** (01409) 231282), producing large wood-fired pots. Sandy Brown works in Appledore and is well-known for artistic tableware. Others include Harry Juniper at **Bideford Pottery** (Rope Walk, Bideford, **t** (01237) 471105), who makes traditional slipware pots, including big harvest pitchers; Philip Leach, son of Michael and grandson of Bernard, who has worked with Clive Bowen and now runs the **Springfield Pottery** in Hartland (88 Springfield; **t** (01237) 4415506, *www.springfield-pottery.com*); and John Leach, Bernard's other grandson, who works out of Muchelney Pottery (*see* p.102).

The **Torridge Valley** between Bideford and the old railway station is beautiful, with tidal water, marshes, reedbeds and woods. The best way to see it is by cycling along the Tarka Trail, following the old railway line. The road runs along the river to **Great Torrington**, an amiable market town with a colonnaded town hall and an elegant pink Pannier Market (a general market is held on Thurs and Sat). Look in on **Nick Chapman's Potter** in Porch House as you drive in from Bideford. Just outside town is the famous **Dartington Crystal**, which emerged in 1967 out of the Dartington Project (*see* p.135). It is one of the the leading glass manufacturers in the country; the factory shop pulls in the coachloads.

Nick Chapman's Potter
t (01805) 622842

Dartington Crystal
t (01805) 626262;
www.dartington.co.uk

Tarka Country

Author Henry Williamson moved to North Devon in 1921 after the First World War and lived there for 14 years, writing stories about the world of 'otters, deer, salmon, water moonshine... the only world in which perhaps there was consistency, form, integrity' and earning himself a reputation as England's favourite nature writer. His bestseller *Tarka the Otter* (published in 1927) follows Tarka's adventures up and down the rivers Taw and Torridge. The otter's journey can be retraced along the Tarka Trail, a 180-mile walking route stretching from the North Devon coast to the top of Dartmoor in a figure of eight centred on Barnstaple, and touching Lynmouth and Ilfracombe in the north, and Bideford, Great Torrington and Okehampton in the south. The trail takes you through moors, cliffs, wooded river valleys and sandy bays. The stretch of the trail between Braunton and Petrocstow follows an old railway line and is popular with cyclists. You can hop on the scenic Tarka Line train to Barnstaple at Exeter St Davids. It takes just over an hour and weaves up the Exe and Tor, crossing and re-crossing the river. Bicycles are available for hire at Barnstaple Station, and then you're off on a good cycle path in either direction. Any North Devon tourist information centre or bookshop can supply you with leaflets and guide books. Otherwise contact the **Tarka Country Tourism Association** or **Coast and Countryside in Bideford** for more details.

The eels of the Two Rivers were devourers of the spawn and fry of salmon and trout, and the otters were devourers of eels. Tarka stood on the shillets of the shallow stream while they twisted and moved past his legs

Tarka the Otter,
Henry Williamson

Tarka Country Tourism Association
t 08707 469 209,
www.tarka-country.co.uk

Coast & Countryside in Bideford
Bideford Station,
t (01237) 423655

ⓘ **Barnstaple**
The Square,
t (01271) 375000,
www.staynorthdevon.
co.uk; open Mon–Sat
9.30–5

★ **Broomhill Art Hotel >**

Festivals and Events in Barnstaple Bay

The **Bideford Folk Festival** takes place over a week in August. Kingsley College is the main venue: **t** (01237) 473931, *www.bidefordfolkfestival.co.uk.*

Where to Stay and Eat in Barnstaple Bay

Broomhill Art Hotel, Muddiford, **t** (01271) 850262, *www.broomhillart. co.uk* (*moderate–expensive*). Two miles outside of Barnstaple, this is a real treat for the eyes with rooms filled with modern art and antiques. The hotel is surrounded by a sculpture garden, which boasts one of the Southwest's largest outdoor collections with more than 300 pieces. There's also a great 'slow food' restaurant, and various events, including jazz concerts, are laid on throughout the year.

The Royal Hotel, Barnstaple Street, Bideford, **t** (01237) 472005, *www.brend-hotels.co.uk/TheRoyal/ Home.cfm* (*moderate–expensive*). Smart Victorian hotel at the eastern end of the old Bideford Bridge looking

ⓘ **Bideford**
Burton Art Gallery and Museum, Kingsley Road,
t (01237) 471455; open Mon–Fri 10–5, Sat 10–4, Sun 11–4

ⓘ **Great Torrington**
Castle Hill, t (01805) 626140; open Mon–Fri 10–4, Sat 10–1

out over the River Torridge. Charles Kingsley wrote part of *Westward Ho!* while staying here. Stylish, antiquey-looking rooms and a formal, multi-mirrored restaurant (3 courses: £23).

Half Moon Inn, Sheepwash, Beaworthy, **t** (01409) 231376, *www.half moonsheepwash.co.uk* (*moderate*). Robust fishermen's inn on a pretty town square in the Torridge Valley, surrounded by thatched cottages. It offers 14 comfortable rooms, a traditional English-style **restaurant** as well as game-fishing (and tuition) on a 10-mile stretch of the River Torridge (salmon, sea trout and brown trout).

Browns Delicatessen, 37 South Street, Great Torrington, **t** (01805) 622900 (*budget*). Lovely little place for takeaway rolls or good strong coffee. There are three tables at the back if you want to sit down for an afternoon tea or a more substantial lunch.

Pannier Market Café, Pannier Market, Barnstaple, **t** (01271) 327227. Good working man's café with views of the market stalls. It serves all-day breakfasts, big mugs of tea and coffee, toasted sandwiches, bacon sandwiches and ham, egg and chips. *Closed Sun.*

The Black Horse Inn, High Street, Great Torrington, **t** (01805) 622121 (*budget*). A cosy inn with a fire serving simple staples: fish pie, sausage and chips, mushroom pie etc. It can also offer three basic guest rooms (*moderate*).

Entertainment in Barnstaple Bay

The Queen's Theatre, Boutport Street, Barnstaple, **t** (01271) 327357, *www.northdevontheatres. org.uk*. Touring theatre and seasonal favourites (such as Christmas pantomimes) held in the auditorium of the old town hall.

The Plough Arts Centre, 9–11 Fore Street, Great Torrington, **t** (01805) 624624, *www.plough-arts.org*. Busy little arts centre with a small auditorium offering a mix of local and touring theatre and bands, world music and arthouse cinema. The café serves wholesome home-cooked dinners. There's also a friendly bar with bottled ales. The work of local artists is exhibited in an upstairs gallery.

Appledore and Around

At the confluence of the Taw and Torridge rivers about two miles from the sea, Appledore has a long history of boatbuilding. In 1970 the largest covered shipbuilding docks in Europe were opened here; recent commissions include two Royal navy survey ships, HMS *Echo* and HMS *Enterprise*. All this goes on out of sight of the pretty Victorian quayside and Georgian terraces. From the quay, there are wide views across the estuary to Instow. Narrow alleyways lead uphill from the quayside, open doors leading into galleries, craft shops and fishing shops. **Sandy Brown** at no.3 Marine Parade is a noted potter. In summer a ferry goes to Instow, which has a long sandy beach. From the coastguard's hut you can see Northam Burrows, an estuarine marsh protected by a shingle ridge. At the top of the town, in a grand Georgian house on Odun Road is the excellent **North Devon Maritime Museum** with models of ships.

Avoid the dreary resort of **Westward Ho!** which was developed in the mid-19th century on the back of Charles Kingsley's book – but without his backing. Kingsley wrote to the company: 'How goes the Northam Burrows scheme for spoiling this beautiful place with hotels and villas? I suppose it must be, but you will frighten away all the sea-pies and defile

Sandy Brown
t (01237) 478219,
www.sandybrown arts.com

North Devon Maritime Museum
t (01237) 422064;
www.devonmuseums. net; open Mon–Fri 11am–5pm, Sat & Sun 2pm–5pm; adm £1.50

the Pebble Ridge with chicken bones and sandwich scraps'. It must be the only place in England with an exclamation mark in its name.

It feels good to get back on the coast road, leaving the busy estuary behind. The picture-postcard village of **Clovelly** in its steep wooded combe is part of a private estate that has never been modernized or developed (it charges visitors for entry, cars are banned so you'll have to park up and walk in). A steep cobbled street leads down past immaculately preserved fishermen's cottages to the stone harbour. Charles Kingsley lived in Clovelly for many years (his sister married the rector), and a small room in one of the cottages has been turned into a Victorian study and dedicated to him. At the bottom of a wooded cliff, around the quayside, are a pub, some cottages and piles of crab nets. In the harbour are a handful of rowing boats (which sit on the grey shingle at low tide trailing rusted metal chains).

There is a good walk two miles east along the beach (at low tide) to **Buck's Mills**, another tiny village with a tea shop. In summer there are boat trips (1.5 hours) to Lundy Island, just off the coast (see p.159).

At **Hartland Point** the coastline turns south. The walk between Hartland and Bude is one of the toughest sections of the Southwest Coastal Path, with some of the wildest coastal scenery. There are few pubs and only a few farmhouses to stay in. There are good walks from wind-battered **Hartland Quay** – all that survives of a port which stopped operating in 1860. The narrow street of old fisherman's cottages and quay stores lead down a slipway to the ruined harbour. Inland there are two good potteries in Harland, including Springfield Pottery (*see* p.162), run by Philip (and Frannie) Leach, son of Michael Leach and grandson of Bernard Leach.

Where to Stay and Eat in Appledore, Clovelly and Hartland

(i) **Clovelly**
Car Park, **t** *(01237) 431781. Open daily summer 9am–5.30pm, winter 10am–4pm.*

(★) **Bradbourne House >**

New Inn Hotel, High Street, Clovelly, **t** (01237) 431303, *www.clovelly.co.uk* (*expensive*). A short walk up from the quay in the heart of the village, the New Inn has eight comfortable William-Morris-inspired room (lots of twirly leafy motifs).

Red Lion Hotel, Clovelly, **t** (01237) 431237, *www.clovelly.co.uk* (*expensive*). A good choice by the harbour, this has several nautically-themed rooms to rent and a renowned restaurant (*booking required*).

Bradbourne House, Marine Parade, Appledore, **t** (01237) 474395, *www.bradbournehouse.co.uk* (*moderate*).

B&B in an elegant Georgian house overlooking the River Torridge with fantastic wooden spiral stairs and three lovely bedrooms (one double, one twin, one single) with private bathrooms. Friendly and helpful owners.

Hartland Quay Hotel, Hartland, **t** (01237) 441218, *www.hartlandquay hotel.com* (*moderate*). Lonely hotel above the old Elizabethan quay with 15 functional bedrooms. Great atmosphere and Wreckers beer.

2 Harton Manor, The Square, Hartland, **t** (01237) 441670, *www.twoharton manor.co.uk* (*moderate*). Beautiful house with oak floorboards, a big fireplace and a golden labrador. The walls are hung with woodcut prints (wood-cutting courses are offered). There's also a studio full of books and paintings. One good-sized twin and one double available, both with Wi-Fi.

West Titchberry Farm, Hartland Point, Hartland, **t** (01237) 441287 (*moderate*). An 18th-century Devon longhouse with three bedrooms plus board games and a woodburning stove in the lounge. Follow the Hartland Point signs from Hartland Village. Walkers will appreciate the offer of a packed lunch and a lift home at the end of an arduous hike. It lies about five minutes' walk from the coastal path.

The Old Farmhouse, Hescott, Hartland, **t** (01237) 441709, *www.old hescottfarmhouse.co.uk* (*budget– moderate*). About three miles from Hartland Point and Clovelly with a flagstone floor and a big pine breakfast table, this B&B boasts three simple bedrooms and comfortable beds.

Cornwall

Above all, people come to Cornwall for one thing, a little bit of magic – to stand atop the violent, wind-ravaged cliff castles from where Arthur once rode out to fight the Saxon invaders, to battle their way through the sultry depths of a make-believe rainforest, and to try and tame the endless rollers of the Atlantic armed only with a wooden board. In the rest of the country, it can sometimes be difficult telling exactly where one county starts and another ends. Borders are often imprecise, perhaps marked by a small 'welcome to' roadside sign, while cultural and geographical differences can be marginal. There's no mistaking Cornwall's uniqueness, however. Delineated by the River Tamar to the east and the sea on its other three sides, this is a region both geographically distinct and with a proud Celtic culture unlike anywhere else England, if England is indeed where it resides – there are plenty in 'Kernow' who'd dispute it.

09

Don't miss

⭐ **Cheesewrings, Hurlers and beasts**
Bodmin Moor **p.171**

⭐ **Swinging in the treetops**
Looe Monkey Sanctuary **p.174**

⭐ **Trekking through the Tropics**
Eden Project **p.180**

⭐ **A seafood empire.**
Padstow **p.184**

⭐ **The blooms of a thousand tropical flowers.**
Tresco Abbey Gardens **p.215**

See map overleaf

20 km

1 0 miles

N

St Martin's

Bryher

Tresco

Hugh Town

St Mary's

Old Town

St Agnes

Isles of Scilly

Trevose Head

Trevone

Constantine Bay

Treyarnon

Padstow

Bedruthan Steps

Watergate Bay

Newquay

Holywell

Trerice

Perranporth

A30

St Agnes

Truro

Redruth

Carn Brae

Trelissick Garden

St Ives

St Ives Bay

A30

Camborne

Zennor

B3306

Chysauster

Penryn

A394

St Mawes Castle

Pendeen

Geevor Tin Mine

Cape Cornwall

St Just

Falmouth

Roseland Per

Pendennis Castle

Carn Euny

Penzance

Marazion

National Seal Sanctuary

Mawnan Smith

Rosemullion Head

A30

Newlyn

St Michael's Mount

A394

Glendurgan

Land's End

Mousehole

Mount's Bay

Porthleven

Helston

Helford

St-Anthony-in-Meneage

Gillan

Treen

Porthcurno

Gunwalloe

Goonhilly

St Keverne

The Manacles

Mullion

Coverack

Kynance Cove

Cadgwith

Lizard

Lizard Point

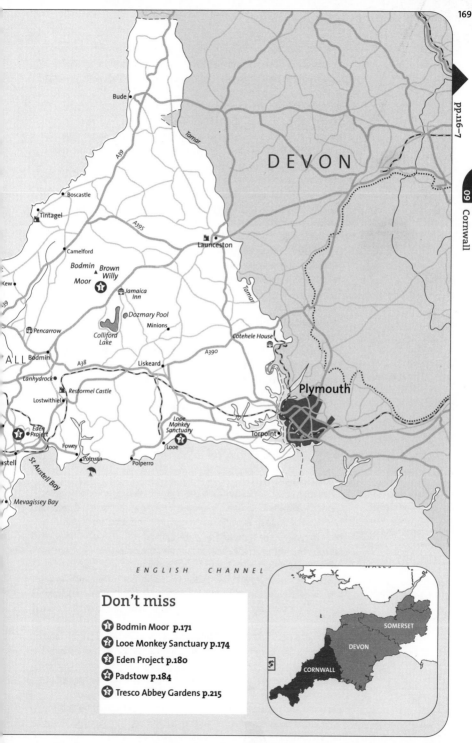

DEVON

Bude

Tamar

Boscastle

Tintagel

A39

A395

Camelford

Launceston

Bodmin Moor

Brown Willy

Jamaica Inn

Kew

Dozmary Pool

Minions

A39

Pencarrow

Colliford Lake

Tamar

Cotehele House

ALL

Bodmin

A38

Liskeard

A390

Lanhydrock

Restormel Castle

Plymouth

Lostwithiel

Eden Project

Looe Monkey Sanctuary p.174

Torpoint

stell

Fowey

Polruan

Looe

Polperro

Mevagissey Bay

St Austell Bay

ENGLISH CHANNEL

Don't miss

1 **Bodmin Moor p.171**

2 **Looe Monkey Sanctuary p.174**

3 **Eden Project p.180**

4 **Padstow p.184**

5 **Tresco Abbey Gardens p.215**

WALES

SOMERSET

DEVON

CORNWALL

Bodmin

The market town of Bodmin grew up around the seventh-century monastery of St Petroc, a Welsh saint who spent most of his life ministering in the Southwest. In the Middle Ages it became one of the region's stannary towns, the centres of tin production that came to dominate the local economic and political life, and its church grew into the largest in Cornwall. Today Bodmin's importance has waned rather, but it's a pleasant base from which to explore nearby Bodmin Moor. In the centre of the main square stands a statue of Athelstan the tenth-century King of England – a slightly controversial choice given the Saxon king's campaigns of conquest against the Cornish – overlooked by the **Shire Hall**. Within is a display on a famous local 19th-century miscarriage of justice when a young farmer was convicted of murdering a local woman, Charlotte Dymond, on the slimmest of evidence. He was executed at nearby **Bodmin Jail**, a macabre Victorian building with granite walls, with an estimated crowd of around 20,000 in attendance, many of whom travelled on specially-laid-on train services. You can tour the jails, which are today populated by a coterie of unhappy-looking mannequins, supposed to resemble historical prisoners.

Bodmin Jail
Berrycoombe Road;
t (01208) 76292;
www.bodminjail.org;
open daily 10am–dusk;
adm £5.50

The Camel Trail

Bodmin Jail stands near to the Camel Trail, a popular cycling, walking and horse-riding route, following the old Bodmin and Wadebridge Railway Line beside the River Camel between Bodmin, Wadebridge and Padstow (12 miles) and on to Camelford (7 miles). The line was built by Sir William Moleworth of Pencarrow to convey lime sand from Wadebridge up the Camel as manure. The line closed in the 1960s in the wake of the Beeching Report, but part of it has opened again for steam-train rides. **The Bodmin & Wenford Railway** chugs its way along a 13-mile section between Bodmin Parkway, Bodmin General and Boscarne Junction.

**The Bodmin &
Wenford Railway**
*General Station,
Bodmin, t (01208) 73555,
www.bodminandwenfo
rdrailway.co.uk, adm
return £11, day rover £15*

Around Bodmin

Five miles north of Bodmin off the A389 lies **Pencarrow House and Gardens**, a lovely Palladian-style mansion, its gardens stocked with rare trees and peacocks. Sir William Molesworth, the 8th Baronet (1810–55) built the mile-long approach drive embanked with rhododendrons, and laid out the formal Italian gardens around the house. He also planted ornamental woodlands around an Iron Age fort.

Two miles west of Parkway station is **Lanhydrock House and Gardens**. A tree-lined avenue runs through the 17th-century gatehouse and knocks on the front door of the splendid neo-Jacobean house, its walls covered in grandiflora, camellia and ivy. It was one of the largest houses in Cornwall when built in the 1630s by Sir Richard Robartes on the land of St Petroc's. Since then much of it has been demolished, leaving only the north wing and its barrel-vaulted long gallery. The 2nd Lord Robartes refurbished the old place in Victorian style. Now it has everything but charm: vintage car rides, a collection of Victorian toys, 910 acres of parkland and meticulously presented interiors. A highlight is Tommy Agar Robartes' dressing-case, laid out on the bed as if he were about to return to the Front Lines in 1915 (he never did).

**Pencarrow House
and Gardens**
*Pencarrow, Bodmin;
t (01208) 841369;
www.pencarrow.co.uk;
open house Apr–Sept
Sun–Thurs 11am–5pm,
garden March–Oct daily
9.30am–5.30pm; adm
£8.50*

**Lanhydrock House
and Gardens**
*Bodmin;
t (01208) 265950;
www.nationaltrust.org.
uk/main/w-lanhydrock;
open house March–Oct
Tues–Sun 11am–5pm,
garden all year daily
10am–6pm; adm £9.45*

Getting to and around Bodmin and Bodmin Moor

By Car/Train

The main A30 route into Cornwall cuts across Bodmin Moor and narrowly bypasses Bodmin town. Bodmin Parkway station is a major stop on the London Paddington to Penzance mainline railway. Services for the Bodmin and Wentford Railway also leave from here. The line now conveys passengers on scenic steam-train rides to Boscarne Junction and back, a 13-mile round trip (*see* p.170 for details).

On Foot and by Bicycle

The Camel Trail is a popular cycling route, following the old railway line beside the River Camel (*see* p.170 for details). You can rent bicycles at Bridge Bike Hire in Wadebridge at the start of the trail near Padstow, (t (01208) 813050, *www.bridgebikehire.co.uk*; from £10 a day).

Bodmin Moor

⭐ Bodmin Moor   The main West Country road (A30) whizzes straight through the middle of Bodmin Moor to the north east of Bodmin town. The smallest of the Southwest's trio of 'wildernesses', Bodmin Moor is like Dartmoor in miniature: boggy and rugged with tinkling streams, murky lakes, thick expanses of grassland and, of course, a smattering of bizarrely shaped granite tors. Near its centre, occupying an appropriately barren and

Jamaica Inn   windswept location, is the **Jamaica Inn**, as popularized in Daphne Du
Bolventor;   Maurier's eponymous tale of moorland smuggling. Today it's a much
t (01566) 86250;   visited and rather tacky tourist attraction with a **Museum of Smuggling**
http://jamaicainn.co.uk   which has displays both on the age-old Cornish practice of customs evasion and Du Maurier herself. The inn still rents out rooms, although anyone looking for a bit of creaky, hidden-panel smuggling authenticity will be disappointed. They're modern, generic and rather comfortable.

Heading south for around a mile from the inn will take you to one of the various sites on the moor associated with local myths and legends, **Dozmary Pool**. This is supposedly the final resting place of Excalibur, King Arthur's magical sword, which was thrown into the water by Sir

The Beast of Bodmin Moor

In the early 1980s reports emerged of a large, black panther-like cat seen roaming the Cornish moors. Dismissed at first as a hoax or perhaps the ravings of a particularly drunken tourist, soon more and more people started coming forward claiming to have seen the same thing. Could it be true? Could there really be a big cat on the loose in the West Country and, if so, where did it come from? No zoos had reported any missing animals. The 1976 Dangerous Wild Animals Act prohibited the keeping of big cats as pets. Perhaps it was an illegal pet that had been released once it had grown too big to handle, the owner fearing the legal consequences if they reported it. The national press became determined to solve the mystery, sending teams of reporters to hunt for what soon became known as the 'Beast of Bodmin Moor'. With hundreds of amateur sleuths also on the trail, it rapidly turned into a cause célèbre. Farmers expressed concern for the safety of their livestock while tourist boards worried about the potential damage that the presence of a dangerous wild animal running loose in the countryside might do to the tourist industry – although, if anything, the mystery served to increase the area's popularity. Before long, the beast had become as famous as that other great mystery creature, the Loch Ness Monster.

Despite all the interest, the 'beast' itself has remained tantalizingly elusive. Unconfirmed sightings have continued to flood in over the last 25 years, occasionally accompanied by some rather (conveniently) blurred photos showing a fuzzy black shape that could be a cat, or a boulder, or a hole in the ground, or anything really. Absolute proof of the beast's existence has been somewhat hard to come by. To this day, it has managed to escape the combined attention of thousands of tourists and press, not to mention an RAF search team, which means that if there is something out there, it's pretty good at hiding itself.

Bedevere as Arthur lay dying at the Battle of Camlann, whereupon a mysterious hand reached out of the water, grabbed the sword and dragged it down into the depths where it was reclaimed by the Lady of the Lake (who presumably still has it). Other nearby sites include the **Stripple Stones**, a circular arrangement of Neolithic stones and **Colliford Lake Park**. Just south of Bolventor the park makes a good stop-off for families, with lakeside walks, an adventure play area and various resident animals, including sheep, cows and poultry.

To the east of Jamaica Inn are some of the moor's most famous prehistoric monuments. The **Cheesewring** is an improbably shaped 9m-high granite monolith, which looks like several large stone discs balanced precariously – and seemingly in contravention of the rules of gravity – one on top of the other, but is in fact a single rock weathered into bizarreness. Nearby stand the **Hurlers**, which comprise two lonely rings of weathered, moss-covered stones – local legend says they were originally men who were turned into stones for committing the sin of playing hurling on a Sunday. To the south stands a Neolithic burial chamber called **Trethevy Quoit**, made up of a giant stone slab balanced on several small ones – it looks a bit like a slightly wonky giant's table

Other notable attractions in the southern moors include the **Carnglaze Caverns**, a collection of vast slate caverns, one of which has been turned into an auditorium, the Rum Store (so named because the Royal Navy stored supplies of rum here during Second World War) and the **Golitha Falls**, a popular beauty spot where cascades tumble over a series of mossy rocks in a nature reserve protecting one of the moor's last remaining swaths of oak woodland. Both lie just a couple of miles from the village of St Neot, which boasts a fine medieval church and which was particularly beloved of John Betjeman.

Heading into the northern moors from Jamaica Inn, it's about a four-mile walk to its highest point, the singularly-named **Brown Willy** (the name is believed to derive from a corruption of the Cornish term *bron ughella*, which means 'high hill', or possibly from *bron wennyly*, which means 'swallow's hill'). The highest hill in Cornwall at 420m (1,400ft), it sits with its twin peak, Rough Tor, around 4 miles southeast of the town of Camelford. It'll take you around three to four hours to trek to the top of the Willy, from where there are great views of the county.

Sometimes all it takes to start up an industry is a vaguely promising name, which presumably explains all the Arthurian hoopla going on in **Camelford**, which has been identified as the site of Arthur's Castle (Camelot) and his last battle (Camlann). The town's **Arthurian Centre** has displays on the legends, myths and sites associated with the legendary West Country king (with all the signs written in a swoopy medieval-ish font). Signs lead from the centre to a sixth-century stone, the evocatively named **Slaughterbridge Stone**, marked in Latin and Ogham (ancient Celtic) inscriptions, which supposedly mention Arthur.

Slightly unpredictably, Camelford is also the site of the **British Cycling Museum**, which traces the history of bipedal transport from 19th-century boneshakers to ultra-modern, ultra-light wind-tunnel-tested flying machines favoured by Olympic riders and Tour de France winners. The museum lies around a mile north of town on the B3266.

Colliford Lake Park
Bolventor,
t (01208) 821469,
www.collifordlakepark.
co.uk; open daily
10.30am–5pm; adm £6

Carnglaze Caverns
St Neot, Liskeard,
t (01579) 320251,
www.carnglaze.com;
Mon–Sat 10am–5pm;
adm £6

Arthurian Centre
Slaughterbridge,
Camelford, t (01840)
213947; www.arthur-
online.co.uk; open
Easter–Oct 10am–5pm;
adm £3

British Cycling Museum
The Old Station,
Camelford; t (01840)
212811; open Sun–Thurs
10am–5pm; adm £3.35

Where to Stay and Eat on Bodmin Moor

ⓘ **Bodmin**

Shire House, Mount Folly Square; t (01208) 74159; open summer Mon–Sat 10am–5pm, winter Mon–Fri 10am–4pm. The centre can provide information on Bodmin, the moor and Cornwall more generally.

⭐ **Lavethan >**

Treverbyn Vean Manor, Twowatersfoot, Liskeard, t (01579) 326105, *www.treverbynvean.co.uk* (*expensive*). Occupying a terribly romantic setting above the wooded Glynn Valley on the southern slopes of Bodmin, this Grade II listed neo-Gothic manor house provides a highly elegant moorland base. Inside it's all very antique with a minstrel's gallery, stone mullion, windows and exposed beams. The two rooms are large and comfortable. Dinner, much of it sourced from hotel's own organic garden, can be arranged on request. **Lavethan,** Blisland, Bodmin; t (01208) 850487; *www.lavethan.com* (*moderate–expensive*). The farmhouse was already a going concern when the Domesday Book was being compiled and today provides a suitably historic setting for exploring the timeless pleasures of the moor, set in its own wooded valley near a tributary of the River Camel. B&B accommodation is offered in three large, tasteful bedrooms, and three self-catering cottages named Tom, Dick and Harry, which cater to four, four and seven people respectively. There's also a lovely walled garden and a heated outdoor swimming pool. **Berrio Bridge House,** North Hill, Launceston, t (01566) 782714, *www. berriobridgehouse.co.uk* (*moderate*). On the eastern side of Bodmin Moor, halfway between Launceston and Liskeard, this pretty white cottage B&B next to the River Lynher has two neat pretty bedrooms.

Countryman Hotel, Victoria Road, Camelford, t (01840) 212250, *www.thecountrymanhotel.co.uk* (*moderate*). Just two minutes' walk from central Camelford, on Route 3 of the National Cycle Network, this is ideally situated for anyone doing some serious moorland hiking and biking. The ten rooms are simple but comfortable with TVs and tea-making facilities. Some have private bathrooms. Breakfast is served overlooking the garden.

Hotel Casi Casa, 1 Higher Bore Street, Bodmin, t (01208) 77592, *www.hotel casicasa.co.uk* (*moderate*). Pretty little white-fronted hotel. There are five quiet, double-glazed en-suite bedrooms, a comfortable bar and lounge.

Prior Cottage, 34 Rhind Street, Bodmin, t (01208) 73064 (*moderate*). Friendly, centuries-old cottage in a quiet secluded part of Bodmin with two nicely furnished bedrooms.

Maple Leaf Café, 1–4 Honey Street, Bodmin, t (01208) 72206 (*budget*). Friendly small café with a courtyard at the back. Good wholesome lunches – home-made soups and pasta bakes – and an espresso machine.

The South Coast: Looe to Fowey

Once through the moor you feel like you're in Cornwall proper at last, with pretty coastal villages and ports lined up before you.

Looe and Around

Sand, sea and shark-fishing are the principal attractions of the south-coast town of Looe. It's a straightforward little place that has so far resisted the gentrification undergone by many of its coastal rivals, with a workaday harbour that still functions as a busy port bringing in coal, timber and fish, and exporting stone and minerals. The East Looe River divides the town into East and West Looe, linked by a seven-arched bridge. East Looe has most of the tourist services – including the majority of hotels and restaurants – as well as a working fish quay, its fishing fleet moored against the river wall, the fish market and packing

Getting to and around Looe

By Car/Train

If you're arriving by car, you can park by the river at West Looe or at Liskeard and continue by train.

The mainline London-Paddington to Penzance **trains** stop at Liskeard, from where you can catch a local train to Looe, along the scenic Looe Valley Line, which runs for 8.75 miles along the old quarry line. The service is operated by First Great Western (t 08457 000125) and takes half an hour.

On Foot

If you're ready for a **walk** after the trip down, ask for the Looe Valley Trails leaflet at the Tourist Information Centre. Mark Camp at Walkabout West, t (01503) 273060, *www.walkaboutwest.freeserve.co.uk*, is a Blue Badge guide who can be hired for day or evening walks.

By Boat

Boat trips depart from East Quay and head out around the bay to Looe Island bird Reserve with its smugglers' caves. Ask at the Tourist Information Centre. The Shark Angling Club of Great Britain (The Quay, East Looe, t (01503) 262642, *www.sharkanglingclubofgreatbritain.org.uk*) runs seasonal fishing trips: two-hour mackerel trips, half-day shark or reef-fish trips or an all-day shark or reef-fish trip (£20/£30 half/full day).

museum
Higher Market Street;
t (01503) 262070; open
spring bank holiday
weekend–Sept Sun–Fri
11am–4pm; adm £1.80

houses on the quayside. Fore Street, behind the quay, leads to a cluster of seafront streets. The 15th-century Guildhall on Higher Market Street houses a **museum** full of fishing-related flotsam and jetsam, such as an old pilchard press, as well as a large archive of local historic photographs.

It's less fussy than some of the other resorts of the Cornish coast. The bucket-and-spades sandy beach is jolly, but you might prefer to go east along the coastal path to **Millendreath Beach**, which is smaller and nicer. You can take a ferry or cross the bridge to West Looe and there are several companies offering 'big game' fishing trips, chief among them the evocatively named **Shark Angling Club of Great Britain**, as well as excursions to nearby **Looe Island**. This 23-acre wildlife sanctuary was, according to legend, where Joseph of Arimathea and the young Christ first set foot on British soil during their brief visit to the country. What can be stated with a degree more certainty is that it today bears the remains of a 12th-century Benedictine monastery and in the 20th century was owned by two sisters who lived there until their deaths (and recounted their experiences in the book *We Bought an Island*), after which the island was bequeathed to the Cornwall Wildlife Trust. Today it is home to large populations of great black-backed gulls and, rather less cutely, rats. According the 19th-century author, Wilkie Collins, in his travel memoir *Rambles beyond the Railway* (1851), the rodents once provided a popular food source for the locals who ate them with 'vindictive relish'. Thankfully the towns' restaurants have improved rather since then.

Looe Monkey Sanctuary

⚄ Looe Monkey Sanctuary
St Martin, Murrayton,
Looe; t (01503) 262532;
www.monkeysanctuary.org;
open April–Sept Sun–Thurs
11.30am–4.30pm; adm £7.50

Just outside of town, heading towards Plymouth, this small area of woodland is home to a colony of leaping, climbing, clambering South American Woolly Monkeys. All the animals were born in the sanctuary and have a pragmatic tolerance of people, which means you can get right up close as they make their way between their various interlinked enclosures. You can also watch bats here. Down in the cellar of the sanctuary house lives a community of horseshoe bats that can be spied on with the aid of infra-red lights and a special camera. The sanctuary's vegetarian 'Tree Top' café serves some pretty decent, locally sourced, sandwiches, baguettes, cakes and Cornish ice cream.

Where to Stay in Looe

Looe

(i) Looe
The Guildhall, Fore Street, t (01503) 262072. Open summer daily 10am–5pm

(★) Cardwen Farm
>>

(★) Mawgan's of Looe >>

Barclay House, St Martins Road, **t** (01503) 262929, *www.barclayhouse. co.uk (expensive)*. One of the town's grandest choices on the slopes of the East Looe river valley. The main Victorian house has ten very stylish bedrooms and there are another eight self-catering units in the six acres of grounds as well as a high class restaurant (3 courses for £24.50) and an outdoor swimming pool.

Beach House, Marine Drive, Hannafore, **t** (01503) 262598, *www.the beachhouselooe.co.uk (expensive)*. A modern and rather luxurious guesthouse positioned on the seafront at Hannafore Point right on the Southwest Coastal Path. The bright, sea-fresh rooms are all named after local beaches. Generous cooked-to-order English breakfasts.

Trehaven Manor Hotel, Station Road, **t** (01503) 262028, *www.trehavenhotel. co.uk (moderate–expensive)*. Set a short hike above the town and estuary, this sturdy old place has a collection of large rooms, most with coastal views, decorated in a pleasing country-house style with plenty of antiques. Breakfast (locally-source, of course) is served in a bay-fronted dining room overlooking the water.

Annaclone, Marine Drive, Hannafore, **t** (01503) 265137, *www.annaclonelooe. co.uk (moderate)*. Friendly B&B on the seafront at Hannafore with three large slightly chintzy bedrooms.

Tidal Court, Church Street, **t** (01503) 263695 *(budget–moderate)*. Modest, old-fashioned guesthouse in a great location in the centre of town, a minute's walk from the harbour.

Around Looe

Talland Bay Hotel, Porthallow, **t** (01503) 272667, *www.tallandbay hotel.co.uk (expensive)*. Lovely old-world country-house hotel at the end of a long track, on the coastal path

between Looe and Polperro, with 21 tasteful rooms (some with sea views), a pool, a croquet law and a terrace overlooking the water.

Cardwen Farm, Pelynt, **t** (01503) 220213, *www.cardwenfarm.com (moderate)*. A seventeenth-century Grade II listed farmhouse offering three bedrooms in a beautiful garden by the River Poll and two self-catering cottages (one with three bedrooms, the other with four). There are also two ponds, one home to Aylesbury ducks, the other to trout.

Eating Out in Looe

Trawlers on the Quay, The Quay, **t** (01503) 263593, *www.trawlersrestaur ant.co.uk (moderate–expensive)*. Long-established seafood restaurant with a great reputation right on the working quay. Dinner is served all year and light lunches too in summer. The menu changes daily according to the daily catch. Mains £15–19. *Closed Mon.*

Mawgan's of Looe, Higher Market Street, East Looe, **t** (01503) 265331, *www.mawgans.co.uk (moderate)*. The management here espouse a super-keen good-food ethos, promising that all the ingredients are locally sourced and free of artificial flavourings and GM additives. Of course, operating a kitchen with a clear conscience isn't enough to get paying customers through the door. The cooing must also be up to the mark, which it most certainly is – lots of fresh fish and seafood from the harbour (Dover sole, sea bass, mussels, scallops etc.) served simply and well, plus some hearty meat concoctions, such as 'trio of lamb noisettes'. *No children.*

Old Sail Loft, Quay Street, **t** (01503) 262131, *www.theoldsailloft restaurant.com (moderate)*. A very yo-ho-ho fish restaurant with a flagstone floor, exposed wooden beams (said to have been recovered from local wrecks), bits of maritime paraphernalia on the walls and a changing menu based on the daily catch.

Anne's Sandwich Shop, The Archway, The Quay, **t** (01503) 265405 (*budget*). Tiny seasonal shop just off Fore Street on the way to the quay, serving huge filled baps, baguettes and sarnies.

Emile's, 1 Barbican Parade, Barbican Road, **t** (01503) 262932 (*budget*). Decent fish and chips.

The Salutation Inn, Fore street, **t** (01503) 262784 (*budget*). A salty, traditional pub (1612) with a tiled floor, leather bench seats, old photos, a small coal fire and low beams. The decent prices and reasonably priced food ensure that it's nearly always busy. Mind your head on the way in.

Treleavens, Fore Street, **t** (01503) 220969, *www.treleavens.co.uk* (*budget*).Delicious home-made Cornish ice cream. You'll also find branches in Polperro (Lansallos Street) and Tintagel (Fore Street).

Polperro

Quaint with a capital 'Q', Polperro is so archetypically pretty, with its dinky little streets and cottages clustered around an equally dinky fishing harbour, that you half-suspect it of being the artificial creation of some particularly cunning tourist board. Its tiny white-washed cottages are real, however. Indeed, despite their wholesome appearance, many were built from the proceeds of smuggling. The town's sandy beaches are as clean and well maintained as you'd hope and, in high season, just as crowded as you'd expect. Down on the front, a 15-strong fishing fleet of netting boats, trawlers and scallopers bring catches of mackerel (and scallops) into the covered fish market on the quay, but the fishermen can't afford to live in the village these days – most of the cottages are second homes or holiday lets – and they don't even use the pubs. The **Polperro Heritage Museum** is located in an old fisherman's store on the slipway at the end of the West Quay, and has a display on smuggling as well as lots of historic photos of the town. Other attractions include a house covered entirely with shells along the Warren – the centrepiece is a depiction of the Eddystone Lighthouse. You can take boat trips from Polperro Harbour along the coast to Fowey.

Polperro Heritage Museum
The Harbour;
t (01503) 272423;
www.polperro.org/
museum.html; open
Mar–Oct daily
10am–6pm; adm £1.75

Fowey

Fowey (pronounced 'Foy') is Cornwall's grandest old harbour town. Its shops sell expensive nautical gear, its streets are lined with excellent restaurants and it's surrounded by green hills preserved for centuries by the local gentry. In the Middle Ages, Fowey was as prosperous as any south-coast port. It traded tin and cloth, ferried pilgrims to Santiago, supported the English in various military campaigns and initiated a few private ones of its own – the medieval Fowey Gallants gained notoriety for their acts of daredevil piracy, terrorizing the ports of France and Spain and the Cinque Ports of southeast England. Today things are much more sedate, the harbour busy with pleasure boats and container ships heading for the china-clay docks. The town is stacked up the hillside behind the quay, with the Gothic mansion of the Treffy family halfway up. The church has a handsome tower and a fabulous peal of bells. Sir Arthur Quiller-Couch, the literary critic and compiler of the *Oxford Book*

Getting to Polperro and Fowey

You can't drive to **Polperro**, but will have to leave your car in the car park and either walk in (10 minutes), take a 'bus' (it's actually a converted milk float) or a horse-and-cart ride (which is the most expensive option, but you do get a free ice cream with a return ticket).

Fowey is on the coast between Mevagissey and Looe, off the A3082. Leave the A390 at St Blazey. Buses link the town with Looe and Liskeard.

---

museum
Town Hall, Trafalgar Square; **t** *(01726) 833513; open Easter–mid Oct Mon–Fri 10.30am–5pm; adm £1*

Dapne Du Maurier Visitor Centre
5 South Street; **t** *(01726) 833616; open daily 9.30am–5.30pm*

of English Verse 1250–1900 who wrote under the pen name 'Q', is buried in the churchyard. Despite its compactness, Fowey is imposing; its narrow lanes and flights of steps echo your footsteps. Large Victorian buildings on the quay include a small one-room aquarium (open summer only), a **museum** filled with all the usual local oddities, including models of sailing ships, old photographs, costumes and the mayoral regalia and the **Dapne Du Maurier Visitor Centre**, which is housed in the same building as the tourist office. The author lived west of Fowey at Menabilly and used the area as a setting for many of her novels. Every May the town plays host to the Daphne Du Maurier Festival, featuring readings, talks and various other live events.

09 Cornwall | Section

Kernow – the kingdom within a kingdom

Cornwall's absorption into England was slow and often painful, and some would argue never entirely completed, hence the revival of Cornish Nationalism in recent decades. The series of conquests and invasions that instilled unity in England during the first millennium AD failed to assimilate Cornwall. There are no Roman villas or Saxon burghs in Cornwall because there was no Roman conquest or Saxon colonization. Until the defeat of King Hywell of Cornwall by Athelstan in 926, Cornwall ploughed a separate cultural furrow, developing its own language, Celtic-Catholic religion, and laws enforced by indigenous kings.

The Norman kings of England made Cornwall an earldom which became, under Edward I, a duchy, the first ever created by an English monarch (today held by Prince Charles). This is at the heart of Cornwall's special situation. The duke was heir to the old kings of Cornwall, with regal powers and a place in Lostwithiel. Tin mining was regulated by the Stannary Parliament, which had its own law-making powers and was exempt from the laws and taxes of Westminster. In practice, all Cornish life came under its jurisdiction. Cornish medieval history is one of collisions between the Stannary Parliament and English monarchs. Henry VII's suspension of stannary government, confiscation of stannary charters and attempts to raise Cornish taxes to fund his own wars in Scotland led to an uprising in 1497. Michael Joseph *An Gof* ('The Smith') led a Cornish peasant army of 15,000 men to London, meeting the King's army (raised for the Scottish wars) at Blackheath. The rebels were no match for professional soldiers, and An Gof was executed at Tyburn. There was a second Cornish uprising in the same year, when a 6,000-strong Cornish army led by the regal imposter, Perkin Warbeck, attacked Exeter. As part of the clampdown, an English force was sent into Cornwall to put an end to the flagrant privateering, smuggling and independent sea battles of the Cornish captains. Ships were impounded with all their gear, victuallers arrested and captains executed in London. The Charter of Pardon in 1508, however, reaffirmed the legislative independence of the Stannary Parliament: 'No act or statute shall have effect in the stannaries without the assent and consent of the 24 stannators'.

The beginning of the end of self-government came with the 1549 Act of Uniformity, which ordered that all church services must be conducted in English instead of Latin. Following a petition to the king – 'And so we the Cornish men utterly refuse this new English' – Humphrey Arundell raised another Cornish army, whose defeat was followed by reprisals: 'Henry VIII's mobsters were the real conquerors of Cornwall', writes Cornish historian John Angarrack in *Our Future is History*.

Around Fowey

There's plenty of good **walking** around Fowey. You can pick up a leaflet produced by the National Trust, listing some of the most popular routes, from the tourist office. One of the most pleasant short walks is the Hall Walk, taking the **Bodinnick Ferry** from Fowey and walking from Bodinnick to Penleath Point along a private promenade, laid out in the 16th century by a member of the local gentry. Another walk takes you from Coombe Farm down to Poldrimouth – the beach where the shipwreck takes place in *Rebecca* – and east along the cliff to Catherine's Point, which guards Fowey Harbour with its Tudor castle and Rashleigh mausoleum. Just beyond the point is Readymoney Cove, once a landing place for smugglers, at the end of a secret wooded valley. The old trading route between Fowey and Padstow is a popular walk, known as Saints Way.

A few miles north of Fowey is **Castle Dore**, an impressive Iron Age fortress guarding the mouth of the River Fowey, which was occupied into the Roman period. **Restormel Castle**, a mile northeast of the old market town of Lostwithiel, is the castle's Norman successor, protecting the river crossing and collecting tolls from traders. Restormel later became the administrative centre of Cornwall and a stannary court. Abandoned following the Civil War, it now lies in picturesque ruins atop a hill and offers great views over the Fowey Valley.

Bodinnick Ferry
car £2.20, pedestrian £1

Restormel Castle
t (01208) 872687; www.english-heritage.org.uk; open April–Oct daily 10am–4pm; adm £3

(i) **Fowey**
South Street, t (01726) 833616, www.fowey.co.uk; open Mon–Fri 9am–5.30pm, Sat & Sun 9am–5pm

(★) **Fowey Hall** >

Festivals and Events in Fowey

The **Daphne Du Maurier Week** arts and literary festival (*www.dumaurier.org/festival.html*) takes place mid-May. Many literary figures attend and numerous events and readings take place. Du Maurier's family home, Ferryside at Bodinnick, is private, but can be seen from the ferry quay.

The **Fowey Royal Regatta** (*www.foweyroyalregatta.co.uk*) in mid-August offers races, Red Arrow jet displays and concerts and ends with a spectacular firework display.

Where to Stay in Fowey

Fowey Hall, Hanson Drive, **t** (01726) 833866, *www.foweyhallhotel.co.uk* (*luxury*). A great choice for families, Fowey Hall is a listed Victorian mansion set above a river estuary overlooking the Channel – it's said to have provided the inspiration for Toad Hall in *The Wind in the Willows*. Its bedrooms (named after characters from the book) are swish and elegant – there are 24 in all including 11 family suites – and there are two family-friendly **restaurants**. Its five acres of grounds boast a covered, heated pool as well as tennis courts. *Children can stay free in adults' room.*

The Marina Hotel, Esplanade, **t** (01726) 833315, *www.themarinahotel.co.uk* (*very expensive*). Handsome yellow-painted Georgian waterfront house with wrought-iron balconies and a patio garden just behind the river wall. Inside it's very boutique with 18 chic bedrooms, some with harbour views. The Nathan Outlaw **restaurant** (*expensive*) specializes in seafood and has an excellent reputation.

The Fowey Hotel, The Esplanade, **t** 0844 50 27587, *www.thefoweyhotel.co.uk* (*expensive–very expensive*). Large cream-painted four-star Victorian hotel built by the Great Western Railway with a pretty garden at the mouth of the estuary. The bedrooms are decked out in period-style furnishings, while the **restaurant**, the holder of an AA Rosette, has huge bay windows overlooking the water.

The King of Prussia, 3 Town Quay, **t** (01726) 833694, *www.kingofprussiafowey.co.uk* (*moderate–expensive*). The inn's current 19th-century quayside building was erected on the site of a 17th-century original said to have been the haunt of the famed local smuggler, John Carter, nicknamed the 'King of Prussia Cove'. Today it offers simple, bright rooms overlooking the water, as well as a good selection of bar meals. *Live music Sat eve.*

The Old Exchange, 12 Lostwithiel Street, **t** (01726) 833252, *www.foye-old-exchange.co.uk* (*moderate*). Cheery B&B housed in the town's old telephone exchange with three good-sized en suite doubles, the largest with a four-poster bed (for which you pay a £10 supplement). The breakfasts are legendary.

The Old Malthouse, West Looe Hill, **t** (01503) 264976 (*moderate*). A 350-year old Grade II listed building close to the harbour with free parking and three simple rooms to rent.

Trevanion Guest House, 70 Lostwithiel Street, **t** (01726) 832602, *www.trevanionguesthouse.co.uk* (*moderate*). Friendly, old-fashioned guesthouse behind net curtains with dried flower displays dotted around the snug little rooms. The building is Grade II listed and parts date from the 16th century.

Golant YHA Hostel, Penquite House, Golant, **t** 0845 371 9019, *www.yha.org.uk* (*budget*). One of the YHA's more impressive offerings set in a Georgian manor house amid 14 acres of woodland overlooking the Fowey Estuary. Most of the accommodation is in large 6–10-bed dorms, but there are private rooms available too. There's a **restaurant** and a kitchen.

Eating Out in Fowey

Food for Thought, The Quay, **t** (01726) 832221, *www.foodforthought.fowey.com* (*moderate*). Consistently excellent restaurant right on the seafront with over 30 years experience and a menu dominated by fish and shellfish. They offer a three-course dinner menu for £19.95.

Sam's, 20 Fore Street, **t** (01726) 812255, *www.samsfowey.co.uk* (*moderate*). Steamy warmth and jazzy music hit you on entering this popular two-floor bistro. You may have to wait a while at the bar to be seated but they will get to you in the end. Specials include big bowls of fresh mussels or oysters. Expect to pay £16.95 for a roasted sea bass fillet. A second

branch, **On the Beach**, recently opened in the town's old RNLI station.

Taipan Restaurant, 1 Fore Street, **t** (01726) 833899 (*moderate*). Decent Thai restaurant with a good reputation and a strong local following. Takeaway service available.

The Other Place, 41 Fore Street, **t** (01726) 833636, *www.theotherplacefowey.com* (*moderate*). The downstairs section serves ice creams and superior takeaway fish and chips, while the upstairs is a highly regarded restaurant. They do a mean fish soup for £5.50 or if you fancy sampling a bounty of fishy surprises, try the Fowey Fish Special, featuring red gurnard, sea bass, monkfish, scallops and mussels for £15.50.

The Lugger Inn, 5 Fore Street, Polruan, **t** (01726) 833435 (*budget*). Perfectly positioned pub, right on the Quayside in Polruan serving local St Austell Brewery beers (Tinners and Tribute) and great, reasonably priced fish and chips. *Child and dog friendly.*

The Ship Inn, Fore Street, **t** (01503) 263124, *www.staustellbrewery.co.uk* (*budget*) A very old St Austell Brewery inn built by the Elizabethan privateer, Sir John Rashleigh, a contemporary of Drake and Raleigh. It has a snug bar, a separate dining room where simple pub grub is served (fish and chips, steak and ale pie, gammon and chips etc) and eight comfortable bedrooms (*moderate*). Mains £6.95–9.95.

Eating out in Polperro

Couch's, Saxon Bridge, **t** (01503) 272554, *www.couchspolperro.com* (*expensive*). Housed in a cheery little white cottage, Polperro's top choice looks very traditional and Cornish from the outside, but within it is much more modern with Charles Rennie Mackintosh-influenced furniture and a chef schooled by the likes of Gordon Ramsay and Marco Pierre White turning out fancy Modern British creations – carpaccio of beef with capers, truffles and parmesan, sea bass on crushed potatoes with horseradish velouté etc. A seven-course gourmet tasting menu is offered Sun–Thurs for £37.95 per person.

St Austell and Around

The only industry left in Cornwall is the extraction of china clay, or kaolin, which was discovered in England around 1746 by a Plymouth chemist called William Cookworthy in west Cornwall and around St Austell, and sold to Staffordshire potteries like Wedgwood. The industry has been boosted recently by the use of kaolin in paper-making and around 18–20 pits are still in operation. All of this is great for the local economy, but makes for a less attractive area visually: mining villages such as Foxhole, Nunpean and St Denis are surrounded by spoil heaps known as the 'Cornish Alps'. The **China Clay Country Park** in Carthew can tell you more about china-clay extraction in the setting of an old refinery.

China Clay Country Park
Wheal Martyn;
t (01726) 850362;
www.wheal-martyn.com;
open daily 10am–5pm;
adm £7.50

Eden Project

⚡ Eden Project
Bodelva, St Austell;
t (01726) 811911;
www.edenproject.com;
open daily 9am–6pm
(last entry 4.30pm);
adm £16 (£15 if booked
online)

Three miles east of St Austell, an old china-clay pit the size of 35 football pitches is now home to the most talked about greenhouse in the country, the botanical garden to beat all botanical gardens. It is the brainchild of Tim Smit (whose first baby was Heligan, *see* p.181), and is essentially a 21st-century update of the Victorian wrought-iron glasshouse except on a much bigger and worthier scale, with a mission to excite the populace about 'the vital relationship between plants, people and resources'.

Some £86 million and 14,000 tons of tubular steel have gone into creating Eden's two space-age 'biomes', each representing a climatic zone and its flora. The largest, at 200m long and 45m high, is devoted to tropical plants with a huge waterfall crashing through palms, mangroves and rubber trees, while the less sweatily intense Mediterranean biome contains plants from Europe, the deserts of Mexico and the South African veld; visit in the evening when the gently wafting aroma of flowers fills the air. Surrounding the two great domes are acres of outdoor gardens planted with species from around the world. It all looks smashing and it's hard to begrudge the price, the queues or the surrounding traffic jams. It certainly brings in the punters, being by far and away Cornwall's most popular visitor attraction, and brings some much-needed cash into the local community.

Cornish Saints

While travelling in Cornwall you'll come across places bearing the names of various saints you've probably never heard of. In the 5th century, Christianity retreated to the western, Celtic fringes of Britain in the face of the Germanic invasions. The open-air, non-hierachical version of Christianity imported from Ireland was also strong in the north of Britain at the time St Augustine started working on the King of Kent in Canterbury (AD 597). The two brands of Christianity came head-to-head at the Synod of Whitby in 664, and Roman Christianity emerged victorious. The key figures of Celtic Christianity were the Irish monk, St Aidan (d.651), who set up the monastery of Lindisfarne on Holy Island, and his disciples St Cuthbert, St Chad and St Cedd, who helped spread the word. In the land of Kernow, west of the River Tamar, Celtic Christianity thrived under a colourful set of churchmen and women like St Ia who, according to legend, sailed across the Irish Sea on a leaf, and St Piran who, even more miracu-lously, arrived on a millstone. Little is known about these early martyrs, but their lives are commem-orated in place names including St Austell, St Merryn, St Ervan, St Erth, St Mabyn, St Mawes and St Ewe.

Getting to St Austell

Mevagissey lies around 15 miles east of Truro on the B3273. **Buses** link the town with St Austell and Fowey. You can also catch a **ferry** from Fowey's Whitehouse Quay to Mevagissey's Lighthouse Quay, which leaves three to five times a day between late April and September (**t** 07977 203394; *www.mevagissey-ferries.co.uk*; single £6, return £10).

Mevagissey

aquarium
The Harbour Office;
t (01726) 843305

museum
Frazier House,
t (01726) 843568; open
Easter–Oct daily
11am–5pm

World of Model Railways
Meadow Street;
t (01726) 842457;
www.model-railway.
co.uk; open April–Oct
10am–5pm; adm £3.95

Narrow lanes wind down through green hills into this tiny fishing harbour. The fishing boats, stacked plastic crates of ropes and nets, and men in gumboots busying between the two are the signs of a small but active fishing community. Otherwise Megavissey is a tourist town, with streets reeking of chips and pasties, and some rather crowded beaches. Have a walk around the harbour wall, where there are great views back into town and along the headlands. A recently revamped **aquarium** in the old lifeboat shed shows the fish that end up in the fishermen's nets. At the end of the quay there's a little **museum** housed in a boatshed once used for building and repairing smuggling vessels, which is full of local fishing and smuggling paraphernalia. The town's other principal attraction is the **World of Model Railways** with more than 30 model trains that meander their way through a variety of miniature landscapes, including tin mines, a fairground and a thatched village.

Mevagissey Walks

There is an excellent stretch of coastline west of Mevagissey, dominated by the two headlands of Dodman Point and Nare head and crinkled with sandy coves. The modest village of **Gorran Haven** is a good place to begin a walk around Maenease Point to Hemmick Beach via Dodman Point, with its massive Iron Age cliff castle. Further west, on the

Caerhays Castle
t (01872) 500025;
www.caerhays.co.uk;
open daily 10am–5pm;
adm £9.50

cliffs above Porthluney Cove, **Caerhays Castle** is a romantic pile built by John Nash in 1808 on the site of the medieval fortress of the Trevanion family, who went broke building it. John Charles Williams stepped in, and was one of the first gardeners to make use of early 20th-century plant discoveries, raising successful hybrids such as the entirely new Camellia x *williamsii* group (J. C. Williams, Caerhays and Cornish Snow are all varieties). West again, there is a walk from the unspoilt fishing village of Portloe east to Tregenna and back along the coastal path. Nare Head is another two and a half miles along the coastal path from Portloe.

The Lost Gardens of Heligan
Pentewan, St Austell;
t (01726) 845100;
www.heligan.com; open
daily April–Sept
10am–6pm, Oct–Mar
10am–5pm; adm £8.50

The Lost Gardens of Heligan

At the head of the Mevagissey valley, the 'lost' gardens were once at the heart of the Tremayne family estate. Their 'rediscovery' in 1990 sparked massive media interest and funds poured into their restoration. In their Edwardian heyday the gardens were hugely diverse, growing exotic fruit in glasshouses and the latest specimens of plants and trees brought back by plant hunters George Forrest, Robert Fortune and Ernest 'Chinese' Wilson. In 1914 all the gardeners disappeared to fight in the First World War, the gardens became derelict and overgrown and

Where to Stay and Eat in Mevagissey

ⓘ **Mevagissey**
St Georges Square,
t (01726) 844 857,
www.mevagissey-
cornwall.co.uk; open
summer daily
9am–5pm, winter
Mon–Fri 11am–3pm

★ **The Salamander Restaurant >>**

Corran Farm, St Ewe, **t** (01726) 842159, *www.corranfarm.co.uk* (*moderate*). Trim, cream-plastered farmhouse looking out over green hills with three tastefully furnished en suite rooms. Guests also have use of a lounge with a cosy open fire. Extras include free Wi-Fi and a complimentary cream tea upon arrival. It borders the Lost Gardens of Heligan. *Closed Dec–Jan.*

Honeycombe Farm, 61 Polkirt Hill, **t** (01726) 843750, *www.bandbinmeva gissey.co.uk* (*moderate*). Family-run B&B perched on a hill over the town with great views out to sea. The rooms are simple but comfortable. Two have sea-facing balconies but cost more.

The Fountain Inn, Cliff Street, **t** (01726) 842320, *www.staustellbrewery.co.uk* (*moderate*). A 15th-century inn with a smugglers' bar and an oak-beamed, slate-flagged front bar. The upstairs restaurant specializes in fish and steaks and there are three bright bedrooms for rent (*moderate*).

The Salamander Restaurant, 4-6 Tregoney Hill, **t** (01726) 842254, *www.salamander-restaurant.co.uk* (*moderate*). Great little restaurant specializing in locally-caught fish and locally-reared meat. Mains £10–£17.50.

were eventually forgotten. Their restoration has been as exciting as their discovery. The location is unbeatable. Walled fruit gardens trap the sun and boast rare examples of horticultural innovation from the 18th and 19th centuries, such as manure-heated pineapple pits and a prefab fruit house designed by Joseph Paxton of Crystal Palace fame. A jungly arm of the garden shoots down the valley where the crowds thin out and you can feel the romantic spirit of the secretive pools, paths and views.

The North Coast: Bude to Padstow

From Hartland Point to Padstow light
Is watery grave by day or by night

The above verse was written by the 19th-century priest poet Robert Stephen Hawker about the magnificent, but murderous, North Cornwall cliffs. Following the coastal path between Bude and Padstow you can at low tide climb down to the sandy beach at Lundy Bay to explore its caves and rock pools. Of the ports of Porthquin, **Port Isaac** and Portgaverne – once busy fishing pilchards and exporting ore and slate from the nearby mines – only Port Isaac, where the TV series *Doc Martin* was filmed has kept its spark. At low tide its beach is littered with seaweed, rusty chains and lobster pots. The village climbs uphill along narrow lanes; buy a pot of prawns, cockles or lobster scraps from one of the shell-fish shops and go for a wander. The coastal path leads off enticingly in both directions.

Bude

A popular family surfing resort, Bude is a bit like a less intense version of Newquay with three excellent sandy beaches: **Crooklets**, the main surfing beach (there's a dog ban in operation from Easter to 1 October); the National Trust-owned **Sandy Mouth**, which is better for beginners (and the more timid) and can offer a network of rock pools for non-surfers to explore; and the main family beach, **Summerleaze**, which has a

Getting to and around the North Coast

Bude is on the A3073, just off the A39, from where the B3263 connects with **Boscastle** and **Tintagel**. Regular daily bus services link the three towns.

Padstow lies on the west bank of the Camel River, 12 miles northeast of Newquay on the A389 and B3276. The nearest mainline **railway** station is Bodmin Parkway, 17 miles away. A regular **bus** service runs from Bodmin to Padstow throughout the day. National Express **coach** services stop at Wadebridge, from where you can catch the same onwards bus.

09 Cornwall | The North Coast: Bude to Padstow

Bude-Stratton Museum
The Castle; t (01288) 353576; Easter–Oct noon–5pm

seawater swimming pool, a mini-golf course and a go-kart track. All three employ lifeguards during the summer months. The small **Bude-Stratton Museum**, housed in a former forge, gently retraces the town's industrial and maritime history.

Boscastle

You feel as if you're still in North Devon here, with the wooded valley and the local links to Sir Richard Grenville, the Elizabethan sailor who rebuilt the quay prior to the arrival of the Spanish Armada. From the old village, it is a short walk down the steep valley to the harbour. Where the river opens out into the sea, a double breakwater shelters a handful of boats. Whitewashed fishermen's cottages huddle around the slipway. Things may look calm and serene now, but in 2004 this was a scene of utter devastation when unprecedented rainfall sent more than 400 million gallons of water hurtling down the valley into the village, ripping apart homes and carrying cars and trees out to sea. It's little short of a miracle that no one died. Most of the flood damage has since been repaired but, despite the facade of normality, there's still an uneasy undertone to the town. No one is exactly sure what caused the flood; whether it was a freak event or the sign of climatic change to come and the townspeople are understandably wary.

From the old village, a footpath leads two miles inland up the wooded Valency Valley to **St Juliot Church**, famously restored by Thomas Hardy in 1870. Hardy, then working as an architect prior to his literary career, met his first wife, Emma Gifford, the rector's sister-in-law here. On the north aisle wall is a memorial to Emma that he designed. A Thomas Hardy memorial window was erected in the church for the millennium.

Heading south to Willapark headland, the coastal path leads across Forrabury Common where you can see the rare, preserved remains of an Iron Age arable-strip farming system. The views are magnificent from the cliff castle.

Tintagel

Tintagel
t (01840) 770328; www.english-heritage .org.uk; open daily April–Oct 10am–5/6pm, Nov–March 10am–4pm; adm £4.90

It's fitting that Arthur, the nation's most charismatic king, should have been born here on this wild, windswept Cornish clifftop. It's a hugely atmospheric place with the ruins perched high above the crashing sea and it takes just a little imagination to picture the young king riding out to battle against the latest Saxon invaders or to hunt for the Holy Grail. As with all Arthurian sites, the evidence linking the castle with the king

King Arthur

In his *History of the English-speaking Peoples*, the great rationalist Winston Churchill was in no doubt about the reality of Arthur: 'Somewhere in the island a great captain gathered the forces of Roman Britain and fought the barbarian invaders to the death... Twelve battles, all located in scenes untraceable, with foes unknown, except that they were heathen, are punctiliously set forth in the Latin of Nennius.' Nennius was a ninth-century chronicler who compiled a history of the old kings of Britain. His work was the main source of the *History of the Kings of Britain* by Geoffrey of Monmouth, a 12th-century Welsh scholar working in one of the religious houses in Oxford. The *History*, which catalogues the reigns of 99 largely fictitious British kings over 2,000 years up to the year 689, is the great source of Arthurian legend. And it is almost entirely made up. There were so few sources for Geoffrey to go on.

During the Middle Ages, further romantic tales were spun around Geoffrey's History, the writers encouraged by Tudor monarchs keen to show off their heroic Welsh pedigree. The most famous, *Morte d'Arthur*, was written by Sir Thomas Mallory, a disreputable Warwickshire knight whose recorded crimes included theft, cattle-rustling and abduction. It was probably written during one of Mallory's spells in prison. The action roams all over Britain, from Wales to Northumbria and Cornwall. It was Mallory's Arthur who entered the modern world, capturing the imagination of the poet Tennyson, who penned his own *Morte d'Arthur*, sparking the 19th-century explosion of Arthurian poems and stories, and the proliferation of Arthurian sites in the West Country.

If you were touring Arthurian sites, you might start at **Cadbury Castle** (*see* p.64), a Somerset hill-fort named as Camelot by the 16th-century antiquarian John Leland, where archaeological digs in the 1960s identified it as one of the largest sixth-century fortifications in Britain. From there, you could head northwest to the North Devon village of **Morwenstow**, home of the eccentric vicar and Arthurian scholar Robert Hawker (1803–74). Tennyson visited him anonymously in 1848, wearing a long black cloak. You can follow in Tennyson's footsteps with Hawker, who took him along the cliffs to see his little retreat, built of driftwood into the cliff-face. Another Arthurian hotspot is the lake into which Sir Bedevere throws the sword, Excalibur, and an arm 'clothed in white samite' rises up to catch it. There are several contenders, including **Dozmary Pool** on Bodmin Moor (see p.171) and **Loe Pool**, on the west of the Lizard Peninsula near Porthleven (*see* p.200), Tennyson's choice.

is practically non-existent. Parts of the site do date back to the 5th century AD, which more or less fits in with the chronology of the 'real' Arthur, but that's about it. Arthur's first association with the site wasn't recorded until the 12th century in the *History of the Kings of Britain* by Geoffrey of Monmouth (*see* box above).

Most of the dramatic ruins on Tintagel Head belong to the 13th-century cliff castle of Richard, Earl of Cornwall. Now it's run by English Heritage, making some Celtic blood run hot – Arthur, scourge of the Anglo-Saxon invaders, in the hands of the English. The ruins straddle a collapsed rock causeway linking the island to the mainland. Follow the track down to the haven below the headland where Tennyson described Merlin scooping the baby Arthur out of the sea. Then climb the wooden steps up to the exposed top of the headland, 250ft above the sea.

Padstow

 Padstow

Best known for its May Day 'Obby Oss' festivities and as the headquarters of **Rick Stein**'s seafood empire, Padstow is a delightfully quaint, typically Cornish coastal town with a working fishing harbour surrounded by picturesque cottages. With some decent places to stay, a great collection of restaurants and some of the most beautiful stretches of coastline, it makes a great base for exploring the north coast.

From the grey slate quayside there are views of rolling green hills across the river, which at low tide become a huge expanse of yellow sand, leaving the boats in the harbour grounded in sludge. The town's name was originally Petrocstow, named after a monastery founded here by Irish missionary St Petroc in the 6th century. These days, some wags have taken to calling it Padstein, since the fish-loving TV chef Rick Stein moved in with a chain of eateries (now standing at four and counting, as well as a cookery school and a deli), which have turned the sleepy old port into gastronomy-on-sea. If you're not just here for the food, the heart of Padstow is its inner harbour, always full of boats – beam trawlers visit between January and April (after the Dover sole) and pleasure boats arrive in summer. There is only a tight huddle of little streets to explore, but it is easy to get lost here, in narrow lanes where the old trade emporiums have been replaced by gift shops and craft boutiques. There is an interesting little **museum** in the old Victorian institute, which tells the story of the town over the past two centuries .

museum
The Institute, Market Place; t (01841) 532752; www.padstowmuseum. co.uk; open Easter–Oct 10am–5pm; adm £1.50

Padstow is famous for its **May Day** celebrations, held annually on 1 May, when a red and blue '**obby oss**' (hobby horse) dances through the town, stopping at houses and pubs on the way. The crowds follow, trying to touch the 'oss's' mask (which is believed to have magical, fertile properties), egged on by accordions and primeval drums. The whole drunken procession ends up at **Prideaux Place**, the grand Elizabethan house of the Prideaux family at the top of the town, set in its own deer park overlooking the Camel Estuary. If you arrive out of season you can watch a video of the May Day dance at the town museum.

Prideaux Place
t (01841) 532411; www.prideauxplace.co. uk; open Easter Sun & May–Oct Sun–Thurs house 1.30–4pm, garden 12.30–5pm; adm £7.50

A foot ferry goes back and forth all day across the estuary to **Rock**, a sailing village with swimming beaches, which are the haunt of rowdy public-school boys on holiday. From there you can walk across the golf course to **St Endoc's Church** and visit the grave of the poet-laureate, John Betjeman. Continue to the unspoilt, fish-tail-shaped Pentire Peninsula where there is an Iron Age fort called the Rumps, or walk to Stepper Point and Trevose Head on the opposite headland.

Where to Stay and Eat on the North Coast

Bude

ⓘ **Bude**
The Crescent, t (01288) 35424, www.visitbude.info, Open daily Mar–Oct 10am–5pm, Nov–Feb 10.30am–4pm.

ⓘ **Boscastle**
The Harbour, t (01840) 250010. Open daily Mar–Oct 10am–5pm, Nov–Feb 10.30am–4pm.

Dylan's Guest House, 12 Downs View, t (01288) 354705, www.dylansguest houseinbude.co.uk (*moderate*). Just five minutes from the shore, Dylan's is a fairly traditional B&B in a Victorian house that's been elevated to the next level by the charm and helpful-ness of its owners. Rooms are of a good size, particularly those at the top of the house with views over the golf course, and are very well furnished with crisp, light décor. Breakfasts are hugely generous and at night the owners will steer you in the direction of all the best local restaurants.

Life's a Beach, Summerleaze Beach, t (01288) 355222, www.lifesabeach.info (*budget–moderate*). Sat amid the cliffs overlooking Summerleaze Beach, this is a fairly standard café in the day, turning out baked baguettes, bruschettas with various fancy toppings, burgers and nachos to a largely surfing-orientated crowd. From 6pm, however, it transforms, as if by magic, into a bistro offering fancy, locally sourced seafood.

Port Isaac

The Slipway Hotel, The Harbour Front, Port Isaac, t (01208) 880264, www. portisaachotel.com (*expensive*). A 16th-century building at the bottom of narrow streets winding down to the harbour with ten light and bright

(i) Tintagel

*Bossiney Road,
t (01840) 779084. Open
daily Mar–Oct
10am–5pm, Nov–Feb
10.30am–4pm.*

(i) Padstow

*The Redbrick Building,
North Quay,
t (01841) 533449,
www.padstowlive.com.
Open summer daily
9.30am–5pm,
winter Mon–Fri
9.30am–4.30pm*

(★) The Seafood
Restaurant >>

rooms spread about its slightly wonky confines, some with sea views. There's a cosy bar and an outstanding **restaurant** which cooks up seafood that's fresh off the boats for breakfast, lunch and dinner (*moderate*).

The Anchorage Guest House, 12 The Terrace, t (01208) 880629 (*moderate*). Cheap and cheerful place facing the sea with clean, tidy rooms for £35 per person per night. The top-floor rooms have great views out towards Tintagel.

The Harbour Restaurant, Middle Street, t (01208) 880237 (*budget–moderate*). Excellent locally caught fish served simply in this slightly tumbledown building.

Boscastle

Wellington Hotel, The Harbour, t (01840) 250202, *www.boscastle-wellington.com* (*moderate–expensive*). This centuries-old place may look like a converted castle, but the crenellated tower is a 19th-century addition. It's a very grand place, back to its best after the devastation of the flood, with large rooms, bags of antique charm and a very good (and surprisingly modern) **restaurant**. There's also a garden where live music is often staged.

The Olde Manor House, The Bridge, t (01840) 250251 (*budget*). Fresh fish – either brought over from nearby Plymouth and Newlyn or caught by local Boscastle fishermen – served well. You can also get a decent cream tea or a snack lunch. The specials board changes daily.

Where to Stay in Padstow

Cross House Hotel, Church Street, t (08717) 168148, *www.crosshouse.co.uk* (*expensive–very expensive*). White-painted, blue-shuttered Georgian house at the top of Church Street. Inside it's elegantly furnished with rich period colour schemes. There are 11 very refined en suite bedrooms. At the back there's a pretty patio garden overlooking the town.

St Petroc's Hotel and Bistro, New Street, t (01841) 532700, *www.rickstein. com* (*expensive–very expensive*). This pretty white-painted hotel set behind a hedge is beautifully furnished and decorated, with attentive staff and a relaxed atmosphere. There's a reading

room with cream-painted wooden panelling and sea-grass matting, as well as ten bedrooms with ornate wrought-iron beds and chairs. The Mediterranean-style **bistro** (*moderate*), Rick Stein's second restaurant, serves seafood, fish and grilled meats at slightly more forgiving prices than his flagship eaterie (*mains £15.95–19.95*).

Althea Library, 27 High Street, t (01841) 532717, *www.althealibrary.co.uk* (*moderate-expensive*). The Althea is cosy and cottagey and snug with two upstairs en suite rooms, a larger downstairs 'puffin' suite with its own lounge, and a guest lounge equipped with games and sofas. Aga-cooked breakfasts are served in a dinky dining room overlooking the south-facing garden. It's just a couple of minutes' walk to the harbour.

Tregea Hotel, 16–18 High Street, t (01841) 532455, *www.tregea.co.uk* (*moderate–expensive*). Elegant, comfortable B&B in a 17th-century townhouse (one of Padstow's oldest buildings). The rooms are slightly on the snug side, an inevitable consequence of the building's age, but bright and airy with cream-painted wood and pretty wallpaper.

Treverbyn House, Treverbyn Road, t (01841) 532855, *www.treverbyn house.com* (*moderate*). Set in its own gardens, this is a very superior B&B occupying a large detached house overlooking the estuary a couple of minutes' walk from the town centre. All five bedrooms are pleasingly decorated with antique knick-knacks. A choice of English, continental or smoked fish breakfasts is offered.

Where to Eat in Padstow

The Seafood Restaurant, Riverside, t (01841) 532700, *www.rickstein.com* (*expensive–very expensive*). The largest and priciest of the four Padstow eateries managed by TV celebrity chef, Rick Stein, this has a huge reputation. And deservedly so, coming up with imaginative arrangements of the fish and seafood, brought straight off the fishing boats into the kitchen and onto your plate. Typical mains include Indonesian seafood curry with monkfish, squid, and tiger prawns. or fillet of brill with fresh summer truffle, slivers of potato, mushrooms and truffle oil. The best value is offered by the £35 three-course lunch menu. Otherwise mains are £28–£44. There are also 16 well-appointed rooms, most overlooking the harbour.

Margot's, 11 Duke Street, t (01841) 533441, http://margotspadstow. blogspot.com (moderate– expensive). This is one of Padstow's very finest restaurants, and no, it's not one of Rick Stein's. It's a friendly little place with just nine tables set amid pink marbled walls hung with paintings for sale. Dishes change all the time but can include such tasty treats as seared scallops with bacon and saffron-poached pear with clotted cream. They do a two-course menu for £18 at lunch. Evenings tend to be booked up months in advance. Closed for lunch Sun–Tues.

Rick Stein Café, Middle Street, t (01841) 532700, www.rickstein.com (moderate). If you can't afford his restaurants you will be pleased with the café, just next door to his delicatessen. It serves good coffee and pastries, as well as light lunches of mussels and other seafood (mains £11.30–16.60).

Stein's Fish & Chips, South Quay, t (01841) 532700, www.rickstein.com (budget) The final and cheapest outpost of the Rick-Stein Padstow empire is this modern take on a traditional chippie, serving battered fish cooked in beef dripping and served with chips for a very reasonable £6.40 (for cod) rising to £10.75 for monkfish. Eat in or takeaway.

The Shipwrights, North Quay, t (01841) 532451 (budget). Good for a pint and a cheap un-gastro meal overlooking the harbour.

Newquay and Around

South of Trevose Head, the coast turns west for a while, so you get sunsets over the sea, fast-changing weather and the Atlantic rollers that have become so popular with surfers in recent decades. The tide goes way out leaving expanses of beach littered with washed-up slate, particularly at Constantine and Treyarnon. The long beach at Porthcothan Bay is the only un-raked beach on the north coast. It still gets fertilized by seaweed when the tide comes in, and the sand dunes are allowed to spread. At low tide there are caves to explore around the headland (but beware the tides, which come in very fast) and the cliff walks in either direction are unbeatable. Further south, the **Bedruthan Steps** are a distinctive series of rocks marching across the green bay between headlands. According to the legends (probably invented in the 19th century), Bedruthan was a Cornish giant and the rocks kept his feet dry across the bay. At high tide, they look like shark fins breaking the surface. At low tide you can climb down and explore the rock pools.

Extreme Academy
t (01637) 860543, www.watergatebay.co. uk/extremeacademy. htm; board/wetsuit hire £6/£10 per day

Further down the coast, **Watergate** is great for beachcombing. Come in winter for the richest pickings of tropical shells and sea beans, swept across the ocean by the Gulf Stream. It is also a popular surfing beach. The giant Watergate Bay hotel complex backing the beach has a surf school, the **Extreme Academy** which offers lessons and hires out boards.

Newquay

If you're coming to Cornwall to experience all that is uniquely Cornish – the age-old fishing villages and traditional inns, the rural crafts and folk dances – then Newquay is probably not the resort for you. Its charms, such as they are, are of a rather more off-the-peg variety, shared

Getting to Newquay

By Car

Newquay is 14 miles southwest of Padstow off the A3058. Traffic congestion can be severe during the peak summer months.

By Train and Bus

Newquay is on the main London–Penzance **rail** route out of London Paddington. National Express **coaches** also run daily from London, Plymouth, Bristol and Manchester. Local First Group services also links the town with Truro and other Cornwall towns, **t** 0845 600 1420, *www.firstgroup.com*.

By Air

Ryanair fly to Newquay from London Stansted (*www.ryanair.com*).

Blue Reef Aquarium
Towan Promenade;
t (01637) 878134;
www.bluereefaquarium.
co.uk; open daily 9.30am
–6pm; adm £7.75

Newquay Zoo
Trenance Gardens;
t (01637) 873342;
www.newquayzoo.org.uk;
open April–Sept
9.30am–6pm, Oct–Mar
10am–5pm; adm £10.95

Newquay Waterworld
Trenance Leisure Park;
t (01637) 853828;
www.newquaywater
world.co.uk; adm £5.40

Steam Railway
St Newlyn East; t (01872)
510317; www.lappavalley.
co.uk; open Apr–Sept
daily 10.30am–4.30pm;
adm £9.50

DairyLand Farm World
t (01872) 510349;
www.dairylandfarmworld
.com; open April–Oct daily
10am–5pm; adm £7.95

Trerice House
Kestle Mill; t (01637)
875404; open Mar–Oct
Mon–Thurs & Sat–Sun
10.30am–4.30pm; adm £7

by dozens of resorts up and down the country. It's a place of happy hours, 2 for 1 clubs, arcades, boozed-up stag and hen parties and bargain burger bars. It's certainly not the place to get to know the 'real' Cornwall. But if you want to put the culture on hold for a day or two and indulge in a little guilt-free hedonism, then Newquay can most certainly oblige.

It's famed, of course, above all for its waves. This is the self-styled 'surf capital of the UK' where thousands come every year to ride the big Atlantic breakers. For the less sportily inclined, it's also got some fine beaches, albeit often submerged beneath a mass of slowly roasting human flesh. Head out of town if you want to do a little solo sunbathing, to Crantock three miles southwest or east to Lusty Glaze and Porth.

Newquay is particularly useful if you've got the little 'uns in tow, with plenty of distractionsincluding a very good aquarium, the **Blue Reef Aquarium**, where you can watch sharks, jellyfish and octopuses from a walk-through seabed tunnel and stroke rays in an open-top tank, **Newquay Zoo**, home to lions, penguins, monkeys, zebras, meerkats and more, and a waterpark, **Newquay Waterworld**, next to the zoo, with slides, flumes and a water cannon. There is also a miniature steam railway, **Lappa Valley Steam Railway** which includes a boating lake, a maze and crazy golf, and **DairyLand Farm World** where you can watch cows being milked and stroke various animals.

A few miles inland from Newquay, **Trerice House** was home to a branch of the Arundells, one of Cornwall's foremost families from the mid-14th to the 17th century. All the heads of the Arundell family were called John, except Thomas who got his lands confiscated for his involvement in the Duke of Buckingham's rebellion against Richard III. A younger brother of one of the Johns married the sister of Henry VIII's fifth wife, Catherine Howard, and bought some monastic estates in Wiltshire at the Dissolution. He founded a junior branch of the family in Wardour, which outlived the quieter Cornish lot. Now you can look around the gardens.

Surfing on Fistral Beach

This is the main show where all the most experienced boarders come to show off their most skilful moves on the beach's famed waves, which break on the sand here having travelled an unbroken 3,000-mile course across the ocean. When the wind is up, they can be pretty fearsome,

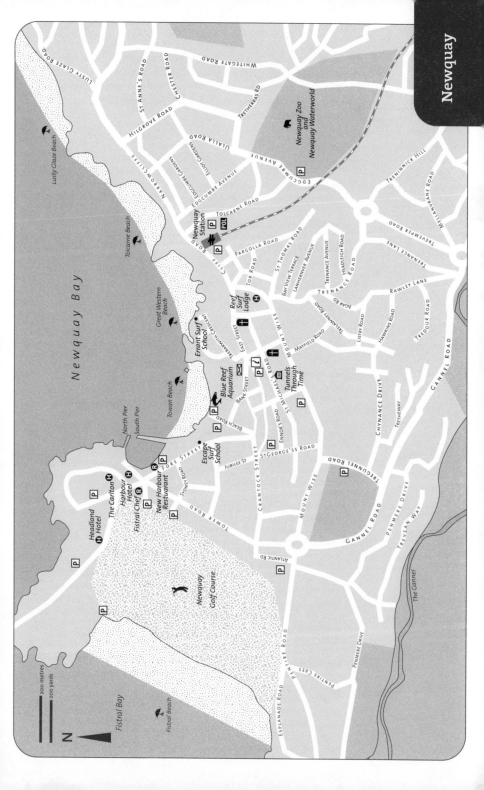

Newquay Bay

Lusty Glaze Beach

Tolcarne Beach

Great Western Beach

Towan Beach

North Pier
South Pier

Headland Hotel

The Carlton

Harbour Hotel

Fistral Chef

New Harbour Restaurant

Newquay Golf Course

Fistral Bay

Fistral Beach

N

200 metres
200 yards

Errant Surf School

Escape Surf School

Blue Reef Aquarium

Reef Surf Lodge

Tunnels Through Time

Newquay Station

Newquay Zoo and Newquay Waterworld

LUSTY GLAZE ROAD

ST ANNE'S ROAD

HILGROVE ROAD

CHESTER ROAD

WHITEGATE ROAD

TRETHERRAS RD

ULALIA ROAD

EDGCUMBE AVENUE

EDGCUMBE GARDENS

ELIOT GARDENS

NARROWCLIFF

TOLCARNE ROAD

CLIFF ROAD

PARGOLLA ROAD

TREBARWITH CRESCENT

TREMANCE ROAD

TREVEMPER ROAD

TRENINNICK HILL

MELLANVRANE ROAD

TRENANCE LANE

BAY VIEW TERRACE

ST THOMAS ROAD

LANHENVOR AVENUE

TRENANCE AVENUE

HEADLEIGH ROAD

TOR ROAD

EAST STREET

MOUNT WISE

RAWLEY LANE

TREMWITH ROAD

ACRE RD

MAYFIELD ROAD

LISTRY ROAD

HAWKINS ROAD

TREDOUR ROAD

GANNEL ROAD

CHYNANCE DRIVE

PRETHEWAY

BANK STREET

BEACH ROAD

SYDNEY ROAD

FORE STREET

TOWER ROAD

JUBILEE ST

CRANTOCK STREET

ST GEORGE'S ROAD

ENNOR'S ROAD

ST MICHAEL'S ROAD

MOUNT WISE

TRECUNNEL ROAD

GANNEL ROAD

PENMERE DRIVE

TREVEAN WAY

ATLANTIC RD

PENTIRE ROAD

PENTIRE CRES

PENMERE DRIVE

ESPLANADE ROAD

The Gannel

POL

which of course is just how the best surfers like them. Fistral has hosted numerous national and international surfing competitions.

For the less experienced there are plenty of surf schools. The following schools have all achieved the highest, level 4 accreditation with the British Surfing Association. Expect to pay in the region of £25 for a half day, £45 for a full day.

British Surfing
Association
www.britsurf.co.uk

ⓘ Newquay
Marcus Hill, t (01637)
854020,
www.newquay.co.uk.

★ Watergate Bay
Hotel >

Surf Schools

Errant Surf School, Trebarwith Hotel, Trebarwith Crescent, *www.errant surf.com*

Escape Surf School, 35 Fore Street, t 07967 497117, *www.escapesurf school.co.uk*

Gwithian Academy of Surfing, Redrussel House, Prosper Hill, Gwithian, Hayle, t (01736) 755493, *www.surfacademy.co.uk*

Where to Stay and Eat in Newquay and Around

Watergate Bay Hotel, on the beach, Watergate Bay, t (01637) 860543, *www.watergate.co.uk* (*expensive–very expensive*). Beachside Victorian slate hotel with white gables and bays that's been turned into a very modern, stylish affair where you're invited to 'design your stay'. The rooms are lovely with oak floors, plasma screens, MP3 docking stations and very smart contemporary décor. Those at the front have ocean views. There's also a surf school, a very swish restaurant housed in a modern annexe, as well as a branch of Jamie Oliver's 'Fifteen' chain (*see below*). For those who don't want to pay top dollar, there are some simpler, cheaper rooms at the rear of the property away form the beach (*moderate*).

Fifteen, on the beach, Watergate Bay, t (01637) 861000, *www.fifteencorn wall.co.uk* (*expensive*). Top-notch if rather pricey cooking served up by the protégés of Jamie's West Country outpost. As with its London predecessor, this is a not-for-profit exercise designed to give deprived local youngsters a head start in the catering industry.

Harbour Hotel, North Quay Hill, t (01637) 873040, *www.harbour restaurant.co.uk* (*expensive*). A lovely, relaxing choice with cosy antique-filled rooms – some with wrought-iron beds, all with balconies and sea views. Out front is a great harbourside **restaurant** (*moderate*), open for breakfast, lunch and dinner.

Headland Hotel, Fistral Beach, t (01637) 872211, *www.headlandhotel. co.uk* (*moderate–luxury*). This imposing red-brick Victorian hotel, standing alone and aloof on Fistral headland, is not the type of accommodation you typically associate with Newquay. Many of its 104 rooms are terribly swanky – and terribly expensive – with grand sea views, but, perhaps realizing the town's mainstream appeal, it also has its 'budget' (or more precisely *moderate*) options, which don't have views. Extras include a swimming pool, tennis courts, a golf course and a **restaurant** overlooking the water.

New Harbour Restaurant, South Quay Hill, t (01637) 874062, *www.new-harbour.co.uk* (*moderate*). At lunch this harbourside favourite offers some great seafood sandwiches – Newquay crab with dill, spring onion and mayonnaise or prawns in Marie Rose sauce. You get a more serious plateful in the evening – perhaps grilled turbot with parsley and almond pesto or lobster pulled directly from the tank out front. A very superior choice.

The Carlton, 6 Dane Road, Towan Headland, t (01637) 872658, *www. carltonhotelnewquay.co.uk* (*moderate*). A nice quiet B&B away from the crowds on the headland with some very grandly appointed en suite rooms, a licensed bar and a shady outdoor patio.

Fistral Chef, Beacon Road , t (01637) 850718 (*budget*). A very high-grade café offering big fry-ups, breakfasts and sandwiches for boarders looking to load up on some carbs. In the evening it turns into a Thai restaurant.

Reef Surf Lodge, 10–12 Berry Road, t (01637) 879058, *www.reefsurflodge. info (budget)*. As with most of Newquay's surf lodges, this offers a rather basic standard of accommodation aimed at boarders who want to spend their time out on the waves. Still, the rooms and dorms here, though small, are clean and well-maintained and it's got a laid-back ambience and a pleasant sundeck. You can learn to surf at the on-site school.

Treyarnon YHA, Tregonnan, Treyarnon, t 0845 371 9664, *www.yha.org.uk (budget)*. One of Cornwall's best backpacking options, the Treyarnon occupies a converted 1930s home on a quiet stretch of beach. Inside it's well equipped with a select café and dining room overlooking the crashing waves. Surf packages are available in summer and log fires roar in winter. Dorm beds from £13.95.

Industrial Cornwall: Camborne and Redruth

The short stretch of the north coast between Perranporth and Hayle is the heart of industrial Cornwall. Camborne was the centre of engineering, while Redruth was the financial and administrative centre. When South Crofty mine shut down, Cornish tin mining, practised in this region for thousands of years, vanished. Camborne and Redruth have merged into a conurbation of old miners' terraces and light industry. Behind them is **Carn Brae**, a rich archaeological site with remains of a Neolithic fortified settlement which, on the evidence of burnt remains and arrowheads, came to a sudden and violent end.

To get a bit more background on the area, stop off at the Cornish Mines and Engines Discovery Centre on the site of East Pool Mine, owned by the Agar Robartes of Landydrock. The visit takes you on a tour of mining that is now firmly in the past. From the engine house you can see the ruins of South Crofty. The star exhibit is a giant 52.5 tonne Cornish beam engine.

Turn right out of the museum and follow signs to the Camborne School of Mines Geological Museum, part of the University of Exeter. The mines school was set up in 1859 to provide engineering training to the tin- and copper-mining industries, which at that time produced half of the world's tin and copper. The well-presented mineral collection is based on local specimens.

There is a 7-mile walk around Carn Brae. Follow the signs to the Mineral Tramway Centre in Penhallic, where you can pick up a walking trail. The two-mile stretch along the Basset Tramway from Carnkie follows the **Great Flat Lode**, considered the best-preserved mining landscape in Europe, and now a World Heritage site.

Gwennap Pit, just south of Redruth following signs off the A393 Redruth–Falmouth road, is the original amphitheatre in which John Wesley preached 18 times between 1762 and 1789, rallying the locals to the temperate, self-sacrificing cause of Methodism. Down on the coast, **St Agnes** has a surfing cove, which provides a nice antidote to all the spoil tips and ruined engine houses. At Trevaunance Cove, the crumbling brown cliffs enclose a ruined harbour, exposed at low tide, and a shingle-topped sandy beach. You could stop for lunch at the Driftwood Spa Inn, or even stay in one of its 15 well-equipped bedrooms .

Cornish Mines and Engines Discovery Centre
Pool, t (01209) 315027; www.nationaltrust. org.uk; open April–June & Sept–Oct Mon, Wed–Fri & Sun 11am–5pm, July–Aug Mon & Wed–Sun 11am–5pm; adm £5.80

Camborne School of Mines Geological Museum
t (01209) 714866; www.ex.ac.uk/cornwall/ academic_departments/ csm/; open Mon–Fri 9am–5pm

Mineral Tramway Centre
t (01209) 613978; open Sun–Fri 10am–4pm

Trevaunance Cove
t (01872) 552428, www.driftwoodspas.com,

Getting to and around Truro

Take the A30 west off the M5 at Exeter. Truro is off the A3076. **Trains** on the main London Paddington to Penzance line stop at Truro. National Express **coaches** operate from the Truro Bus Depot on Lemon Quay via Plymouth and Exeter to London.

Boat trips to Falmouth sail from the town quay between May and October. The crossing takes 30 minutes.

Truro

Truro has all the hallmarks of an English country town: a Victorian cathedral, county courts and a county museum, but of course it's really Cornish. It's a fine old town, originally one of the Cornish stannaries, now jolliest on Saturdays when its four markets – the covered Pannier Market, Food Market, Tinner's Court Market and Farmer's Market – coincide. There are winding streets, elegant Georgian buildings, interesting little shops, as well as the museum and cathedral to explore. It's a shame, though, that the river has been expunged from the centre of town. It silted over in the 18th century whereupon Truro lost its then thriving shipped trade to Falmouth. Today the old quays look at each other forlornly across an ugly car park.

The old **Coinage Hall** on Boscowan Street was the source of Truro's early wealth and status. Tin ingots from the local mines were stored here to await the industry's quality-control tests and get the Duchy stamp before the tin could be traded and shipped out from the quays. **Truro Cathedral**, a mighty Gothic rocket shooting right out of the town, was built on the site of the old 16th-century parish church when Cornwall got its own diocese in 1876, but it wasn't completed until 1910. It is Britain's first brand-new cathedral since St Paul's was built in London in the early 18th century. Inside is some rather good stained glass but outside it seems rather too big, dominating the skyline every which way, and rather pompous.

Pomposity is a theme that has continued on Lemon Street where several grand Georgian mansions were built for the town's industrial magnates. Crossing Lemon Street from Lemon Quay, you can pick up the river, which ducks and dives to the attractive Victoria Gardens near the railway viaduct.

The town's main shopping streets are Boscowan Street and River Street, where the **Royal Cornwall Museum** has displays on the town's long and proud past, albeit told from a rather Anglocentric viewpoint. The Rashleigh Gallery has models of the giant beam engines that used to power the local industry as well as colourful displays of minerals.

Truro Cathedral
14 St Mary's Street; t (01872) 276782; www.trurocathedral.org. uk; open Mon–Sat 7.30–6pm, Sun 9am–7pm; guided tours are offered Mon–Sat at 11am and 2pm; adm free but donations welcome

Royal Cornwall Museum
River Street; t (01872) 272205; www.royalcornwall museum.org.uk; open Mon–Sat 10am–5pm

ⓘ **Truro**
Municipal Buildings, Boscowen Street, t (01872) 274555, www.truro.gov.uk; open summer Mon–Fri 9am–5.30pm, Sat 9am–4pm

Where to Stay in Truro

Alverton Manor, Tregolls Road, t (01872) 276633, *www.alvertonmanor. co.uk* (*expensive*). Amazing stone Gothic-Victorian building on the edge of town, formerly owned by the Bishop of Truro, with a bell tower, mullioned windows and crenellations.

There are 33 comfortable rooms and a traditional **restaurant**.

Mannings Hotel, Lemon Street, t (01872) 247900, *www.mannings hotels. co.uk* (*moderate–expensive*). This big old town-centre hotel has been given a modern revamp and now boasts light, airy, if somewhat generic looking, rooms aimed at its core business clientele. There's a brasserie and bar (*see* below) and free Wi-Fi.

Bay Tree Guest House, 28 Ferris Town, t (01872) 240274, *www.baytree-guesthouse.co.uk* (*moderate*). A simple Georgian townhouse with four decent, reasonably priced rooms and generous breakfasts. *No credit cards.*

Cliftons Guest House, 46 Tregolls Rd, t (01872) 274116 (*moderate*). Friendly, comfortable guesthouse occupying a tall Victorian townhouse with bay windows, set above the main road into town. There are six clean rooms.

The Townhouse, 20 Falmouth Road, t (01872) 277374, *www.trurotown house.com* (*moderate*). An easy-going B&B with 12 rooms, five minutes' walk from the cathedral. There's no restaurant, but you're welcome to order a takeaway to eat in their dining room. Wi-Fi access throughout.

Eating Out in Truro

Saffron >

Saffron, 5 Quay Street, t (01872) 263771, *www.saffronrestauranttruro.co.uk* (*moderate–expensive*). This great little bistro takes its local sourcing seriously, changing its menu daily

according to the available produce. Expect plenty of inventive meat and fish choices, and extreme difficulty booking a table (it's popular). They offer a great value three-course menu from Mon–Sat for £19.50. *Closed Sun.*

Mannings Bar and Grill, Mannings Hotel, Lemon Street, t (01872) 247900, *www.trurorestaurants.co.uk* (*moderate*). Smart business-style bar where sizzling platters, hot chicken salads and Thai steamers are served to an accompaniment of gently tinkling background music.

Piero's, Kenwyn Street, t (01872) 222279 (*moderate*). Large, long, airy Italian pizza-pasta restaurant with occasional live music. *Closed Sun.*

Lettuce and Lovage, 15 Kenwyn Street, t (01872) 272546, *www.lettuceand lovage.com* (*budget*). Small, friendly vegetarian restaurant with sunny décor and a menu filled with pizzas, salads and rostis. Vegan options available. *Open Mon–Sat 10am–4pm.*

Mandarin Garden, 114 Kenwyn Street, t (01872) 272374 (*budget*). Looks un-promising from the outside, but serves excellent Chinese food. Take-away service available. *Open eves only.*

Falmouth and Around

Falmouth

We are in a very wild and barbarous place which no human being ever visits, in the midst of a most barbarous race, so different in language and custom from... the rest of England that they are as unintelligible... as to the Venetians.
The Venetian ambassador, Falmouth, 1506

Falmouth is the once-mighty port of this coastline, tucked into the third largest natural harbour in the world (after Sydney and Rio, albeit these days rather less celebrated than its more exotic rivals). Its name tells only part of the story, as it sits on the mouth not only of the River Fal, but also the rivers Percuil, Tresillian, Truro and Restronguet, not to mention several other creeks. The wide open estuary is always full of little sailing boats cutting across the path of huge containers. Dotted around the green edges are tiny hamlets and some of the best walks in Cornwall.

Falmouth's dramatic history of piracy, privateering and lawlessness, which once gave visiting ambassadors the jitters, is viewed by many in Cornwall, not as barbaric, but as an unofficial Cornish foreign policy whose enemies and allies were often at odds with those of the government in Westminster. Still, in the mid 16th century, Falmouth joined in with the national 'take-what-you-can-from-Spain' policy, essentially going to war against Spanish shipping. The men of the Killigrew family, who feature prominently in the town's swashbuckling history, amassed

Getting to and around Falmouth

By Car

Falmouth is 12 miles south of Truro on the A39, 10 miles north of the Lizard Peninsula and 58 miles southwest of Plymouth.

By Train/Coach

There are regular branch line services to and from Truro, which lies on the main London Paddington–Penzance line. National Express runs services from London via Truro.

By Boat

Enterprise Boats run a ferry service between Falmouth's Prince of Wales Pier and Truro from May to Oct: t (01326) 374241; *www.enterprise-boats.co.uk*.

King Harry's Cornwall Ferries, which runs most of the local ferry services also offer two-hour 'Orca Sea Safaris' of the local coast: t (01326) 319417, *www.kingharryscornwall.co.uk*, adm £39.50, although, despite the name, your chances of spotting a killer whale are pretty slim. Seals, dolphins and, in summer, basking sharks are more likely to put in an appearance.

private fortunes by plundering Iberian ships in the harbour and provisioning pirates and privateers who operated from the Helford River. In the 18th century the town began to develop along more respectable lines as a Royal Navy base and packet station, acting as the Royal Mail's point of departure for its overseas mail services, and as a major supply port for the British Empire.

The Fox family of Quaker traders came to Falmouth in 1762 and over the next hundred years developed the docks and shipbuilding industry, pouring profits into flamboyant gardens around the Helford River.

The town itself is workaday, although much enlivened by the half-decade old National Maritime Museum in Discovery Quay (see below). For the most fun way to reach the collection, leave your car outside town at the Ponsardon car park and try the **Park and Float service**, which involves a 20-minute boat ride to the Prince of Wales Quay. There are a few knick-knack shops and restaurants on High Street and Church Street, parallel to the quays, which get more glamorous the nearer you get to the **Customs House Quay**, built by John Killigrew in 1670 and now a pleasant maritime spot.

Park and Float
King Harry's Cornwall Ferries; t (01326) 319417; www.kingharrys cornwall.co.uk; adm £15 including museum

National Maritime Museum

National Maritime Museum
Discovery Quay; t (01326) 313388; www.nmmc.co.uk; open daily 10am–5pm; adm £8.75

Falmouth's main tourist attraction is visually impressive and seriously hands-on. The exhibition kicks off with a series of large screens showing you what it's like to race in a regatta and experience a storm at sea. From here displays chart the rise of the post office's fleet of packet ships which set sail from from Falmouth for America and once made the town the second busiest port in the British Empire. For boat enthusiasts, the highlight of the museum will undoubtedly be the **Flotilla Hall**, filled with small craft from around the world – from yachts and launches to dinghies and canoes. The display includes numerous prize-winning sail boats. The less nautically inclined may prefer the 'Lookout', a tower providing 360° views of the harbour, coast and estuary with telescopes on hand to help you pick out the details in the distance. At the base of the tower, you can watch the tide rise and fall in the harbour through huge glass windows – stay long enough and you'll see it move an astonishing five miles. The museum also has a good café with views across the harbour.

The Ria Coastline

This fabulous coastline is shaped by rias – drowned river valleys formed when the sea level rose in Neolithic times. These long, narrow, deep-water inlets, flanked by woodland that comes right down to the water's edge, are used as a harbour by vast container ships, an uncanny juxtaposition.

Pendennis Castle
Pendennis Headland;
t (01326) 316594;
www.english-
heritage.org.uk; open daily
Apr–June & Sept
10am–5pm, July–Aug
10am–6pm, Oct–Mar
10am–4pm; adm £5.70

You can walk to **Pendennis Castle**, past Falmouth Docks, or drive. Built as a coastal defence during the reign of Henry VIII, the castle was besieged by the parliamentary forces in the Civil War – it took them over five months to starve the Royalists into submission. Today it offers great views along the shoreline, but still retains a military atmosphere. Its defensive position was so good that it was expanded to face new threats over the centuries. In the summer the castle puts on various family entertainments including a 'Tudor Kitchen Experience' (see what Henry III used to have for lunch) and a medieval-themed jousting tournament.

From Flushing there is a 4.5 mile walk around Trefussis Point to Mylor Bridge and back down some quiet lanes, or you can go on to **Restronguet Creek**, just under a mile northeast of Mylor Bridge, where there's one of the region's most atmospheric pubs, the **Pandora Inn**, set in a wonderfully gnarly 13th-century thatched building by the water. The Upper Deck restaurant serves superior pub grub.

King Harry Ferry
King Harry's Cornwall
Ferries; t (01326) 319417;
www.kingharrycornwall.
co.uk; daily every 20mins
7am–9pm; adm £4

Roseland Peninsula

Trelissick Garden
Feock, t (01872) 862090
www.nationaltrust.
org.uk; open Feb–Oct
daily 10.30–5.30,
Oct–Jan daily 11–4;
adm £7

One of the most staggeringly lovely corners of Cornwall is the Roseland Peninsula on the eastern shore of Falmouth Haven, almost cut off by the sinewy tidal arm of the River Fal and dissected by the River Percuil. If you are driving from Truro or Falmouth, take the **King Harry Ferry** between the beautiful, densely wooded banks of the River Fal past ships docked in its incredibly deep waters. **Trelissick Garden** is on the western side of the ferry crossing. The gracious 18th-century parkland drops steeply down to the Fal estuary, while the fabulous gardens of rhododendrons and camellias were planted by the Copelands, a Staffordshire Spode china family who moved down to Cornwall and bought the neo-Georgian mansion in 1937.

foot ferry
May–Sept every half
hour 8.30am–5.30pm;
adm £4.50

St Mawes Castle
St Mawes; t (01326)
270526 www.english-
heritage.org.uk; open
Apr–June Sun–Fri 10–5;
Jul–Aug Sun–Fri 10–6;
Sept daily 10–5; Oct–Mar
Mon and Fri–Mon 10–4;
adm £4

Take the **foot ferry** from Falmouth to St Mawes. There is a beautiful 2.5- mile walk from St Mawes to St Just in Roseland church via **St Mawes Castle**, a miniature clover-leaf Tudor fortress on a clifftop, built at the same time as Pendennis on the opposite headland to guard the entrance to Falmouth Haven against the Spanish. It is almost homely, with its elaborate coat of arms, Latin inscriptions and waterside garden of spiky exotic plants. Continue along the path to **St Just Church**, located beside a wide, salty creek. People come from miles just to see its flamboyant churchyard, with not a sinister old yew tree in sight, but palms, rhododendrons and enormous cabbage swamp plants beside ponds instead. The last ferry back to Falmouth is at 5.30pm.

In summer a second foot ferry from St Mawes crosses the **Percuil River** to Place, from where you can pick up the coastal path to **St Anthony's Point** at the southernmost tip of the peninsula, with interesting 19th-century and Second World War fortifications. Walk from there around the cliffs to **Porthbeor Beach**, and back to the ferry.

Helford River

The Helford River is the westernmost of the rias, tucked in behind the Lizard Peninsula. It is also the most unspoilt, with its little pirate coves and secretive wooded creeks. There are some grand private houses on either side whose gardens slope down to the water. The wide river presents a serious obstacle to travel; only a foot-ferry crossing connects the southern villages – collectively known as the Meneage – with urban centres like Falmouth and Truro. The coast path cuts inland from Rosemullion Head to the ferry crossing, then back along the southern side and around Gillan Creek. The best way to see the river is on a **boat** from Falmouth to Gweek (the limit of navigation), or by hiring your own sailing or motor boat (for anything from an hour to a week, try Helford River Boats below). If you are coming by car from the north, park in Mawnan Smith and walk down to the shore, then west along the coast path to **Glendurgan Gardens** or east to Rosemullion Head. Glendurgan was built in the 1840s by the Quaker Alfred Fox, but the valley gardens date back to the 1820s. As Falmouth's chief shipping agents, the Foxes were perfectly placed to get hold of exotic trees and shrubs from as far afield as China. Alfred's nephew Robert raised hybrid rhododendrons at Glendurgan. A gate leads from the gardens, which contain a large laurel maze, to the village of Durgan, the limit of navigation at low tide. In the 1850s Charles Fox created an even lovelier little paradise in a steep ravine to the west called **Trebah Garden**, which start just outside a pretty 18th-century house, from where they descend 200 feet down a steep ravine to the Helford River. In between is an exotic mass of thick, lush vegetation. Huge palms and ferns tower overhead, gnarly 100-year-old rhododendrons block your path, while koi carp regard you lazily from their pools. Make your way to the end and you'll be rewarded by the sight of a private beach, where you can have a picnic or take a quick secluded dip.

From **Helford Passage** there is a seasonal ferry service to Helford, an idyllic village in a quiet inlet. These days every house in Helford is a holiday home, so there's not even a semblance of normal life, although it was once such a busy port that it had a Customs House of its own. From Helford, you can walk via Kestle to the head of **Frenchman's Creek**, one of the most enchanting creeks of all, especially at high tide when the water laps the trees. It was made famous by Daphne du Maurier who gave the creek its name. A path leads down its east side through woods.

boat
Falmouth Pleasure Cruises; t (01326) 212939; www.boattrips-falmouth.co.uk; two sailings a day at 11am & 2pm Mon, Tues, Thurs–Sun and 12 and 2.30pm Wed

Glendurgan Gardens
Mawnan Smith; t (01326) 250906; www.nationaltrust.org. uk; open Feb–Oct Tue–Sat 10.30–5.30; adm £6.40

Trebah Garden
Mawnan Smith; t (01326) 252200 www.trebah-garden.co.uk; open daily 10.30–6.30, last entry 5; adm £7.50

Helford Passage
Helford River Boats; t (01326) 250770; www.helford-river-boats.co.uk; April–Oct according to demand; adm £5 return

Gillan Harbour, a late medieval port in Gillan Creek, is separated from the Helford River by Dennis Head, where the ramparts of an Iron Age cliff castle are mixed up with Royalist fortifications from the Civil War. Make time to look at the lovely 15th-century St Anthony's Church in the village of the same name on the north bank of the creek.

Where to Stay in Falmouth and Around

Falmouth

⭐ The Greenbank Hotel >

ⓘ Falmouth
*Prince Of Wales Pier,
t (01326) 312300; open
daily 9.30am–5.30pm*

The Greenbank Hotel, Harbourside, t (01326) 312440, *www.greenbank-hotel.co.uk (moderate–very expensive).* A large cream-painted 17th-century hotel on the water's edge looking out towards Flushing and St Mawes, this is beautifully decorated with a tiled entrance lobby and period furniture in the oh-so-elegant bedrooms. Enjoy the views from the excellent **Harbourside Restaurant**, which specializes in seafood (*moderate*).

Dolvean Hotel, 50 Melvill Road, t (01326) 313995, *www.dolvean.co.uk (moderate–expensive).* This award-winning B&B is one of the best in Falmouth with 11 fresh, comfortable bedrooms. It's a short walk into town.

Cotswold House Hotel, 49 Melvill Road, t (01326) 312077, *www.cotswold househotel.com (moderate).* Across the road from the Dolvean, this is homey, extra friendly and efficient. Some of the bedrooms have sea views. Rooms drop into the *budget* category if booked for a week or more.

Hawthorne Dene, 12 Pennance Road, t (01326) 311427, *www.hawthornedene hotel.co.uk (moderate).* The clean lines and stark modernism favoured in many of the region's other B&Bs get short shrift in the Hawthorne. Here it's all about antique clutter and Edwardian charm. Several rooms have sea views, all have interesting period details plus flat screen TVs (as a concession to modernity). It's a five-minute walk to the seafront.

⭐ Budock Vean >>

St Mawes

Hotel Tresanton, St.Mawes, t (01326) 270 053, *www.tresanton.com (luxury).* This incredibly elegant white-walled Mediterranean-style hotel now comprises a cluster of fancy houses, but began on a small scale in the 1940s, gradually earning its reputation among the well-to-do yacht crowd. Today all the rooms have balconies with sea views and are adorned with antiques and local artwork, while a gorgeous mosaic-tiled restaurant spills out on to a sunny terrace on warm days. Book in advance for lunch (*moderate*) and dinner (*expensive*).

The Idle Rocks Hotel, Harbourside, t 0844 502 7587, *www.idlerocks.co.uk (expensive–very expensive).* Right on the seawall, this is a good, relaxing choice with 27 individually decorated rooms, the most expensive of which have sea views. There's also a well-respected **brasserie**, the Water's Edge, the holder of two AA rosettes, with a terrace looking out over the harbour.

The Victory Inn, Victory Steps, t (01326) 270324, *www.victory-inn.co.uk (moderate).*On the hill behind the quay right in the heart of the village with two charming, well-equipped rooms, and a very good seafood **restaurant** (*moderate*) and a terrace overlooking the bay . It's friendly and quaint.

Helford River

Budock Vean, Helford Passage, Mawnan Smith, t (01326) 250288, *www.budockvean.co.uk (luxury).* One of Cornwall's very grandest choices set in luxurious, manicured splendour on the north bank of the Helford River amid 65 acres of subtropical gardens. The bedrooms are splendid, the self-catering cottages even more so, and additional facilities include an indoor swimming pool, sauna, outdoor hot tub, restaurant and 9-hole golf course.

The Riverside, Helford, t (01865) 400825, *www.theriverside-helford.co.uk (budget-moderate).* A delightful, large cottage with terraced gardens and six bedrooms that can accommodate up to 12 adults and five children. Cooked breakfast, dinners and wine are provided, as well as a motor launch and sailing dinghies. It's available for weekends in winter and by the week in summer. It's charged per head, minimum eight people (dropping to six in term time).

Eating Out in Falmouth and Around

Bistro de la Mer, 28 Arwenack Street, **t** (01326) 316509, *www.bistrodelamer. com* (*moderate–expensive*). While many places call themselves a 'bistro' this is the real deal offering French-inspired takes on local ingredients – escargots de bourgogne, Hereford steak fillet au poivre etc. – and a serious wine list.

⊛ Hunky Dory >

Hunky Dory, 46 Arwenack Street, **t** (01326) 212997, *www.hunkydory falmouth.co.uk* (*moderate*). Lovely, light fresh restaurant decked out in natural woods, sea blues and whites, serving some of the town's very best seafood – such as sea bass with saffron, mussels and king prawn paella or cod in prosciutto with parmesan mash and parsley vinaigrette.

Powell's Cellar, 9 High Street, **t** (01326) 311212 (*moderate*). At the bottom of the high street, this sells seafood and steaks plus various other interesting concoctions, such as deep-fried vegetable parcels with tomato coulis, and stilton crumble with broccoli and sweetcorn. *Open eves only.*

The Seafood Bar, Lower Quay Street, **t** (01326) 315129 (*moderate*). Tucked

away in a basement, halfway down Quay Street, with a good local reputation. Try their renowned sea platter. *Open evenings only.*

Gylly Beach Café, Cliff Road, **t** (01326) 312884, *www.gyllybeach.com* (*budget–moderate*). On the seafront with outdoor seating overlooking Gyllyngvase Beach and a rather stylish wood-panelled interior, this environmentally-conscious place serves simple, locally sourced meals from morning till late. The highlights are the barbecues from 5pm onwards Fri–Sun.

The Chainlocker and Shipwrights, Quay Hill, **t** (01326) 311085 (*budget*). Good old-fashioned pub right on the quay serving local beers (such as Skinners Cornish Knocker) and basic fish and chips. Established in 1742, this is one of Falmouth's oldest pubs.

The Shipwright's Arms, Helford, **t** (01326) 231235 (*budget*). Cosy, cute thatched pub with a terraced patio overlooking the water. They serve a good range of local ales, including Sharp's Doom Bar and Skinners' Betty Stogs, as well as food in the evening (best to pre-book).

The Quayside Inn, 41 Arwenack Street, **t** (01326) 312914 (*budget*). Sit outside and enjoy the views across the harbour towards Flushing and St Mawes. They serve wonderful food: try the hand-carved ham, beef and stilton pie or huge hands of bread. It puts on live music on Fri and Sat nights, and is popular with local students.

The Lizard Peninsula

South of the intimate wooded fringes of the Helford River, you emerge into the flat, windswept plateau of the Lizard Peninsula. The serpentine rock of which it is made, found nowhere else in England, is exposed around Kynance, Mullion and Coverack in the form of contorted black, red and green cliffs. **Lizard Point** separates the sheltered harbours on the east side of the peninsula from the wave-battered bays on the west. You can walk round.

The B3293 skirts around the Helford River and its creeks to **Coverack** on the eastern coast. Unusually for a Cornish harbour village, Coverack sits above a wide bay. Its small harbour is sheltered behind Dolar Point. From here, looking north you can see Lowland Point (a 1.5 mile walk from Coverack), an Ice Age beach formed by the upward movement of the land when rising temperatures melted the great ice sheets that formerly pressed down on this area. From the point you can see the **Manacles** reef, where many a ship has been wrecked. Nowadays divers flock to the reef in search of treasure. You can continue to **St Keverne**, cutting inland to a narrow lane. The leaders of the 1497 Cornish uprising, Michael Joseph *An Gof* ('The Smith') and the lawyer Thomas Flamank are commemorated in St Keverne with a plaque on the church wall, adapted from *An Gof*'s famous last words at Tyburne:

'MICHAEL JOSEPH *AN GOF* AND THOMAS FLAMANK LEADERS OF THE CORNISH HOST WHO MARCHED TO LONDON AND SUFFERED VENGEANCE THERE JUNE 1497. THEY SHALL HAVE A NAME PERPETUAL AND FAME PERMANENT AND IMMORTAL.'

Up the hill (in the direction of London's Blackheath, where the peasant 'host' met Henry VII's 25,000-strong army) are statues of the Cornish rebels – *An Gof* depicted rallying his men – erected in 1997 in the spirit of Cornish revival.

A vertiginous lane is the route down to **Cadgwith**, a workmanlike fishing village of thatched cottages with crab boats pulled up on the tiny beach, a good fish shop and singing in the pub. You can walk north along the coastal path to **Carleon Cove**, at the foot of the Poltesco Valley. The ruins behind the beach once belonged to a thriving pilchard factory (1,347,000 fish were caught in two days in 1908), later a serpentine works. Or you can head south on the coastal path to Lizard Point. It's a fabulous section of coastline. On **Bass Point** stands the old Lloyds Signal Station, which telegraphed London shipowners news of their ships entering the Channel, and a lookout that logs all passing shipping. You can stop for tea or drinks on the terrace of the old Housel Bay Hotel, whose guests have included George Bernard Shaw and Lewis Carroll.

From the Lizard village green, footpaths lead south to **Lizard Point**, where there are two cafés and a shop selling trinkets made of serpentine. The Lizard is the gateway into the English Channel, and the first sight of England for ocean shipping – it's not always a welcome one; hundreds of boats have been wrecked on the submerged rocks that extend more than a mile out to sea. In the days when the French and Spanish were always about to invade, its beacon was the first in a chain of communications flashing along the south coast. A concrete path zigzags down to the old lifeboat shed in Polpeor Cove, which operated from 1859 until 1961. In heavy seas, the lifeboat men used to crawl down so as not to get swept off. You can see the slipway where the lifeboat was hauled up off the beach to the shed in bad weather.

lighthouse
t (01326) 290202;
www.trinityhouse.co.uk;
open June & Sept
Sat–Wed 11am–5pm,
July daily 11am–6pm,
August daily 11am–7pm,
Oct Sun–Wed
11am–4pm, Nov–Dec
noon–4pm; adm £4

On the headland stands the old twin-towered **lighthouse**, built in 1752, and still operated, by Trinity House. It's the biggest lighthouse complex in the world, standing 19m tall and once accommodating six keepers' families, although it has been fully automated since 1998. You can see the engine room where a powerful foghorn was operated by three enormous steam engines – two blasts a minute when visibility dropped below three miles.

East of the lighthouse is the **Lion's Den**, a hole in the cliff top created by a collapsing sea cave. To the west is Kynance Cove – steps lead down to the serpentine inlet. Its sandy beach, guarded by fearsome crags and caves with boulders piled up by the sea beneath the red-black cliffs, becomes completely inundated at high tide.

Mullion, a mile or so from the sea, is a complete toytown village with its own one-way system, council estates, fire brigade, schools and shop. From Mullion, three roads shoot down three valleys to **Mullion Cove**, **Poldhu Cove** and **Polurrian Cove**. The harbour at Mullion Cove is a perfect green square basin that looks like a swimming pool. Beyond the cove Mullion Island – a bird sanctuary – forms a natural breakwater. There's a good 1.5 mile walk south from the harbour up Mullion Cliff to Bosvean. North of Mullion, Poldhu Cove is a lovely spot, its dunes enclosed by headlands. The first long-distance radio signal was sent across the Atlantic from Marconi's cliff-top wireless station here. The coastal path leads on to **Helzephron Cliff** ('Hell's Cliff'), a good spot for a swim, via **Gunwalloe Cove**, which has a dramatically sited church, St Winwaloe's, right next to the beach with a detached rock belfry. If you fancy putting a little purpose into your beach exploring, the pirate John Avery (more commonly known as 'Long Ben') supposedly buried an as-yet-undiscovered horde of gold somewhere in the sands around here.

Helston and Porthleven

Helston is the Lizard's most serious urban centre. It was once a stannary town and has the handsome Georgian townhouses, large civic buildings and air of slightly faded self-importance to prove it. It's at its jolliest in May when the town is festooned with flowers and bunting is flung up across the high street in preparation for the Furry (or Floral) Dance held on the Saturday closest to 8 May. Big crowds arrive to watch the elegantly dressed dancers (top hats and tails for the boys, puffy dresses and wide-brimmed hats for the girls) twirl their way through the thronging streets. You can find out more on the background to the ritual at the town's **Folk Museum**, housed in the town's former market. It also has items of local craft paraphernalia as well as a display on local hero, and pugilistic prince, Bob Fitzsimmons, who won the world middleweight, light heavyweight and heavyweight boxing titles – he must have packed quite a punch. A blue plaque marks the house in which he was born.

Folk Museum
Market Place;
t (01326) 564 027;
www.cornwall.gov.uk;
Mon–Sat 10am–1pm

Porthleven, just past Helston, has a terrific man-made harbour, built in the early 19th century after crowds had helplessly watched the man o' war HMS *Anson* being wrecked a mile east. Recovered cannons from the ship can be seen by the harbour and outside the Folk Museum. On the water's edge are Victorian warehouses and the town council which occupies Bickford-Smith building, a former scientific and literary institute with a distinctive clock tower.

To the south there are good walks around **Loe Pool**, a lake separated from the sea by a shingle bar (park at Penrose, Highburrow, Chyvarlow, Degibna or Helston). It is one of the contenders for the 'great water' into which Bedevere throws Excalibur in Tennyson's Morte d'Arthur:

'A broken chancel with a broken cross,
That stood on a dark strait of barren land.
On one side lay the Ocean, and on one
Lay a great water, and the moon was full.'

Getting to and around Helston

Helston, the main hub of the Lizard, lies near the South Cornish coast on the A394. It's linked to Truro by regular **buses** operated by First Group (**t** 0845 600 1420, *www.firstgroup.com*). The T2 route links Helston with many of the local towns, including Coverack and St Keverne.

Flambards

Flambards
Helston;
t *0845 601 8684;*
www.flambards.co.uk;
open daily Apr–Jul 10–5;
Aug 10–5.30; Sept–Oct
10.30–4.30; adm £16.50

A theme park without a theme, **Flambards** just outside Helston off the A394, has a charmingly eclectic range of attractions that will keep families entertained for an afternoon. Alongside a couple of very nifty rollercoasters, a log flume and swinging pirate ship, you'll find a reconstructed Victorian village with over 50 buildings to wander through, each decked out with period furniture, decorations and even period food; a reconstructed Second World War street (shown ravaged by Blitz bombs); a weather station, where you can watch live satellite transmissions from space; and an exhibition showing how wedding fashions have changed through the centuries. There is also a petting zoo, an adventure playground, a soft play area for toddlers, an interactive science centre, some sedate fairground rides, a garden centre and the Cornwall Children's Eye (a rival to the rather larger Ferris wheel in London). In summer, there are occasional evening firework displays. It's a bit strange but holds together very well, giving kids plenty of opportunity to run around and let off steam.

National Seal Sanctuary

National Seal Sanctuary
Gweek, Helston;
t *(01326) 221361;*
www.sealsanctuary.co.uk; open daily 10am–dusk; adm £13

A few miles further outside Helston in Gweek (follow the A3083 then the B3293), the **National Seal Sanctuary** has been ministering to the needs of the region's marine mammals since the late 1950s. A few seals have made the sanctuary their permanent home. Most, however, are just temporary residents passing through while their ailments and injuries are seen to. The largest sanctuary of its type in Europe, it releases over 30 seals a year back into British coastal waters. With a good audiovisual display on the work of the sanctuary, regular talks by the sanctuary's keepers and lots of feeding-time fun, the sanctuary is both educational and enjoyable for the kids. The seals are best viewed at the underwater observatory, where you can see them gliding and skimming through the water. Guided walks are available through the local woods and there's also a small farm to visit.

Where to Stay and Eat on the Lizard Peninsula

Very Expensive
Housel Bay Hotel, The Lizard, **t** (01326) 290 417, *www.houselbay.com*. Family-run three-star Victorian hotel with half of its well-equipped 21 rooms looking out towards Lizard Point. The **restaurant** specializes in local produce. It's a short walk down the cliff path to Housel Cove.

The Bay Hotel, Coverack, **t** (01326) 280464, *www.thebayhotel.co.uk*. Comfortable family-run hotel in its own gardens with sea-facing rooms and a restaurant on the coastal path behind the sea wall, overlooking the bay. It's just a few steps down to the beach. Cheaper weekly rates offered.
The Polurrian Hotel, Mullion, **t** (01326) 240421, *www.polurrianhotel.com*. Big, bright white hotel on the cliff tops with 39 recently refurbished rooms,

an outdoor pool and gardens sloping down towards the headland. Additional facilities include a restaurant with views across the bay, an indoor pool, leisure club, tennis and squash courts.

Moderate

Cadgwith Cove Inn, Cadgwith, **t** (01326) 290513, *www.cadgwithcove inn.com*. Seven sea-facing rooms in a 300-year-old inn and very good pub meals of fish, including monkfish and lobster, caught fresh from the cove. Stay longer than three nights and your room rate drops by 20 per cent.

Penmenner House Hotel, Penmenner Road, The Lizard, **t** (01326) 290370. An 1850 house just off the coastal foot-path, this was visited by the poet Rupert Brooke on his way to a rom-antic rendezvous with the under-age Noël Olivier. He met up with the gang of so-called Cambridge Apostles here and put the world to rights over dinner – a letter from Brook to Noël bears testimony. The B&B is clean, bright and family-run with six taste-fully furnished bedrooms, all with sea views. It's a short walk to the village.

St Mellans House, Meaver Rd, Mullion, **t** (01326) 241881, *www.stmellans.co.uk*. A pretty Edwardian house set in its own large garden on the way into the village, with five bedrooms (a mixture of en suite and shared bathrooms). It offers good breakfasts, comprising kippers, smoked haddock, eggs and summer-fruit pancakes.

The Caerthillian, Lizard Village, **t** (01326) 290019, *www.thecaerthillian. co.uk*. Large, bright-blue Victorian B&B

with four spacious bedrooms, a few steps from a village pub.

The Paris Hotel, The Cove, Coverack, **t** (01326) 280258, *www.pariscoverack. com*. An Edwardian inn on the quay, named after the SS *Paris* passenger liner which foundered on the Manacles in 1893. It has four simple rooms, a cosy bar and a restaurant offering fresh fish, simply prepared and panoramic sea views.

The Top House, Lizard Village, **t** (01326) 290974, *www.thetophouselizard.co.uk*. Eight smart and clean, recently revamped en suite rooms in a 200-year-old village pub serving traditional fare and Sharps ales, brewed near Padstow. Photos of lifeboats and wrecks decorate the walls.

Valley View House, Porthallow Cove, St Keverne, **t** (01326) 280370. Charming 3-bedroom B&B in a picturesque cove.

Budget

The Blue Anchor Inn, 50 Coinagehall Street, Helston, **t** (01326) 562821, *www.spingoales.com*. A 15th-century inn where monks used to produce mead and which today is the site of a small brewery turning out lethal 'Spingo' ales. It's a very traditional place with a skittle alley and a covered beer garden.

The Old Cellars, Cadgwith, Ruan Minor, **t** (01326) 290727. In the tiny fishing/smuggling village of Cadgwith, this serves morning coffee and cream teas in the courtyard, with delicious home-made doughnuts, plus lunches of local crab, cod and fresh pollack caught off the beach.

Penzance and Mount's Bay

Penzance, Britain's most westerly town, is the main port of Mount's Bay, providing a stepping stone to Land's End and the Isles of Scilly. It can strike you as dreary, characterized by busy roads and industrial estates, or quaint in a workmanlike way (especially around the old harbour), depending on your mood. Mount 's Bay has been busy for thousands of years. Today it's all go, from the old dockside warehouse buildings behind Wharf Road beneath the pinnacled tower of the church along the arms of the bay to the detached islet of St Michael's Mount, with boats, cars, helicopters and trains in a state of near-constant activity. In the Bronze Age St Michael's Mount was the local hub of activity. Later it was Mousehole and Newlyn.

Getting to and around Penzance and Mount's Bay

The A30, the major trunk road of the West Country, which continues on from the M5 (from Bristol and Birmingham) and A303 (from London) at Exeter, takes you all the way to Penzance. Great Western Trains run regularly from London Paddington, via Bristol Temple Meads, Exeter and Truro. National Express runs services daily from London, Bristol and Exeter.

But Penzance was a late bloomer, finally making a name for itself in the 1550s when it became the major tin port and administrative centre for West Cornwall. Three hundred years later half of Cornwall's tin was being exported from Penzance to destinations across the globe, including Turkey, Portugal, Spain, Prussia, Norway and Sweden, all of whom had vice-consuls stationed in town. Twenty-first-century Penzance seems almost disinterested in tourists, leaving all that to Mousehole, St Michael's Mount, Newlyn and St Ives.

Park in the large car park by the railway station, once part of the old harbour. Several streets take you into town. **Chapel Street** leads past the town church (there are superb views from the churchyard over the bay) with a pleasant mix of shops, restaurants and interesting buildings, such as the flamboyant **Egyptian House**, a 19th-century building with a strange Egyptian-style facade built by a local mineralogist to hold his collection of rocks; the Chocolate House tearoom, with its seafaring sign, candy-twist columns and nude nymphs; and the Admiral Benbow pub topped by a statue of an armed smuggler on its roof. The **Union Hotel** on Chapel Street used to be the town's assembly rooms where news of Nelson's death and the victory of Trafalgar was first told on the mainland – a Penzance fishing boat intercepted the British warship HMS *Pickle* that was carrying the good/bad news to Falmouth. It was immediately passed on to the Major of Penzance, who let everyone know in what is now known as the Nelson Bar. The town's lighthouse museum has now closed, as has its maritime museum, the contents of which were transferred to Falmouth's new collection (*see* p.194). That leaves the **Penlee Gallery and Museum** as the main repository of culture. It's housed in a handsome Italianate mansion that once belonged to an 18th-century Penzance merchant. Permanent exhibitions cover farming, mining and fishing, as well as one or two extraordinary events in local history, such as the Spanish raid of 1595, seven years after the Armada, when 200 troops set fire to Newlyn, Mousehole, Penzance and Paul before being chased off by soldiers from Plymouth. Its art exhibition inevitably includes numerous Newlyn School paintings (*see* p.204). There's also a good café, as well as pleasant gardens to stroll in.

Penlee Gallery and Museum
Morrab Road;
t (01736) 363625;
www.penleehouse.org.uk;
open daily Easter–Sept
10am–5pm, Oct–Easter
10.30am–4.30pm;
adm £3

Market Jew Street is the main shopping street at the top of the town, its unusual name apparently deriving from the Cornish 'marghas yow', meaning Market Thursday. The shops are mainly down-at-heel, but at one end is the magnificent green domed and porticoed Victorian guildhall (now a bank). In front stands a statue of local inventor Humphrey Davy holding up his greatest invention – the miners' safety lamp. One or two lanes lead uphill to little galleries, selling crafts and art.

Newlyn

Newlyn is best known for its modern fishing harbour and market, and its turn-of-the-2oth-century regional arts scene. There are one of two things to detain you here. On New Road, the recently revamped, re-opened and very jazzy looking **Newlyn Art Gallery** is probably the best contemporary art galleries in the West. First opened in 1885 it shows constantly changing displays of works by modern artists from around the world, both here and at its smaller outpost, **The Exchange**, which is housed in the town's old telephone exchange.

Newlyn Art Gallery
New Road;
t (01736) 363715;
www.newlynartgallery.
co.uk; open summer
Mon–Sat 10am–5pm,
winter Tues–Sat
10am–5pm; adm free

The Exchange
details as above

There are a few galleries and shops (where you might pick up a tin of pilchards made at the local works and decorated with pictures from the Newlyn School) at the head of the quay around Fisherman's Mission on North Pier, which boasts a ship weathervane made of Newlyn Copper, a distinctive type of repoussé copper work popular in the town in the late 19th century. To get a sense of the old fishing harbour that so enraptured the Newlyn painters, walk along the narrow road between the modern fishmarket and the Victorian iceworks to the old quay, as painted by Walter Langley. It's now a little green at the foot of a village area known as Fradgen. Most of the Newlyn artists lived in the colourful cottages in the Fradgen and Trewarveneth Street.

St Michael's Mount

St Michael's Mount
t (01736) 710507;
www.stmichaelsmount.
co.uk; open April–Oct
Mon–Fri & Sun
10.30am–5.30pm,
guided tours available
in winter

The castle on **St Michael's Mount** looks as a castle should look: dramatic, mysterious and almost utterly impregnable. The mount, which lies a few hundred yards offshore from Marazion a couple of miles east of Penzance along the coast road, is reached at low tide along a splendidly romantic narrow brick causeway and at high tide (providing the sea is calm), when it is marooned on its cone of granite, by ferry. The fairy-tale battlements belong to the Aubyn family home. Colonel John Aubyn bought the old Benedictine priory-turned-post-Dissolution barracks in 1659. Subsequent refurbishments have retained (and even enhanced) its Gothic appearance, with the addition of some Chippen-dale furniture and an Old Master painting here, and a new Victorian wing there. The harbour at the foot of the hill was rebuilt in 1727 to stimulate trade in tin and copper. Summer crowds trek across the causeway like the medieval pilgrims to the priory (who came to see the

The Newlyn School

The heyday of the Newlyn School of art was 1880–1930, just before St Ives took off – and in all honesty eclipsed it. The earliest Newlyn painters had all studied impressionism in France and thought that Newlyn looked just like the little French fishing villages they had been painting, with a similar quality of light. Walter Langley (born in Birmingham) was the first of the Newlyn painters to settle here, in 1882, followed close behind by his friend Edwin Harris (also a midlander). However, it was the arrival of Irishman Stanhope Forbes, and particularly his *Fish Sale on a Cornish Beach*, painted in a gale on the sand between Newlyn and Penzance, that first drew national attention to Newlyn. The group painted out in the open as their French teaching dictated ('en plein air'), depicting ordinary life laced with a bit of Victorian melodrama and often annotated with poignant lines of poetry or Shakespeare.

Godolphin Arms Hotel
West End, Marazion;
t (01736) 710202;
www.godolphinarms.co.uk

jawbone of St Appolonia of Alexandra, patron saint of toothache). Get yourself up to the 14th-century priory church at the top of the island, from where the views rekindle any magic lost in the crowds.

Back in **Marazion** there are a few galleries near the seafront and a couple of good restaurants, including the **Godolphin Arms Hotel**, which serves lunches on the terrace overlooking St Michael's Mount.

(i) **Penzance**
Station Approach,
t (01736) 36220; open
summer Mon–Sat
9am–5pm, Sun
9am–1pm; winter
9am–5pm, sat
10am–1pm.

(★) **The Summer House** >

(★) **Penzance Arts Club** >

Where to Stay in Penzance and Mount's Bay

Very Expensive

Abbey Hotel, Abbey Street, **t** (01736) 366906, *www.theabbeyonline.co.uk*. This hotel is very pretty, set in a fine historic house, containing bits of 17th and 19th century architecture, above the harbour. The rooms are grand and elegantly cluttered with French armoires, armchairs and lots of antiques. It also boasts a top-notch **restaurant**.

Expensive

Ednovean Garm, Perranuthnoe, **t** (01736) 711883, *www.ednoveanfarm. co.uk*. Roomy, arty place in a converted 17th-century barn occupying a stunning location in gardens overlooking Mount's Bay. There are three super-luxurious bedrooms with sitting rooms, silk wall hangings and DVD players.

Ennys, Trewhella Lane, St Hilary, **t** (01736) 740262, *www.ennys.co.uk*. Lovely house in a delightful spot with large bedrooms and even larger suites in an adjoining Grade II listed granite barn. There are also some self-catering cottages to rent.

The Summer House, Cornwall Terrace, **t** (01736) 363744, *www.summerhouse-cornwall.com*. A charming Grade IIlisted Regency corner house tucked behind the Queens Hotel. It's beautifully furnished and decorated with dark wooden floorboards and sunshine-yellow walls and comfy old sofas. There are five, fresh, summery bedrooms and a very good-value seafood **restaurant** (*open summer only*).

Moderate

Penzance Arts Club, Chapel House, Chapel Street, **t** (01736) 363761, *www.penzanceartsclub.co.uk*. A cultural centre-cum-hotel, this offers an elegantly scruffy venue for various arty local happenings – most hosted in the bar-lounge – and four B&B rooms, the best of them with stripped floorboards, art on the walls and showers in glass boxes in the corners. It's all very easy-going – old sofas dotted around the house, paintings stacked up against the wall and breakfast whenever you like. The owners organize painting holidays and poetry workshops.

The Pendennis, Alexandra Road, **t** (01736) 363823, *www.geniusloci.co.uk*. A tall, gabled Victorian house on a quiet street, with eight rooms (seven en suite) and a cheerful breakfast room. Its front-garden blooms won first prize in the hotel category of Penzance's 'Britain in Bloom' competition. Free Wi-Fi available.

Budget

Estoril Hotel, 46 Morrab Road, **t** (01736) 362468, *www.estorilhotel.co. uk*. A very good value B&B set in an attractive Victorian house where rates start at £20 per person per night. There are nine clean, comfy bedrooms.

Penzance YHA, Castle Horneck, Alverton, **t** 0845 371 9653, *www.yha. org.uk*. The setting is so fantastic, in a Georgian mansion set in wooded grounds, that you can almost forget it's a YHA. It offers the usual range of hostel facilities, including a café, games room, kitchen and camp-ing facilities. Dorm beds from £15.95.

Eating Out in Penzance and Mount's Bay

Expensive

Chapel Street Brasserie, 12 Chapel Street, **t** (01736) 350222, *www.chapel streetbrasserie.com*. Good-quality brasserie in a light, brightly painted setting. They offer an early dinner set menu between 6 and 7.15pm – two courses for £12. Things are a bit more pricey after that. Live music, typically jazz, is laid on every Sunday from 7pm.

Moderate
The Summer House, Cornwall Terrace, t (01736) 363744, *www.summerhouse-cornwall.com*. Attractive airy restaurant spilling out onto a leafy patio on warm evenings. The kitchen serves up delicious Mediterranean-style home cooking, such as fillet of red mullet with black olives and fresh basil followed by warm apple tart.

Budget
Turk's Head, Chapel Street, t (01736) 363093, *www.turksheadpenzance.co.uk*. A medieval pub, the oldest in Penzance, this serves some very good pub food, including plenty of fresh fish, and a decent pint. A tunnel,

dating back to its smuggling past, leads from the pub to the harbour.

The Renaissance Café, Wharfside Shopping Centre, Market Jew Street, t (01736) 366277. At the wharfside near the railway station, overlooking the harbour, this has high ceilings, fans, lamps and big, bright paintings. It's friendly and welcoming.

Entertainment

The Acorn Arts Centre, Parade Street, t (01736) 363545, *www.acornartscentre. co.uk*. The old Victorian chapel has housed Penzance's arts centre for more than 30 years, hosting mainly comedy, music and films (with some drama) in its 255-seat auditorium.

St Ives

Pretty, white-washed St Ives wraps itself around the rocky headland of St Ives Head on the western rim of St Ives Bay, the last stop before Land's End Peninsula. Tate Gallery St Ives arrived on the seafront in 1990, reversing the fortunes of the declining harbour town and its seasonal seaside attractions. Due to the Tate's success, small commercial galleries are flourishing all over town, and restaurants and hotels have improved immeasurably. The harbour, tucked into the headland, adds grit to the galleries, while the town's three sandy beaches jolly it all along. In the height of summer the place absolutely heaves.

Ditch your car en route into town, as the small centre gets jam-packed in summer. Beneath the main road into town, the east-facing **Porthminster Beach** is the main family beach in St Ives, but you are more likely to drift from the quayside to **Porthgwidden Beach** – in a sheltered

Modern Art in St Ives

Artists have been painting St Ives since Turner first sketched it in 1811. By the 1890s they were coming down in hordes on the railway and using old sail lofts as studios. By 1920, when Bernard Leach set up his Japanese-influence pottery with Shoji Hamada, there was a small community of artists living in the town, who came together to form the St Ives Society of Artists in 1927. Alfred Wallis, a retired fisherman with a local rag-and-bone business, is the unofficial patron of St Ives artists past and present. He had no art training and didn't pick up a paint brush until he was widowed at the age of 72. After then, he couldn't stop, painting on bits of wood and old marmalade jars. In the 1920s Ben Nicholson and Christopher Wood discovered him while on a trip to the town and started to copy his unsophisticated style, turning their back on art-school conventions like perspective. Nicholson married the abstract sculptor, Barbara Hepworth, in London in 1933 and they moved down to St Ives on the outbreak of the Second World War. Hepworth bought her Trewyn Studio in 1949, the year of the famous split in the St Ives Society of Artists over abstraction in art. The avant-garde broke off and formed the Penwith Society, leaving the figurative painters to their own devices. Artists like Nicholson, Wood, Hepworth and Naum Gabo were internationalist in their outlook, but shared enough common values, and the landscape of St Ives, to be called a school. The St Ives School is considered Britain's most influential 20th-century art scene.

rocky niche in the headland – or the mile-long **Porthmeor Beach** on the other side of the headland, which is north-facing and gets the big Atlantic rollers. In the old fisherman's mission above the harbour, **St Ives Museum** is full of interesting everyday flotsam and jetsam from the old town before it caught art fever.

To get your bearings, stand on the end of St Ives Head (otherwise known as The Island) and look back. Beneath you, **Tate Gallery St Ives** looks like the Starship Enterprise in disguise; striking and monolithic, but like a jumble of houses full of balconies and small windows. It was built to exhibit the work of the St Ives School – which it does – but its diverse gallery spaces also feature quarterly changing displays of 20th-century art, usually with a Cornish connection. There's a great café on the top floor with views over Porthmeor Beach.

Behind it in the hillside cemetery is the tiled grave of **Alfred Wallis** (near the chapel) made by the potter Bernard Leach who first opened a studio in St Ives in 1920. The inscription reads: ALFRED WALLIS/ARTIST & MARINER, with a picture of a man climbing up steps through a lighthouse door. Wallis was a fisherman who took up painting when he retired, and caught the attention of the artist Bill Nicholson with his naive paintings of boats on old bits of driftwood and cardboard. There is a plaque on the wall of his old cottage in Back Road West, just along from the Tate Gallery.

St Ives Museum

Wheal Dream;
t (01736) 796005; open
Easter–Oct Mon–Fri
10am–5pm, Sat
10am–4pm; adm £1.50

Tate Gallery St Ives

Porthmeor Beach;
t (01736) 796226;
www.tate.org.uk/stives;
open March–Oct daily
10am–5pm, Nov–Feb
Tues–Sun 10am–4pm;
adm £5.65 or £8.55 with
entry to the Barbara
Hepworth Museum

09 **Cornwall | St Ives**

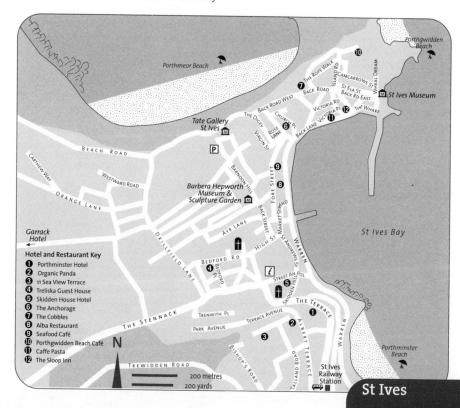

Hotel and Restaurant Key
1. Porthminster Hotel
2. Organic Panda
3. 11 Sea View Terrace
4. Treliska Guest House
5. Skidden House Hotel
6. The Anchorage
7. The Cobbles
8. Alba Restaurant
9. Seafood Café
10. Porthgwidden Beach Café
11. Caffe Pasta
12. The Sloop Inn

St Ives

Getting to St Ives

St Ives is on the North Cornwall coast, a short hop off the A30 on the A3074 or B3311. **Trains** and National Express **coach** services run from Penzance and London Paddington.

Barbara Hepworth Museum and Sculpture Garden
Barnoon Hill; t (01736) 796226; www.tate.org.uk/stives/ hepworth; open March–Oct daily 10am–5pm, Nov–Feb Tues–Sun 10am–4pm; adm £4.65 or £8.55 joint ticket with Tate St Ives

The old studio of the sculptor Barbara Hepworth, Nicholson's former wife, is at the bottom of Barnoon Hill. It became the **Barbara Hepworth Museum and Sculpture Garden** shortly after her death in 1975. The complex of delightful, ramshackle workshops with low, sloping roofs, turns its back on the town, facing into Hepworth's garden. In 1951, she came to live here when her marriage with Ben Nicholson broke down. There is a small exhibition in her old living rooms (stripped of all domestic memories), while her workshops and garden are a sculpture gallery and her memorial. Her dusty, whitewashed stone workshop is kept just as she left it – old hand tools lying around, her overalls on a hook and notes to herself pinned to the walls. She produced more than 600 original pieces in wood, stone and metal, living alone, eventually setting fire to herself smoking in bed, aged 72.

Expensive contemporary art is now sold at the **Wills Lane**, **Millennium** and **Belgrave** galleries, while a raft of others sell a hotchpotch of local work.

Bernard Leach Pottery
Higher Stennack; t (01736) 799703, www.leachpottery.com; open March–Oct Mon–Sat 10am–5pm, Sun 11am–4pm; Nov –Feb Tues–Sat 10am–4pm; adm £4.50

About a mile out of town, taking the steep road called the Stannack from the top of the High Street, the **Bernard Leach Pottery** has a workaday atmosphere that belies the quality of the work produced here. Leach founded the pottery in 1920 following time spent studying in Japan with a young Japanese potter named Shoji Hamada, who slept on a camp bed in the workshop, and developed a craft tradition that has influenced every studio potter since. It is still a working pottery. The house is filled with pieces by the entire Leach family and Hamada, and items donated by ex-students such as Michael Cardew. Look out for the fireplace decorated with Bernard Leach Tiles.

★ **Blue Hayes** >>

ⓘ **St Ives**
The Guildhall, Street an Pol, t (01736) 796297. Open Mon–Sat 9am–6pm, Sun 10am–4pm

Where to Stay in St Ives

Luxury
Porthminster Hotel, The Terrace; t (01736) 795221; www.porthminster-hotel.co.uk. Overlooking the bay, set above subtropical gardens, this offers a very superior range of rooms and suites, with either garden or sea views. There's also a bar, a lounge, a fitness centre and indoor and outdoor pools.
The Garrack Hotel, Burthallan Lane, t (01736) 796199, www.garrack.com. A 1920s house, blanketed in Virginia creeper and set in gardens high above Porthmeor beach, this offers 24 three-star rooms and very good evening meals in its **restaurant** (*moderate*).

Very Expensive
Blue Hayes, Trelyon Avenue, t (01736) 799098, www.bluehayes.co.uk. This 1920s house attracts a dedicated following drawn to its grand, spacious and stylish bedrooms and superb terrace overlooking the B&B's pretty grounds and out over the water. The the Master Suite, has a four-poster bed and private balcony (from £95 per person per night). The lesser suites are around £20 cheaper.

Expensive
11 Sea View Terrace, 11 Sea View Terrace, t (01736) 798440, www.11stives.co.uk. This has great views out over the waves. The interior sights aren't too bad either with three luxury suites

adorned with modern art and boasting LCD TVs and DVD players.

★ Organic Panda >

Organic Panda, 1 Pednolva Terrace, t (01736) 793890, *www.organicpanda. co.uk*. If the environmental cost of your holiday gives you sleepless nights, try the Panda, whose eco-friendly policies – it uses reclaimed timber furniture, biodegradable washing products and scrupulously recycles its waste – will help assuage your guilt. It's also very comfortable, and a bit funky with modern art adorning the stark white walls. The breakfasts (organic and locally sourced, of course) are a treat. There are just three bedrooms, so book early.

★ Seafood Café >>

Primrose Valley, Porthminster Beach, t (01736) 794939, *www.primroseonline. co.uk*. In a great location by Porthminster Beach, the Primrose is a very boutique B&B. Its ten rooms come in a variety of styles, from modern and stark to old-fashioned, cluttered and cos, – but all have been done to the highest specifications. A beauty therapy room, locally sourced breakfasts and an environmentally friendly ethos complete the picture.

★ The Alba Restaurant >>

Moderate

Skidden House Hotel, Skidden Hill, t (01736) 798619, *www.skiddenhouse. co.uk*. Centuries-old B&B in an excellent position just up from the sea with en suite rooms, blue-painted shutters, white walls and flower baskets. It's within easy walking distance of several restaurants.

The Anchorage, 5 Bunkers Hill, t (01736) 797135, *www.anchoragestives. co.uk*. Four rooms and generous breakfasts in a Grade II listed early 18th-century house just off the quay.

The Cobbles, 33 Back Road West, t (01736) 798206, *www.thecobbles.co. uk*. Super-friendly B&B with cosy clean rooms in the centre just a minute or so's walk from the harbour.

Treliska Guest House, 3 Bedford Road, t (01736) 797678, *www.treliska.com*. One of St Ives' new breed of B&Bs where the emphasis is on smart, modern décor and designer touches. The owners are as friendly and welcoming as tradition dictates. Rooms are stylish if a little small, the breakfasts are generous and guests get free use of a cappuccino machine.

Eating Out in St Ives

Porthminster Beach Café, Porthminster Beach, t (01736) 795352, *www.porthminstercafe.co.uk* (*moderate*). Excellent seafood restaurant right on the beach with views out towards Godrevy Lighthouse. It's open spring and summer only, daily from 9am, for morning coffee, lunch (*budget*) and dinner (*moderate*).

Seafood Café, 45 Fore Street, t (01736) 794004, *www.seafoodcafe.co.uk* (*moderate*). Getting food the way you want it at the Seafood Café couldn't be easier. Go to the refrigerated display of fish and seafood (John Dory, cod, monkfish, halibut etc., all hauled in locally), pick the one you like the look of, tell the kitchen how you'd like it cooked and add your choice of sauces and vegetables. And, if you're still not happy, it's probably your fault.

The Alba Restaurant, Old Lifeboat House, Wharf Road, t (01736) 797222, *www.thealbarestaurant.com* (*moderate*). Run by a protégé of Rick Stein, this offers a modern English menu of line-caught fish and seasonal vegetables in a split-level venue that was once the town's lifeboat building. One of St Ives' top choices.

Porthgwidden Beach Café, Porthgwidden Beach, t (01736) 796791, *www.porthgwiddencafe.co.uk* (*budget-moderate*). Fresh local produce and lots of seafood, served for breakfast (from 8am, dishes include scrambled eggs with smoked salmon), lunch (crawfish-tail baguettes, fish and chips) and dinner (*moules mariniere*, grilled scallops and confit duck leg). Prices get more expensive as the day progresses, but are still reasonable.

Caffe Pasta, The Wharf, t (01736) 798899, *www.caffepasta.co.uk* (*budget*). Modest little place on the quayside selling a range fairly priced pizza and pasta choices.

The Sloop Inn, The Wharf, t (01736) 796584, *www.sloop-inn.co.uk* (*budget*). This no-nonsense old boozer provides a nice old-fashioned contrast to all the boutique hotels and modern seafood restaurants. Expect real ales, low ceilings, booth seating and plenty of locals.

Land's End Peninsula

Land's End Peninsula is the western extremity of Britain, beyond the deep bays of St Ives and Penzance. Although the interior is a patchwork quilt of fields dotted with farmhouses, the battered north coast between St Ives and Pendeen is harsh, backed by rough hills, scree-slope moors and the shattered relics of prehistoric life. You would hardly believe it, but Bronze Age Penwith was the most populous part of Cornwall and St Michael's Mount was its port. On the western rim of the peninsula, there are more than a thousand known archaeological sites, most still prominent in the landscape: stone circles, cliff castles, stone burial chambers (quoits) and Bronze Age villages with strange tunnels called *fougous*. The prehistoric structures echo the natural tors and rocking stones so closely that it is often hard to tell them apart. Not all the archaeology here is ancient. Along the cliffs there are also the ruined engine houses and chimney stacks of 19th-century tin mines. At that time the bays were busy with pilchard fisheries too. The main shoals would appear in mid-July, southwest of Land's End, swimming into the Channel in oily swarms (the last great pilchard catch was at St Ives in 1907). To tour Land's End, base yourself in St Ives, Penzance or a farmhouse B&B further west and explore on foot.

Mousehole

Mousehole, just around the southern headland of Mount's Bay, is yet another picturesque granite fishing village. It is remembered as the home of Dolly Pentreath (d. 1777), the last native speaker of the Cornish language (until its revival), and the setting of the Penlee lifeboat disaster of 19 December 1981 when the entire crew of the *Solomon Browne* drowned trying to save a coaster in mountainous seas beyond Lamorna Cove. There is an excellent walk south along the cliffs to rugged Lamorna Cove (where a café serves pizza, pasta and good breakfasts) with its granite quarries, up the Lamorna Valley and back via Kemyel. Mousehole is today rather filled with second homes which can give it a bit of a ghost town feel out of season. Still, both locals and newcomers get together to celebrate the town's slightly peculiar pre-Christmas ritual – eating a fish pie, known as a star gazey pie, made from seven types of fish, with the fishes' heads and tails sticking out of the top of the pie. According to the tales, the pie's origins date back to a terrible winter several hundred years ago when a raging, unrelenting storm prevented the town's fishing boats from putting out to sea for weeks. Eventually, to stop the villagers from starving to death, one brave soul, Tom Bawcock, battled out across the waves and miraculously managed to catch enough fish to feed the town. He landed seven different types which he had cooked with the heads and tails showing so people could see what was what. The festival is held on 23 December, also known as Tom Bawcock's Eve.

Over the Top and Around the Coast from Mousehole

The Newlyn–Treen road crosses the Lamorna Valley and soon you'll see a sign to the **Merry Maidens**, the best-preserved of Cornwall's stone circles, dating from the late Neolithic era-early Bronze Age. Treen, with its

Getting to the Land's End Peninsula

Nine miles from Penzance, 18 miles from St Ives, 290 miles from London, 886 miles from John o' Groats and 3,147 miles from New York, Land's End is off the A30. A regular **bus** service runs from Penzance.

general shop, pub and car park, is the starting point for a walk to the most famous *logan* or rocking stone in Cornwall. The path heads south through the stone gateway of Iron Age cliff castle **Treryn Dinas** on the rocky headland. The **Logan Rock** is inside the castle. All these headlands are fabulous to explore, with their smooth, grey anthropomorphic rocks and cliff-top views. You can follow the coast path east to **Penberth Cove** or west to Prothcurno.

The road sweeps down the valley to **Porthcurno**, past a complex of 1950s buildings – all that is left of the training college for the telegraphy station at the back of the beach which, at its height in the early 20th century, was the largest in the world and the hub of the British imperial communications network: 14 buried cables ran up the beach and out across the world. The Eastern Telegraph Company chose the site in 1870 because it was out of the way of major shipping lanes, with deep sand to bury the cables. In 1929 it merged with the radio telegraphy side of the Marconi Company to form Cable and Wireless. You can mug up on the history of telegraphy at the **Porthcurno Telegraph Museum**, housed beneath the old telegraph station, where there is a working replica of Marconi's spark transmitter, which sent the first radio signal across the Atlantic in 1901. The small hut on the beach was the physical terminus of the cable links with the former colonies. From here the 14 cables stretch underwater as far as Gibraltar, Bombay, the Azores and Brest.

Porthcurno Telegraph Museum
Eastern House;
t (01736) 810966;
www.porthcurno.org.uk;
open April–Nov daily 10am–5pm, Nov–Mar Sun & Mon 10am–5pm;
adm £5.50

Up the headland above Porthcurno is the open-air **Minack Theatre**, cut into a rocky gully in the cliff in the 1930s by Rowena Cade, daughter of a Derbyshire industrialist. You can visit all year, although productions (usually Shakespeare) are staged only in summer. It looks like it has strayed from Ancient Greece, with its amphitheatre of stone seats. Behind the stage, it's a sheer drop to the sea ('break a leg' indeed). The site also has an exhibition on Ms Cade's life with photographs and audiovisual displays.

Minack Theatre
Porthcurno,
t (01736) 810181,
www.minack.com

Land's End

Land's End
Sennen;
t 0871 720 0044;
www.landsend-landmark.co.uk; open Easter–Oct daily 10am–5pm; adm £10.95

The theme park on **Land's End** is one of England's most depressing tourist spots, ruining a spectacularly beautiful headland and landmark. By approaching on foot from Sennen Cove along the coastal path, however, you can still appreciate the natural grandeur of the site. On a clear day you can see the lighthouse on **Wolf Rock**, nine miles off shore. It is one of the most remote lighthouses in Britain – a keeper was once driven mad with fear during a sustained storm, leading to a rule that there should always be two keepers.

To the north of Land's End, behind the long sandy sweep of **Whitesand Bay**, is the most popular beach in Penwith. Amenities are at its southern end, at Sennen.

Not far away, taking the Sancreed turn off the A30, is the excavated Iron Age village of **Carn Euny**. The existence of round houses and a more elaborate courtyard house indicate to those who know about such things that the village developed between 200 BC and AD 400, although there was a settlement on the site as early as the Neolithic era. You can see a stone tunnel, or *fougou*, here. It's about 15 yards long and built of drystone walls, the earthen roof supported by granite lintels. No one knows why the *fougous* were built, but smugglers later found them useful for hiding contraband.

The North Coast

St Just is the centre of the now defunct tin- and copper-mining district of Penwith, stretching north to Pendeen. Cape Cornwall is a dramatic place to begin a cliff walk north to the headland of Pendeen Watch, taking in ruined engine houses dotted along the cliffs. **Geevor Tin Mine** was the last working mine in West Cornwall, closing in 1992. It is a huge and complex place, where you can learn about the intricate mechanics of ore extraction, through the crushing, sifting and purifying processes. It's all quite modern and not very romantic but nonetheless provides a fascinating glimpse of the old industrial Cornwall. In the museum a model of the underground workings show 70 miles of levels under the sea, the furthest extending more than a mile from the shore. In the 1960s, Geevor took over the workings of nearby **Levant Mine**, a Victorian cliff mine disbanded in 1930 because miners were no longer prepared to descend 2,000ft underground on a ladder. The crumbling brick chimneys around the site are known as calciners. The 1840 engine house contains the only Trevithick beam engine in Cornwall, still regularly steamed up.

You could spend an entire holiday tracking down Stone Age–Iron Age antiquities here. From a car park east of **Pendeen**, on the B3318, a track leads along a Tinner's Way across the moor to **Chun Quoit**, a perfectly preserved Stone Age chamber tomb built of four upright megaliths supporting a massive capstone. From here, a path leads up to the stone ramparts of **Chun Castle** on the top of the hill. It is the only Iron Age hill for in Cornwall built of stone. On the slopes beneath it you can still see the outlines of the prehistoric fields.

Chysauster Iron Age Village, just off the Gulval-Gurnard's Head road between the A30 north of Penzance and the B3306 coast road, is not to be bettered archaeologically anywhere in England, and is also intensely atmospheric, wild and overgrown. The nine excavated courtyard houses, preserved with thresholds and fire grates, date from the first three centuries AD, when the rest of Britain was increasingly Romanized.

From the tiny stone farming village of **Zennor**, a few fields away from the cliffs, you can walk up Zennor Hill to **Zennor Quoit**, a Stone Age chamber tomb with a monumental entrance. In Zennor there is a café in the old chapel (or you can drink beer in the **Tinner's Arms**). The lane between the church and the pub leads to **Zennor Head**, following the coastal path around the sheer headland, with terrific views back towards the dome of the granite moorland. The longer walk south to Pendeen is one of the most dramatic, empty and wild sections along the Southwest Coastal Path.

Geevor Tin Mine
Pendeen;
t (01736) 788662;
www.geevor.com, open
Sun–Fri 9am–5pm; adm
£8.50

Levant Mine
Trewellard, Pendeen;
t (01736) 786156;
www.nationaltrust.org.
uk; open Mar–Oct Wed
& Fri, also Sun
June–July; adm £5.80

Chysauster Iron Age Village
t (07831) 757934;
www.english-heritage.org.uk;
April–Oct daily
10am–5pm; adm £5

Tinner's Arms
t (01736) 796927

Where to Stay and Eat on the Land's End Peninsula

The Old Coastguard Hotel, Mousehole, t (01736) 731222, *www.oldcoastguard hotel.co.uk* (*expensive–very expensive*). Fabulous, stylish place to stay with antique grey woodwork and simply fantastic sea views. Twelve of the hotel's 14 bedrooms are in the lodge, opening out into subtropical gardens.

Boscean Country House, Boswedden Road, St Just, t (01736) 788748, *www.bosceancountryhouse.co.uk* (*moderate*). An imposing, solitary whitewashed building set in three acres of neat gardens. Its recently revamped rooms come with either sea or countryside views.

Gear Farm, near Zennor, t (01736) 795471, *www.gearfarmcornwall.co.uk* (*moderate*). Through Boswednack, just before the Gurnard's Head Hotel, this wonderful farmhouse must surely have the best bathroom in Cornwall with long views over dry-stone walled fields. The very friendly owners have one B&B bedroom to offer in the main house, plus three large self-catering cottages.

The Cornish Range, 6 Chapel Street, Mousehole, t (01736) 731488, *www.cornishrange.co.uk* (*moderate*). A very spick-and-span seafood restaurant housed in a former pilchard-processing factory. It serves fish from local nets and veg from local farms.

There are also three very pretty en suite rooms for rent (*moderate*) all named after local Newlyn artists.

The Gurnard's Head Hotel, near Zennor, t (01736) 796928, *www.gurnards head.co.uk* (*moderate*). An old pub standing alone on the coastal road between St Ives and Land's End, a short walk from a Celtic hill fort, this offers good food, paintings for sale on the walls and cosy comfortable rooms. There's live folk music on Wed/Fri eve.

Tregeraint House, near Zennor, t (01736) 797061 (*moderate*). Run by a local potter, this is a wonderfully remote place, flanked by hills and Iron Age remains, outside Zennor, with three comfortably rustic bedrooms and a roaring open fire in the breakfast room.

Logan Rock Inn, Treen, St Levan, t (01736) 810495 (*budget*). This conforms to the standard country pub template – a flagstone floor, low wooden beams, horse brasses, an open fireplace, local ales on tap etc. But it also serves some superior food in generous portions. There's a little beer garden at the rear.

The Ship Inn, Mousehole, t (01736) 731234, *www.shipmousehole.co.uk* (*budget*). This stately old pub is the place to tuck into the local boggle-eyed delicacy star gazey pie (see p.210), the day before Christmas Eve. The rest of the time it's a decent inn with a good range of ales and eight double bedrooms (*moderate*).

The Isles of Scilly

The Isles of Scilly are an archipelago of about 50 islands and countless rocky islets 30 miles beyond Land's End. Five are inhabited: St Mary's, Tresco, St Martin's, St Agnes and Bryher. You could walk around the coast of St Mary's, the biggest, in an afternoon. The rest, with Tolkienesque names like Biggal of Gorregan, are left to the seals, birds and gales. The isles are said to be the drowned land of Lyonesse of Celtic legend, home of Tristram and Lady of Lyones. They are in fact sinking. In the early Middle Ages the islands were connected at low water. Now they're divided by narrow sea channels with romantic names like Garden of Maiden Bower.

There are hundreds of miles of Scilly coastline, with deserted sandy beaches and rocky coves to explore. The inland heathland is peppered with prehistoric remains, including a Neolithic chambered tomb particular to Scilly. The climate is particular too, warm even in winter, filling the fields with daffodils and lacing the hedgerows with wild flowers – the fleshy mesembryanthemum and dwarf pansy – which don't grow on the mainland. The cut-flower industry started in 1868 and is now the mainstay of the island's economy, along with tourism. The rocky islands guarding the English and Irish channels are notorious ship-wreckers. Take a boat trip around Bishop's Rock lighthouse to see the lethal **Western Rocks**. Scilly is the main landfall for many rare migrating birds, far from extinct, who stop off here in spring and autumn. In October the islands are overrun with birdwatchers. B&Bs are booked up months ahead, launches are packed out, and every evening the birdwatchers' log is brought out in the Scillonian Club in **Hugh Town**, and sightings recorded. The twitchers long for wild westerlies to blow vagrant American birds across the Atlantic.

Scilly is a remarkable place to be outdoors, so pack wet-weather clothes at any time of year. Base yourself in Hugh Town, the main population centre on St Mary's, and explore the islands by boat and foot. By the end of your stay you'll have a ruddy-cheeked glow.

Isles of Scilly Museum
Church Street;
t (01720) 422337;
www.iosmuseum.org;
open summer
10am–4.30pm; adm £2

On a rainy day pop into the **Isles of Scilly Museum** in Hugh Town to see the archaeological finds – the most impressive of all a 2.5ft long Iron Age sword in an ornate bronze scabbard. Salvaged wreckage includes a Greek vase from HMS *Colossus*, Nelson's store ship at the Battle of the Nile, wrecked off Samson in 1798, and flotsam from Sir Clowdisley Shovell's fleet, wrecked off the Western Rocks in October 1707 returning from the Wars of the Spanish Succession. On the ground floor is a fully rigged 19th-century pilot gig.

On a sunny day no one sticks around in town. Everyone is out walking in remote places and finding deserted beaches. St Mary's is at the hub of the islands and by doing a complete lap of it you glimpse them all: the bare hills of Samson; the southern beaches of Tresco and St Martin's to the north; the scattered islets to the east; the mouth of the English Channel to the southeast; and waves churning over St Agnes and Annet to the west. From the half-hour Garrison Walls Walk, at its best in the early evening, you get a panorama of the western islands. Stay on the lower path, where you get views of Bishop's Rock lighthouse over Annet, the twitcher's paradise of St Agnes and the Gugh, and down into Porthcressa Bay. If you head north to **Porthmellon**, you can follow the coastal path past mesembryathemum-covered walls round the west side of the island to **Harry's Walls** and the 16th-century fort, an excellent lookout towards the bare hills of Samson and the golden sands of Tresco, with Bryher inbetween. From Porthloo beach aim for the telegraph mast nearest the shore and you'll come to the prehistoric sites on **Halangy Down**. The stone remains of a Bronze Age village are built on terraces up the hill. At the top of the hill, **Bant's Carn** chambered tomb is about 1,500 years older.

The northern face of the island lacks all habitation and roads. **Bar Point** on the northernmost tip is a wild spot backed by dunes, ferny slopes and angular pine trees. The sandy coastal path towards Toll's Island takes you to **Innisidgen Carn**. Further south, you can reach remote, sandy Pelistry beach over a sand bar at low tide.

Getting to and around the Isles of Scilly

Note that you can't travel to or from the islands on Sundays.

By Air

The 'Skybus', a small 17-seater plane, flies between Land's End Airport and St Mary's seven times a day Mon–Fri, 8.30am–5.30pm and five times on Sat; cost £129 return. Skybus services also link the islands with the airports at Newquay, Exeter, Bristol and Southampton. British International Helicopters also offer flights 6 days a week from Penzance to St Mary's; £174 rtn: t (01736) 363871, www.islesofscillyhelicopter.com.

By Boat

Isles of Scilly Travel, the company that operates the Skybus, also operates the *Scillonian III* passenger ferry which departs once a day from Penzance at 9.15am Mon–Fri, and twice on Saturdays at 6.30am and 1.45pm, between April and October. Tickets cost from £80 return. For plane and ferry services, contact Isles of Scilly Travel Centre, Quay Street, Penzance, t 0845 710 5555, www.ios-travel.co.uk.

Once you're there, the **St Mary's Boatmen Association** has ten passenger launches motoring around the islands in summer. Tickets are available from the kiosk on St Mary's Quay; t (01720) 423999, www.scillyboating.co.uk; direct returns to any island are £7.60, circular trips are £11.

By Bus, Taxi, Bicycle and On Foot

You can catch a **bus** from Hugh Town across the island and walk back, or do the same by taxi (try Island Taxis, t (01720) 422126). **Bicycles** can be hired on St Mary's from Buccaboo Cycle Hire at Porthcressa, t (01720) 422289. Guided wildlife **tours** and archaeological **walks** around the island are run by Island Wildlife Tours (42 Sally Port, St Mary's, t (01720) 422212, ww.islandwildlifetours.co.uk) and Scilly Walks: t (01720) 423326, www.scillywalks.co.uk.

09

Cornwall | The Isles of Scilly

Porth Hellic beach, on the southeastern coast, is all scrunchy shingle and shells. At the back of the beach is a monument marking the spot where the body of Sir Clowdisley Shovell, admiral of the British fleet, was found after his boat HMS *Association* was wrecked off the Western Rocks in 1707. You can follow a nature trail up the Holy Vale stream, along a magical path where the embanked roots of trees part like processional swords to guide you over quaggy ground.

Between Porth Hellic and Old Town the coastal path crosses heathland past huge rocks projecting into the sea. Take note of the 'Warning Aircraft Stop' sign; continue with a green light over the runway of St Mary's airport, or stop if it's red.

Plain **Old Town** sits on a beautiful green headland. It was once called Porthenor and boasted a castle, quay and church, but fell into decline when Hugh Town grew in the 16th century. It now boasts two cafés and a churchyard packed with sailors' graves. Detailed epitaphs include one 'who died at Rio de Janeiro of Yellow Fever on his voyage to the Cape of Good Hope aged 21' among the shipwrecked. The obelisk at the top belongs to Louise Holzmaister, one of 300 fatalities of the 1875 wreck of the *Schiller*, a New York-bound German liner which ran onto the Western Rocks in fog.

Beside the modern lighthouse on Peninnis Head, the rocks resemble Hepworth sculptures. On Tresco, the second largest island, you can walk to **Cromwell's Castle** and **King Charles' Gate**, continuing on to the lush subtropical **Tresco Abbey Gardens**, the island's chief attraction. This wonderful collection of more than 20,000 tropical plants – gathered from all over the world – was first planted in the early 19th century on the site of a ruined 10th-century Benedictine abbey. Today the blooms flourish amid the island's Gulf Stream-boosted climes – so much so that

✪ Tresco Abbey Gardens
t (01720) 424105;
www.tresco.co.uk; open
daily 10am–4pm;
adm £9

even in winter there will still be more than 300 plant species in flower. More sobering views are on display in the garden's Valhalla Museum, which contains 30 figureheads recovered from ships that foundered on the islands' rocky coasts.

Another trip could take you to St Agnes and The Gugh (pronounced 'goo'), to see the **Old Man of Gugh**, an isolated Bronze Age standing stone, 9ft high.

(i) Isles of Scilly
*Hugh Street,
St Mary's,
t (01720) 424031,
www.simplyscilly.co.uk.
Open summer Mon–Fri
8.30am–6pm, Sat
8.30am–5pm, winter
Mon–Fri 8.30am–5pm.*

(★) Atlantic Hotel >

Festivals and Events on the Isles of Scilly

There are twice-weekly **gig races** in summer and in late April or Early May St Mary's hosts the World Pilot Gig Championships.

Where to Stay and Eat on the Isles of Scilly

Star Castle Hotel, St Marys, t (01720) 422317, *www.star-castle.co.uk (luxury)*. An atmospheric place with large, tastefully decorated rooms housed in the 16th-century fort above Hugh Town. There are also two good **restaurants** (*the seafood conservatory restaurant is open summer only*) and a small, cosy bar in the old dungeon.
Atlantic Hotel, St Mary's, t (01720) 422 417, *http://atlantichotelscilly.co.uk (very expensive–luxury)*. About 100 yards from the quay, this is a marvellous choice. All of its 25 rooms are comfortably furnished and most have sea views. There's also a very good **restaurant**, Tides, offering locally sourced fish and ocean vistas.
The Harbourside, The Quay, St. Mary's, t (01720) 422352, *www.harbourside scilly.co.uk (moderate–expensive)*. The more you pay the better your view will be from this waterside B&B. It's a friendly place that's been in the same family for 30 years, and is just a couple of minutes' walk from the restaurants and shops of St Mary's.
Evergreen Cottage, The Parade, Hugh Town, St Mary's, t (01720) 422711, *www. evergreencottageguesthouse.co.uk (moderate)*. A beautiful old 1700s captain's cottage with a garden overflowing with flowers, cosy en suite bedrooms and a wide selection of books for when the night draws in. It's opposite the town hall.

Hazeldene, Church Street, t (01720) 422864, *albat.williams@talktalk.net (moderate)*. Two chintzy, cosy en suite rooms (one with a bath, one with a shower) are offered in this family home occupying a typical old Scillonian granite cottage. The friendly owners cook a mean breakfast.
Juliet's Garden Restaurant, Seaways Flower Farm, St Mary's, t (01720) 422228, *www.julietsgarden restaurant.co.uk (moderate)*. On the headland above Porthloo Beach, and below the golf course, this well-regarded establishment, which began as a simple tearoom in the 1980s, now serves soups, light lunches and crab sandwiches in the day and offers a more sophisticated menu of fish and meat choices come evening.
The Atlantic Inn, Hugh Street, t (01720) 422323 *(budget)*. This local pub has tons of character, a good range of ales (five at the last count) and a separate family dining area serving decent pub grub – fish pie and the like – at decent prices. Organizes weekly quiz nights.
The Galley Restaurant, The Parade, t (01720) 422602 *(budget)*. This tiny long-established place is the island's only fish-and-chip shop. Downstairs you can get a takeaway cod and chips for under a fiver, while upstairs is a small sit-down dining area with a more extensive menu featuring skate, John Dory, lemon sole, mackerel and sea bass.
The Mermaid, The Bank, St Mary's, t (01720) 422701 *(budget)*. Just about the first building you encounter upon stopping off the ferry, this is a great place to sit with a pint (try 'Scuppered' by the local Ales of Scilly brewery) and get your bearings. Its décor is proudly old-fashioned and it enjoys an intensely loyal local following. Decent pub grub served out the back.

Further Reading

AA, 50 Walks Series; *Somerset* (2009), *Devon* (2009), *Cornwall* (2008). Comprising 150 walks through the three counties for all abilities.

Austen, Jane, *Northanger Abbey* (1817). The social swirl of Georgian Bath as seen through Austen's not always favourable eyes: "Do you know I get so immoderately sick of Bath". *See* also Austen's Bath-set *Persuasion* (1818).

Betjeman, John, *Cornwall: A Shell Guide* (1935); *Devon: A Shell Guide* (1936). Though long out of print, it is still sometimes possible to pick up old copies of Betjeman's 'motoring' guides to the counties at second-hand bookshops – or through Amazon – although you may have to pay several hundred pounds for an original copy. More readily available, and cheaper, are copies (particularly audio copies) of *Betjeman's Cornwall* (1988), a collection of the poet laureate's poetry and prose in praise of the county.

Blackmoore, R. D., *Lorna Doone* (1869). Love, romance, family feuds and swashbuckling adventure on the Exmoor wilds at the time of the Monmouth Rebellion.

Brindle, Steven and Cruickshank, Dan, *Brunel: The Man Who Built the World* (2006). The life and influence of the towering figure of the industrial age, the man who linked the Southwest with the outside world and, according to a poll taken by the BBC, the 'second greatest Briton ever'.

Burton, Anthony, *Richard Trevithick: Giant of Steam* (2002). The tragic story of the Cornishman who did perhaps more than any other to hasten the progress of industrialization in the early 19th century, through his invention of the first railway steam locomotive, and yet perhaps benefited least of all, dying in poverty.

Conan-Doyle, Sir Arthur, *The Hound of the Baskervilles* (1901). Sherlock Holmes solves the mystery of the great beast with 'blazing eyes and dripping jaws' prowling the lonely depths of Dartmoor. Many of the book's locations are based on real places. *See* p.154.

Du Maurier, Daphne, *Jamaica Inn* (1936). Du Maurier helps to create Bodmin Moor's tourist industry with her tale of secrets and smuggling at the 'stark and forbidding' inn, which still stands today (*see* p.171). *See* also Du Maurier's other Cornish-set novels: *Rebecca* (1938) and *Frenchman's Creek* (1942).

Eglin, John, *The Imaginary Autocrat* (2005). The life and times of the man largely responsible for placing Bath at the centre of Georgian society, the scene's self-styled 'master of ceremonies', Beau Nash.

Hardy, Thomas, *A Pair of Blue Eyes* (1873). A tragic love story set on the North Cornwall coast where Hardy lived and worked as a junior architect prior to his career as a writer.

Kingsley, Charles, *Westward Ho!* (1865). Both a tale of derring-do of the Elizabethan era and a love letter to the North Cornwall coast. The town of the same name was created as a direct consequence of the book (and not much liked by the author).

Payton, Philip, *Cornwall: A History* (2004). Thoughtful, in-depth study of the county's 'often contradictory' history by the University of Exeter's Professor of Cornish Studies.

Quiller-Couch, Sir Arthur, *The Delectable Duchy* (1893). A selection of 'stories, studies and sketches' of Cornish life by the Fowey-based author who wrote under the pen name 'Q'.

Rowse, A. L., *A Cornish Childhood* (1942). The Cornish poet's autobiography paints an evocative picture of the West Country during the early years of the 20th century.

Smit, Tim, *Eden* (2001). The story of one man's struggle to create a Cornish rain-forest. If you enjoy Smit's tales of the Eden Project, you could also hunt out his account of the discovery and restoration of 19th-century estate, *The Lost Gardens of Heligan* (2000).

Sugden, John, *Sir Francis Drake* (2006). The definitive account of the Elizabethan era's greatest adventurer and pirate.

Williamson, Henry, *Tarka the Otter* (1927). The rivers and countryside of 1920s North Devon as seen through the eyes of a young otter. *See* also p.163.

Index

Main page references are in **bold**. Page references to maps are in *italics*.

1st edition published 2010

Cadogan Guides is an imprint of
New Holland Publishers (UK) Ltd
London • Cape Town • Sydney • Auckland

New Holland Publishers (UK) Ltd
Garfield House
86–88 Edgware Road
London W2 2EA

80 McKenzie Street
Cape Town 8001
South Africa

Unit 1, 66 Gibbes Street
Chatswood, NSW 2067
Australia

218 Lake Road
Northcote
Auckland
New Zealand

Cadogan@nhpub.co.uk
t 44 (0)20 7724 7773
www.cadoganguides.com

Distributed in the United States by:
Interlink Publishing Group, Inc.
46 Crosby Street
Northampton
Massachusetts 01060

Copyright © Joseph Fullman, 2010
© 2010 New Holland Publishers (UK) Ltd

The publishers would like to thank Guy Macdonald for the factual material in chapters 5, 6 and 9.
Cover photographs: © Ian Woolcock/Alamy (front), © Kevin Britland/Alamy (back)
Photo essay photographs: © istockphoto.com, except p.9 (Tate St. Ives), p.10 (Cheesewring, Bodmin), p.11 (Lost Gardens of Heligan), p.13 (Blackpool Sands): © Pictures Colour Library; and p.11 (tulips at Eden Project): © Kevin Britland/Alamy.
Maps © Cadogan Guides, drawn by Maidenhead Cartographic Services Ltd
Cover design: Jason Hopper
Photo essay design: Sarah Gardner
Editor: Guy Hobbs
Proofreading: Elspeth Anderson
Indexing: Isobel McLean

Printed in Singapore by Craft Print International Ltd.
A catalogue record for this book is available from the British Library

ISBN: 978-1-86011-425-0

The author and publishers have made every effort to ensure the accuracy of the information in this book at the time of going to press. However, they cannot accept any responsibility for any loss, injury or inconvenience resulting from the use of information contained in this guide.

Please help us to keep this guide up to date. Although we have done our best to ensure that the information in this guide is correct at the time of going to press, laws and regulations are constantly changing and standards and prices fluctuate. We would be delighted to receive any comments concerning existing entries or omissions.